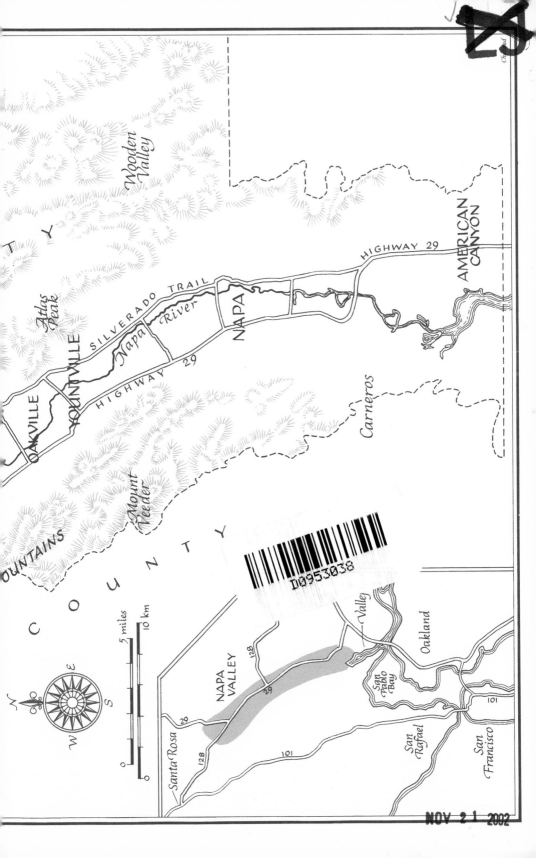

The Far Side
of Eden

BOOKS BY JAMES CONAWAY

The Big Easy
(FICTION)

*Judge: The Life and Times
of Leander Perez*

The Texans

World's End
(FICTION)

The Kingdom in the Country

Napa

Memphis Afternoons
(MEMOIR)

The Smithsonian

America's Library

The Far Side of Eden

The Far Side *of* Eden

NEW MONEY, OLD LAND,
AND THE BATTLE FOR
NAPA VALLEY

James Conaway

Houghton Mifflin Company

BOSTON • NEW YORK

2002

For information about permission to reproduce selections from
this book, write to Permissions, Houghton Mifflin Company,
215 Park Avenue South, New York, New York 10003.

Visit our Web site: www.houghtonmifflinbooks.com.

Library of Congress Cataloging-in-Publication Data
Conaway, James.
The far side of Eden : the ongoing saga of Napa Valley / James Conaway.
p. cm.
ISBN 0-618-06739-6
1. Napa Valley (Calif.) — History. 2. Wine industry — California —
Napa Valley — History. 3. Napa Valley (Calif.) — Social conditions.
4. Napa Valley (Calif.) — Economic conditions. I. Title.
F868.N2 C65 2002
979.4'19 — dc21   2002075939

Printed in the United States of America

Book design by Robert Overholtzer
Endpaper map by Jacques Chazaud

QUM 10 9 8 7 6 5 4 3 2 1

Portions of this book have appeared, in altered form, in
Preservation, Outside, Worth, Civilization, and *Food & Wine.*

AUTHOR'S NOTE:
The names of two characters have been changed, at their
request, and the pseudonyms Norm and Pat substituted.

For Shainah, Morgan, and Shion

THE HOPE OF THE WORLD

Woe to those who join house to house,
who add field to field,
until there is no more room,
and you are made to dwell alone
in the midst of the land.

ISAIAH 5:8

CONTENTS

The Far Side
of Eden

PROLOGUE

A T THE SOUTH END of the valley, the Carneros hills roll in great earth swells down toward San Pablo Bay, and at the north end the lowering presence of Mount St. Helena sits like a cork in a bottle of opaque green glass.

The Napa River between these two points covers just thirty miles, and the valley floor is only a couple of miles wide at its most commodious, yet here, under skies oceanic in depth and color — a blue impossible in most of the world's climes — there occurred over the course of the twentieth century something truly remarkable: agriculture withstood the assault of development that overwhelmed the rest of this coveted bit of California, and the product of that effort — wine — was made into a symbol of privilege.

Meanwhile the valley, as is often said, became the envy of the world. But in the last quarter century some of the idyllic character has disappeared, and the valley, like the rest of the country, felt the pressure of opposing views about what it should be and what it should look like. In the 1990s those tensions came forcefully into play here, and I was drawn to the struggle in the belief that it embodied rudiments of the American character and held clues about the future of the American landscape.

I had already written a book about Napa Valley, from research done in the late 1980s, entitled *Napa: The Story of an American Eden*. I had not been back for several years. When I did return I was surprised to find many additional vineyards, more traffic, new mansions high in the rugged but not inviolable hills, and a heightened sense of glamour; I also heard on all sides contending views and strongly expressed expectations that each view must prevail. Some people wanted only material prosperity, others only to capture the moment in time, and these were clearly on a collision course.

I moved back for a time, the highway drawing me in like memory, past the outskirts of the city of Napa in the south, into those broad expanses of vineyard like unfurled bolts of corduroy planted also with houses and recent manifestations of the booming tourist trade. I actually live on the other side of the continent but here felt, in a way, that I was home, too, or at least in some approximation of it: more than a tourist, less than a citizen.

I knew something of the valley's history and topography, having hiked in the bracketing, north-south–trending mountains that to the unknowing eye are secure in their ruggedness and isolation — the Mayacamas range on the west, dense with redwood and Douglas fir, separates Napa and Sonoma valleys, and the Howell range on the east, droughty, with a denser mix of chaparral amid the conifers, walls off the farther reaches of Napa County — and I knew that the valley supported great biological diversity. In addition to some of the finest *Vitis vinifera* on earth there was a good complement of California's native oaks, steelhead trout, deer, black bears, and a few spotted owls.

The valley's story, like California's, is essentially one of success, but in my absence some volatile elements had been added to the human mix, and they were potent indeed. The engines of commerce and electronics had carried the country into the greatest hegemony in human history, producing unimaginable new wealth, and a disproportionate amount of it had found its way into the valley. At the same time, there had flowered a school of protest with no roots in the commodity that had made the valley famous and was in fact hostile to it. These two elements were new, and already on the way to a showdown.

I found a place to live, in St. Helena, one of four "up-valley" towns: a room with a bed and table, windows shielded by mock orange trees, a sun-washed kitchen and a deck. There was a good restaurant just down the block, but I used it infrequently. I listened to the sprinklers each night, and awoke each morning to a fresh world, the exuberance of roses and mallows lining the fence replaced by the smell of baked earth that is so Napan. A few steps led to vineyards that surrounded the town and made available to the lowliest visitor open, matchless vistas of mountains and sky.

The months I spent in that little house were happy and productive, and I am grateful for them. It was the end of the nineties, that lost decade so full of hope and opportunity, and it seemed to me, in that place, at that time, that the future lay out there, just beyond the garden.

I still believe that what happened in Napa Valley is relevant to the rest of the country, however altered now are our interior landscapes. How people living in a contained, beautiful part of America dealt with threats to established order is in large part what this book is about. The account is factual, and it is important to note that the story isn't over yet. In this new century ideals share equal space only if they are lucky with hard global reality; meanwhile, the valley's fate is being fixed in the long weave of ambition and desire, wealth and restraint, vines and the wildness of chosen places.

I

A VINEYARD OF
ONE'S OWN

I

SOMETHING HAD HAPPENED, something momentous, something involving money, lots of it — what didn't at century's end? — but more complicated and subtle. It pervaded the lives of Americans considered blessed by any standard, with houses close to some of the best restaurants on earth, the value of their property on a near-vertically ascending plane, their views of a gorgeous pastoral dream: mountains, agriculture as old as human history, wild mustard blooming in the spring and, in autumn, the air perfumed by fermenting wine as precious as that of Bordeaux, Burgundy, and Champagne.

San Francisco lay just across a sparkling inland sea, but the finest things could be had right here, too, at stations of the new cross — truffles at Sunshine Market, demi-glace at Dean & DeLuca. Appetites were enhanced by the best weather in a state famous for it, and the proximity of visiting Hollywood and other sorts of stars imbued existence with a certain *frisson*. And even if there were five million tourists a year to deal with, well, those already here in the Napa Valley were the envy of all who weren't.

Yet something was wrong. People disagreed over when "it" had happened, and why, but not about the effect: a real, and growing, sense of loss.

They felt it while sitting in a long line of cars on Highway 29, looking up at once pristine slopes dense with conifer and chaparral, studded now with "steroid houses," "muscle houses," "McMansions," all contemptuous names for places built not to live in but as monuments to finance, visited by absentee owners. The locals felt it overhearing conversations about vanity vineyards, "cult" cabernets, and gardens with "water features" to cover the traffic noise.

If they wanted to buy a house to actually live in, or to trade up, they had to listen to sales pitches not about the valley's illustrious history, its neighborliness, schools, and churches, all the old-fashioned values, but about the proximity of Tra Vigne and the French Laundry. If they owned a house already, they had to wait for a carpenter or a plumber because these tradesmen worked for the owners of the muscle houses or redone Victorians, and then the locals had to pay fees often inflated by the presence of so much outside money.

Worst of all, they had to listen to the stories. Many of these featured limousines but were otherwise interchangeable. "I was pruning my roses when this couple gets out," began one such account. "He's got on wraparound shades and a five-hundred-dollar shirt with not enough buttons, bought in Beverly Hills, and she's wearing haute safari from wherever."

The visitor might also be driving a new Lexus and looking nerdy in pressed jeans and granny glasses, sure sign of a Silicon Valley weekender. These were the young beneficiaries of the computer boom, and realtors referred to them as "the children."

The procedure was much the same: "He says, 'I'll give you . . . ,'" and here the figure varied among the millions, but was never less than one. "I tell him the house isn't for sale. He doubles the price. I have to go inside to get away from him." Later, the visitor calls and triples the offer.

The problem was, many of the stories were true, like the one about the house that sold for one-point-three, already an amazing sum for such a modest place, and then the new owners "tweaked" the landscaping — added some exotics and a stone wall — and sent to France for a containerful of furniture. They put the house back on the market for two-point-nine-five and received three instant offers for more. During escrow, an unsuccessful bidder offered the buyer point-five just to step aside — half a million dollars to get out of the way.

There was the house listed for four, bought by a venture capitalist who had seen it only once. Upon seeing it a second time, he decided he no longer fancied it and resold the house at a half-million-dollar loss to a thirty-five-year-old working in the acquisitions department of a major bank. And there was the cottage in the town of St. Helena, listed for point-nine-two-five, bid up to one-point-three. After that, everybody with a three-room Victorian guesthouse with one and a half baths thought it was worth one-point-three, and it was.

Houses that were not for sale were auctioned off without the knowledge of the owners, who were presented with offers as faits accomplis. Weekend guests bought their hosts' residences. One such couple reportedly paid millions, first stipulating that everything had to be left as it was, right down to the terrycloth bathrobes, since they didn't want to be bothered with purchasing their own things or didn't know what was required. Not that it mattered. Experts materialized to perform that function for the newcomers, many of them living in San Francisco and tripping up on commission. They advised on the creation of cunning archways, the buying of period settees or Mayan urns, the planting of herb gardens "with a culinary bias," the buying of wines from the Oakville Grocery, the joining of Meadowood Country Club, the ordering of cut flowers from Tesoro's, the hiring of chefs and the vetting of maids and valets and the planting of the ultimate symbol of success, more important even than a house — a vineyard of one's own.

Everybody who mattered suddenly had to have one. This link to ancient tradition was the latest, best way of transforming money into status, though what the newcomers really wanted was a vineyard *and* "a cabernet" made from its fruit that would be highly ranked by the critics and set them miles ahead of other merely wealthy people. The locals couldn't afford these wines but had to listen to weekenders talk about them.

And they had to listen to the story about the woman with a vineyard of her own who sold her mauve Bentley because it had no rack for holding lattes, and the story about the couple building a glass house containing smoke machines, and the story about another couple with monogrammed toilet paper, each square resembling an illuminated manuscript. You laughed at the stories, but they had an effect.

Life began to feel like a lottery, or like Renaissance Spain, the gold ships coming in and their sails overshadowing all past custom and convention. Their modern equivalent was the stretch limo, the pilot fish of the nouveau riche lurking in restaurant parking lots and in the shade of olive trees on landscaped lawns. Much of this bullion had been mined down in the Santa Clara Valley, once lovely orchards since paved over and rechristened with that unlovely moniker Silicon, symbol of the greatest economic expansion in human history, a chemical that transmitted electronic impulses and churned assets, changing the world, spinning off money to computer whizzes and venture capitalists, dot-commers, "IPO sluts," entrepreneurs, investment bankers, retailers, media- and consumer-related accumulators of capital, all belted to the marvelous economic engine of the fading American century. And not a few of them were disciples of personal gratification, and self-serving.

And there were the speculators, a category to which every winery owner and, in fact, many householders now belonged. That fact alone was galling. With the acceptance of it came another realization, even sadder, that in a few short years many longtime residents had gone from being members of a community to serving as its adjuncts. So many of the big old houses now belonged to outsiders the locals were unlikely to get to know, and so eventually, it seemed, would all the valley. These old-timers would be performing some service for the new people, if they weren't already, even though the locals were relatively rich on paper. If one of them sold a house or a little vineyard, he couldn't afford to buy another, not "up-valley." He couldn't compete at the wine auctions that raised money for the schools and hospitals, couldn't get a new kitchen countertop put in, couldn't get a table at Bistro Jeanty or even at Green Valley Café because of all the tourists drawn by the celebrity.

Things were out of whack, not just in the real estate offices but also in the hills. Out of sight, larger muscle houses were being built, and caves dug to gargantuan dimensions to contain activities not related to wine, and outlandish embellishments put in. There was the persistent story of a canal built on a high dry ridge, complete with an operating lock and a barge that could be boosted up and down, this in a fragile place where water was scarce. Some people thought this a charming diversion, and others thought it disgusting ego gratification and bad taste, but they didn't say so because for the most part people in the valley were accepting souls, polite, reluctant to criticize.

This was just another story, no worse than the one about the woman who moved from the Midwest to a house in the hills costing millions so she could make cheese and sell it to the CIA — the Culinary Institute of America. Thus a substance once the byproduct of mere agriculture had been elevated to a symbol of culture. For the first time in human history, people were spending fortunes to make chump change and in the process be associated with the most basic sort of enterprise — agriculture — which in this incarnation had become glamorous. It made no more economic sense than the muscle houses and vineyards on steep land where forest had stood, and people marveled at the cost of it all. Planting those steep slopes cost upward of a hundred thousand dollars an acre just to get the vines in, not counting the purchase price, unjustifiable on the economics, not arrived at by trial and error, as in the old days, but simply ordained, bought, and written off.

There was no space left on the valley floor for such "vanity" vineyards, but they had to go in somewhere, for the social and financial enhancement they promised, and that meant the hills. The visible new vineyards and muscle houses amounted to a fraction of what was going on out of sight, or so it was said; in the rainy season, development high in the Mayacamas and the opposing range to the east tinged the reservoirs of drinking water and turned the Napa River murky. There was too much happening up there for most people to keep track of and still live their lives. More and more of them worried about what it all meant, where it was all going, what was being lost.

2

ONCE UPON A TIME, wine was made in basements in the eastern states by immigrants who never envisioned it as either a serious financial or a social enhancement. In Napa Valley, those with names like Krug, Beringer, and Schram made in the late 1800s a commercial success under the amazing California sun, and their ranks came to include a Finnish sea captain, Gustave Niebaum, who used a fortune from Alaskan fur to try to match the quality of Bordeaux chateaux, and Georges de Latour, the industrious Frenchman who imported vines from his native country and founded Beaulieu Vineyard in the first year of the new century.

Napa Valley was renowned for wine by then, but many of the early viticultural lights were poor and struggling, dimmed by a decline in the nation's economic health in the early years of the twentieth century and by the pestilential attack of the vine louse, phylloxera. Many were extinguished by Prohibition. From then through the 1950s grape growers and a few winemakers held on to enclaves in this lovely place that came to be dominated by calf-and-cow operations and prune groves. Then in the 1960s ambitious dropouts from corporate and academic America moved in, and a second, inexorable ascendancy toward fame began.

These offshoots of the Aquarian age, these idealists and glimpsers of an alternative to certified American success, met in a rural setting far removed from the ferment of North Beach and Haight-Ashbury, from Los Angeles and Chicago and Cambridge and Washington, D.C. They began to make and to pour wines competitive with those of Europe, and the beam of celebrity fell across their "boutique" wineries tucked into the folds of coastal mountains. That was the dawn of the commendable, difficult winemaking renaissance in a place that still had more in common, agriculturally, with Iowa than it did with Tuscany or the Médoc.

In the 1970s "the valley" still meant just that, a vernal plain bordering the Napa River that began in a narrow wooded apex in the foothills of the Mayacamas and ran south for thirty miles to San Pablo Bay, broadening in the journey to several miles in width and containing all the land anybody could want for planting grapes and building a little barrel cellar, if you were daring or foolish enough to try. Even big wineries like the hulks lowering in the distance were cautionary tales in their own right, described in one of the many books written about the valley as "white elephants all, and all for sale, with weeds in the yards and blank windows staring back into the illusions of the founders."

The hillsides — small mountains, really, if steepness and the dramatic effect of rock and redwood signified — seemed as close as your hand before your face. These were wild places, inaccessible, seemingly impossible to plant; the relatively few moving up there favored isolation and cheapness, without either a care or a clue. Their terrain was not much of a factor in the life below and connected only by threads — narrow roads, individual needs, and a tradition as old as human history, going back to the seedbed of civilization — to an agrarian culture struggling on the valley floor.

By the beginning of the 1990s, the perspective of value had reversed, at least for vineyards — the hills were up, the valley down — and the renaissance was approaching its zenith. The newly endowed arrivals, early beneficiaries of what would be the resounding boom in the nation's fortunes — businessmen, entrepreneurs, academics, heirs, collectors, impostors — were less eager to make wine than to associate with one of the oldest expressions of husbandry and cultural accomplishment, needing — requiring — a recognized testament to their material and spiritual worth.

Some locals thought this change began when Gil Nickel, owner of Far Niente Winery, paid more than one hundred thousand dollars an acre for undeveloped land along the highway and thus crossed the magic frontier. Some said it started when Al Brownstein crossed another magic frontier by charging a hundred dollars for a bottle of his Diamond Mountain cabernet sauvignon. Some said it began when the movie director Francis Ford Coppola purchased the historical flagship Inglenook and turned it into a wine-cum-movie roadside attraction, and still others said it began with the ascendancy of the corporations in the valley and their worship of the bottom line.

A woman who had lived long in the valley thought it began in the mid-1980s when the country saw evidence of a new kind of prosperity, one that would bear up people who found themselves in the right place at the right time. Their new money came from electronics and stock deals, and from tourist exploitation and all manner of commercial activities now an essential part of an emblematic place — Napa Valley — undergoing dramatic and possibly catastrophic change. And over the course of the next decade these examples would prove to be anything but arbitrary, their common objectives, money and status, linking them — though they might be only slightly acquainted — in an unbroken story of varied parts and contrasting visions.

She had first encountered this at a dinner party where she was seated next to what she considered the embodiment of "new money" — a short, boyish entrepreneur named Garen Staglin. At least she thought he was an entrepreneur. It wasn't easy determining what new people actually did to make money, not like in the old days when it was made in manufacturing, medicine, banking, and what was then simply and unceremoniously called business.

Staglin — dark hair, ready grin — had a reputation for accumulating large sums in ways related to insurance and to these new computers everybody was talking about. He had made money almost from the moment he emerged from Stanford University, and she asked how he had managed to concentrate on his career at a time when so many people were still agonizing over the war in Vietnam. "Oh, I didn't pay any attention to that stuff," Staglin told her. "I just got on the elevator and pushed 'Penthouse.'"

He and his wife, Sharilyn — Shari, out of South Dakota, short like her husband and with his intensity of ambition — showed up at functions reserved for successful owners of wineries and those willing to contribute to their causes. The Staglins had purchased a historic property in Rutherford that had once belonged to that Parnassan of Napa's early wine success, Georges de Latour, courtly

Old World figure, avatar of decency and foresight, father of one of the most famous eponymous wines in the valley, Georges de Latour Private Reserve. By owning a piece of the old de Latour estate, the Staglins had rooted themselves in the most competitive *terroir* — soil in which vines are planted — in America. This could quickly vault them into the higher ranks of the "vintners," a largely symbolic term used nowadays for those who owned wineries, or at least grapes that could be vinted in one of the rented spaces available throughout the valley.

The original vineyard had been planted under the supervision of another Parnassan, the late, legendary André Tchelistcheff, a White Russian émigré who had advised in his sixty years as a professional enologist most everyone who mattered in American fine wine. The sale of the de Latour parcel to the Staglins was significant because it represented the latest in a string of disastrous business decisions by de Latour's heirs and because it involved the arrival in Napa Valley, never a stranger to new money, of a new degree of brashness.

A large fortune, it was always said, was needed to make a small one in the wine business. But new money from well-placed capital and stock options flowing into *Vitis vinifera* now had different expectations. Status was the primary one, the new vintners wanting accolades associated with a vineyard and a wine of one's own — a pedigree — but they also wanted to make money from this and related endeavors. They were willing, sometimes eager, to confuse fine wine with other businesses — that is, to use wine to boost other, related and unrelated financial schemes, just as wine was used to create formerly nonexistent social standing, to prove that a person was "a winner" and, by contrast, that a person's critics were losers.

That, the woman thought, was different.

According to Staglin, he first considered moving to Napa Valley after having another dinner, this one with a resident of the valley named Andy Beckstoffer. Two decades before, Beckstoffer had himself been an *arriviste* and an example of unwelcome change, acquiring considerable land and influence through the ineptness of the Heublein Corporation, which then owned most but not all of the old Inglenook and Beaulieu estates. Beckstoffer had worked for Heublein, and his large chunks of valuable vineyardland had been financed in part with Heublein money. Staglin had met Beckstoffer through the Young Presidents Club, as he had met Michael

Mondavi, son of Robert and one of the valley's "lucky spermers," those who had vineyards and jobs because they had inherited them. Both men had encouraged Staglin to move to paradise.

Beckstoffer gave Staglin the name of a real estate broker who might be able to introduce him to de Latour's heirs. The broker knocked on doors and eventually knocked on that of Dagmar de Pins, granddaughter of old Georges de Latour and one of the original lucky spermers. She was married to Walter Sullivan, mastermind of the ill-advised, much lamented sale of Beaulieu Vineyard to Heublein back in the sixties. The loss of the family winery was still mourned by Dagmar, but her husband relished disposing of his wife's property to finance their comfortable existence, a fact evident to all who floated balloons with dollar signs on them in the vicinity of Walter Sullivan. He and Dagmar maintained a country estate in France and a house in San Francisco as well as remnants of the old de Latour estate in Napa Valley, and they spent a good deal of time in cooking schools.

The Staglins were invited to San Francisco by Dagmar "to see if we were suitable," as Garen put it, though in fact they had been invited at Walter's instigation to determine how much money they had. Over cocktails Dagmar de Pins Sullivan told the Staglins that the Rutherford property they coveted would go to the Sullivans' children, not to the Staglins. She had said the same thing about Beaulieu before that fabulous realm was sold to Heublein through the machinations of Walter, who again put out vibes contrary to his wife's wishes. The broker thought Walter could not pass up a real estate deal and that Walter would persuade Dagmar to sell the vineyard to Garen, just as he had persuaded her to sell Beaulieu to Heublein when its executives first came nosing around the valley.

The broker advised Garen that his offer should be accompanied by sufficient evidence of intent — cash. Garen slipped a check for fifty thousand dollars under the broker's door on Father's Day, 1985, to accompany a formal offer of more than a million dollars, still big money then. The broker tracked the Sullivans down in Venice, where they were learning to produce new dishes from Julia Child, and Walter agreed on principle to the sale. But he insisted that it be kept secret until he could cajole his wife — again — into disposing of the something near sacred to her that would prove — again! — to be a lot more valuable than Walter thought it was.

The men came up with a code name for the deal, Project Basil, a reference to the Sullivans' current area of culinary interest, so Dagmar wouldn't know until it was too late that one of the last vestiges of her family's presence in the valley had been bartered away.

Not long afterward, the vineyard put in by Tchelistcheff was pulled out and replanted with new, disease-resistant rootstock. It would produce wine that the Staglins hoped would set them on a lofty second-career path occupied by Mondavis and Rothschilds, ultimate proof of the transformational qualities of wine. The Rothschilds were wealthy bankers before entering the wine business, and the Mondavis had been Central Valley dealers in produce. A vineyard still brought respect in quarters where it was not otherwise available — in Paris, for instance, where the Staglins dined at La Tour d'Argent and were not offered the best wine list by the sommelier, even after Garen told him that he owned several companies in the United States. Then Shari told the sommelier that they also owned a vineyard in Napa Valley, one that had been owned by the legendary Georges de Latour, and out came the good list.

In 1991, a bulldozer cut into the base of the Mayacamas Mountains above the vineyard, and a structure rose that was no common residence: a long, fenestrated, Palladian tribute to California's eclectic architecture, the hue of "Rutherford dust," a double entendre referring to both the shade of the vineyard's inestimable dirt and the reputed taste of the cabernet it produced, a taste first identified by Tchelistcheff and used as a successful marketing tool for most of the century, proof of geographical taste distinctions in the ongoing squabbles over Napa Valley vineyard appellations.

Now Rutherford dust was the official color of a house with a broken roofline suggesting an entire Tuscan village, the tiles varied in shape and color to resemble those that had originally been made on the thighs of Italian artisans, as Garen Staglin liked to point out.

He told everyone that the house was a link to ancestors in the Old Country. His father's name was Stagliano, another "talking point" in what was becoming a concentrated marketing effort blending California ambience with the images of family, wine, and art. The association of these things had long informed selling, following the example set by Robert Mondavi years before when he proved that fine wine moves best through channels lubricated with the personality of the creator and his or her association with "family values" and the finer things of life, including works of the imagination.

The Mondavis claimed to "sculpt" their wines; press releases from various wineries spoke of "the art of winemaking." There were impressive art collections in private museums that also had wine-tasting rooms, or houses specially constructed to show off art collections. The Staglin house featured a loggia, a fountain, and a pebbled courtyard, entered between columns bearing the lacquered ceramic sculptures of the Staglins' Jack Russell terriers, Sami and Mister Deuce. The twenty-two-foot ceilings provided ample wall space for their assemblage of contemporary paintings, and under the colonnade out back stood an eighteen-foot granite harvest table designed by a sculptor who also artfully arranged boulders in front of the house.

The Staglins envisioned visitors arriving in cars, passing the boulders to enter a winery dug into the mountainside, tasting and buying wine, and then strolling the grounds in appreciation of four million dollars' worth of art and many more millions' worth of real estate.

"Windshields just don't do it the way wine does," Shari would say, a reference to one of her husband's most successful businesses, a company that replaced shattered auto glass nationwide. Garen also sat on the boards of what he called "information solution technology companies." But these endeavors didn't allow one to rethink corporate strategy while overlooking one's own cadre of regimented vines. They didn't allow one to "get out of the box and into nature," as Shari put it. They didn't allow trips abroad for sampling the culture and business acumen of Bordeaux and Burgundy, or the exposure of a Staglin wine to the public.

Quality was foremost in the ongoing American wine success, but also important was a style of marketing very different from the traditional European approach, the personal representation of one's wines and the mystique of the successful vintner.

To build their winery, the Staglins needed the approval of their neighbors, and this they failed to obtain. Their application was denied by the county after they had bought the historic vineyard, put in expensive trellising, hired a good winemaker, built a stunning house with authentic tiles, and paid an artist to design a label reminiscent of the best of Bordeaux, one bearing the likeness of a contemporary sculpture owned by the Staglins, Stephen DeStaebler's

Winged Woman Walking, "inspired by Nike in the Louvre," as Shari pointed out. "Nike represented excellence to the Greeks, competition, and victory," she added, the valley's reigning values, and now, after Garen had gotten on the elevator and pushed "Penthouse" and done everything a person could possibly do to get there, they were being denied their victory.

One night their neighbor, Jack Cakebread, woke up to the sound of running generators. A large, florid man with a fierce countenance, alternately charming and abrasive, Cakebread was from Oakland, where his father had owned a garage and had taught his son the inner workings of the internal combustion engine. But Jack had chanced upon Napa Valley in the late sixties and had bought land, some of it for as little as eight hundred dollars an acre, and had since built his brand into one of the most successful of the so-called high-end wines. His striking modern wooden winery out on Highway 29 would soon be matched by another, second winery nearby, a double-barreled assault on the country's disposable income in the best years ever for selling wine.

Cakebread had also founded an organization known informally as the Breakfast Club, a secretive group of two dozen powerful vintners and their representatives who met regularly at his winery for sauvignon blanc and scrambled eggs and the discussion of government regulation, incompliant elected officials, and troublesome environmentalists. Jack thrived on less sleep than his peers: to bed shortly before midnight, up again around four o'clock and out into the darkness to walk his land, now worth upward of one hundred thousand dollars an acre. A sign in his winery read, "Aren't I lucky! The harder I work the luckier I get!"

And the luckier he got, the harder he worked: redeyes to Japan or France, back to Napa Valley for some clean shirts, and off again in the opposite direction. Sleep was nonproductive, he thought, a necessary pain in the butt, and here was a new arrival in the valley making him sit up in bed with only half of his requisite four hours.

Cakebread looked out the window and saw a bunch of trailers parked side by side on the Staglin property under a bank of lights. He went out and asked the driver of one of the huge mobile lounges — it was slipping backward in the mud, right down his property line — what the hell was going on. He learned some things that made him less happy. The trailers were part of an artistic assault on the neighborhood by Walt Disney Pictures, about to remake a film called *The Parent Trap*. Over the next month the engine of popular culture would fill this formerly bucolic setting with humming machines and a small army of cinematic factotums, to earn the Staglins both money and recognition.

The Staglins, Cakebread learned, had consulted another Napa Valley resident partial to filmic endeavors, Francis Ford Coppola, who had advised them to let the film unit in and had told the Staglins what it would cost Disney to build a set similar to that provided by their house, with its artworks and tiles replicating those made on the thighs of Italian artisans. The Staglins had divided that figure by the number of days Disney wanted to film and come up with a per diem of about ten thousand dollars, not a bad return on static real estate.

There was nothing Cakebread or the other neighbors could do about it. Napa County has strict zoning requirements, but there were temporary exceptions to be had. The irony was that Cakebread, an ardent free enterpriser, was forced to admit that unlimited money could have undesirable effects when located next door. The relentless rise of the stock market had produced too many fistfuls of cash and not enough knowledge of life as anything but an investment opportunity. People coming to the valley found or created a bit of vineyard and grew some "rocket juice" — Cakebread's term for good Napa Valley cabernet that had propelled many fortunes, including his own, upward — and then they required a house, and then a winery.

Cakebread hated the disruption of the rural byway that dead-ended in the former quiet of the Mayacamas, hated the fancy new Staglin stone wall that broke the seamless continuity of the land, and hated what he called a lack of the courtesy that should characterize country living. He told people, "The Staglins are the worst thing to happen here since the Wine Train. They're the Dennis Rodmans of Napa Valley."

But the Staglins applied for another winery permit, and would eventually get it in the waning years of the nineties, by espousing the right cause: the American Center for Wine, Food and the Arts. It was the ultimate project of the aging Robert Mondavi, a symbol of the valley's exalted success in part due to the association of wine and art, and an indication of the country's fascination with luxury.

Still the reigning monarch of the valley, Robert was no longer at the head of the famous winery bearing his name, now a public corporation run by his elder son, Michael, that lucky spermer. The Center, Robert's passion, was to cost a great deal of money. Garen Staglin had agreed to provide one million dollars for it and to raise more money from the heads of other corporations. When complete, the Center would have a room in it named for the Staglins — the Tasting Bar, or perhaps the Gallery of the Senses. The Staglins were, they told people, "kindred spirits" with the Mondavis and also in love with food, wine, art, and music.

Mondavi went to see Jack Cakebread and urged him not to oppose the Staglins' winery. This was ironic, since Jack had served as a stalking horse for the Mondavis for years, taking up causes that the Mondavis believed in but didn't want to be associated with — like standards for reserve wines, a cause dear to the Mondavis but anathema to Ernest Gallo and so politically difficult. Although Jack took his old friend Robert up to his house to show him how close a Staglin winery would be, and although Robert said, "You've got to protect yourself," he didn't offer to help.

The Staglins' ostensible promotion of their wine took them all over. After a week's bicoastal sojourn — to Nantucket and to Seattle, where they discussed their wines and the Staglin "vision" with restaurant owners, proprietors of wine shops, and devotees of Bordeaux and Burgundy who recognized the appeal of the California alternative — they returned to stroll in their vineyard, the setting sun igniting the eastern mountains. They were in an expansive mood. "Our house has one of the highest recognition factors in the country," Garen said, of the effects of *The Parent Trap*, the Staglin Family Vineyards Web site, and a short film about them shown repeatedly on a commercial airline, called *Dream Living.*

"Our wine allows us to go anywhere in the world and entertain," added Shari, reaching up to turn down the collar of her husband's polo shirt. "It's a legitimate expense, and a connection with the earth."

Garen pulled some grapes from a cluster and handed one to her;

together they "sampled the sugars." Their winemaker arrived in a minivan with her son, fresh from soccer practice, and over the stone wall they palavered about when to pick, the winemaker trying hard to accommodate the Staglins' "sense" of the optimum moment. Then Garen and Shari drove into Rutherford for dinner.

Outside La Toque, a red Ferrari worth a quarter of a million dollars, too fast to drive on Napa Valley's roads, was parked as a statement of a customer's wherewithal while he traveled the valley in a limo. Garen explained that he and Shari are investors in the restaurant: "We cash-flow this thing on sixty-five covers a day," he said.

After they were seated, Shari, in a silk blouse of palest mauve, smiled up at La Toque's sommelier as he filled their glasses from a bottle of Staglin Family Vineyards chardonnay, a counterpoint to the sautéed figs with lime and ginger and seared Muscovy foie gras. Later, Garen tasted the Staglin cabernet and found there "a cornucopia of flavors" that suited the medallions of rare lamb and local chevre, antiphons to the wine's primal chant. He mused about the qualities of the Staglin vineyard, formerly the de Latours', and the practice of "manageable agriculture that doesn't require the attention of a major corporation." With it, he could make money in a more relaxed manner, with only three full-time employees, no outside investors, and a mode of existence more copasetic than that of a run-of-the-mill CEO. He and Shari derived more satisfaction from this than from activities traditionally associated with wealth, he said, like polo ponies or yachts. "Building a brand is more fun than winning the Block Island sailing race."

"And it can also go on for *centuries*," she said. "We've met vineyard-owning families in France and Italy that have been there for *seven hundred years* . . . Awe-inspiring."

"We're doing the succession thing — our children are involved."

Garen passed a hand across the scene: well-dressed people eating expensive food, handing bottles of wine back and forth between tables like ducal celebrants, attended to by culinary acolytes on the very edge of America. "Wine is all about these things," he said at last. "When you can say you have had dinner with Garen and Shari, and talked about *The Parent Trap*, you've had a whole reinforcing experience."

And then, "We've got a lot of lifestyle here."

3

THE SANTA CLARA VALLEY, at the south end of San Francisco Bay, had once been as beautiful as any in California, an agricultural idyll obliterated by its late-twentieth-century makeover. People up in Napa Valley were acutely aware of this and wondered aloud if their valley's fate could be the same in the twenty-first. The question was more often answered in the affirmative now, as the two valleys came together in ways that said much about values at the high end of American achieving. One was the symbol of quick, unbounded wealth, the other of the good life that had come to entail, in addition to pleasure, cultural authentication. Simply being rich was no longer enough, and since these two geographical founts of money and legitimacy lay only sixty miles apart, it was inevitable that the newly monied denizens of the former would be drawn to the charms and social opportunities of the latter, and that there would be problems.

All the traffic in Napa Valley could not be blamed on the northward migration from the other valley, not with five million tourists annually. But in spring "dot-commers" and related beneficiaries of the stock market were an outsized factor in valley life. They vacuumed up plants at the nurseries and construction material at the building-supply outfits and tended to be blamed for the muscle houses, angular frame slope-clingers, stucco mishmashes, and monumental stone boxes with driveways cut brutally into the earth. Many of these had been put up by developers, retailers, and various other trophy-house collectors, serial builders having become epidemic all across the nation. Some of those rich folk also owned getaways in Snowmass or the Hamptons, Provence, Tuscany, and elsewhere, and their decidedly immodest off-road vehicles, symbolic of their ability to go anywhere in safety and comfort, ascended on weekends like metallic insects on the vernal skin of a sleeping beast.

Even in winter, when bluish smoke rose from the fires of vine cuttings, big, bright SUVs passed under volcanic rocks with deep striations, eyed by buzzards tilting overhead, lending the scene a medieval quality.

Robert Bressler was in some ways representative of the dot-com wealth newly arrived in the valley, and in others highly individualistic. He considered himself lucky to have earlier been in the right place at the right time, by which he meant the Massachusetts Institute of Technology in 1971. There, writing a graduate thesis about how computers talk to each other, a budding electronic engineer before anyone had come up with the handle "computer scientist," he got involved in a Department of Defense project called ARPANET, which for all practical purposes became the Internet.

Bressler went on to join a technology company. He discovered that he had an aptitude for understanding where networking was going when it was about to go bonkers. He was then recruited by Sun Microsystems, a pubescent general in the happening electronic revolution, which made him a vice president. Bearded, bespectacled, precisely spoken, Bob Bressler began to think of himself as the Johnny Appleseed of networking, a partaker of shared visions for the future. The best way to succeed on the wild digital frontier, he realized, was for engineers to work together toward a common goal, with lots of elbow room. Put a stake in the ground way out there and let the engineers work toward it. One stake in the ground was "special purposes devices," bits of hardware that performed specific functions and did not need a big mainframe.

The analogy of profitable networking he liked to use was that of the toaster: better to have something that simply makes toast than a toaster oven that does a lot of other unnecessary things and is complicated and more expensive. "In the old days," he says, "the computers arrived in trucks, and the software in envelopes." As a result of his and others' innovative thinking, "the computers began arriving in envelopes, and the software in trucks."

By then Bressler, as a vice president, was well endowed with Sun stock, which would split five times between 1994 and 2000, making a lot of things possible for Bob and his wife, Stacy, that had never seemed possible before. They were living in Los Altos Hills, minutes from a company that was challenging others in the neighborhood as well as the mighty Microsoft, up in Redmond, Washington. Internet supremacy was the grail, and the Bresslers' lives were dominated by the feverish, driven ways of a valley nicknamed for a microchip component.

Fabrication and miniaturization, it seemed, had been projected directly onto the human persona. Every bit of turf was fought over, from the latest software to mountain bikes. In restaurants, the Bresslers would look around to see who was seated near them, and talk in code so no secrets would be revealed. There were so many stakes in the distance, people were tripping each other up trying to reach them, but there was little felt human intercourse or bonding. People were either transients or out to steal your vision.

The Bresslers took all this for granted until some friends invited them to attend a wine auction up in Napa Valley, and there they saw that things could be different. The auction was a sophisticated party where you could have *fun* — unusual, even unorthodox behavior in Silicon Valley. You didn't have to stand around talking in code, just swirl cabernet in a tulip-shaped glass and meet nice people, and the next year the Bresslers returned.

Then they made a decision many people of means make when overlooking comely vineyards seemingly untouched by the ambition and acrimony in the world: they called a realtor. They bought a modest house and started coming up on weekends. They found themselves thinking of Silicon Valley as a distant battlefield and of Napa as home, and decided to move up full time. He would commute to Silicon Valley a couple of times a week. Still wearing his Sun Microsystems hat, he thought he could in his spare time put Napa Valley on the Internet, helping people who were interested in selling wine electronically. And maybe they would explain wine to him.

Before long, the Bresslers had sold their first house and bought another, not an architectural expression of geek hubris in the hills, but a big, utilitarian structure in the up-valley town of St. Helena. It met their standard that they had to be able to walk everywhere from it — to Tra Vigne and the Green Valley and other restaurants, to the renovated movie theater and Main Street Books and the Model Bakery. Their new friends had told them they would never find such a house that was suitable, these being people who for the most part were recent arrivals themselves and already had their vineyards and their labels and assumed the Bresslers, too, were looking for a modern-day castle keep with plenty of space for vines.

The Bresslers ordered the construction of an insulated wine room, an early step in any renovation. It cost eighty thousand dollars and was capable of holding eight thousand bottles of the right stuff, meaning many of Napa's most famous cabernets that few people could afford even if they could find them for sale, with either a historical pedigree — Heitz Martha's Vineyard, Stag's Leap Cask 23, Phelps Insignia, Dunn's Howell Mountain, and so on — or, more impressive, cult status — Dalla Valle, Screaming Eagle, Grace, Bryant Family, and others elbowing their way up the critics' statistical ladders. Then their eyes turned toward the land.

The property already included a little acre-and-a-quarter vineyard planted to runty vines in a long-gone, less sophisticated time, and this might have satisfied them, being the down-to-earth millionaires they were, in jeans and baggy sweaters, with a pool table in their living room and a droll sculpture of a standing lower torso, also wearing jeans. But then they met the vineyard manager, and everything changed.

Vineyard managers are necessary adjuncts of the good life in Napa Valley, more important than personal trainers or personal chefs, and in the valley they come neither easily nor cheaply. This one had a crooked smile, a tendency to swear, and a reputation for excellence at any cost which, translated, meant anywhere from twenty-five thousand to seventy-five thousand dollars to replant a single acre of vines, and another ten thousand to thirty thousand dollars an acre a year just to maintain it.

This vineyard manager was an outgoing native with curly black hair and a lopsided grin named David Abreu, of Portuguese descent, who had grown up in the valley and learned vineyard work the hard way, by doing it. Abreu was the most talked about vineyard manager in the valley now, which some thought meant in California, some in the world, a "vineyard manager to the stars" sought after by the likes of Garen Staglin and others who could afford him.

Abreu came over and looked at their vineyard and laughed in that slightly manic way of his. He said, "Here . . . hey," and began to pleasantly curse, calling theirs "a toy vineyard." The Bresslers had to hire a winemaker, too, for between one thousand and four thousand dollars a month, and not just any winemaker. Mia Klein, partner of Tony Soter, architect of the famous Spottswoode wines, had for years made the cult cabernet Dalla Valle, and she and Dave and the Bresslers had a fine debate about rootstock. Dave agreed to a close planting, three feet by five, for a mere six thousand dollars, and Mia to someday make the wine in one of the valley's custom crushers — commercial wineries offering pressing and storage facilities to small producers — for forty dollars a case. And the Bresslers would have to buy their own French oak barrels for storage at six hundred and fifty dollars apiece.

What fun, the Bresslers thought. Even with a toy vineyard, where the economies of scale were not in your favor, more money could be made than was spent, given the astronomical price of Napa Valley boutique cabernet sauvignon with the right provenance, meaning it had been put together by the right people and carefully positioned. Hadn't the Grace family turned one acre of grapes into a cult wine of the nineties? The Bresslers would hire someone to do their label, the twenty-first-century equivalent of a coat of arms; such a "package," including foils and letterhead, could cost more than one hundred thousand dollars to design. But first they went label shopping at Dean & DeLuca, picking out the sort of label they liked, imagining what their name would look like on a lovely dark bottle.

Gradually the vineyard became more to them than a toy. They were able to buy an adjoining four acres, and quickly did so, and Dave Abreu took that on, too. By then the price of it all had risen considerably. Abreu now said, when asked how much money would be required, "Whatever it takes."

The Bresslers could afford him and they could afford Mia Kline. Bob Bressler was, as he often said, modestly, standing there in his running shoes, clean jeans, and bulky sweater, cell phone attached to his belt, "a capitalist." He and Stacy would eventually produce a thousand cases a year. Robert Parker, the famous wine critic, would no doubt taste their wine because he liked Abreu and he tasted all the wines originating in Abreu vineyards, and all the wines that Mia made, and usually ranked them highly. The Bresslers' wine would flow out to the world through fine restaurants and the Internet when the time came. All this was predicted from what was still a scruffy patch of hobby vines but might someday be a cameo Lafite or Stag's Leap.

In the process something else was being demonstrated by these avowed capitalists: making money had become a necessary component of social and cultural authentication; it was perhaps the primary distinction between the new fortunes of the day and those of the past, as if John D. Rockefeller had tried to marginally increase his fortune with some commercial enterprise in his side yard.

Meanwhile, at parties, people inquired after the Bresslers' vineyard and after their intentions for their wine; suddenly, Bob and Stacy were *in*. Their involvement in a vineyard and a cabernet aspiring to cult status was an indication of serious intent and the great distance they had traveled in a short time — from the rigors of take-no-prisoners electronic innovation to the joys of vintnerhood.

Some of their new neighbors had reservations about all this. The neighbor just to the west, Roland Wentzel, was a successful entrepreneur, not in computers but in furniture, the owner of three upscale outlets called Traditions who had come to the valley in 1990 to "turn back the clock." He had conducted a survey of the Bay Area and concluded that St. Helena was the only small town left with a small town's characteristics. These included an independent economy, so people did not have to get into their cars to go shopping, and schools close enough so children could walk, and the movie theater and restaurants close enough for the parents to do the same. And there was agriculture within the town limits.

Farming was a vital part of the ideal community, Wentzel believed, and of nature, too, evident in the long westerly view of the Mayacamas Mountains that included Douglas fir and some redwoods, evidence of the rapidly disappearing wild California past. A soft-spoken Ph.D. with a degree in resource economics, he had earlier come under the tutelage of the agricultural economics theorist Siegfried Ciriacy-Wantrup, at the University of California, Berkeley, and in Paris had studied "peri-urban" agriculture — farming in the presence of an ever-expanding population.

Napa Valley's agriculture was increasingly peri-urban. Wentzel thought the county had done a pretty good job with maintaining it, largely because of long-standing zoning restrictions, and he wanted to be part of it, but not obtrusively. The idealized small-town environment he prized would not have been possible without vineyards like the old one that came with his property, and with the house next door. Grapevines had postponed subdivision and provided open space, as well as that connection to nature.

Wentzel did not hire a vineyard manager to take care of his, and he didn't tear out the old, unchic grape varieties but worked them himself, going against what he referred to as "the dilettante fashion of these times."

He and his wife, Barbara, built a lovely, pale orange Mediterranean house with lots of doors and beams from a monastery in Spain. In addition, they planted Lombardy poplar trees on the eastern boundary, to form a *petite allée* to define the dirt road there and contribute to the rural aesthetics. An *allée* was a traditional European walk or drive lined with evenly spaced trees — yews, hornbeams, or sycamores — but the Wentzels' *allée* was defined by fast-growing poplars that would also screen what they considered a less than aesthetically pleasing house being built next door.

The owner sold it unfinished to a developer, who made some cosmetic changes and put it up for sale again. The developer also informed the Wentzels that he, not the Wentzels, owned the dirt road and one side of the *petite allée*. That was a surprise to them, but such things were happening in Napa Valley. Re-surveys and lot-line adjustments were common now in a place where property boundaries had once been casual considerations, before real estate became synonymous with getting rich.

Roland Wentzel wrote a letter to the broker saying that he was under the impression that he owned the *allée* and assumed it would be preserved in any case. He learned that the prospective buyer was a dot-commer named Bressler.

One day Wentzel saw a bearded man in glasses and blue jeans drive up in a car and get out. He was smiling, as Wentzel remembered it. "He said, 'Hi, I'm your new neighbor.' Then he told me how rich he was and that he was going to sue me."

Bob Bressler would dispute that account. "I didn't get in my car and drive over there," he said. "I was coming home from somewhere and saw him, and simply stopped." He would deny threatening to sue because "that would have been illogical."

A subsequent survey proved that the Bresslers did indeed own the *allée*. They granted the Wentzels an easement to use it anyway, and decided to cut down one row of trees, acting on the advice of Dave Abreu, the vineyard manager, whose sole interest was vines. The Bresslers had learned that grapes, not trees, were what Napa Valley was all about, that if you wanted to be taken seriously, you had to be willing to go to the mat over quality cabernet sauvignon. The trees not only took up space but would also shade the young vines, and they were, as Bressler pointed out, "only *poplars,* for God's sake."

The truth was that neither Bressler nor Wentzel stood to lose anything substantial. Failure to produce a sought-after, expensive wine would not appreciably affect Bressler's fortune, nor was Wentzel financially prohibited from tearing down his little guesthouse and building a *petite allée* on his own property. And whoever failed to get what he wanted could well afford to move somewhere else and start over again. What really transpired was a contest of wills among people accustomed to getting what they wanted: vineyard owner, vineyard manager, and neighbor were all convinced of the rightness of their position and unwilling to compromise. The argument was not about grapevines, profit, peri-urban aesthetics, or the need for yet another cult cabernet, but about the importance of winning, and a direct reflection of corporate values projected on a small, increasingly fragile part of America.

Some perspective on this was provided by Samson Bowers, a tall, courtly, aging St. Helena city councilman — white goatee, white buzzcut, tennis shorts — who lived for a time in the Wentzels' guest cottage, liked the poplars, and after learning that the Bresslers intended to remove one row of them, decided to help out. Not officially but artistically, by making a scale drawing of the *petite allée* and plotting the angle of afternoon sun and proving that cutting the trees would do away with only about eight feet of shadow for a short period each day.

Bowers had bailed out of advertising in Manhattan at age forty-seven and come west, never regretting it, living first in Carmel Valley and fleeing its commercialization, already the second time he had witnessed such a phenomenon. He grew up in upstate New York, and on the wall of his St. Helena condo hung a photograph of his ancestral home, a brick Georgian with a fireplace in every room, Bowers being descended from the man who had been given a patent for thirteen thousand acres by King George III in the eighteenth century.

That land came to include Cooperstown, and Bowers had watched it transformed from a lovely American community into a parody of the same — Baseball, USA — with a Hall of Fame, "museums," souvenir shops, baseball paraphernalia emporiums, and fast-food outlets. He didn't want the same thing to happen to St. Helena, threatened by sheer wealth and by people pressing in from all sides. Newcomers to the valley didn't vote, as Bowers often pointed out, and didn't attend Rotary or the other less glamorous gatherings. "They want all the services they had in cities," from specialty protein to "Julieted" nails. "And they always drive their cars."

Bowers walked everywhere — the supermarket, the library — and increasingly found himself opposed not just to automobiles but also to the concept of private property, a surprising position, he realized, in one whose ancestor was given land by the king of England. St. Helena had six thousand citizens, three traffic lights, and no Mc-Donald's. The closest thing to a fast-food stop was Taylor's Refresher, home of the ahi burger, heavenly fish tacos, and of course wine. "The only way to keep the town small is to deny the overblown plans of outsiders, commercial and otherwise," Bowers said repeatedly. "But 'no' is a word Americans have a problem with."

The "yuppiefication of the valley," as he put it, was symbolized by the Napa Valley Wine Auction, which raised large sums of money from people competing to show how much of it they had, and by the fact that few of the almost three hundred vintners "ever get their hands dirty." Both things he saw as the unhealthy result of a national economy empowering a relative few without inculcating in them a commensurate sense of responsibility.

Bowers calculated at the time that the Bresslers' new vineyard would contain twenty-eight hundred vines per acre when completed. That was six times the number that would have gone in under the old planting system, before yield and quality became as much social as financial concerns. Each of the vines would require water, and water was already a contentious issue in the valley. All an observer had to do was to project the elements in this little conflict over a row of poplars onto the rest of the valley to see the scope of the problem of vineyard development. In the end, Bowers believed, the big battles — including the one over the hillsides — would be between private property proponents and those advocating shared community values.

The trees were cut, Roland Wentzel contending that about thirty poplars fell to make way for roughly as many cabernet vines, but Bob Bressler claiming that only twenty-four fell, and this allowed him to put in four additional rows of vines because he no longer needed turnaround space for the tractor. The capitalist also claimed that the additional vines would produce at least three hundred bottles of wine worth, if all went well, about twenty-five thousand additional dollars a year.

The Wentzels continued to look at the toy vineyard and at the Bresslers' house and tried to be philosophical about both. But then they put their lovely Mediterranean villa, with its monastery beams and old-fashioned, wide-spaced vineyard, on the market for five million dollars. They moved up to Mendocino County — no one asked if they still intended to turn back the clock — to relatively unspoiled country. There they, too, put in a commercial vineyard and planned to build a winery.

4

THE STRIVING after success and its effects was limited to neither the entrepreneurs nor the beneficiaries of the recent boom in electronic commerce. The outsized desire to achieve went back even further than the 1960s, when ambitious dropouts, professors, doubting businessmen, dreamers, and emotional refugees had embraced the un-American vine and sought in Napa Valley an existence outside the corridors of presumptive behavior. They had names like Davies and Winiarski, Forman and Barrett, and they didn't know where they fit into the relatively simple life of the valley then, its recognizable groups roughly divided into the social set (Ramsey, Hart, Daniel, de Latour), the mavericks (Stewart, Heitz, McCrea), the colorful misfits (bohemians and other borderliners), and, of course, the Italians (Martini, Mondavi, many others). All the groups mixed in those "old days": raucous evenings at steak houses, occasional square dances or cocktail parties at the end of a dirt road. At that time everybody felt part of something larger, whatever their intentions or their net worth, but that had changed.

The groups were now as diverse at the top as at the bottom, with mostly new names and new credentials. The old social set had vanished, the new one containing a few lucky spermers and holdovers but dominated by new money and notoriety. The mavericks tended to be investors in peculiar commodities outside the valley who agreed to pursue the things — wines, acceptable causes — important within it; the misfits were investors in peculiar commodities outside the valley who took no part in valley life, dropping in, levitating out, corporate and New Age pashas. Even the Italians were different.

A bulldozer operator cutting a foundation for a mansion overlooking the valley floor or clearing chaparral for a vineyard still came across the odd redwood stake, hammered into the earth in another era. And if the driver knew the valley, he might say, "Ah, the Italians."

Their names are mostly forgotten, as are the men and women who put minds and backs into what became a triumph of transplantation. They were once as exotic as the Chinese coolies they replaced in the fields, identified by hard cheese, stubby smoldering toscanos, and unpronounceable names. The Italians took up the tough tasks and seemed to enjoy them, their warm, explosive speech echoing through the vineyards and their smiles in the old photographs full of teeth. They paid homage to grapes few people had heard of and no one dreamed would someday have a devoted following here as "Cal-Italos" and "super-Tuscans." The names suggested foreign potentates, saints, and weather — barbera, sangiovese, nebbiolo. They drank local "zin" (zinfandel) and "pets" (petite sirah) with gusto, in great quantities.

Their cooking varied beyond the imaginings of the Californians — how could there be so many different kinds of noodles? And they were loyal. Take on one Italian, take on all. Unfazed by the stupendous effort required to plant and tend grapes by hand, they had unbounded confidence in other endeavors, insisting on their due, maintaining *bella figura,* gradually buying up plots in the Central Valley and in the narrow coastal defiles, farming land no one else wanted, including the hillsides. The already wealthy owners of those Victorian piles built in the late nineteenth century in Napa and Sonoma couldn't outlast the paisans, whose favorite game involved bowling without pins and who pursued life on a level of emotional intensity exhausting to the uninitiated.

There was nothing that could not be contended. "An argument," as one descendant recognized, "is an Italian conversation."

Mostly they worked. It was as if the Protestant ethic had been grafted onto the Catholic mysteries. The outcome of all this energy was not limited to wine, food, and opera. There were Italians in the bank in San Francisco, and so a large segment of the wine industry was nurtured. Italian fortunes came to be exemplified by two

names famous in the California vineyard, Gallo and Mondavi. Ernest
Gallo showed California how to sell wine with a single-minded
competitiveness that left the competition dry-mouthed. Eventually
he turned bottles with handles on them into sleek Bordelais shapes
containing French varietals and sold them at prices no one ever
thought Gallo wines would aspire to. But more than anyone in Napa
Valley, it was Robert Mondavi who boosted the appreciation of fine
California wine.

The Mondavis had been preceded in the valley by Louis Martini,
an imposing figure in a black cloak, a gifted winemaker but proud,
terminally argumentative, thoroughly Italian. Had Martini possessed
a talent for public relations, there would never have been the Robert
Mondavi phenomenon. Robert and his brother, Peter, began in
Sunny St. Helena Winery with their father's money, Robert dreaming of oak barrels and a product to compete with the best, which
then meant French. But his and Peter's arrangement — an echo of
the Gallo brothers' anthem, "I'll sell all the wine you can make if
you'll make all the wine I can sell" — faltered after too many Italian
conversations, and Robert went out on his own.

So relentless was his selling and so great was his success that he attracted a Frenchman — the Baron Rothschild — to Napa Valley in
the 1970s, a coup and a watershed. But now, at the end of the twentieth century, the Robert Mondavi Winery was a publicly held corporation where Italian conversations abounded between Robert's
two sons, the lucky spermers Michael and Tim, with their sister a
distant moderating force. What would happen to the corporation
when the old man died was anybody's guess.

The most famous Italian in the valley might still be Robert, but
increasingly attention focused on another name, one with fame related not to wine but to the spinning of celluloid fantasy and, increasingly, to tourism.

"Don Corleone's desk will be in the entrance hall," said the handsome young woman serving as a tour guide, talking about the desk
used in the film *The Godfather.* "It's a statement, you know, of Francis's accomplishments."

The year was 1996, and Francis Ford Coppola had recently purchased the old Inglenook winery from the Heublein Corporation. "Francis brought in specialists from the films," she added, and had concept drawings for the staircase done by the production designer who worked on *Apocalypse Now* and *The Godfather*. The display cases for his wine, on sale, were designed by a movie conceptualizer, and those for his T-shirts by yet another. "There have been so many changes" — the removal of the modest fountain once out front to a nearby hillside, the parking of a red Tucker, star of another of Coppola's films, in the second-floor gift shop until the finishing of the Memorabilia Room, a showcase of cinematic marginalia. Fifteen woodworkers had been brought in from Nevada just to build the winery's central staircase and were living in the winery's shell. The three-story modified Gothic edifice hummed.

Out in the courtyard, men were putting the final touches on a concrete reflecting pool and pergola. Nearby sat the gunboat that appeared in *Apocalypse Now*, its plywood showing through flaking gray paint, to be redone and moved into some undecided public viewing space. Francis — it was the sanctioned reference for employees — had rechristened grand old Inglenook chateau "Niebaum-Coppola," thus associating the early symbol of the valley's ability to produce fine wine with the new owner's unrelated vocation.

This was to be symbolized by placing Don Corleone's desk across the entrance hall from Gustave Niebaum's oak-paneled Captain's Room. Costumes from *Bram Stoker's Dracula* were to be draped on mannequins arranged on the stairs, the guide added, to greet visitors who made their way to the second floor on risers made of poison-wood imported from Belize, where Coppola owned a resort. The balustrades would be of Belizian jobillo, the carved fruit bowls on the newel posts of Belizian granadilla. The design would be "Europeanish," said the master carpenter, an imposing bearded figure in new Carhartt coveralls. "We got the concept and sort of massaged it . . . We opted to do it all by hand because, when Francis looks at it, he wants to be able to see the craftsmanship."

The tasting room on the second floor would be fitted with movie screens for a "multimedia tasting experience," including a film about Niebaum-Coppola. There was more than one Tucker available for viewing, and a large trove of movie paraphernalia elsewhere on the property, ready to be brought forward when the exhibits needed refreshing. Visitors would pay to get a tour of the winery, and pay again for the tasting and for some souvenir from what promised to be a large trove of wine-related products, and some very distantly related.

If the valley's stunning, often jarring new architecture symbolized the remove between new arrivals and locals, so had the historical buildings when they first went up. Inglenook was, in contemporary parlance, a nineteenth-century steroid structure that once reigned over a gorgeous, totally rural landscape dedicated to the creation of one idealized product — wine — and modeled on Old World antecedents. Designed by a Vermonter, Hamden McIntyre, who was not an architect but a talented builder with an eye for classical form, Inglenook had belonged to the wealthy Niebaum, seafarer and fur trader, and for more than a century had reflected the aspirations and vulnerabilities of a New World Eden.

Now Napa Valley ranked second only to Disneyland in popularity among tourists. Most of the five million annual visitors were accustomed to spending more than five dollars for distraction, and at Niebaum-Coppola they would certainly have the chance. Selling T-shirts and wine was a common practice all over the valley — some other historical structures, notably Beringer, had also been burnished beyond the luster of their former selves — but at Niebaum-Coppola, née Inglenook, this commerce took on heightened intensity.

A patina of the past appealed to visitors who wanted a brush with wine culture and a few mementos but none of the scruffiness associated with true agriculture. There were many devices in the valley for luring visitors — Sterling's ski lift, Mondavi's concerts — and winery tours had become increasingly important as avenues to further profits from direct sales of wine and clothing. Niebaum-Coppola was in a unique position to capitalize on another — the most — romantic California industry, movies.

Inglenook's intransigent stone and towering symmetry resisted this reinterpretation, however. The winery's proportions had been carefully worked out as functional, if not beautiful, and the renovations struck some old-timers as incongruous. No wine was to be made here; the alterations all suggested crowd control, and the imperial reflecting pool would mirror a structure devoted as much to

Hollywood as to Bordeaux. Francis told a newspaper reporter that in planning the retrofit he had tried to imagine what Gustave Niebaum would do, but Niebaum had allowed no tourism and no deviation from the narrow path of a great wine estate. He had strode through the winery in a pair of white gloves, searching for dirt, and the idea that this traditionalist would have allowed costumes from a melo-drama to be placed on a theatrical central staircase, or would erect a movie prop in the shadow of hard-wrought Victorian sensibilities, was absurd. But today no one seemed to care.

Francis and his wife, Eleanor, had already purchased and moved into Niebaum's house when they acquired Inglenook. A lovely Victorian with Eastlake influences and a broad wraparound porch reminiscent of a ship's deck, the house sat a quarter of a mile west of the old win-ery. Francis had wanted a retreat from the pressures of filmmaking, or so he told people at the time, and he wanted to make a little wine from his own vineyard, a reminder that his father had once pursued the same hobby in a Brooklyn basement.

In the Niebaum house the Coppolas entertained lavishly, using what they referred to as "natural" servers, people from the valley who dispensed food with a smile. Most of the arrangements were made by outsiders, and restaurants in San Francisco were often paid to come to Rutherford and prepare feasts, from Italian to Moroccan, and caterers brought in. Everything had to look just so, the same fac-totum system that surrounded the making of films prevailing at these events. More than one person was on hand to make sure the candles on the porch were lighted at precisely the right moment and spaced properly to assure "continuity" in every detail, and make sure everything seemed spontaneous.

The pay was good, the labor unending and exhausting. Some locals were thrilled by the presence of celebrities like Madonna and George Lukas, Robert De Niro and Robin Williams. Anthony Hopkins once stopped by the kitchen before departing and, seeing some leftover fava beans, slipped into his role as Hannibal Lecter in *The Silence of the Lambs*. The thrilled kitchen workers watched Hopkins disappear into the darkness and felt a tinge of fear even as they laughed at the idea of a cannibal in the house built by the con-servative, strait-laced Niebaum.

When Eleanor had women friends over, Francis insisted on being included, the center of attention, and the guests found him childish, if winning. His financial difficulties were often discussed by acquaintances and by staff. Francis used the house, with its ancient, overspreading live oak out front, to impress potential investors in movies and other enterprises. Strangers were immersed in family activities as if they belonged, Francis himself cooking the pasta, everything *abbondanza:* food, wine, talk, Napa Valley bounty of all sorts ladled up in a kitchen that had served the relatively meager needs of the Niebaums and their heirs, the Daniels.

The renovations in the house, like those in the winery, showed how much California and the world had changed in a century. Francis had used the old stable to make the first vintages of Niebaum-Coppola wine, which he called Rubicon, the beginning of the methodical transformation of a movie director into a founder's spiritual heir, and after he bought the winery, too, he needed all the help he could get.

John Skupny worked for Caymus Vineyards and there earned a reputation as an effective, straightforward, pleasant administrator, a blond Californian with a degree in fine arts and that rarity among winery managers, a sense of humor. Down there by the Napa River, a few stones' throw from Inglenook, he had dealt with the irascible old Charley Wagner and his son, Chuck, and with Randy Dunn, fresh out of Davis and not yet on the heights of Howell Mountain, and had learned most everything about power cabernets, from production to marketing to the delicate managing of myth and reality.

Skupny went to work for Francis in 1992, before the Inglenook winery was purchased. Niebaum-Coppola had some assets in addition to the vineyards that had come with the house, including a good winemaker, Tony Soter, of Spottswoode fame, a new press, and a determination on the part of the owner to develop a more elegant style of cabernet. Liabilities included limited working facilities — the wine was made where carriages had once stood, and it shared storage space upstairs with reels of film — and a lot of inky, older Rubicon that badly needed selling.

Wine had to be moved through an old-boy network of distributors, the narrow part of the hourglass. The producer was on top and the consumer on the bottom, and the old boys in the middle didn't like aged wine without stellar rankings by Robert Parker or *Wine Spectator*. Skupny's challenge was to find someone willing to bet that Rubicon would improve and, until it did, to move the present inventory. Francis was gracious when Skupny brought the distributors and big names in the trade by the house, entertaining them, making them feel special. And Skupny pointed out that Niebaum-Coppola intended to increase the quality of the wine while cutting production, making the wine rare and raising the price at the same time. Production of Rubicon went down to two thousand cases, very small, but that meant another Coppola brand had to be invented to broaden the market.

A wine consultant and the new winemaker sat down together and fashioned something from cabernet franc and merlot, and they called it Francis Coppola Family Wine. Skupny put it out for eighteen dollars a bottle, and it sold like crazy during a recession. They also decided to make a brand of zinfandel called Paternino, a tribute to Francis's Italian grandfather. The winery had trouble with the Bureau of Alcohol, Tobacco and Firearms because there was to be a picture of the Statue of Liberty on the bottle, but the label was finally approved because, Skupny thought, the BATF got preoccupied with Branch Davidians down in Waco.

At that point wine was small potatoes in Francis's larger financial basket. But he told Skupny he wanted to be on first base if Heublein ever decided to sell Inglenook, the regal chateau standing out there to the east facing Highway 29, and they could move into the big time. Skupny knew Heublein's history and all the baggage it carried in the valley, symbolized by the big, ugly storage facility built in front of the winery shortly after Heublein acquired it, spoiling the view from the highway. He knew Heublein could never recover from decades of bad decisions and that someday the corporation would have to unload a property also burdened by an unhappy family history.

Niebaum's great-grandnephew, John Daniel, a conservative pillar of rectitude, had been married to a woman known variously as beautiful, talented, and destructive. Her name was Betty, and she had made much of John Daniel's life miserable. Her hatred of the winery contributed to his decision to dump the family heirloom in the sixties;

in Daniel's eyes, Heublein soon devalued the Inglenook name, which had been carefully made into a symbol of excellence, by producing a great deal of cheap wine and plastering it with that proud name. Daniel had refused to sell any wine that was not first rate, a standard that had prevented him from ever making a profit, and otherwise hewed to the line laid down by Niebaum in bygone times. After selling out he had to watch an invasive corporation use out-of-valley grapes to fill jugs — sacrilege, in his view, and a possible factor in Daniel's subsequent suicide.

John Skupny knew all this. He knew that the corporation would now like to unload Inglenook, but assumed the price would be unapproachable by an independent operator like Coppola, even with his occasionally massive cash flows. But Skupny, like others in the valley, dreamed of the old chateau's passing again to "local" control, and feared its being taken over by another corporation more ambitious than Heublein.

One night in 1994 he received a call from a friend in the business who told him, "Your worst nightmare is about to be realized. Heublein's being sold to Canandaigua."

Canandaigua was huge, Canandaigua was foreign (the East Coast), Canandaigua was rich. Skupny couldn't sleep. Then his friend called back and said, "It happened. They bought everything but the crown jewel." He meant the old winery and its ninety-three acres. They didn't know what to do with it, and Skupny saw this as the big chance.

He called Francis the next morning and told him, "Work it from the top." Francis was acquainted with the right people at Grand Metropolitan, the conglomerate that owned Heublein, and he could get in touch with them while Skupny worked the person divesting Heublein here on the ground. It was decided that movie director and divestor would meet, but first Skupny "scripted" Francis: "Don't remind this guy that you tried to buy Inglenook ten years ago, because he'll see how much you want it." The strategy was to convince Heublein, instead, that selling to Francis was the morally correct decision. It would exonerate the company for what was widely perceived as a destructive tenure in the valley, when Heublein had ushered in the corporate presence, altering the perception and the operation of Inglenook and of Beaulieu Vineyard.

Spike Lee's movie *Do the Right Thing* had just come out. Francis had seen it, and Skupny thought he was influenced by the notion of doing the right thing. Francis invited everybody to meet on his porch late one morning, to sit out there as if on the deck of a crenelated white ship sailing through a sea of vineyards, all very cordial and low-key. But the Heublein people were tight with information. If they agreed to sell, they would still demand the right to buy grapes from the prized Inglenook *terroir,* and that Francis replant the vineyard. Also, they would demand a lease-back on the ugly storage facility out front, to house their barrels.

They wouldn't come up with a dollar amount and wanted Francis to make an offer. He and Skupny thought they were being used to push up the price while Heublein shopped Inglenook around among other potential buyers. Francis came up with another strategy — preemption. The chief financial officer of Zoetrope, Francis's company headquartered in San Francisco, part of the Coppola team, worked out how Inglenook would fit in with Francis's other businesses, while the staff in Rutherford studied the inventories provided by Heublein. And the attorney who acted as Francis's guardian had to be convinced that it was all a good idea. At last a purchase agreement was produced, and Francis wrote a check for a million dollars in the little house near the stable that served as his office. Skupny walked the check over to the big house so Eleanor could countersign it, then walked it back again. Francis was giddy, Skupny would remember. He asked if Skupny played poker, and when he answered yes, Francis said, "Good."

Skupny delivered the purchase agreement and the check to Heublein. The next day the guy called and said okay, and Skupny got into his car and drove over to Inglenook and stood out in the courtyard, under the massive façade overgrown with ivy, and called Francis on his cell phone. Skupny told him, "It's yours."

The final price was just over nine million dollars. Heublein would take back about half that amount in a note; Francis's cash would all come from *Dracula.*

After a day in San Francisco with the lawyers, when it was a done deal, Skupny drove up to the old carriage house through a setting little changed in a century. Navalle Creek, lined with stone by Chinese laborers, wound down to the broad plain of Rutherford. He told the winemaker, "A year from now we won't be able to remember what this was like," and called the staff into the library above the stable and told them, "Everything's going to change."

The final agreement was six inches thick; Skupny's hand grew tired signing it. Francis didn't get the Inglenook name, but he got everything else he wanted — vineyards, property, architecture, Rubicon . . . *tutti*.

The logo was redesigned and all labels made similar. That was the fun part. Francis constantly came up with creative ideas: a rum from Belize to be stored in old Rubicon barrels, a grappa from Oregon, bottled water from a spring up on the mountain. Not all of it worked out. Any profits were to go to the mother ship, Zoetrope, but meanwhile there were huge expenses involved — renovating old Inglenook, replanting, redesigning. The money had to come from somewhere, and it had to come fast.

When the winery was stripped, before all the new equipment went in, Francis threw a party and invited everybody in Rutherford, St. Helena, and Oakville. The comedian Don Novello was the master of ceremonies. There was a battle of the bands, fireworks, and two cakes — one for the Coppolas' acquisition of the Niebaum house, the other for the acquisition of the winery — both devoured.

Francis hired Dick Maher, a short, feisty former Marine who drank soda from a customized Howitzer shell. Maher was supposed to build the business, to go from zero to sixty in about a year. He had a long, spotty history in the wine business. While working for Heublein, Maher had been the brand manager of the cola-flavored bubbly wine called I Love You, and while working for Seagram had earned a reputation as a corporate ass-kicker, capable of either affability or unpleasantness, whichever was required. Maher had headed up Christian Brothers after it was bought by Grand Metropolitan, another swallowing-up of an old Napa property by the alien conglomerate.

Maher hired a winery manager not from the wine business but from a large retailing company, and the writing was on the wall, Skupny thought. In addition, Francis always had some guru type around, first a studio guy, then a young economist, then somebody else idea-oriented, enthusiastic. This person would say, "I've been thinking about something, Francis. Why don't you . . ." And Skupny would think, "Who the hell owns this place, anyway?"

Traveling with Francis was great fun. He was a world-class gourmand, a consumer of life. In New York, Skupny watched Francis be-ing interviewed by Charlie Rose and five other journalists. Francis taught Skupny the importance of the journalistic file, by which he meant any newspaper or magazine story that became part of the public record. He taught Skupny to make sure he was always the source of a story, never *the* story, a crucial distinction. Francis was, of course, always the story.

Together they staged a Niebaum-Coppola celebration party at the Four Seasons, and it sold out. Francis sat up on the dais, sur-rounded by ingénues, and confided to Skupny, "I feel like a Roman emperor."

Skupny concentrated on the "hospitality" issues, getting customers into the chateau while the renovation was being done. Everything was to be "related"; synergy was the high concept. For instance, guests at Francis's lodge in Belize would watch Francis's movies while drinking Francis's wine. Gift packets at Niebaum-Coppola might include a Coppola movie and a Coppola wine of the same vintage, along with a Niebaum-Coppola T-shirt. But there were limits to what they could legally do, part of the controversial winery definition passed a few years before that prevented the sale at winer-ies of anything unrelated to wine. But historical structures had a great advantage, one that would prove decisive: whatever had been sold before, whatever had been done, was grandfathered — that is, exempt.

Skupny was told, as he later recalled it, "to access the rights to eve-rything ever sold here, to establish precedents." He pored over all the old Inglenook inventories. There had been a cheese deli then, so they could sell cheese now. A knife had been used to cut the cheese in the old days, so presumably today they could also sell cutlery. That was the idea. But where, Skupny wondered, were the limits?

The emphasis was on sales and on the look of the place. Enhance the merchandise. Enrich the visitor's experience. Creative consul-tants put the decision makers at Niebaum-Coppola in touch with designers of various sales emporiums; a woman responsible for ex-hibits at the San Francisco airport was hired. Another woman was brought in who could "source" special merchandise — a buyer's buyer. Meanwhile, Skupny went through all the old tax records and folders full of old photographs, and saw some that gave him goose bumps. He thought of two immigrant families — Niebaum and Coppola — ending up in the same place, at different times, with nothing else in common. But Francis worked the symbolism, calling Skupny on the telephone from all over — New York, Lisbon — with new ideas for exploiting the Niebaum connection.

Skupny still had to dispose of the old Rubicon wine. And there remained the big question of grapes. Niebaum-Coppola vineyards could supply only a fraction of what was required for the new, cheaper wines, so where would the rest of the fruit come from? Francis and Maher wanted to ramp up fast, but no wine that contained less than seventy-five percent of Napa Valley fruit could qualify for the coveted Napa Valley appellation. Napa Valley grapes were too precious and hard to find to put into inexpensive new lines, but there was another route: cheap Central Valley and central coast fruit trucked in and made into wine sold with just the Napa Valley address on the label. Heublein had done it in the past, and so presently were Beringer, Mondavi, Sutter Home, and many others. Invent new brands under the proprietary name, since most buyers don't notice or don't care, and watch the revenue roll in.

The day of the Christmas party, 1995, Dick Maher told Skupny he was fired. Holiday time, season of good will, adios. Skupny had by then taken care of all the tough stuff, including moving old Rubicon, and if truth be told was tired of it all. Niebaum-Coppola had gone from sixteen to seventy employees in one year, and in the process Skupny had missed a lot in his children's lives. Maher had convinced Francis, or so Skupny surmised, that concern with "the right thing" would lead to failure. And Skupny was tired of Maher's posturing, what he called "the Marine thing, all that bullshit." Skupny knew as much about the business as anybody, he would do fine on his own, and he went home.

This treasure, this Inglenook, might survive in perpetuity because of all the commercialism, Skupny reasoned. The heavy merchandising and publicity were bullets in the war for tourist dollars. But at other times he thought of what Inglenook could have been, and he shuddered.

5

O FTEN THE IMPULSE and the wherewithal to build anew in the valley came not from tourism or electronics, not from commerce, bonds, banking, or retail, but from real estate. The notion that a lot of expensive cabernet sauvignon, too, was rooted in money from bricks and mortar, condos, resorts, and all the guises of what was generally known as development was not part of the promotion of fine wine. But at the outset of that now lost decade of the nineties, the effects of development overshadowed all else.

"The *feng shui* isn't the best — too much *chi* running around."

The statue on her newel post had wings and a shield, and seemed Mediterranean, while those in the dining room alcoves were definitely Asian. A Spanish chandelier overhung a huge vase of exotic dried flowers. The angels on the heavy mirror frames in the sitting room, blowing horns, might have been Italian, their silent heraldry reverberating amid all the marble. "We did some odd things," she admitted, like the phone room with the big chair. Another small room was "a perfect shape. They call it *bagua*," one side representing money, one representing relationships, a third side representing something indeterminate. She shrugged. "Yada yada yada. I don't want to know too much about *feng shui*. Then you get crazy."

Nell Sweeney had bright blond hair cropped short, a very large diamond, and a Southern accent. She could be very amusing, but her gaze behind steel-rimmed glasses was unswerving. She spent a lot of time at home and abroad looking at and buying furniture and other things in quantity, and some of these ended up here and some in rooms of the Embassy Suites, owned by her husband.

The large painting of a peasant on a horse was bought in Hong Kong, where "in the translation from English to Chinese I ended up with a barnful of stuff I didn't want." She designed this house herself, to reflect various cultures. "I call it French and Italian. I just put everything together and hoped it would come out with some style."

The house was roughly the length of two basketball courts and clung to the edge of a near-precipice overlooking the Silverado Trail and the breadth of the valley. The fig arbor out back flanked the swimming pool; in the loggia was another massive chandelier. Shrubs, trees, and flowers in heavy terracotta planters were backed by the distant flanks of the Mayacamas and by blue sky. "Our emphasis is on the views — you can see the fires in Dry Creek from here."

The framed sheet of a Gregorian chant on the music room wall may or may not have been old. "I don't know, I just bought it." The living room tapestries were of indeterminate age and provenance. Nearby stood another statue. "I don't know who she is. I just buy and buy. We have to outfit all those suites."

Such omnivorous practicality extended to the wine cellar, where she kept her fur coats, too. In addition to California wines, "we do some French, some Italian. We go to all the auctions." The reception room outside the cellar had a vaulted ceiling painted with a phoenix, symbol of the winery, Vine Hill. "The artist mixed the paint with eggs to make it look like stucco."

A party was about to get under way. The chef, brought in for this occasion, wore the traditional black-and-white-checked trousers and white blouson; she gingerly touched the coffee service already arranged on the presentation island. The expected guests, all women, regularly gathered to view one another's property enhancements, and it was Nell Sweeney's turn. Her enhancements entailed the removal of a wall between the culinary and consumption chambers (kitchen and breakfast room) and the installation of modern, and ancient, conveniences. The aromatic essence of hot scones escaped the silent authority of the interior environmental controls, while out front, beyond the potted palms, tires whispered in the pea gravel.

Her husband, Chuck, had worked for a quarter of a century in the hotel business when suddenly it came to him: travelers — businessmen, vacationers, whatever — didn't have to be stuck in a cubicle.

For a little more money they could have a suite, and feel special. It was, he liked to say, "a novel product. Suites, not rooms."

He had been coming to Napa Valley since the seventies and bought the site of the historic Vine Hill Winery in the eighties. The Embassy Suites chain proved so successful that he and Nell decided to move to the valley; they had vineyards put in and applied for a winery permit when those were still easy to get, since the old Vine Hill had burned long ago. Soon they were making fifteen thousand cases, split evenly among cabernet, merlot, and chardonnay.

They saved a spot up on the hill for a five-bedroom house, and had to dynamite to get it in. The plan and then the house were very controversial. Citizens from all over the valley stood up in public meetings and complained of having to look at it every time they drove up Silverado Trail. Chuck, a big man who waved his hands a lot, wasn't easy to intimidate. He often told his wife, "These people are looking for spotted owls and three-toed frogs. They're on a mission. Ignore them and they'll go away."

"Why would anyone be foolish enough to spend millions of dollars on a house that would slip down a hillside? It's jealousy. I told Chuck I was going to drive up and down the Silverado Trail taking photos of old car bodies and make a big deal of that!"

The new space was full of attractive women: several gold belts and pashmina scarves, a disproportionate number of blondes. "I don't like kitchens that look like kitchens," Nell told them as they helped themselves to coffee and the chef's delicate baked fare. Indeed, this kitchen looked as much like a combination library and food display unit, with leather-bound volumes of Cook's voyages, high-backed padded chairs arranged on harlequin tiles, a chandelier made of stag antlers. "The pizza oven takes forever to get going . . . This exhaust fan is strong enough to pull your hair out."

The handsome antique rotisserie was turned by an elaborate device suggesting a cuckoo clock, with spinning cones and a heavy stone counterweight. "We saw this thing in some castle, and Chuck said he had to have one. We tracked the guy down."

A guest asked about the saucers. "I never saw a piece of china I didn't like. I'm looking for something in gold and green that can be put into the dishwasher. I sent Thomas to England, but he couldn't find it."

No one asked who Thomas was; it didn't signify. Talk was of other shopping venues, the flea market in St. Tropez. The party moved incrementally into the marble foyer and adjoining rooms, chatting, balancing saucers, an egalitarian bunch: a heavy contributor to the local arts, the wife of the owner of one of the largest wineries, the wife of the owner of a large wine distributorship, the wife of a builder of nursing homes, two caterers whose services would be needed eventually but who now were indistinguishable from the women who would be hiring them. One white pantsuit told another, "We just built two houses, but we're not living in either of them. Yours in yet?"

"Half."

"Are you a kitchen person or a garden person?"

"Oh, I'm both."

A downturn in the stock market could be seen in a switch from decomposed granite to arbor mulch, but for the moment there was no dearth of decomposed granite. There was concern about criticism in the valley — of development, even of vineyards. "Their complaints are so stupid," said the hostess, of the critics. "They criticized us building on a hillside. We're on *top* . . . Why don't they talk about the nice things?"

She listed them: the new iris farm near Lake Berryessa, the skeet-shooting club, another club called Second Growth for lucky spermers, a retired race car driver living in the valley . . .

"And the beekeepers!"

"And that woman who witches wells!"

The store of scones, French butter, and marmalade had been seriously impacted. This was just the first round of a prearranged tour that would take them all to a house in St. Helena, for a viewing of the plantings and a lecture. But not everyone knew where it was. "Just follow the red Jag," said a pashmina.

They mounted their respective SUVs, bright in the California sunlight, and in a flurry of air kisses and Palm Pilots hied off to the ornamental town garden.

Jayson Pahlmeyer came to real estate, and to wine, from an entirely different direction.

He wasn't sure just when he made the decision to produce a wine that would drop you to your knees, but it was back when he worked as a General Services Administration lawyer in Washington, D.C., and encountered a substance — Bordeaux — that engendered a passion uncommon in an Oakland boy. His native city was famous for the Hell's Angels and the Black Panthers, and forever stigmatized by Gertrude Stein's alliterative assessment, "There's no there there." But he went back there, and then there was a business there, one with his name on it.

Jayson and a partner made some real estate deals in the eighties, and one of those involved fifty-five acres about an hour to the north of Oakland, in the Coombsville area of Napa County, scrub-covered slopes at the south end of the valley that had been passed over by the big wineries and boutique vintners and the corporations busy buying up the flats. Jayson and his partner wanted to do a residential development, starter mansions, but then he learned that Napa County had pretty strict zoning laws.

A Freudian might have seen other motives in a savvy attorney-developer in the go-go years making such a mistake. What Jayson Pahlmeyer really wanted was not an upscale subdivision full of mock Tudors, Spanish missions, and cantilevered sun decks, but a wine bottle with his name on it. This relatively erudite ambition seemed misplaced in a big, rangy guy with a hawklike profile, swept-back hair kept in place with a dab of something, and gold-rimmed glasses. But he was also a risk taker, and he proposed a crazy idea to his partner: plant a vineyard instead.

To Jayson's surprise, the partner agreed. So they had a weather station put up, to measure rainfall, temperature, wind and sun exposure, with good results, and then they went to Bordeaux. This was a suspect move in Napa Valley, where most everybody interested in growing fine wine grapes went to the University of California at Davis — simply "Davis," mother to the wine boom — but Jayson Pahlmeyer was different, dreaming of his Bordeaux-style red wine that contained all the various grapes in those famous blends, some unobtainable in Napa. And if an aspiring vintner wanted a great Bordeaux-style wine from great Bordeaux grapes, Jayson reasoned, then the aspiring vintner must transport himself to the Médoc, home of the ultimate blend of cabernet sauvignon, merlot, cabernet franc, petit verdot, and malbec.

The French vintners thought him mad and gave him this advice: plant corn. Jayson would later use this and the rest of his French experience as part of his sales rap: that he learned about vine spacing there, and focused on the mystery of the great French wines, which of course meant drinking them, the unique, overpowering flavors of the '45 Mouton-Rothschild and the '47 Cheval Blanc, called by him "incredible synergies." He got to the point where he didn't have to taste such wines to appreciate them, he said. Just smelling them was enough. He dreamed of such an aroma in a wine of his own, a Pahlmeyer nose, and gradually, by dint of enthusiasm, persuaded the French to help him isolate what he judged to be the five best clones of the classic varieties.

Some people back home thought this an apocryphal story, but Jayson told often of buying French budwood — shoots to be budded onto rootstock — knowing it couldn't be taken legally into the United States and so shipping it to Canada. There his partner supposedly carried it across in the trunk of his car, one load at a time, and shipped each load by Federal Express overnight to Napa Valley. On the ninth crossing, Jayson claimed, a border guard stopped him, searched the car, and found the smuggled budwood, covered with wax and wrapped to keep it dark and dormant. Soon not only U.S. Customs was involved but also the Bureau of Alcohol, Tobacco and Firearms and the U.S. Department of Agriculture, all wanting to know what had happened to the plants already on the other side of the American continent.

The story grew into a full-scale domestic drama that went like this: a plea bargain included a seventeen-thousand-dollar fine and an agreement to hand over the rest of the budwood, something Jayson had no intention of doing. Instead, he and his partner purchased an equal amount of California budwood from a local nursery and had it ready at their vineyard when five cars full of state and federal authorities rolled up. They confiscated this "contraband" and rolled off again, and a year later the California Department of Agriculture thanked Jayson and his partner for handing over alien plant material that, they said, was riddled with viruses and other diseases. Jayson wanted to tell them that it was their own hotshot vineyard fodder they were talking about, but couldn't, not without blowing his whole operation.

★

Whatever the truth, Jayson wanted the best. What was the point of doing all this, he asked people, "if I don't make a wine that drops you to your knees?" He considered his competitors to be the best producers in France — Lafite- and Mouton-Rothschild, not Stag's Leap and Chateau Montelena. The best wines in Napa Valley were already in the ninety-eighth and ninety-ninth percentile in terms of quality, proven by the famous Paris tasting in 1976 when California had bested France, but the Americans were still engaged in what Jayson called "edge work," a phrase used by gonzo journalist Hunter Thompson, whom Jayson admired. It summed up what Jayson felt *he* was doing, functioning not on ludes and cocaine and Wild Turkey but on the pure ether of global demand and his own heady expectations.

These bumped up against the realities of winemaking in northern California. Since he had no producing vineyards of his own yet, he had to buy grapes from someone who did, to start the money flowing in, and then find someone to make the wine before it could be sold. There were custom crushers around the valley, but sometimes staff rotated, and space was at a premium. Custom crushing was often synonymous with enological chaos, he thought. One day your wine was in one part of the cellar; when you went back a week later it was somewhere else. Or someone leaves the barn door open, as happened to Jayson's first vintage, the sun beating down on imported staves, heating what lies within, a recipe for disaster. Then the cellar he was using was sold and his wine had to be moved to yet another one.

Heat-stressed, peripatetic, this cabernet was not going to drop anyone to his knees, Jayson decided. He intended to make only four hundred cases and sell in bulk any wine that was left over. The wine ended up at the cellar owned by the son of a food writer who was also a professional pilot, and Jayson was pleased with the taste of it. Adversity had made it interesting, he thought. He let others taste it, and although they didn't drop to their knees, they were impressed.

One day, by chance, Jayson was standing around the cellar talking about his new wine when one of the rising stars of California cabernet arrived in an old pickup. He was Randy Dunn, the squarely built, taciturn pro who reminded Jayson of Robert Redford, with his reddish-blond mop and a beard to match. Dunn worked for Caymus Vineyards and made his own wine high on Howell Mountain; he was becoming famous for big, flavorful, heavily structured cabernets and an unwillingness to suffer fools. He would hang up on aficionados demanding to buy his wine and tell uninvited visitors to his ranch that Randy Dunn didn't live there.

Dunn tasted the Pahlmeyer wine and, while Jayson waited, pulled air into his mouth over the wine, closed his lips, and breathed out through his nose, forcing the aromas up into his nasal passages. He sloshed the wine around in his mouth. He spat it out. Then he stood there.

Well?

Finally Dunn said, in that laconic way of his, "Not bad. Don't mess it up."

Don't mess it up. Of course not! But how? . . . Dunn was already driving away, his accolade hanging like a hot-air balloon in the bright, glorious morning.

Later, Dunn called Jayson and told him he was considering using some of Jayson's leftover wine in his own Napa Valley blend, less prestigious than his Howell Mountain but still very good indeed. Jayson couldn't believe it. The great Randy Dunn wanted his cabernet, and what's more, Dunn would make Pahlmeyer's wine for him in the future, for a while. And he would introduce Jayson to distributors who would help him get his wine on the market. Dunn would help this unknown lawyer from Oakland obsessed with a blend — Bordeaux — perfected in a distant land millennia before, and Jayson said yes, yes, yes.

Chardonnay was hot. Jayson decided to make one of those, too. A practical decision. He chose Merryvale as the custom crusher because he knew the winemaker, who could get him a discount. Jayson designed his own label — pink and turquoise, to the horror of all who saw it — and sold it all at five dollars a bottle. He couldn't believe how much money could be made, even at that price. Hey, wine was profitable! It wasn't starter mansions, but it might one day match, and complement, the real estate deals.

Looking back, Jayson would say that two coincidences put his wine on the map, the first being the visit from Randy Dunn, who introduced it to Robert Parker, publisher of *The Wine Advocate* and a tectonic force in the global wine market, on one of Parker's much-heralded visits to California. The artful blend of cabernet and other varietals that Dunn had put together for Jayson received ninety-four points out of a possible hundred in Parker's ranking system, a single event that catapulted it into the ranks of what were already being treated as cult objects.

The second coincidence involved Jayson's chardonnay, and a phone call. It came from the production manager of a movie being made, no big deal in California. The production manager had seen a ranking of the chardonnay — the pink and turquoise label had been replaced by something more acceptable by this time — in *Wine Spectator*. It, too, had been ranked in the nineties, not astronomical but well ahead of the pack. The production manager wanted a case of it to use in the movie, not for the quality but for the wine's unusual name — Pahlmeyer — and its relative inaccessibility. And the production manager wanted it for free.

"My chardonnay costs twenty-five dollars a bottle," Jayson told him, and hung up.

Then he recalled hearing that a bottle of Taittinger appearing in *Top Gun,* with Tom Cruise, had garnered a hundred and fifty thousand dollars' worth of free publicity. The appearance of a can of Budweiser in another movie had supposedly received two hundred and fifty thousand dollars' worth of free publicity. This new movie, *Disclosure,* would star Demi Moore, Michael Douglas, and, if Jayson went along, a bottle of Napa Valley chardonnay with his name on it. He called the production manager back.

When the movie came out, Jayson went to see it. The plot turned on one person's trying to get another person into bed, with his wine as a seduction tool. Jayson thought, "So what?" Then his telephone began to ring, and it never really stopped. Requests for Pahlmeyer wine also came in the mail — by the bagful. He could have sold four hundred thousand cases of Pahlmeyer chardonnay if he'd had them. When the movie was re-released it started all over again. Ditto after the European release, and the television rerun. Each successive wave brought more calls and more mail.

Somewhere in there Jayson began to see that success depended on something totally unpredictable, mysterious, and, if lightning struck — and lightning had — uncontrollable.

6

BACK IN THE late eighties, cusp of the nineties, the allure of a vineyard of one's own brought large amounts of capital to the valley, and some of this was inherited, not "made." The natural — original — beauty of the finite landscape was already being altered by the most successful small-scale agricultural crop in America, but few of the new arrivals understood or readily accepted the idea of restraints. These existed in Napa County in the form of zoning and land-use laws, but the newcomers — and some longtime residents — rebelled against the notion of limits, even as that notion worked its way to the forefront of national consciousness. During the 1980s, the United States had lost almost one and a half million acres a year of open space, including farmland and wildlife habitat. From San Francisco to Nantucket, the Outer Banks to Tucson, Americans were decrying the sprawl of houses, retail outlets, industrial parks, and roads.

During the 1990s, the loss of open space had grown to more than two million acres a year, fifty thousand of those in California. But the impetus to build gathered strength everywhere, including Napa Valley, which had proven so successful by denying some aspects of it. The population growth rate in the valley had been about two percent a year since the 1970s, only slightly less than India's, most of this in the cities of Napa and American Canyon. But there were still thousands of plots outside the cities' limits that could be built on, and this so-called unincorporated area had begun to resemble an image of itself, scattered with idiosyncratic architecture like that found in Carmel, Santa Fe, and the Hamptons. Vineyards on formerly wooded slopes were part of that trend, and an intensified struggle for quality and recognition.

Delia Viader, Argentine by birth, Californian by choice, had studied the concept of freedom as expressed by Saint Augustine. She had continued to pursue the subject at the Sorbonne, in Paris, with Jean-Paul Sartre as an instructor, sparring with the existentialist philosopher. Sartre had regularly made Delia weep, not out of fear or humiliation, but frustration. Sartre insisted that everyone in his class be purged of preconceptions, not an easy thing for a young woman raised as a Catholic and unaccustomed to losing arguments; Delia Viader did not take easily to contradiction, even by the author of *Nausea* and *No Exit,* friend of Albert Camus, and lover of Simone de Beauvoir.

But Sartre made her see that nothing is perfect and that sometimes you have to settle for the best temporary solution while looking farther out, toward perfection.

She grew up in France. Her father was made military attaché to the United Nations, and Delia moved from Paris to Boston, studied at the Massachusetts Institute of Technology and then at the University of California, Berkeley, in the mid-eighties. "California was the place to be," she had decided, and she persuaded her father to purchase ninety-odd acres in Napa Valley, on the side of Howell Mountain. She moved there in 1988, overlooking a blue lake and a stretch of valley as beautiful as any in Burgundy or the Loire, and an investment, as she told her father: she would supervise the planting of the grapes, and arrange financing and permits.

"I'll give you two years to entertain yourself," he told her, "then we'll see."

Pretty, diminutive, with big green eyes and a penchant for dark blazers with gold buttons, Delia Viader convinced a bank that she could "make something out of a pile of rocks." She got in touch with Dave Abreu, reputedly unfazed by the difficulties and risks on steep hillsides. If Abreu said something couldn't be done, she had been told, then it wasn't possible.

The vines would be closely spaced, as they were in France, one every five feet or so. That meant about two thousand vines an acre, with vertical trellising, the latest thing. It would be difficult, said Abreu, but ultimately no problem. He had gotten his feet wet at

Newton Vineyards, across the valley, where planted slopes were very steep.

Here on Howell Mountain, it would cost the Viaders about two million dollars, for everywhere there were rocks, rocks of all sizes. Whatever their size, Delia referred to them as "pebbles," even those that had to be blasted into smaller "pebbles" and then raked out by bulldozers. The volcanic soil was to be "ripped," with six-foot steel fangs dragged through the earth, dislodging rocks by the thousands that ended up in walls and planters, in the house that would stand above the vineyard, in sediment control ponds, and eventually in a little subterranean winery, and still there would be rocks.

The money ran out, and Delia went down to Silicon Valley, "where risk is a fact of life," and got more. "It's like trying to get a ball of snow downhill," she would say. "As long as you keep it moving, it's all right."

She kept it moving. In the autumn of 1989, young vines protruded from a steep slope deprived of ground cover, the soil free not just of pebbles now but also of native plant life. That time of year, storms can sweep in from the Pacific Ocean with suddenness and intensity. Everybody involved in the Viader vineyard hoped the rains would hold off until the earth was furred with a million blades of tenacious new grass.

Tom Burgess lived just south of the new vineyard, and he watched as the soil was ripped and the vines planted next door. He had steep vineyards, too, but his were terraced, horizontal — the old method — and he still had his rocks, a pain to farm around but a lot less costly to leave in place, and more stable.

There had been a time when Burgess's vineyard was the only one on this stretch of Howell Mountain, called Souverain Cellars then, the creation of the notoriously tight-fisted maverick Lee Stewart, one of the pre-sixties pioneers, a dreamer, novelist manqué, and workhorse. Stewart had proved that good wine could be made amid all the rocks, after learning his skills from André Tchelistcheff and imparting them to a number of younger vinous aspirants, among them Warren Winiarski, founder of Stag's Leap, who were willing to commit themselves to servitude.

Burgess bought the property, changed the name to his own, and began a long, slow process of learning and expansion. Formerly an airline pilot, he had maintained some independence within the society of vintners, supporting the cause of limited growth when others were more reluctant. Burgess had dynamited many a hole to plant a vine, and he employed Viader's contractor to clear more of his land, after the Viader vineyard was in, so he could expand his vineyards the following year.

There were no regulations about what degree of slope could and couldn't be planted in Napa County, but Burgess and others worried about the steep vertical rows and rock-free soil at the Viader place under a lowering sky. Then in October dark clouds rolled over the Mayacamas from Sonoma County. It rained and rained as only it can in those temperate zones washed by cold, deep, unpredictable oceans. And it rained some more.

"The resulting heavy runoff into Bell Canyon Reservoir caused excessive damage to the City of St. Helena's Police Range as well as a small arm of the reservoir receiving a silt flow from two recently cleared hillsides . . . The steep slopes, which were deep in dust from having been recently worked, acted as a funnel at two points . . . This flow cut its path to bedrock along the way and buried the shooting range with mud, making it unusable . . . The results of the surveys suggest that, indeed, the flowing of silt-laden water and debris has caused some damage to the aquatic systems . . ."

The report produced by the California Department of Fish and Game did not appear until three months after Tom Burgess woke up and saw a gully at the bottom of his property, close to the Viader line. He soon learned that the runoff had colored the reservoir serving St. Helena. The mud had also inundated the police firing range. If there were things a vintner absolutely did not want to do, they had to include harming the local drinking water and annoying the cops.

He and Delia Viader appeared to have done both. They had also given impetus indirectly to a movement already under way to create regulations about what could and could not be developed in Napa Valley's hills, after similar but less spectacular failures on Diamond Mountain. Knowing that blame would flow from this, and maybe lawsuits, Burgess took his camera and drove up to the Angwin airport. He owned a little Marchetti, the most powerful single-engine plane in the neighborhood, so fast and steady that third-world countries sometimes bought Marchettis and armed them with machine guns, creating an instant, low-rent air force.

Angwin had a short runway and tricky crosswinds that made taking off and landing a challenge, but that was no problem with the Marchetti. Within a minute or two Burgess was at a near-stall over his property; from that vantage point it seemed clear to him that the erosion had come from the adjacent property, run down and across the new vineyard, and cascaded across the bottom corner of his land. He took lots of pictures, and then descended to face the music.

Delia Viader would not admit that runoff from her property reached the reservoir. But she had a stone wall built at the bottom of the vineyard, and a basin to trap suspended dirt on its downward migration next time. She made sure she was seen working on the problem and thus helped deflect the assignment of guilt. It came anyway, from the newspapers and from a more potent source, word of mouth. She blamed the uproar on the fact that she was a woman and a foreigner, not on the possibility that she had authorized Dave Abreu to put in a steep vineyard too late in the season. She had seen steeper ones in Switzerland and Germany, where it rained a great deal, and the inclines of the vineyards in China, she said, were just incredible.

She thought the controversy and the discussion of regulations reflected the loss of personal freedom. This notion had changed radically from the time of Saint Augustine to the present; what had been a classical, elegant view of existence and free will had become in modern times a fractured thing, succumbing to the destruction of values during World War Two. It was all right there in her Ph.D. thesis, she told anyone who asked, like the assertion that greater personal freedom may have followed the destruction of values but that personal accountability had not. Instead, it went into sharp decline, so that nowadays people expected to be told what to do. If they did something they weren't supposed to do, this was considered someone else's fault rather than their own.

Delia Viader considered this the crucial fallacy of contemporary life: if you are always a victim of circumstance, what of free will? The contradiction seemed never to have occurred to her: invoking Saint Augustine while opposing the spirit of the law in the place she had chosen to live.

She refused to accept blame for what had happened. Dave Abreu had not, she said, misled her about what was and was not possible in the hills; Delia Viader was no victim! Neither would she admit the fact of the disaster, pointing out that no fish had been killed in the reservoir, that the drinking water remained potable. She had, she said, simply replaced pebbles with vines, and if the earth looked as if it had been turned upside down, well, it had, and would someday look quite different. And she avoided paying even a small fine.

Abreu learned some of his trade from Ric Forman, winemaker, vineyard manager, and general troubleshooter, first for Sterling Vineyards and then for Peter Newton. Abreu had simply appeared at Newton Vineyards one day, back from Vietnam and in need of a job, and Forman had shown him a few things. Products of St. Helena High, Abreu and his friends were working stiffs, locals but not lucky spermers. Dark-haired, bright-eyed, Dave had a curious, profane, funny way of talking — "Here . . . hey . . ." — characterized by some as "Rutherford-speak." He was driven to succeed, taking odd vineyard jobs around the valley, and remembered in the business for asking all manner of questions, as in, "Here . . . hey, how does pH work, anyway?"

Randy Dunn hired him to prune atop Howell Mountain, and on cold winter mornings Abreu would come into his house to warm his hands by the stove, where Lori Dunn, Randy's wife, was struck by his gentleness and good humor. He also worked for Caymus Vineyards, on the valley floor. Before long he began to call himself a consultant and use his friend Buddy Meyer to do the bulldozing. Buddy's father had sold the land on Spring Mountain to Peter Newton, and Buddy still lived at the base of Newton Vineyards, as did Abreu. He would tell people he had sold Newton a rock pile and that Newton had built a house up there on a rattlesnake den, and laugh at the folly of it.

But Newton Vineyards was where Abreu started. Peter Newton's was a notable success; he also had a leggy Chinese wife, an octagonal house, and a Mercedes that glided down the steep winding road from his opulent, stylish outpost, running the gauntlet of industrial implements at the bottom belonging to Buddy. Visitors to Newton

— and there were many, drawn by the wines' quality and the dramatic aspect of winery, house, and gardens, but not by the rattlesnakes that did indeed sun themselves on the tarmac — couldn't help but notice the contrast between the men at the bottom of the hill, in their coveralls and Big Ben shirts, their boots and billed caps and air of indifference, and Newtonian sophistication above.

A keen distinction had arisen between perceived privilege exemplified by the Newtons and kick-ass earthmoving competence below. When trees in heavy containers of imported soil arrived from northern California and Oregon aboard big flatbed semis that could barely navigate the steep winding road, the dirt movers would come to the rescue, but not without choice words about Newton's imperial ways and Newton's fancy wife. Some visitors thought the people at the bottom of the hill deliberately kept their neighborhood looking countrified, and put in speed bumps, just to tweak those living above. The irony was that Newton had paid good money for land that at the time did not seem so valuable, and had provided work for those at the bottom, a classic case of new lord and old freeholder.

Some of the Newton vineyards seemed, from a distance, cut into rock, one row five feet above another. Decades later, little would grow on some sections; every time it rained, the creek at the bottom of the hill would change color with sediment making its way down from the high slopes of the Mayacamas where Meyer and Abreu had hunted and fished as boys. There they had become men, and yet they helped transform it and similar land. Even woodlands adjacent to new vineyards were bulldozed, to destroy any cover for what might be enemies of vines, work that would be done because some people wanted it done and were willing to pay anything for it.

Abreu seemed, among all the vineyard managers, best able to understand the extraordinary needs of the newcomers. He told others in the business who questioned his methods, in no uncertain terms — he and his brothers knew how to take care of themselves — "Here . . . hey, I've got a job to do."

He was no longer just a learner but a professional. Delia Viader's was not the last of his controversial projects, but the first of many. He, the projects, and his new clients would become significant factors in the discord in the valley, as well as in the still ascendant reputation of its wines. Likewise, Delia Viader was not through with audacious vineyard practices. She would continue to pursue "freedom" as she in-terpreted it, which apparently extended to challenging gravity on the slopes of Howell Mountain.

Years later, another Napa Valley vineyard manager would angrily declare, of all the problems arising out of hillside development, "A brass plaque should be put up in Delia Viader's vineyard saying, 'It started here.'"

7

H AD TOM BURGESS turned his single-engine Marchetti
away from the Viader vineyard, he might have passed over
the lofty holdings of Dunn, and other, older vineyards carefully insinuated onto Howell Mountain. Heading south, toward the
silvery intimation of San Pablo Bay, he would have overlooked
a mostly wild amalgam of chaparral and conifer, the established
plantings of Chappellet and a few new, raw additions to the canon of
the perfect cabernet, and some new houses. And if he had come
back up the west side of the valley, he would have flown over Mt.
Veeder, Hess, and Mayacamas vineyards, Newton on Spring Mountain, Sterling and smaller gems on Diamond Mountain, everything
contained within this gorgeous entity, this valley and the hills defining it, vineyards hanging up among the trees like apostrophes in a
long, elegant passage written by the Creator about sublimity and the
agrarian dream.

Out on the flats, the broad carpet of grapes was beginning to look
a bit moth-eaten, evidence of phylloxera, the plant louse once again
invading the vineyards after a hiatus of a century. But the bare spots
in the hills were new vineyards belonging to recent devotees of
"mountain fruit," pilgrims seeking the flavor bombs of stressed,
runty grapes forced to dig their roots deep into rocky soil and struggle for sun exposure and warmth, tough guys with character — that
was the argument.

But the new vineyards bled soil into streams that flowed into the
Napa River, and in the rainy season the muddy river sometimes
spread over the valley floor. Increasingly, people complained, not just

of the flooding but also of the water's opacity, the extremely various levels of the water, the very character of their river.

The man who had to listen to them was their representative on the county board of supervisors, his bailiwick the wealthy, sometimes contentious up-valley. His name was Mel Varrelman, and he operated out of a bungalow on a back street in St. Helena with a blue awning printed with the words "Go, Bears," a reference to the football team of the University of California at Berkeley. He had studied chemistry and physics there and gone to work as a policeman on the graveyard shift in St. Helena while he got his teaching certificate; he had then taught in the St. Helena public school while twice serving as a St. Helena city councilman. Now a certified financial planner and many times elected supervisor, he liked to say of politics, "Call it a career."

The poems he wrote to overcome the stress of combined professions, poems that his wife collected in loose-leaf notebooks because she knew Mel wouldn't bother, began to flag at the outset of the nineties. This was not because he had less stress or less poetic impulse, but because he no longer had the time or the will to write them. Everything else was taking a back seat to politics. Varrelman probably talked to more constituents on the telephone than he talked to customers. In open shirt and V-neck sweater, banked by family photographs, he juggled the demands of vintners, developers, ordinary citizens, and clients, using soft-spoken good humor tempered by skepticism. This went back to his experience as a cop on the graveyard shift and in the halls of the public school, good, maybe essential training for any elected official in small-town America, riven as the country was with competing interests and a wide divergence of incomes and ambitions.

Varrelman had come to believe that growth was the key issue. It wasn't schools, doctors, crime, but growth. New structures, new vineyards, newly cleared land. The problem — he didn't like talking about this because it was so sensitive politically — was that growth had to end eventually. Inexhaustible land did not exist, in fact had never existed. This was a western notion going back to Thomas Jefferson — the closest thing to a philosopher-prince since Marcus Aurelius — who believed that the Louisiana Purchase would provide a frontier for a thousand generations of Americans. But it had begun to run out some time ago.

Manifest Destiny hadn't really arrived in Napa Valley, Varrelman liked to say, until the outset of the twentieth century. Now, in 1989, so near that century's end, neither America nor the valley was predominantly the community of hearty, democratic yeoman farmers that Jefferson had envisioned. Napa Valley had agriculture, but also much macadam, tourist facilities, trophy houses, runoff, and prohibitively expensive wine. How this had come about in the last two decades was very interesting, he thought, and had begun with something known as the Williamson Act.

Passed in 1965 in Sacramento, that piece of legislation had allowed county assessors to consider land use in determining the taxable value of farmland. This made it easier for farmers to stay on the land because the income from farming, not the potential for residential development, was the basis for taxation. Then a formal agricultural district had to be established. This would have its own zoning and other laws that prevented or limited activities not related to farming. At that time, the county's population was expected to double — from about one hundred thousand people — by the year 2000, so such protection was obviously necessary, and fortuitous.

In 1968, the board of supervisors — well before Varrelman's time there — created the Agricultural Preserve Zone for the floor of Napa Valley, over great opposition. Some people wanted to subdivide their property for house lots and other commercial activities, and others opposed the preserve on ideological grounds, as a form of socialism. New arrivals fleeing suburbs elsewhere in California, among them some aspiring vintners, knew the dangers posed by houses. A minimum lot size of twenty acres was then established, instead of the existing one-acre zoning, which amounted to a small revolution in county politics and local land use; it was the first such "ag preserve" in the United States and an example for other counties to follow. A few of them did, notably nearby Marin, with good results, but very few established the large, minimum-acre building plots that would prove to be the key to preserving farmland, even with the existence of an agricultural preserve.

The twenty-acre minimum was soon doubled. In California, the environmental movement was gathering strength in the sixties as well-educated urbanites moved "back to the land" in places other than Napa, slow growth was gaining a footing in political agendas and in the popular lexicon, and "nature" was ascendant in the public mind.

The first Earth Day was held in 1970, the same year Napa County's planning director, Jim Hickey, came up with the first plan for a greenbelt in the San Francisco Bay area. Over the ensuing years the board of supervisors would shift back and forth between conservative and relatively liberal, but a resistance to restrictions on land use persisted among some vineyard and winery owners, even after a court challenge to the ag preserve failed.

In 1989, in the midst of Varrelman's tenure, a strong effort got under way, backed by the Napa County Farm Bureau, to limit by law the amount of out-of-county grapes allowed in officially designated Napa Valley wine. This would assure continued quality and limit the growth of wineries seeking to expand production with trucked-in fruit. This was the "winery definition" fight, another turning point for the valley, and it was clearly revealing those among the vintners and vineyardists who were for agriculture and those who favored development and tourism. All these were emotional issues, and added to them was the controversial idea of limiting building plots in the hills to one hundred and sixty acres. And then along comes a torrent of muddy water flowing into Bell Canyon Reservoir.

It seemed to Varrelman that Tom Burgess had been trying to protect his land and got caught by a freak storm; Varrelman wasn't so sure about Viader. What he knew was that fouling a municipal water supply was a sure way to rivet public opinion, and he hoped it would sway the public to support new land-use proposals.

A new hillside ordinance would include mandatory erosion control plans for slopes between five and thirty degrees, mandatory use permits (which meant having to do an environmental impact report) for everything between thirty and fifty degrees, and mandatory variances for any slopes steeper than that. Soil catchment basins would also have to be built at the base of steep new vineyards, and any earthmoving — clearing and ripping — would have to stop well before the rainy season.

No-brainers, Varrelman thought. A thirty-degree slope was very steep, something you realized when you went out and looked at it, yet the provisions of this new hillside ordinance would be unique in California, a state with lots of hillsides and a reputation for environmental concern. Once again Napa County was blazing a trail in land use, just as it had with the creation of the ag preserve in 1968. And once again a significant element within the population resented the rules being considered.

Varrelman was surprised — seated at his desk, the telephone cradled between chin and shoulder, arranging financial reports, the stuff that paid the bills, and smiling — how vineyard owners, potential vineyard owners, and some of the big boys who didn't even own hillsides called to denounce any limitations at all. But after the Bell Canyon mess most of those calls stopped, and the hillside ordinance finally passed two years later.

Plantable land had run out on the valley floor, and yet new people clamored for more vineyards. Existing wineries and grape producers sought to expand, and they too turned to the hills. Now when people spoke of the border wars they referred not only to disputes over the effects of erosion, like that between Viader and Burgess, or to clashes of ego and ambition, like the one involving Jack Cakebread and Garen Staglin, but also to skirmishes over noise, dust, "lifestyle," and the encroachment of one cabernet's critical rating upon another's. And there was among the inevitable collisions that of old money with new.

Tom May was a Du Pont, owner of a grape-growing plot called Martha's Vineyard — named for his wife, not for the island off the coast of New England — that had become famous after Joe Heitz put its grapes into his vineyard-designated cabernet, way back. A courtly man with a compulsive laugh, May had in the sixties joined Jack Davies of Schramsberg, Louis Martini, Jr., and others to fight for the creation of the ag preserve, standing up in public meetings and reading aloud statistics about grape production, indicating that prospects were good for wine in the valley and asking that the land be protected.

May's neighbor, a more recent arrival, Bill Harlan, was the valley's developer extraordinaire, the son of the manager of a meat-packing plant, who had created the Meadowood Resort, home of four-hundred-dollar-a-night duplexes amid the remaining live oaks, and the quaintly named Southbridge in St. Helena, an amalgam of restaurants, a hotel, health club, condos, and offices, all announced by a tasteful wooden sign planted near the railroad tracks. Harlan had gotten this commercial potpourri through the St. Helena City Council because he was better prepared than his opponents. At Pacific Union, the company he had helped found, he exercised the protocols of soothsayer, his partners handling the finances and mechanics of skyscrapers and designer communities while Harlan kept his finger in the developmental wind. But real estate apparently hadn't brought the recognition Harlan wanted. He once asked Mel Varrelman why people didn't like him, and Mel had laughed and said, "Take a vow of poverty, Bill."

Thin and ascetic-looking, with blue, marble-like eyes and a collection of dramatic sombreros, Harlan had gone from developer to "lifestyle vintner" in a relatively short time, and from lifestyle vintner to cult-wine producer in a shorter one. The idea of Harlan waking up each morning worrying about the weather, tasting tannic young cabernet, and comparing the finished product to blackberries or old cigar boxes had once amused people, but Robert Parker and *Wine Spectator* had both cottoned to Harlan's cabernet.

The vineyard from which his wine sprang had been planted above Tom May's property. One day May ventured out and found a fence where no fence had been before. May stared at it, incredulous. This was his land — or at least he thought it was — and had been for donkey's years, and now a fence had crept in from the border, a fence belonging to Bill Harlan. May complained and learned that a new survey had been done, and old assumptions about the property proved erroneous.

Land was now so valuable in Napa Valley that even a sliver running along your border could improve your net worth by thousands, perhaps hundreds of thousands, of dollars. Found money had more attraction than the earned sort because it demonstrated luck, cleverness, and an ability to gain from the past. Those old guys settling Napa Valley hadn't a clue, designating property corners as they had with rocks and creeks and trees, and abiding by handshakes that any fool could overturn in court. All you had to do was call in one of the many experts in property matters now roaming the valley, savvy surveyors accustomed to the border wars, armed with lasers.

Bill Harlan stated publicly that all he wanted was a "win-win situation." But he and May ended up in a legal battle, increasingly common for neighbors. People said that if the decision went against Harlan he would shrug it off as just another real estate possibility that didn't pan out, whereas if May lost, it would kill him.

The fences were built not by the new landowners but by those who worked for them. It was the vineyard managers and contractors who went up into the hills, cleared and ripped the land, planted the vines, and did any rough thing needing to be done in the high, scenic country. Many of these were referred to as "cowboys," local parlance for men with experience and brass, their adversary not so much a client's neighbors as nature itself. Farming hills full of rocks left by millions of years of grinding tectonic plates and shedding Sierras and spewed out by innumerable volcanoes, hills dense with chaparral, tough manzanita, and trees big enough to kill, was no easy job. Vines were tender young waifs that needed protection from bugs — phylloxera, leafhoppers, pernicious wasps — and from fungus and other enemies hiding in soil and brush.

A cowboy would clear away all the wild stuff, "shoot" (dynamite) the earth, and drive through it a piece of iron (a Caterpillar) costing as much as a house, fitted with the six-foot steel spikes; he would push other men (Mexicans) and other equipment, crowd deadlines so as not to lose a year in the growing cycle, and reshape a natural feature when called for. There were, the cowboys argued, large investments being made in land and "improvements" by people — dot-commers, investment bankers, entrepreneurs, developers, media beneficiaries, inventors and purveyors of small devices of great aggregate value — accustomed to getting what they wanted when they wanted it, and the amount of money they were willing to pay was simply incredible.

The May-Harlan controversy remained a sideshow in the bigger battle over development and the right — the obligation — of the county to write and to enforce laws for the hillsides. The Viader project and the silting of various reservoirs had been seen by some as the end of the old, freewheeling ways, but it was becoming clear that they were not. The conflicts resulting from continued development would be long, broad, and bitter, and Mel Varrelman, supervisor and financial planner, was just one person whose life was dominated by them.

8

THE "WORD" made the rounds of the valley in record time now, in e-mails that had superseded faxes that had superseded messages left with receptionists and on machines that had superseded stories swapped over fences and in dusty meeting halls. It seemed that exchanges between those picking up newspapers at Keller's and the Ranch Market and Styrofoam containers at the Napa Valley Coffee Roasting Company, the Oakville Grocery, or Gordon's were briefer now, more to the point. Everybody was in a hurry. Lunches at Celadon, Mustard's, and Tra Vigne, Pilates classes, dinner parties held in houses with styles once seemingly anathema to agriculture — aerodynamic rooflines, negative-edge swimming pools — took on a transitory quality, as if something better and more interesting lay always just around the corner.

Dinners were given themes, "appreciation" being one of the more popular, a way of paying homage to one's surroundings and one's possessions and at the same time complimenting the guest of honor and other invitees. An appreciation dinner might be held for the owner of a new restaurant, a new house, a new exotic species of garden adornment, a new activity, a new cause, a new wine — anything. It served much the same function as events held in the name of charity: moral affirmation of all involved, and a chance to socialize.

There could be problems. For instance, the dinner party held in appreciation of Christian Moueix, heir to Château Pétrus in Pomerol and owner of Dominus in Napa Valley, was for his stark, angular winery designed by the Swiss architects Herzog & de Meuron, which stood on the edge of what was once Napanook Vineyard, near Yountville. The property had belonged to John Daniel, of Inglenook, and had been sold to Moueix by Daniel's daughters, the statuesque Robin Lail and Marky, a poet who lived in Washington State. The possible problem was that another guest, Bill Harlan, had in the past also been closely associated with Robin, she having introduced both men to the valley. Both Harlan and Moueix had regularly made Robin cry, and both were indebted to her for more than either cared to admit.

Others were apprehensive about how the men would react to each other in close proximity, but they needn't have worried. Harlan knew the value of associating with an accredited Bordelais, and Moueix knew the value of a testament by locals that his stunning winery was not just a monument to ego. So happy was he with his appreciation dinner that he afterward left a case of Dominus on his hostess's doorstep.

Another favored ritual was the reconciliation dinner, trickier than the appreciation dinner because it often involved disputants in the border wars.

Pritchard Hill stands to the south of Lake Hennessey, on the east side of the valley, a steep, wooded enclave. It overlooks the reservoir — water impounded behind Conn Creek Dam for the drinking of Napa — an azure gem that, depending on the season, is set in either a green profusion of grass and wildflowers or parched, dun-colored slopes susceptible to lightning and arsonists.

For many years an idyll reigned on Pritchard Hill, planted in the sixties by Donn Chappellet but mostly ignored by the newcomers to the valley below. In the late eighties some prospective new neighbors arrived, self-made aspiring pastoralists who wanted small vineyards of their own and a remove from the engine of California commerce. One of these was Greg Melanson, founder of a company with the droll name of FYI, Inc., that provided services to lawyers. It had been fun and exciting to run, and when it stopped being fun he had taken it public and bought thirteen acres on the south side of Pritchard Hill with the proceeds.

Melanson grew up in Brentwood, California, listening to a freeway, and he wanted something entirely different in middle age: a small vineyard in a peaceful setting. With some help from the Chappellets he got one. A pilot as well as an entrepreneur, he flew up with his wife aboard his four-seater helicopter on weekends and landed on the helipad next to their tasteful Tuscan villa. They said of their lives in Napa Valley, "You just feel complete."

One morning the Melansons woke up to the sound of machines operating on the opposing slope: D-8 Caterpillars, clearing chaparral and live oaks. The steep property had been bought by an investment banker with Goldman, Sachs, Joe Wender, whose only claim to fame, as far as Melanson knew, was that he was engaged to be married to Ann Colgin, an employee of auctioneers in Los Angeles and the flamboyant owner of a cult cabernet. A month later the clearing was finished and the D-8s gone, and the Melansons thought they might feel complete again, but then the D-9s arrived. And the dynamite. The blasting shook the furniture in their house and covered everything in a thick coating of dust. Almost as bad as the blasting was the constant scrape of steel on stone.

Boulders began to pile up at the bottom of the property, and Melanson called the vineyard manager, Dave Abreu, and asked him to stop working on the weekends, when the Melansons were *in situ*. Then he called the contractor, a Calistogan named Richard Stadelhofer, who owned the big machines, to little avail. Finally he got Wender's telephone number from Cyril Chappellet, Donn's son, and called this stranger. As Melanson later told the story, Wender said that the project had tripled in size and that things had gotten out of hand. The two of them agreed to meet after the Pritchard Hill appellation roundtable at the Chappellets'. There Melanson found Wender to be a good listener, good at processing information, even a good guy — a rarity in an investment banker, in Melanson's experience. Investment bankers led you to the altar and then cashed out; they were one reason so many initial public offerings of stock crashed and burned.

What Melanson couldn't understand was why a guy like Wender would spend millions of dollars to develop a hillside that would probably never earn it back and that caused such enmity among the neighbors. Then he met Wender's fiancée, Ann Colgin, saw first-hand the lips adorned with distinctive red-orange lipstick used for signing labels on bottles of her wine, not with a signature but with a big, bright, puckered, Evita-esque *Don't cry for me, Napa Valley* open-mouthed smack — and heard Wender saying yes Ann, no Ann, and he understood.

She had come to the valley, so the story went, from Waco by way of Vanderbilt University and Sotheby's, already married to someone else. The couple attended the Napa Valley Wine Auction. Working for an auction house had provided her with certain insights, like creating the perception of value through scarcity, an essential element in moving collectibles that included wine. Ann Colgin's wine business accounted for a bit more than two hundred cases of cabernet a year when Melanson met her, and the wine sold for more than one hundred dollars a bottle when it could be found. Her winemaker, Helen Turley, apostle of extremely ripe fruit procured at any cost, had helped garner recognition from Robert Parker. So sought after was the Colgin cabernet — according to the stories she told — that a woman sent a copy of her divorce settlement to Colgin to prove that she, and not her husband, had retained their coveted position on the Colgin mailing list. Another fan supposedly swapped a Mercedes for a single case.

Such stories were not limited to her wine and could be heard with variations about dozens of others; they appeared in an adoring wine press without challenge. The writing often emphasized wealth and style of living as measures of quality as important as the wine itself; whether or not the stories were true mattered far less than the fact that they were read and repeated. Colgin posed for such a publication, supposedly in celebration of country life, by sitting on a dusty slope of the new Pritchard Hill vineyard in her jeans, leather boots, and hallmark lipstick. In the background lay bare dirt, a large displaced boulder, and a piece of heavy equipment associated with mining.

Colgin already owned a house down on the outskirts of St. Helena, where another house had stood that had belonged to Josephine Tychson, founder of Freemark Abbey, probably the first woman winemaker in Napa Valley. Colgin had proudly announced this fact before she had that historic structure demolished. There the neighbors complained that the new frame, taupe and cream Victorian replacing it resembled a spec house in an upscale tract development,

the black wrought-iron railings so . . . Texas, the ersatz Greek am-
phora, the terracotta maiden, concrete pineapples, and virginal white
flowers contrasting starkly with the image of those wet, red-orange
lips planted on labels of Colgin rocket juice.

The view of the remnant of Pritchard Hill that appeared in the magazine did not include the boulder pile of Brobdingnagian proportions, the one that Melanson's houseguests always gaped at. It was an
industrial rather than an agricultural artifact, and it reminded some
onlookers of the hydraulic goldmining that had done such damage
to the Sierra Nevada in the previous century. Mountainsides were
apparently still being moved to get at glitter.

Melanson tried to explain the pile away, making excuses for his
neighbor, saying the pile was necessary for producing additional
Colgin cabernet that could be sold at a high price, that someday the
pile wouldn't matter. But it just sat there. Melanson brought in a
landscape architect to see whether he thought the pile could be
"mitigated," but the architect told him nothing would grow there, it
was just too big. The rock pile dwarfed the big Cats and the excavators, which in turn dwarfed the pickups clinging to the slope, dust
devils dancing in their wakes, dwarfing in turn the all-terrain vehicles ridden by Mexican laborers that shuttled up and down with
insectile persistence.

At a point midway through the creation of the vineyard, some of
the boulders came loose from the pile and rolled down into the
creekbed. There they broke a two-inch plastic pipe supplying water
to the property belonging to another neighbor, Bob Long, and close
enough for one of Long's employees to hear this. The rocks didn't
menace him, but they certainly got his attention. They got his boss's,
too, and Long called the water division of the Napa County Department of Public Works and told them what had happened, that boulders were now sitting in the bed of a creek that fed Lake Hennessey,
a municipal water supply.

The Department of Public Works contacted the Regional Water
Quality Control Board in Oakland, where an environmental specialist named Tom Gandesbury looked into the problem. It seemed
to Gandesbury that the boulders had been stacked too high on a
bank, as he put it, with "a soft, chewy center" prior to being disposed

of, and that the disposal had never taken place. The boulders were not massed in an engineered manner, Gandesbury thought. It was scary. He discussed the problem with a representative of the Resource Conservation District in Napa and was told that the rock pile was beyond erosion control, that the whole thing could come tumbling down.

The Regional Water Quality Control Board issued a cleanup and abatement order and asked for a winterizing erosion plan anyway, one that involved the owner's hiring geotechnical and subsurface consultants. These experts recommended rebuilding the pile with D-9s, long-arm excavators, and six-wheel dump trucks, extremely expensive reparation. This was undertaken, and, looking at the effects, Gandesbury thought it had to be the most costly vineyard installation in human history.

The people who had caused the problem were in his opinion driven by profits so great that the penalties, if there were any, seemed insignificant. They were willing to risk money and legal action because new regulations might emerge at any time that would curtail their plans.

Some guy had "gone nuts" on a bulldozer, Gandesbury concluded, cutting a road "through hill and dale" so steep that it became a cliff. "Somebody just put a line on a map, and the driver went ass over teakettle."

There should be a regulation on how much rock could be pulled out of the ground for a vanity vineyard, he thought. For the moment, though, there was nothing more his agency could do. If the rock pile, or part of it, went down the hill the following winter, the Regional Water Quality Control Board could impose a big legal penalty.

Other agencies and individuals got involved, part of the damage control. The county district attorney's office investigated but took no action. The Fish and Game warden inspected and told Wender's contractors to remove the tumbled boulders by breaking them up by hand, since mechanized equipment wasn't allowed in the creekbed. The county planning department looked into the situation, but that agency had only two inspectors. Their priority was grading, not rock piles, some of their assignments wild-goose chases in the opinion of Ed Colby, a member of the department. He issued stop-work orders and red tape was put on machines — "red-tagging" — to shut down occasional jobs, but it was an impossible task checking all such development.

Vineyard developers weren't required to have the permits, the owners were. And too many of them thought paying thousands of dollars for violations was just part of the cost of doing business. He thought the rock pile went beyond what ought to be allowed, but it was up to the DA to charge the owner. Colby wasn't surprised that no charges were brought against Wender, Abreu, or Stadelhofer, that in the end no one paid a cent in fines.

Greg Melanson fired up his helicopter and rose slowly on the prevailing westerly breeze. He tilted to the left and passed over the rock pile, its size more apparent from the air. He could see the paths left in the chaparral by the boulders as they plunged to the creek below. He gained altitude, swinging farther to the left — east — topping the ridgeline, and it became apparent that the Wender-Colgin project was only one of many. The tops of the ridges were laid bare; another huge rock pile reared on the horizon, this one belonging to someone else, an Olympian entrance ramp to God's interstate. Beyond it, dumped rocks fanned the headwaters of a stream feeding Rector Reservoir, which held Yountville's drinking water. Some clearings went to the very edge of the canyons.

Melanson had reconciled himself to change, he said, to the prospect of a Colgin winery rising after the vineyard was finished, even to the sound of air conditioning compressors. He added, "People like that get in over their heads, they didn't know what they were doing. I don't blame them." He blamed vineyard developers.

The reconciliation dinner held on Pritchard Hill by the Longs, the neighbors of Wender and Colgin whose water line had been severed by the plunging boulders, was referred to as a "get-together." It included Wender-Colgin, and there was no mention of the rock pile still standing above their property line or the gravitational unpleas-

antness associated with it. Afterward, as they prepared to leave —
this story was told on the steps of the St. Helena post office the very
morning after, and later denied by Bob Long — Ann Colgin turned
to her host and said offhandedly that the phone call he had made to
the county had cost her fiancé a million dollars. But she didn't dispute the fact that the Longs gave a good dinner party.

9

LEIGHTON TAYLOR would always remember two things about the bulldozing of Pritchard Hill: the smell of California bay crushed beneath steel treads and the sight of Anna's hummingbirds dive-bombing machines in a desperate attempt to halt the destruction.

He and his wife, Linda, native Californians, had in 1989 bought an old bungalow and some senescent walnut trees on a few acres up behind the Chappellets, east of the Melansons and far from the Wender-Colgin rock pile. The place had been a U.S. Bureau of Land Management homestead harking back to predevelopment days in the Golden State, and the Taylors had put in a small vineyard and made some wine, aging it in rented space down in Napa — one of the Kinko's of the wine world — so wine wouldn't dominate life at home. He had a degree from the Scripps Institute of Oceanography in San Diego and had worked at the aquarium in Hawaii for many years before coming back to the California Academy of Sciences, and now he wrote books about aquariums and other things in the beautiful, remote place they had chosen for retirement.

A couple from New York with money — computer search engines — had bought the adjoining property, hired Dave Abreu and Richard Stadelhofer, and everything had changed. Leighton Taylor, who knew something about biology, thought what was happening to those steep slopes wrong. The 1991 hillside ordinance was supposed to have prevented such things and had been hailed as visionary, but the county didn't get the picture. The inspectors didn't come out and supervise. The Department of Conservation, Development and Planning, he thought, should be called the Department of Development, Planning and Maybe Conservation.

Someone from the Resource Conservation District, one of those vaguely affiliated agencies with no clout, did take a look at the job, but nothing happened. Someone from the Department of Public Works came out and said the contractors needed a permit to continue. According to Taylor's observations, blasting and rock removal went on for another forty-five days.

It was a typical progression: wealthy people want a vineyard but are absent and distracted by other things, and they turn all the decisions over to strangers and are told not to worry, that they'll get the best. The cost is irrelevant. A different landscape results, and soil is brought in, creating a different place entirely. It doesn't matter to the new people that it's different, just as it doesn't matter to them how much they pay, because they didn't know the land in the first place, and they don't have to earn the money back.

Well, it matters to other people, Taylor thought. It sure as hell matters to the hummingbirds. From time to time he had to remind himself that he wasn't looking at Bosnia. He acknowledged that someday the view would include comely vineyards, but at what ultimate cost? He thought there should be some way for wine producers to credibly indicate on a label that their wine was made from grapes planted and grown in a responsible manner. The same results could be obtained with methods less destructive, but the logic that prevailed was always the same: *get it done.*

Taylor wasn't opposed to vineyards or wineries but to people who didn't follow the rules. One day he encountered Dave Abreu at a meeting at county headquarters, in Napa, and he told him that he considered the property next to the Taylors an ecological disaster. Abreu pointed out that Taylor lived in an agricultural area, and told him that he should have bought the three hundred acres himself. The problem was that Leighton Taylor didn't have the required nine million dollars.

When Donn Chappellet first came to Pritchard Hill in 1967 Napa Valley was turning the corner from prunes and cattle to grapes. Chappellet had made a lot of money in industrial food service and vending and wanted out of that dog-eat-dog business. He didn't want his kids growing up in Los Angeles. Owning a winery seemed a good alternative to vending machines, and Napa the antithesis of urban superficiality.

He looked in the hills for property, on the advice of André Tchelistcheff, who thought vineyards up there would cost forty percent more to farm and that the yields would be half those on the valley floor. But the grapes would earn twice the price because they would be that much better. Chappellet checked out Mayacamas Vineyards, on the west side of the valley, but found it too rough and deer-ravaged, and then found sixty acres on Pritchard Hill, where grapes had been grown as early as the 1870s. He bought the property and gradually added to it, and he joined the Napa Valley Vintners Association. In 1968 that organization had only eighteen members and was racked by the fight over the creation of the agricultural preserve.

The Chappellet winery was built the following year, the first new one since Robert Mondavi's mission-style shocker down on Highway 29. Chappellet settled in to producing fine wine, wearing Hawaiian shirts and operating out of a big leather chair in the airy reaches of an enormous A-frame with long views. He took up soaring in gliders in Calistoga and sailed on his boat from San Francisco to Tahiti. Distributors beat a path to your door in those days, asking only if you made good wine. The stuff seemed to sell itself.

Ten years later you had to sell it — dinners, pep talks to staff, events — and that took money and effort. The number of wineries mounted until there were more than two hundred in the valley. Chappellet was concerned about too much growth and thankful for the remove of Pritchard Hill. Still, he had to market his wine, and he hated marketing. With distributors it was the squeaky wheel that got the grease, and he was glad to be able to turn such duties over to his sons, Cyril and, later, Jon-Mark, too. Now it was they who did the squeaking and the heavy lifting in a family business that, by Napa standards, was downright old when success clobbered the valley in the late nineties and pushed the number of operating wineries above three hundred.

Cyril Chappellet was a big man like his father, with full, chestnut-colored hair and certain inherited advantages. Development of new vineyards in the neighborhood could not be opposed by his family in good conscience, since they had put in their own, but wholesale cutting of live oaks on the property adjacent to the Chappellets' was a shock, even if it was legal. Cyril and Jon-Mark talked to Dave Abreu about leaving some of the trees, which belonged to the Bryant family, owners of the label of the same name and a recognized member of the cult of cabernet. The oaks numbered between eight hundred and a thousand, Cyril estimated, and when they had started to fall in great numbers he made some inquiries. He learned that the Bryants' winemaker, Helen Turley, had told the owners that she wanted as much new vineyard as possible.

The Bryants lived in far-off St. Louis. There was a big difference between the people who lived on the premises, Cyril thought, and those who didn't. Residents felt the change of seasons and closely watched the progress of projects under way, whereas the absentee landowners saw, heard, smelled, and felt nothing. They didn't understand the natural processes and didn't fully appreciate the critical importance of trees and water. There was a history of competition for the creek bottom between the properties now owned by Long and Wender, for instance, that had been going on for decades.

The Bryants shared water rights with four other landowners. All of them could be severely affected by their new vineyard and the new winery that was to follow. All the neighbors were concerned. The label on the Bryant wine included the fashionable word "family," but the project didn't look very personable, caring, or familial to Cyril. And there was the problem of the road, a steep, at times tortuous lane winding up from the shore of Lake Hennessey that had never been intended for heavy trucks. A new Bryant winery would greatly increase this kind of traffic, and unless the Bryants addressed this and other concerns, the neighbors intended to challenge their application for a winery permit.

This was the equivalent of a declaration of war. And there was the additional problem of a cave. The Bryants wanted one, like most everyone else, and Cyril had been told that Helen Turley wanted enough underground space for a single level of French oak barrels, so it would look like Bordeaux. That meant about eight thousand square feet of subterranean space, according to Cyril's calculations, plus another six thousand square feet for the winery: a huge hole. Where would the thousands of cubic yards of spoil go?

The live oaks began to fall on the adjacent slope while the Chappellets watched. One hundred trees, two hundred, three hundred . . . Contractors today were a different breed, Cyril thought; there was no part of the valley too remote or steep to be developed if you threw enough big machines and dynamite at it. This had led to basic alterations in the landscape. The Wender rock pile struck him as one of the Eight Wonders of the World. Abreu had been up there all the time, and in Cyril's opinion Dave would rather do the job now and explain later.

When there were only three oak trees left, Cyril went over and confronted him, and Abreu said, "I've got a job to do."

"Yes," said Cyril, "but be neighborly." He had known Dave at St. Helena High and thought his biggest shortcoming was public relations. Cyril added, "Cut those last three trees, and we'll do a lot-line re-survey. There'll be all sorts of problems."

The three live oaks were left standing. Cyril concluded that Dave saw them as an affront and all trees as nothing more than impediments.

Some of Abreu's friends thought his attitude toward the land went back to his experiences in Vietnam. In the war, the vineyard manager to the stars had been assigned to artillery and stationed north of Da Nang, where he had hooked up with a colonel in communications, driving his jeep. Abreu "got into areas that were pretty hot," as he told it, but that was about all he would say. Growing up in a large, struggling family had engendered both ambition and a frugality about personal revelation.

Somewhere between the time of Abreu's return from Vietnam and the controversial vineyard development for Viader, Wender-Colgin, Bryant, and Jayson Pahlmeyer, the gentleness and generosity of spirit observed by others had been replaced in Abreu by wariness and what longtime acquaintances called "self-orientation." This was attributed to a combination of extraordinary success and inarticulateness, the result being the realization by Abreu that you don't have to compete on a social level to be a leader, that you don't even have to know everything about viticulture to succeed.

Lack of finesse, and of leavening by Stanford or Berkeley, may have made Abreu verbally abusive on occasion, but it didn't mean he was ever at a loss for words. "Any fruit that has its nose hanging out can get nipped," he would say. And, "If it's hanging out in high temperatures and, here, hey, as your fruit goes into *véraison,* you're getting close to your harvest, and . . ." He talked and he talked, subjecting Robert Parker, on his annual visits to the valley, to hours of Rutherford-speak about vineyards, climate, and cabernet, an inexhaustible fount of technical expertise and admiration for luscious, costly wines. One witness to these sessions compared Abreu to a vinous Elmer Gantry in his fervor and his ability to move the hearer.

Parker was already an admirer of the proverbial small producer and the big palatal hit, of pushing the rocket juice envelope on steep slopes and letting the fruit hang out there, pervious to the insects and the elements, whether in California or in Europe. Parker's numerical ranking system had been devised decades before as a way into the market, and it had worked; his ranking of the '82 Bordeaux in *The Wine Advocate* as "the vintage of the century" sold an inordinate quantity of the '82s in the United States when they were released in 1984. Later evidence that it was not the vintage of the century mattered not at all.

At that time, the market in France was flat and the Bordelais realized that they had to expand to survive. The French would not pay twenty dollars for a bottle of wine, and neither would the Germans. England's economy was in the doldrums and so couldn't float Bordeaux on the residue of traditional Francophilia. The Japanese would pay twenty dollars a bottle, but there were too few of them. That left the Americans. The rising tide of prosperity and wine appreciation coincided nicely with the floating of the young government lawyer that Parker was, in love with an uncharacteristic vintage and eager to proselytize its wonders: overripe fruit and lots of extract by French standards.

Some Bordelais realized that Americans not only liked these big, showy, oaky, alcoholic wines but were willing to pay more than twenty dollars a bottle for them, and while they scoffed at Parker and the idea of the vintage of the century, they altered their winemaking regimes to produce similar wines. Some became advocates of overripe fruit, members of the academy of the macerated grape. One of these was Michel Roland, of Château Bon Pasteur, who ran an enological laboratory in Bordeaux and served as consultant to some

California wines, among them Harlan and Merryvale. He reinforced the love of superripe fruit and a powerful assault on the palate in Parker, who looked for disciples of this style — small, zealous producers, so-called *garagistes* — all over the world, including California.

Helen Turley and Dave Abreu were such disciples, and Abreu seemed to have considerable influence with Parker. Such a close connection was a powerful de facto recommendation for any vineyard manager or winemaker with prospective clients, but not as big a one as the perfect score of one hundred that Abreu's wine received in *The Wine Advocate*. For in the intervening years he had become a vintner as well as vineyard manager to the stars, with six hundred cases made from grapes grown near Buddy Meyer's house, in the very shadow of Newton. Abreu's cabernet was nearly impossible to buy and consequently more sought after and, of course, expensive. It netted Abreu about three hundred thousand dollars a year in extra income, or so he said, and he spent only a few days a year dealing with it, someone else handling the winemaking, bottling, and mailing: Napa Valley gravy.

The critic reportedly invited Abreu to come east, to travel with him in France. The tradition of critics distancing themselves from the criticized did not prevail in the wine world. Strict adherence to objectivity, and blind tasting, had given way to elaborate interchanges between those making and those evaluating a glamorous product, and the only complainants were those producers who received low scores.

Prospective clients visiting Abreu's office, in a little industrial complex in south St. Helena, were surprised by its simplicity. Vineyard workers stood around under the arcade out front. Inside, the floor was stacked with survey maps, blueprints, bottles of cult wines in cardboard cases. Dave's cubicle was hung with framed maps of the Côte de Beaune and the Côte de Nuits, an indication of Abreu's catholicity, since he made cabernet, not pinot noir. Visitors' hopes were held hostage there, or in Dave's black and silver pickup with the spray tank in the back, while Dave decided whether or not to consent to work for them.

He did the interviewing — of IPO beneficiaries, sports team owners, dot-commers — and asked if they intended to make wine.

They had to go for the whole package if they wanted Abreu — a vineyard, a recognized winemaker, and a winery. But the key was "a great piece of ground." He drove them to some vernal bit of valley and told them in no uncertain terms what was required — three-by-five vine spacing, "major, major rocks removed" — and that the price was whatever it took. That meant not just upward of one hundred thousand dollars per acre but also ten thousand a year after development as a management fee.

Competitors were jealous of Abreu. "He's a libertarian" was a typical remark. "He doesn't have respect for authority" was another. "Bullheaded. But he seems to have a magic touch. He's making a bloody fortune, and saves everything, buys a truck and drives it forever. Swears constantly. A great guy, single-minded, good work, disastrous projects — all true."

Some were afraid of him: "He's the fox in the woods, always watching for advantage. Cunning — a demonic nature with an angelic façade. All his actions have cold-hearted motives. He never says thanks, never admits he's wrong. Narcissistic may be the best word for him, but he wouldn't know what it means."

Asked about his own success, Abreu would say, "I've got a natural talent for recognizing greatness out there."

He threw an appreciation party for Colgin and Wender after the resculpting of the rock pile and the cutting of the Bryants' live oaks; attending was an enviable collection of old-line vintners, *arrivistes,* and lucky spermers. One celebrant estimated that Abreu spent fifty thousand dollars on the wine, all of it French, to prevent the guests from sniping at each other's creations. That proved, once and for all, that you didn't have to go to Stanford or to Berkeley to be smart.

10

DISPUTES OVER property lines, water, roads, trees, and dirt were not limited to Howell Mountain, Pritchard Hill, or Atlas Peak farther south. On the other side of the valley, on Mount Veeder, on both sides of the Oakville Grade, up Spring Mountain — in fact, along the whole breadth of the Mayacamas — and down in Carneros and on the flank of Mount St. Helena and over in Pope and other valleys subsidiary to the Napa River, vineyard managers and property owners pushed at the limits: viticultural, aesthetic, natural.

The stated objective of all this activity was the production of a wine better than a neighbor's, better than "the best," or at least more profitable, at whatever cost. This was rooted in the striving personality of "the vintner" and in the consuming desire for a pedigree in the form of a label commanding respect in the press. Some blamed the vintners' natural competitiveness, and some blamed the two wine-ranking publications thoroughly ensconced in Napa Valley's consciousness. But the real source was cultural.

The distillation of half a century of affluence and emphasis on the material had altered the landscape and, in some cases, the people. Winning had edged out other values, such as restraint, prudence, and candor about the product; the measure of winning was acquisition, not intellectual or spiritual accomplishment, and so the avatars were those with the most — real estate, art, stock options, the adoration of strangers who paid such prices, and the accolades of those who tasted and ranked.

Jim Laube arrived in the Napa bureau of the *Vallejo Times-Herald* in 1978 with a master's degree in history and economics from San Diego State and a somewhat educated palate. He had visited Napa while a student, when you could hit all the wineries in Napa and Sonoma in a couple of days. That was before all the competition and specialization, when Louis Martini was making thirty different wines, disciples of the Reverend Sun Myung Moon were living in Pope Valley, Coca-Cola had just bought Sterling Vineyards, and the county supervisors were, as usual, arguing about land use.

Laube covered such stories and in his spare time was a stringer for *Wine Spectator,* a brash new magazine out of New York that belonged to Marvin Shanken and was zeroing in on California's second most glamorous product. Twenty-five bucks for a story, ten for a photo, those were the going rates. Laube prided himself on being a working journalist from the age of sixteen, when he covered sports for a newspaper in Anaheim and "Follow the bread crumbs" was his motto.

Here all the crumbs led to wine and the people behind it. He went to tastings and symposia and learned about grape types and pest control. He did straight-up features, no criticism. That was for punctilious Brits like Hugh Johnson and Michael Broadbent. What Laube had wanted to do was write biographies, and in a way that is what happened, although the form was abbreviated and the subject the infinitely varied persona of *Vitis vinifera* in northern California.

When the *Spectator* moved to San Francisco in 1983, Laube joined the staff. Those were heady days. California wine was rising fast in popularity, and so was the *Spectator.* Marvin Shanken had a nose for trends among those sectors of the populace best able to afford them, and a provocative way of presenting them: always try to turn a subject — wealth, beautiful houses, expensive cabernets — into as big a *thing* as possible, take an idea and make as much out of it as you can. This was the opposite of a newspaper's approach, which was to make big subjects comprehensible, and it was fun.

Even when the ideas weren't good ones, they improved with defeat, emerging bigger and better the second time. Then the magazine went from news gathering to consumer information. In those days Burgundy and Bordeaux still mattered most to wine-drinking Americans, so European wine received more coverage. Shanken got to know the business side, visiting wine shops à la Ernest Gallo and asking why the magazine wasn't stacked next to the cash register, and he got to know his readership. It was predominantly professional, passionate about wine, and the *Spectator* homed in on it, sending out surveys and questionnaires, asking precisely what sort of wine was drunk and where it came from, and the results came back loud and clear: cabernet (and to a lesser degree chardonnay) and California.

The concomitant trend — fantasy was perhaps a better word — was the prevailing interest in an "upscale lifestyle." Everybody wanted one. As soon as the *Spectator* geared itself to that desire, with profiles and photos of the wealthy also endowed with vineyards and wineries, circulation took off. Advertisers were in close pursuit. Wine reviews were just part of the *cuvée* then, but Shanken launched a series of focus groups, paying people in trade and consumer affairs to answer detailed questions, and he discovered that even real wine enthusiasts and professionals consulted the *Spectator* before making final decisions about which wine to buy. So the number of reviews increased.

Wines were usually slotted into four categories, but after Parker introduced the numbers rating, the editors of the *Spectator* saw the ease and effectiveness of this device and switched. Most every wine in the world was shipped to their offices. By the beginning of the nineties editors were specializing in regions, and Laube ended up with California. For practical purposes that meant Napa and Sonoma, with some slopover from the rest of the state.

There was a string of good vintages in the nineties. Increasingly, the bread crumbs led to a new tier of people wanting recognition and willing to spend a lot more money to get it than did their predecessors. Meanwhile, consumers were growing more knowledgeable and demanding. *60 Minutes* produced a segment on wine, implying that drinking it was good for you, and that provided another kick up the ladder for volume, quality, and price.

Laube moved his office to Napa, where he devoted most of his working hours to tasting wine. Bottles showed up on his doorstep uninvited. He sometimes asked for specific wines from producers, and when he was tasting in certain categories he purchased some others. He might spend several days with three hundred versions of a specific grape variety, or he might mix varieties, always first eating a bowl of cereal at seven A.M. and brushing his teeth. Reds in the morning, whites after lunch. He figured that one of three things could result. If he said a wine was great and nobody else thought it was, he would be hung out to dry. If he said a wine was crummy and others thought it was great, this would be taken as proof that he didn't know what he was talking about. But if most people agreed with him, he would be considered more or less on the mark.

That is what happened. Laube would admit that he had "a California palate," but the definition of that, like so many things in wine parlance, was imprecise. In general it meant an appreciation of assertive tastes and wines that "introduce themselves" — that is, make a strong first impression. The problem was, a large gray area existed between great and crummy.

Enough readers agreed with Laube often enough to keep subscribing to the *Spectator,* and their number reached about three hundred thousand. By that time Laube, like Parker, could singlehandedly make a success out of an obscure producer or bolster a sagging reputation. He could significantly affect the balance sheet of corporations — including Marvin Shanken's. Laube could have had lunch on somebody else — and breakfast and dinner — every day of the year if he had chosen to. His lack of accessibility, like his rakish salt-and-pepper mustache and newsman's gimlet eye, unsettled some vintners and offended others whose wines received less than a ninety on his celestial scale. But he and his wife rarely went to wine-related events, living a conventional life in the city of Napa — except for all the empty bottles that went out with the garbage.

Laube tasted all the wines blind, but he tasted some more than once. He admitted that once the identity of, say, an Opus One was known, and the wine had received a mediocre rating, he might taste it blind again. Similarly, if a wine was ranked either very high or very low, he might taste it blind again. Laube thought this fair, but his critics thought it indefensible. The devil, they said, was in the second chances.

In the spring of the millennial year, the *Spectator* published an article by Laube entitled "California's Cult Wines: Who They Are and Why They're Red Hot." True to the magazine's origins, the article made the subject as big as possible. In the process, it revealed little about the pasts and practices of the owners, some of them considerably less than glamorous. The fact was that all these people had made their money in activities having nothing to do with wine. Of the nine most celebrated vintners in the article, two were real estate developers (resorts, condos, and Santa Barbara starter mansions), one was a real estate agent, one the fiancée of an investment banker, and one a stockbroker.

The article was widely read and commented on, in the valley and elsewhere, and seen as a canonization of the cult of the macerated grape.

Mark Pope had decided in the early nineties that he wanted to sell what he called "the high-end, ultra-premium lifestyle stuff with a blue jeans approach." He founded a company called the Bounty Hunter with two possible public personas: one traveling in a green '54 Chevy pickup with a three-legged Jack Russell terrier sidekick named Tripod, the other an irreverent Banana Republic type out of the 1880s, both searching out "the best of the best."

Pope had settled for granny glasses and collarless shirts, but he had found what he was looking for. His initial offering was of Diamond Creek, Forman, Hanzell, and Pahlmeyer, all of them snapped up, and in the late nineties he had two boxcars full of catalogues offering for sale many wines not easily available at prices merely high as opposed to inordinately inflated. "If the wine's not great, we don't sell it," he would say. "You can shop our catalogue with a dart."

His success lay in "delivering a sense of place, giving people a fifteen-minute vacation" in a bottle. This harked back to the French notion of the taste of the land, once the ultimate expression of viticultural craft that was being lost in Napa to a modish concentration of ripe fruit and high alcohol. Pope obtained the wines by dint of this enthusiasm for the basics of winemaking, persistence, and a bluntness endearing to his customers. "People want plain-speak, they don't want to chase points. You can't drink points. We have the wines with the points, but we don't talk about points. You live by points, you die by points."

Some of the acknowledged cult, or "trophy," wines he did not sell, considering them "over the top, conspicuous by their bodaciousness," including several hailed in the *Spectator*. The interchangeable terms of "cult" and "trophy" applied to dozens of wines and were at once a source of envy and derision. Some winemakers felt either resentful if their wines were not thought sufficiently cultish, or guilty if they were. They recognized problems inherent in wines praised by Laube and Parker but were afraid to speak out.

Another term for the product began to emerge, in reaction: "limo wines." Limousines were the symbol of new money, conspicuous consumption, cluelessness, and, most important, *otherness.* Limo riders mostly came from elsewhere — usually from a southerly direction — in too formal clothes, depending on their mode of transport to signal their wherewithal and their remove from reality. Enthusiasts were known to bring limo wines *to* the valley in limousines, gather with other like-minded collectors in one of the fine restaurants, and drink their treasures with a suitable amount of fanfare.

Some speculated that there was a direct connection in *Wine Spectator* between the number of square inches of advertising and the ratings of particular wines, a common allegation for which no proof was offered. Laube and his colleagues vigorously denied it, but the effects of the ratings on price were not denied by them or by Parker. "It's scary to see prices continue to go up," Pope would admit. "Everybody's grabbing what they can, while they can. Dare I say greed enters into it?"

The winemaker stood at the window of a house with a view, but to say whether it was easterly or westerly, and of what section of the valley, was not allowed. Views, like geography, amount to identity in Napa Valley, and Pat had stipulated that, if an interview was to be granted, no clue could be offered. Pat did not wish to be known for voicing sentiments common among peers but kept to themselves, because the effect of such sentiments in the outside world was not good for business or for the image of "the vintner."

At the same time, Pat felt compelled to speak out, being profoundly dissatisfied with the status quo and unhappy in a celebrated cradle of contentment. As a younger person, Pat had made a mark and prospered here, but no longer enjoyed what was transpiring in the valley. The setting was still beautiful — no one could deny this — and the work still challenging, but the innocence was gone. "Wine has become a talent show," Pat began, speaking slowly, carefully, "one that disregards the synergism between man and nature. It isn't who can capture the *terroir* anymore, but who can capture the wine writer."

New wines impressed the wealthy neophyte while offending the real connoisseur because they had no balance, no finesse, just power — the bane of modern existence. Some cult wines "don't belong on the shelves where wine is sold," Pat added, "they belong in the sauce department." To state this publicly would be akin to calling someone's child a juvenile delinquent in the society of which Pat was a respected member, a society far touchier than it once was, intolerant of criticism from within and hostile to it from without.

"In the forties and fifties and sixties, there were no cult wines. The *Wine Spectator* contrived the idea, and we fell for it. What a mean thing to do, making people salivate for wines that aren't very drinkable and can't be bought for less than two hundred dollars a bottle. That magazine has taken the wholeness out of everything by adding glitz. Consequently, the winemakers try to impress the wine writers rather than the wine drinkers." Pat paused. "We need to get back to basics, to stop feathering the engines to see how much we can charge."

Pat hated the point system for rating wine. "Are paintings in a museum on a point system?" Pat blamed it in part on Robert Parker, "a groupie, also a nice guy," on whom Pat's success, too, depended. "You have to make Parker feel like he's part of the team, you have to talk to him endlessly about your wines and tell him how good they are . . . Everybody used to just let him taste, until they realized that was the wrong way to do it, that you had to talk to him and be very patient. If he tasted blind he wouldn't come up with those findings. Although he may not realize it, the findings aren't impartial, they're engineered by the winemakers."

Parker's preference for "big, obtuse" cabernets influenced the winemaking of "the superstars," Pat went on. "Some of these winemakers are making extract, not wine. They've lost sight of wine as something that goes with meals. It's not the Holy Grail, and it costs too much. Does it make sense to pay eighty dollars for something that's gone in ten minutes?

"We've elevated wine to a specialty category. We've lost the wholesomeness. The idea of cult wines gives ammunition to the neo-prohibitionists by making wine sound like a drug. The only point of all this competition and fancy marketing is outdoing someone else. The wines dazzle while they insult the palate, but young winemakers are scared not to make them."

Nuances of soil were lost, balanced wines harder and harder to find. Meanwhile, available land was running out. Of the total half-million acres in the valley, less than forty thousand were planted in grapes, but relatively few suitable acres were left. And these were mostly in the hills, steep and often forested.

"If you could stand above the valley and look down on all this, you would see that everybody is bumping into everybody else, trying to get in. The question is always 'Why?' Because the market has gone crazy, providing money in unprecedented quantities. The amount of it spent on frivolity is amazing. Wine has become a post-yuppie thing, the next step after owning a BMW. And if you don't know the best cabernet and who makes it, you're embarrassed.

"As in a nuclear explosion, all the elements are insignificant in and of themselves, but devastating together. We have huge wealth, billionaires willing to spend any amount of money to be here, to be in the new club. Well, I put in decades of work to be able to charge fifty dollars for a bottle. Then some billionaire arrives and simply hires people to do what I had to learn, dumping money on the table. This makes everything more expensive for everyone, including wine. You can't go to a meeting nowadays without someone whispering, 'Where is this going? Is wine really worth this much money? How much more can we glamorize this stuff?'"

It was just afternoon, but already the shadows were lengthening.

"We're all so spoiled — pigs in glass houses. We don't want Napa Valley revealed as Nirvana and wrecked. We don't want more people coming in, but they are. Something will happen because of the greed. A little bit would be good, but if it's worth doing, it's worth overdoing. Very few people can live here now with restraint and dignity. The room is full, everybody's very nervous, we're at the top in terms of money and fame, and nothing grows forever."

II

PASSION ON THE LAND

11

FOR WEEKS they worried about the numbness in his right arm, which he attributed to paperwork and his wife to a darker source. Their doctor in the valley was of little help, so they crossed the mountains to Santa Rosa, in Sonoma County, passing familiar, ordered vineyards, peeper green in spring, and in autumn, when bathed in the angled light of the setting sun, a smoldering gold. The specialist performed some tests and in a moment of unprecedented honesty — brutality was a better word, she thought — told them that her husband had an incurable disease and only two years to live.

People often said of them, "They're charmed." Handsome, poised, seemingly above the contentiousness of the times, Jack and Jamie Davies were not physically imposing but had a collective presence, she with the yellow eyes and a feline loveliness surviving into middle age, he with the foursquare directness of Welsh ancestry, his hair gone gray now but his energy and determination undiminished. Together they had created — on their own, decades before — a product consistently ranked with the best, and the two of them were often cited as worthy examples of the valley's early, hard-wrought, phenomenal success.

Founders, keepers, institutions: that was Jack and Jamie Davies. They made at Schramsberg a unique substance, sparkling wine, compared by a Benedictine monk in an earlier time to liquid stars, and they had beaten their own path, starting in 1964, one that had led through the tangle of manzanita and California bay on an eastern slope of the Mayacamas Mountains, under towering trees, to a reclaimed Victorian with a high, broad porch. There they had reared three sons and in a board-and-batten winery proved that wine can support a family — especially when there are several outside investors. The path girded the earth now, a testament to foresight and hard work — a president of the United States had taken their wine to China, another served it in the White House — but suddenly the way had grown narrow and the shadows deeper than any thrown by redwood and Douglas fir.

Jack could not, would not believe the diagnosis. A seeker after solutions, by nature an optimist, assertive of the best possibilities in any situation, he could not accept the sentence of a neurological disorder with an incomprehensible name, no known cause, and subtle if persistent effects. "Let's identify this thing and deal with it," he would say, and Jamie would say yes and agree to help. There was little in the realm of opinion they did not share, but in this matter their views diverged, despite what she told her husband, and they would come into alignment only through a slow, inexorable process.

They had come north as a young couple from southern California, he a former business executive who turned his back on a large commercial enterprise, she an artist, pregnant with their third child. They were branded city slickers by the locals, who thought their ambition to make sparkling wine ludicrous and their choice of a big wreck of a house, abode of bats and creeping things, crazy. It had been built for an itinerant German barber named Jacob Schram in the nineteenth century. He had made wine tasted by Robert Louis Stevenson, and the writer generously spoke of the valley's potential for producing "bottled poetry." If there were ghosts at the top of Schramsberg Lane, surely they included those of the sickly Stevenson, the fierce-looking but fond German winemaker Schram, who had traveled Napa's rough roads in a wagon, and the Chinese coolies who had gouged out his caves.

Now, thirty years after the Davieses' arrival, Jack emerged from the house in the mornings and walked across to the winery and climbed rough-hewn stairs under a massive eucalyptus tree to the office. There he talked to distributors and to members of what was a privately held partnership, took part in tasting trials, and generally threw himself into the molding of the wine and its market. But he grew tired more quickly, and a look came into his eyes that Jamie had never seen there, not resignation but a deepening awareness of life's limitations.

They decided to go beyond California's borders for an answer to the question of his malady that was more acceptable to Jack, but at the Mayo Clinic the prognosis was no better. Jack's disease was real, and terminal. The doctor suggested that they stop by a room on their way out and buy devices for lessening Jack's difficulties with eating and buttoning his shirts, but Jack disdained this. He called it a macabre "gift shop," and he and Jamie went back to Napa Valley to as bleak a homecoming as any she could remember.

They had traveled widely together in the affairs of Schramsberg — to the East Coast, to England and Europe — and to third-world countries on their own, collecting rugs, masks, knowledge. They were a team, the Davieses: droll, at times unsettlingly self-contained, but outgoing, pulling together in harness, their obligations overlapping, the seams absorbed in the common fabric of family and profession.

Jack had always set the tone; Jamie worked things out. It was Jack who gave the boys the run of the place when they were young, and Jamie who worried about their turning into "wild Indians" and getting lost or injured in Schram's old caves or in the wooded defile between Spring and Diamond mountains, where Ritchey Creek ran cold and clear through a landscape little changed in a century. During the boys' snuff-dipping phase, Jack had railed against the filthy habit, while it was Jamie who found and threw away the Copenhagen tins.

Those Davies boys. There were three of them, and their parties in the vineyard were famous. They would fill grape gondolas with water and haul them up to be used as mobile swimming pools. Jack rarely interfered with this or other expressions of youthful exuberance, but on serious matters he always had a word of advice. Now the boys were all acting like Jack, saying, "Let's get control of this thing," insisting on *doing* something. They were no more able than Jack to accept the fact that the disease might be incurable.

His office hours grew shorter. Some mornings Jack would go back to the house and Jamie would take over. It was not an easy time in the wine business in Napa Valley, which had gone from carefully creating a world-renowned product to aggressively exploiting it.

Most of the genteel aspects of the profession were a memory now. Continued success meant expensive promotion. Survival entailed crucial decisions about style, marketing, and vineyard acquisition at prices unheard of a few years before. There was a glut of champagne on the market, making the decisions even trickier. In addition, Schramsberg's aging board of directors was not the best for the changing times. Some minority shareholders wanted out of the partnership, which meant finding buyers and liquidating shares, and that had never been easy.

Production costs were rising, and salaries, with no end in sight. Jamie was proud of what had been created at Schramsberg and wanted it to endure, but sometimes she felt that she, family, shareholders, and staff were swimming against the tide, their founder in trouble, and all the emphasis nowadays on big red wines. Their oldest son, Bill, had left the family business to pursue his ambition of farming rice organically in the Sacramento River delta; their middle son, John, lived in Alaska, advising investors in the surging stock market, and was a bit of a wild card. The youngest, Hugh — Huey — was an eager recent addition to the Schramsberg staff, but untested.

The founder would be a hard act to follow, if and when it came to that. One of Jack's strengths was his willingness to listen to anyone. Those meeting him for the first time were often surprised by his receptiveness, when successful vintners were supposedly haughty, self-absorbed, and uninterested in the opinions of those beyond their ranks. Jack would not only listen but would also respond, directly and without sentimentality, whether an assertion struck him as sound or unreasonable. Analysis often edged out emotion; his reaction to suggestions for change at Schramsberg could be daunting. So it was surprising when Jack allowed the lamas into their lives.

The year before he got sick, at a retreat held by a friend in Oakville, Jack and Jamie listened to a Tibetan monk discuss death, dying, and the meditative state, just months before they would find themselves in need of such reflection. While the lama spoke, a February storm raked the valley, the wind unrelenting, the lightning illuminating a bruised, angry sky. Everyone was moved by the experience. Jack and Jamie were impressed with the lama's positive approach to life and the way his religion complemented, rather than dominated, others' beliefs. The generosity of spirit attracted them in a way their own Presbyterian and Congregationalist faiths did not. Since neither Jack nor Jamie was particularly religious, she was struck by her husband's strong response to the monk's teaching.

A bond formed between her husband and this affable monk in his saffron robe with the beaming countenance. Jack and Jamie began to attend other retreats and lectures, and read about Buddhism, a difficult subject made more so by murky English renderings. They practiced meditation and stayed in touch with the lama and an associate who spent much of his time traveling the state. Jamie was gratified to see the change in Jack, this rational, successful Republican and long-standing member of the Bohemian Club shedding unneeded elements of his life. He seemed to look toward the unknowable future from a different vantage point, and she thought, "Sometimes help comes out of thin air."

Without actually saying it, Jack acknowledged the irreversible change in their lives. He seemed to be telling Jamie, by example, "You can do it all, you don't need me." This was consistent with his nature, she thought, and with their past together. Jack had always given her complete freedom, acting as if there was nothing she couldn't do, and that was a source of strength for her. But what she could not do was to get Jack to use the computer or dictate memos. An inveterate transcriber of his own thoughts, he abandoned writing altogether when his hands failed him, and drifted into his own space. He never spoke of his illness, being a child of the silent generation and of the Depression, and his silence was harder on the boys than on her.

When Bill Davies heard from a business associate that his father had Lou Gehrig's disease, he was irritated. He demanded, "What are you talking about?" He and his brothers had known their father was ill, but not how ill, and now the severity of the situation settled in. Jack had mentored them all, and they all wanted some formal statement from him, something official: precious words acknowledging lessons learned, expectations met, peace found. But Jack just smiled on them, his words becoming fewer and fewer until finally they ceased.

Even breathing became a trial. The county sent a nurse with a machine to assist him, but Jack sent her and the machine away. It was winter and he sat before the fire in the big house, staring into the flames. The Victorian's high picture window looked onto dark conifers under a sky breaking clear and blue some afternoons. Bill and his wife, Gail, moved into the house for a time with their son, little Jack. Bill remembered entering the house for the first time when he was a child, after he and his father had driven up from Los Angeles in an International pickup, and being awed by the wildness of the place, the vast rooms, plaster falling from the ceilings. The two of them had eaten ice cream in the moldering kitchen and watched a deer in the overgrown garden, framed against the mountainside where he was to grow up following game trails and scrambling into caves with his brothers.

Jack seemed to glimpse in the baby a sign of renewal, of one life ending and another beginning. Watching his father watch little Jack, Bill saw a tacit recognition that life is reduced in the end to the essentials of love and family.

The Mexican gardener left abandoned birds' nests on the outdoor table, and Jamie thought, "Everything is of this place, everything comes back to it. We are on the land for a short time."

When she and Jack had first arrived in Napa Valley, their mountain redoubt was already imbued with history. That helped inspire them, not just to make wine but also to be good parents, good citizens. A family was a boon to society, they thought. Good stewardship of a place benefits others. Jack refused to leave it now, even to be hospitalized. At night, lying in the room with him, Jamie would listen to him falter, and be afraid; then he would breathe again.

One morning at dawn Jamie awoke to discover that Jack had stopped making the effort. She felt deprived and unbearably sad that he had died without her knowing, and for a long time she sat alone with him. He would have expected her to deal with this, she knew, and she went out and told the others, and asked that flowers be brought from the garden to be scattered on and around Jack's bed, making of it a bank of color and fragrance and of the room a bower.

Jack had once told his youngest son, after Hugh had injured a knee, "Listen to the doctors." In a reversal of roles, Hugh had said the same thing to Jack, but his father had come to terms with the disease in his own stoical, inscrutable way. He had left jobs unfinished, Hugh thought. Schramsberg had problems, and so did the valley. Jack and Jamie had worked, back in the sixties, for the creation of the agricultural preserve, even as they built a business. The idea of the ag preserve had since then taken on the quality of holy writ, but now, in the 1990s, even it was being questioned, and there was a loss of comity among proponents of farming, development, and the environment, and sharp battle lines drawn over the valley's future.

After the ag preserve fight, there had been another, over a four-lane highway up the middle of the valley proposed by the California Department of Transportation. That would have altered the place absolutely and forever, and although it had been defeated, the plan could be resurrected at any time. It was the last such fight in which Jack was totally involved. During the winery definition controversy at the end of the eighties, he did speak before the Napa Valley Vintners Association of the need to require at least seventy-five percent of Napa Valley grapes in wines claiming to be of the valley. This he did despite resistance from some of his peers who saw great opportunities for expansion and profits with fewer restrictions on grape origins and on activities that tapped the lucrative tourist trade.

A concern for the environment had taken with Hugh at an early age. He had traveled widely, and whenever he returned to the valley he felt the shock of change most evident in the big, dramatic houses he thought of as "castles" and in the numbers of tourists and the amenities provided for them. He had complained of this to his father, and about the unappealing notion of success in America, saying that he would seek some alternative in life. His father had told him, "You don't want to be a basket weaver, son."

Whatever he chose to do, his father was saying, Hugh must be *in* the world, not removed from it.

He remembered the days following his father's death as a swarm of grief and regeneration. The Tibetan lamas appeared on the periphery of the family's mourning, directing, bolstering, in charge while not seeming to be. After Jack was cremated and some of his ashes spread in the vineyard, Hugh, his mother, and his brothers walked in the places Jack had walked and they gathered on the bank of Ritchey Creek in Jack's favorite grove of redwoods. From some of

Jack's ashes they made stupas, and scattered flower petals on the water which drifted downstream, toward the sea.

The day of the memorial service, the lamas simply disappeared, their work done. So many flowers had arrived at the house that Jamie couldn't accommodate them all. Restaurants and friends sent more food than they could possibly eat. Hundreds of mourners gathered in the vineyard, some seated on folding chairs and others standing, and for four and a half hours they listened as people came forward and spoke of Jack Davies.

Hugh was pulled at by conflicting emotions. He had asked his father near the end if he had any idea where he was going, meaning some sort of afterlife, a bold question. Hugh had received no indication that Jack did know, but he received no indication, either, that Jack was worried about it. Now, standing with his mother and his brothers, Hugh — the tall one, almost gangly, a family anomaly in steel-rimmed glasses, more at home in hiking boots and a down vest than a suit — evinced an eagerness even in grief that contrasted with the memory of his late father's reserve.

At the ceremony's conclusion a cage of white doves was brought forward and the door thrown open. In a burst of wings the birds rose, immaculate white silhouettes against the numinous, depthless sky.

12

"I F NAPA VALLEY can't be saved, no place can."

That sentence had been spoken by Jim Hickey more than a decade before, and often repeated, and in the intervening years he had come to doubt that any place can be saved once it acquires the stamp of significance: a subliminal glow, a nimbus attracting people with all the expectation and fervor of religious pilgrims, and none of the devotion.

Unrestrained, tourists devour the thing they love. This was not a popular sentiment nowadays, not when everybody was looking to get a piece of the tourist action. With the death of Jack Davies, Hickey — a big man with a stentorian voice and a white goatee, retired now — was reminded of how different things had once been, how fragile the valley had become.

The memorial service triggered memories, not all of them pleasant. Hickey had been hired right after the creation of the ag preserve to head up the county planning department, and he had tried to implement the spirit of the new law and to otherwise limit activities antithetical to agriculture — not just housing, but also the winery expansions that had little to do with making or selling wine. Later, he had helped put some clamps on wineries through passage of the winery definition, and was fired in 1990 for his efforts by a new board of supervisors elected by a small group of pro-development vintners, a bitter pill after nineteen years of dedicated service.

It was one he swallowed without complaint. He and his wife, Virginia, had traveled modestly after that, as befitted a retired planner and civil servant, but Hickey could not get Napa Valley out of his mind. Wherever he went, it was with him. Hickey had always been a devotee of good land use, believing that the valley personified many of the problems facing the nation. He was reminded of what could happen to it in Massachusetts, where he and Virginia had gone in search of Plymouth Rock and the spot where the Pilgrims landed. All they could find when they got out of the car at the seashore was a building and a fence. In the gift shop they looked at all the replicas of the *Mayflower,* and finally Hickey asked, "Where the hell is Plymouth Rock?"

They were directed to a walkway built around a hole, and in the hole was the object of their search. The Hickeys could pay to have their photograph taken with Plymouth Rock in the background. It was then that Hickey had a vision of the Napa Valley of the future: the ground was paved over, the hills built out, and valley life transformed into one large, all-encompassing touristic enterprise, with theme parks and water slides, condos, convention halls, overhead trams, and all manner of diversions. Those willing to pay to see the real Napa Valley were directed to a stockade where they would mount a rampart overlooking a green half acre planted to cabernet sauvignon and containing a little reproduction winery, and the guide would say, "There's Napa Valley. You're not allowed to take photos, but you can pose with it over there for our official photographer."

Back home, Hickey drove around the valley in his blue pickup, looking at all the change. He would plant a meaty hand on the truck's roof and swing himself into the cab. A large body was of no use to a man after he was done with high school football, he had decided. He no longer wore the scabbard on his belt that had contained the professional planner's tools, mostly pens. He usually traveled alone through the valley because Virginia didn't want to see all the zoning violations — signs, balloons, advertising banners, all components in her husband's glacier theory, the one postulating that every such violation, relatively insignificant in itself, provided an example for others to emulate or to copy, and they added up and eventually coagulated, like snowflakes, constituting a powerful force, a glacier, that could not be stopped once it began to move.

Judging by the evidence, the glacier had formed and was moving. Once everybody had been in favor of agriculture and talked about it as the highest use of the land, but today everybody wanted a piece of the visitor pie. That was a remarkable change. Tourists did not live in the valley and were the antithesis of agriculture, neither understanding the process nor tolerant of it. Farming was messy and it got in the way of activities like wine tasting and shopping, but tourism was the primary objective of those doing business in the valley now, including many of the wineries.

In the eighties, the county's attitude about the land had been protective. Then things got more profitable, and people began to say, "Why not allow a little development?" The winery definition had been crucial because many wineries really wanted to be shops, with the making of wine incidental to retail sale of wine and other things. Some wineries also wanted to be restaurants, galleries, museums, social and entertainment centers, coffee bars, B&Bs, or a combination of these things. Snowflakes. And the glacier groaned.

There were eight million people living in the Bay Area and another two million would soon arrive, according to official projections. The pressure was on in this, the last undeveloped wrinkle in the overall landscape, an anomaly with a powerful attraction, both as a glamorous destination and as a green magnet for urbanites and exurbanites. Napa County's growth had so far been mostly absorbed by the cities and towns, but they were filling up, pushing at the boundaries, boxed in by vineyards. Housing was relatively expensive everywhere, prohibitively so up-valley, where building continued apace. If the eight thousand plots left in the unincorporated area were built upon, that would bring roughly twenty thousand new people onto agricultural land, with disastrous effects also on ground water and wildlife habitat, to say nothing of the effect on the views and the quality of life of human beings.

This was happening all over America, but in Napa Valley the contrast between residential and commercial clutter and open space was quite evident, and the lesson clear for the rest of the country: act to restrict growth or lose your chance. Wine and agriculture were involved in a struggle with stronger market forces, and the outcome had relevance for all.

Everywhere Hickey drove he saw evidence of this. South of the city of Napa development proceeded. There were plans afoot for a huge destination hotel that would further clot the roads, and factories had already been erected for the production of things having nothing to do with wine, using up valuable space. Projects often permuted for the worse. For instance, land designated for a golf course to serve the industrial park was sold a couple of times, the plans getting further and further from the original concept, the new players looking for the biggest moneymaker only, regardless of its impact. Hickey was reminded of the old planning grants after World War Two for stimulating the economy and providing jobs, which made people in Napa, still a backwater, say, "We better get our share." The same argument was being used now for tourism.

The total commitment to agriculture Hickey had known as a young man was gone, the ag preserve a historical curiosity to the new people. They had heard of it but were ignorant of what it actually meant. What it meant was that Napa County had come up with an innovative, carefully crafted land-use alternative with zoning that discouraged residential development and prevented at least some commercial activities in the countryside unrelated to agriculture. The politicians still hailed the ag preserve publicly, but in private often backed more development, and this had to be resisted.

Hickey had done what he could. He had sat in front of the county board of supervisors for all those years, using his influence to keep the lid on, and that was too much for some powers in the valley. There had been signs at the end that the supervisors planned to dump him. The county counsel told Hickey, "You're always causing trouble." If Hickey hadn't raised the idea of a winery definition, the county counsel added, it would never have come up.

But Hickey had thought it a good idea and had never been shy about expressing his opinion. If he had been Joan of Arc, he might have subsequently run for supervisor himself. But Jim Hickey wasn't Joan of Arc, he was just an aging man with an enduring interest in the valley. He wrote letters to the editor and threw them away instead of mailing them. He refused to say, "Back in the good old days . . ." But still the changes rankled him and the glacier's movement saddened him.

To wile away the time, he had served as president of the Land Trust of Napa Valley, then joined the Elks. He was proposed for Exalted Leading Knight but turned it down, and was made secretary by default. He accepted out of duty. The Elks was full of men about his age — former car dealers, bankers, and so on — doing public service in a low-key way, nothing fancy, no wine auctions, but organizations like it were dying all over America for lack of new members. The baby boomers weren't interested in joining the Elks or any other group that took time away from their own pursuits. The old Upper Napa Valley Association, an anti-development coalition that had once enthusiastically sought controls on growth, was moribund.

Hickey was working on a history of the ag preserve, a civic enterprise to make sure people didn't forget how it had come about and why. At first he thought he might produce a pamphlet for high school students, then decided to go for greater depth. The problem was, most of the people involved were dead — Jack Davies, Louis Martini, the old supervisors and civil servants. It amused Hickey to discover how many of those left claimed to have had a crucial role in creating the ag preserve. Not that it really mattered who had done it. Hickey wanted the story out there as an example, so it would not be thought of as something passé, if sacred, a shrouded compact instead of a living thing.

Meanwhile, he drove around a valley full of challenges to the past: neighborhoods in Yountville, originally built so the valley's workers would have a place to live, gentrified now. The workers lived in the city of Napa or in another county altogether. Sometimes grape pickers slept under the bridges, in season, but that was a relatively small percentage of the workforce, and transient. Many of the wineries reminded Hickey of department stores, the houses of those on slopes above Malibu. These things were all related to the success of wine, including tourism. New investment had been attracted by the valley's reputation and its ability to please. The new homeowners in the hills and many of the new vintners had bought a piece of fame; they were tourists who had remained.

One day he turned into the long, tree-lined driveway of what had once been Inglenook and was now Niebaum-Coppola. He remembered when Heublein built the barrel storage facility out front, the hue and cry, but the more recent transformation of a historical structure into a tourist destination had elicited not one word of protest. This was symptomatic of the times. Now he gazed in amazement at the buses parked at the curb, at the alien pergola and the big new fountain. He parked his pickup in the company of limos and rental convertibles and crossed the gravel courtyard.

Inside the big old winery, he stood before the grand staircase and looked at the movie curios in cases and read the plaque on the wall that equated Gustave Niebaum and Francis Ford Coppola — *Men of Vision . . . separated in birth by nearly 100 years . . . natural, powerful partners . . . based on the deep, inexplicable determination of each man to dream impossible visions . . . Today, two extravagant imaginations . . . woven into this architecture as a double life story . . . Their common dedication to life at its best finds beautiful harmony here . . .* — and he said aloud, in amazement, "God love a duck."

Norm had gone to work at Niebaum-Coppola Winery when the wines still bore the mark of Tony Soter and Inglenook still stood, in Norm's mind, as a symbol of perfection. Intensely interested in wine and in the valley, Norm had educated himself at his own expense, on a meager income, in what good wine should taste like, an education that included an occasional first-growth Bordeaux, grand cru Burgundies, and vintage ports he could not really afford. But the romance of wine was real to him, despite the fact that he lived in modest surroundings, with no view of vineyards, and neighbors more likely to drink beer than cabernet sauvignon.

Because Norm wanted to work close to what he thought of as the source, he had gone to Inglenook, the physical embodiment of Gustave Niebaum, Hamden McIntyre, and John Daniel, bearer of the great historical weight of the valley. Norm remembered Inglenook when Heublein still owned it, most of the towering nineteenth-century structure off-limits to visitors, just a tasting room on the ground floor and a run-down courtyard with a sixties feel. The wine was mediocre at best, but then after the sale in 1995 to Coppola, Norm had dropped by again. Some of the activities there were odd, he thought — movie stuff, boxes of merchandise — but the wines showed promise. Visitors could taste various vintages of Rubicon and the "estate wines" — cabernet franc, merlot — and something called Gustave Niebaum Claret, which was then being made with Napa Valley grapes, and the improvement was obvious and exciting.

He had returned yet again after the remodeling of the chateau and felt he had stumbled into a Disneyland for adults. Displays, a grandiose staircase, costumes, movie awards. He went into the Rubicon Room, full of clever display cases, and felt he was on Rodeo Drive in Beverly Hills. At the tasting bar, he had to pay seven and a half dollars to sample the wines, and he realized that the old Inglenook was no longer a place for ordinary people serious about wine. It had been reinvented for those interested only in living vicariously. Norm decided to give Coppola the benefit of the doubt, that all this was to produce profits for improving and increasing production and returning Inglenook to its former glory, and he went to work for this splashy new operation. As the wine's quality and availability rose, he reasoned, the trappings would fall away.

He had some business experience, and he was immediately struck by the hierarchical nature of management. Those at the top, he thought, knew a lot less about wine than about selling things. Worse, the fact that they had less experience with wine than those they were managing, like Norm, contributed to the high rate of turnover among disgruntled employees. Norm kept his head down, doing what he was told, keeping his opinions to himself in the interest of the greater good.

Every day he joined the long line of workers driving north that began before dawn, part of a broad migration from places distant and diverse, from the tule marshes bordering San Pablo Bay to tract houses in the East Bay to communities north of Mount St. Helena, separated from their jobs by tortuous roads. But on they came as day assembled itself in the valley — carpenters, plumbers, gardeners, bricklayers, secretaries, clerks, receptionists, cooks, waiters, pourers, managers — an endless procession of cars and bodies making themselves available for the demands of the valley.

Long before people emerged from the bed-and-breakfasts and the inns and big houses, there were other people drinking coffee from thermoses while they measured and hoisted and rearranged, sorted tiles and replaced inventory, pulled weeds and corks. One of the problems with obtaining a decent wage for winery staff was the job's allure. People were willing to work for little money because of the perceived glamour, and some people — retirees and those financially independent and drawn by the glamour — sometimes worked for nothing, just to be associated with fine wine.

Norm soon saw that Niebaum-Coppola did not have enough

Rubicon to sell. Less expensive wine was in great demand at the winery, and new labels were already in the Niebaum-Coppola works. Norm also watched the efforts of the winemaking staff, which was supposedly dedicated to producing the finest taste possible from the famed Rutherford Bench vineyards. He thought their skill and good intentions were subverted by the requirements of the new bulk wine operation.

When the line was introduced, and called Francis Ford Coppola Presents, Norm felt that his naive assumptions about quality triumphing had been laid to rest. He blamed himself for being disappointed, for expecting the dedication represented by old Niebaum to reemerge. Niebaum hadn't cared about money, he had simply wanted to make the best wine, and that was unrealistic today. Most of the grapes in the new Niebaum-Coppola wines were not from Napa Valley but from the central coast and the Central Valley, where rows of cheap fruit ran to infinity. Some of the wines were made elsewhere and trucked in, and the tourists snapped them up, too, either unaware of the origin of the grapes or indifferent to it. The wine was affordable and a "good value" — that was the selling line — and the clincher was that the bottle bore the name of a famous movie director.

The commercial aspects of the winery — the salesmanship — continued to bother Norm. What, he wondered, did hand-blown wine glasses, skin-care products, cigars, bathrobes, bocce balls, miniature sailboats, and all the other stuff for sale have to do with making and selling fine wine? There were people working upstairs in the winery offices who did little else but pore through specialty catalogues, ordering things to be sold downstairs. The employees were instructed to associate the Coppolas with all the products, and "Francis" with all activities in the winery, whether or not he was actually involved, all part of the concept of integrating wine, movies, and product.

If Francis was making a movie somewhere, the employees weren't to say so. They were to say Francis was intimately involved, an artist who was sharing his "vision" with visitors not for money but for the satisfaction of bringing pleasure to others. A matronly public relations woman was brought in from New York to lecture the staff about this and other things. She had a Nancy Reagan hairdo, and she told them that no one was to speak to the press about the winery, the Coppolas, or anything else. All such queries were to be passed upstairs, whence they would be passed to her, and she would handle everything. From Manhattan.

Norm saw Francis in action in the winery, and the supposed similarity between him and Gustave Niebaum struck Norm as ludicrous. In his disillusionment he began to speculate about what Niebaum would have thought of the movie director. Norm reminded himself that it was only a job, but increasingly he wanted to tell the manager above him and the woman with the Nancy Reagan hairdo to shove it.

Two occurrences nearly put him over the edge. The first was a proposal for the use of the bonus that was supposed to go to the staff in the tasting and merchandising rooms. They had exceeded their goal — sales each month were approaching half a million dollars — but instead the bonus would go toward remodeling the Pennino Room. That meant buying a beautiful new cash register, the manager said, arguing at a Saturday meeting with employees that the register was really a gift to them, that it would make their lives easier. Dissent bordered on mutiny. "My God, you guys are being so negative," the manager lamented. "Can't we find just one positive thing about this?"

Management by objective failed for once and the employees got their bonus, but the bitterness lingered until the incident with the monogrammed bedroom slippers. Not just any slippers, but custom-made panne-velvet ones lined with grape-colored silk and embroidered in silver with the logo of the Francis Coppola Diamond Series, another affordable wine that Norm disliked. The slippers were the Christmas bonus for a staff that had brought in millions of dollars during the year, and Norm couldn't believe them. He had friends working at small boutique wineries who had been rewarded by the owners for much more modest profits with checks, real money for those who needed it. It was a sad commentary, Norm thought, on a big winery that had become very profitable very fast with the crucial assistance of people who shared none of this exponential growth except the burden.

Norm had mastered a subject — wine — he couldn't really afford, thinking that would make him part of something important, historically and viticulturally. Instead, this knowledge had made him a threat to people who knew little about the substance they were supposedly devoted to. And for all his efforts during this particular year he had been given a pair of monogrammed bedroom slippers that sat on the floor of his closet. He wouldn't wear them, but he couldn't avoid looking at them, either. Every time he did, he got a little angrier.

13

THE HILLS behind the Eisele house retained a vernal irides-
cence, exuberant despite the lack of rain. Green engulfed
the opposing mountainside, distant, drooping digger pines
shading the lower slopes, with lighter chaparral and a fresh swipe of
chlorophyll where new oaks had taken hold. The dense understory
of grass had arisen since cattle were banned from the steep property years before, punctuated now by blue larkspur and delicate wild
iris. Amid the profusion of new growth was bunch grass and European varieties of groundcover that had taken firm hold in California, their seeds capable of lying dormant for a decade before
germinating. But the little native oaks springing up were an encour-
agement.

Cattle still ranged on the neighbor's land, where the lush mix of
species was absent. No trees took root to replace the big ones that
had been fire damaged back in the sixties and were bound to fall.

Volker descended through poison oak, Indian paintbrush, and
blue-eyed grass. He was conditioned by thirty-odd years of political
jousting over environmental issues. There had been some victories
involving water, habitat, and development. The biggest problem, the
one engulfing all the others, was still growth: there were too many
people here presently, and more on the way — too many people
in the valley, in the Bay Area, in California. The state was the de
facto nation of the West, the brightest beacon within the beacon of
America, with the sixth-largest gross national product on earth. A
recent study suggested that the interstate highway between San
Francisco and Sacramento that skirted Napa Valley would in the

future have to be a dozen lanes, and perhaps as many as sixteen. All those people wanted prosperity and a place apart.

He approached his house, a frame Victorian with a cupola and thousands of handmade square-headed nails. Volker's wife, Liesel, a landscape architect, had created a yard and patio on the east side, beautiful in its simplicity, with a vegetable garden to one side. Here her husband paused and gazed out over the vineyard. It was managed now by their son, Alexander, who had grown into a handsome, reserved young man with his parents' blue eyes and with an uncharacteristic brawn. While Volker favored sweaters and bulky trousers, Alexander always wore the sturdy shoes, Levi's, and soft cotton shirts that were the uniform of the working valley, from Mexican pruner to lucky spermer to Silicon Valley turnaround artist sampling his sugars.

Alexander's fair hair was worn short and his smile cracked white in the California sun. He had proven the study of international business relevant to the raising of cabernet sauvignon and merlot in high Chiles Valley, tributary to the Napa River, and had talents his father had been forced to recognize. Like his ability to deal with the Mexicans who lived in the little house near the old winery at the edge of the walnut grove. Alexander had grown up with the Mexicans, and so making the transition from friend to boss had been difficult. He had devised methods for doing the work more efficiently, division of labor being applicable to the vineyard primarily in winter, one worker making the big cuts with the electric shears while another follows, cleaning up and piling cuttings in the rows. His father hadn't been so sure about all this in the beginning, but had allowed authority to pass to his son. A useful side effect of having a competent vineyard manager, Volker had discovered, was that he had more time to devote to the business of selling wine and trying to save Napa Valley.

A graybeard of "the movement," he had attended Berkeley but his impulse for social change had long since been channeled into the land, and particularly Napa County land. Volker had been involved in every environmental issue affecting agriculture following establishment of the ag preserve in 1968, and there had been a lot of those. Not just a grower but also a producer of wine — Eisele Family Vineyards cabernet was unmistakably Bordeaux in style, meaning subtle and balanced — Volker had in recent years entered the Napa

Valley Vintners Association, as was his right, despite the fact that some of its members disapproved of his past activities and what they called his present "agenda." Volker's sibilant English still rang out in NVVA committee meetings, the German accent unmistakable, the arguments difficult to refute and having to do with restraint on activities at odds with the health of land and water.

Looking back, he could plainly see crucial accomplishments since 1968. The first of these was the forty-acre-minimum lot size in the hills, in 1973. Then came the winery definition in the late eighties, when Jim Hickey had asked rhetorically, "What is a winery?" and set off an internecine battle pitting growers against vintners or, more specifically, growers against those vintners who were ideologically or constitutionally opposed to regulation — avowed individualists, adamant free enterprisers, closet developers. The winery definition had resulted in some limitations on their activities, though not enough. The rancor it caused had resulted in the election of a reactionary, pro-development board of supervisors in November 1988, with help from the Napa Valley Vintners Association. That had prompted talk among those most concerned about the valley's future of an extraordinary solution: remove all zoning decisions from the hands of politicians.

At that time Volker had called one of the "good" supervisors, Mel Varrelman, and proposed lunch at The Abbey restaurant in St. Helena. Also meeting with them was a political ally of Volker's, Duane Cronk. Volker told the two men, "We need to do an initiative," a device for putting issues of concern on the ballot, allowed under California law, so they could be decided by the voters instead of the legislative body. If approved by fifty percent plus one of the voters, an initiative became law. But first it had to be drafted with the help of an attorney, and then a campaign had to be launched to get the issue on the ballot by collecting thousands of signatures beforehand.

Volker and other allies in this new struggle raised money, some of it from like-minded vintners, and they hired the San Francisco legal firm of Shute, Mihaly & Weinberger to write the initiative so it would stand up to the inevitable court challenge after the vote.

Then they obtained signatures with the help of volunteers stationed outside supermarkets. If approved, the initiative would mean that any proposed change in the county's existing land-use provisions would have to be put to a popular vote. In effect, this would transfer the power from the politicians to the people. The pols could no longer grant zoning exceptions, rezone, or lower the minimum lot size and undo the good effects of twenty years of restrictions.

The new law would remain in effect for thirty years, and so the organizers called the initiative Vision 2020. It was officially known as Measure J, and it passed. This was recognized as a large victory and a major threat to professional developers in Napa County and all over California. If Measure J was allowed to stand, pliant elected officials couldn't intercede on developers' behalf anywhere in the state, and of course Measure J was immediately challenged in court. Volker persuaded county officials to hire the San Francisco law firm that had written the initiative to defend it. In the initial legal skirmish in superior court, in 1991, the county prevailed, but that decision was appealed by the opponents to a higher court. The county won in the appeal proceeding, too, and the case headed for the California supreme court.

It was freighted with the ambitions of both sides, having assumed real significance beyond Napa. Other counties — Stanislaus, Monterey, Amador, Sonoma, Ventura — were emulating Napa, or trying to, by launching and sometimes passing initiatives of their own. Measure J was the mother of them all, and concern mounted in the construction industry, the big architectural firms, among suppliers of everything from concrete to cupolas. This opposition marshaled its considerable resources for the final fight before the state's highest tribunal.

Shortly before oral arguments were heard by the supreme court in 1994, Volker met one of his many critics at a meeting in Pope Valley, and the man told him dismissively, "We're gonna kick ass."

The man was wrong. The state supreme court voted five to two to uphold the law, stating explicitly that voters had the right to amend the General Plan for the county and that land use was a matter of local authority, even when those limits extended decades into the future. Measure J was constitutional, and thereafter all land-use decisions concerning agricultural land had to be voted on by the people. It was a stunning, far-reaching victory with broad implications, and in the ensuing years many people would claim to be its author.

The day after, Volker and Liesel got up before dawn to take a bus to the San Francisco airport for a flight to Hawaii. Before the bus left the station, the Napa County counsel drove up, still in his bathrobe, fairly jumped out of his car, and dramatically handed Volker a copy of the supreme court decision. It was a rare moment, and Volker subsequently had the satisfaction of reading the decision while winging west across the Pacific.

Measure J was no panacea. He knew that. It simply slowed development, bought time while something more effective could be conceived of and nurtured to life. Even as Measure J moved out of the foundry of the courts, there glowed in the cauldron of civic action a new link to extend and tighten the county's zoning restrictions to the hillsides. Those steep, lovely, precarious heights needed extra protection beyond the forty-acre minimum. Volker, already chairman of the Farm Bureau's land-use committee, talked to the Bureau's executive committee about the possibility of establishing a minimum lot size of one hundred and sixty acres in the watershed, meaning the hills. That this seemingly colossal property bite could be justified anywhere other than on the valley floor was already Napa County Farm Bureau policy.

The president was leery, so the Bureau sent out a survey, and learned something very interesting: people generally do not understand lot size. They are opposed to subdivisions, houses, and roads, and at the same time they think one hundred and sixty acres is too large a lot. Some people in the county still wanted to subdivide for family members or to earn extra money by selling off a smaller parcel — the same objections that had been raised to the creation of the ag preserve in the sixties — but eventually most Farm Bureau members saw the light and came around.

Opponents called the proposal "snob zoning" when it was really the opposite — land was worth more subdivided and therefore was more exclusive. In truth, the new zoning would drastically reduce, on paper, the value of big real estate holdings of families with open-ended financial needs. In this age of unparalleled consumption, children and grandchildren were already accustomed to inheriting, some of them members of a new class that had never worked and never intended to; other families had problems of succession that could most easily be worked out by trading reparceled land. The more valuable the land, the better the outcome.

But criticism of development in the hills had brought radical environmentalists with no connection to agriculture forcefully into the argument, and ordinary citizens' complaints had also grown louder. A one-hundred-and-sixty-acre minimum might act to lessen anti-vineyard sentiment, or so some supporters of the idea hoped.

In 1992, Volker was elected president of the Farm Bureau, and he decided it was time to move. There was a slow-growth board of supervisors in place, and Measure J had provided good evidence of public support for growth limitations. Also, water was of concern in the county, and protected hillsides meant some protection for ground-water reserves and for the quality of the Napa River, which had already gotten the attention of the U.S. Environmental Protection Agency because of its declining steelhead population.

Volker persuaded the county board of supervisors to hold hearings on the new one-hundred-and-sixty-acre zoning for the hills. These proved nasty, the big landowners complaining bitterly and many smaller growers in the room silent because their clients, the vintners, might retaliate if they spoke in favor of the new zoning. There were surprises. Daryl Sattui, who for decades had operated a very profitable picnic grounds next to his winery on Highway 29, stood up and voiced his support. This owner of a large, self-generated fortune proved that even an adamant free enterpriser with money and real estate at stake was willing to forgo options in the long-term interests of uncluttered views and all they implied.

During the hearings Volker received a telephone call from the political operative of the Robert Mondavi Winery, telling him that his bosses opposed the new zoning proposal. The winery had recently gone public and was having financial difficulties, the wine boom not yet rolling and its major asset real estate. The Mondavi stance was a clear indication of the danger posed by the growing corporate presence in the valley. As long as times were good, the corporations would go along with prevailing sentiments about agriculture, open space, all the folderol about wine and culture, but in a serious downturn they would take profits where they could, and the greatest profits — greater even than a vineyard producing hundred-dollar-a-bottle cabernet — were in houses.

The measure passed, but this time Volker had gone too far. It was one thing to stymie residential construction on the valley floor by professional developers, quite another to have an impact on the net worth of people who owned extensively in the hills and considered themselves social bedrock. A few powerful vintners decided that Volker had to be neutralized, and they went after him through their allies on the Farm Bureau. Volker lost his seat on the board in the subsequent election, but he wasn't giving up, not yet.

Even avowed proponents of good land use, apostate Republicans who had in the past been his allies, like the grower who had often said to him, "Don't be so *radical*, Volker," now stopped speaking to him. It was a bitter disappointment but not entirely surprising: past associations, high ideals, were all fine in their place, but in Napa Valley as in much of America it had come down to money.

Volker went into his house and on into the kitchen. He was making dinner tonight while Liesel worked hard, as usual, on a landscape architectural project. In her most pessimistic moments she believed that the preserved natural beauty of Napa Valley would eventually be lost, no matter what they did in trying to forestall it, but Volker resisted this fatalism. After the establishment of the hundred-and-sixty-acre minimum, things had quieted down in the valley for a few years, but in 1997 a new fight had erupted over control of the Farm Bureau and its policies.

Since then, fortunately, good younger members had come up through the ranks, with strong connections to agriculture. Hugh Davies was one of them, son of Jack and a bona fide member of the vintner aristocracy but committed to the land ethic. There was Hugh's friend Tom Gamble, a grower, and Beth Novak Milliken of Spottswoode Winery, Rich Salvestrin, Jon-Mark Chappellet, and a few others. Volker was counting on them in the looming struggles over the direction of the Farm Bureau and the Vintners.

Wild turkeys had gathered in the neighboring field, a flock of matrons in black bombazine. Afternoon sunlight rendered the opposite mountainside unreadable, its shadows capable of concealing lions and boar. No one would ever build up there on less than one hundred and sixty acres, but what the new zoning and Measure J had not done was protect the hillsides from vineyard development. Few had then foreseen the extent of the clearing to come, or the reaction and, with it, the rise of a different sort of environmental activist, one well outside the wine and vineyard business who would make Volker Eisele and his young friends seem downright benign.

14

GROWING UP, she spent whole summers with her sisters on a lake in northern California and hiked and fished the Eel River with her parents. She witnessed the depredations of logging and the decline of the steelhead, that mysterious, muscular, silvery, seagoing trout that spends most of its life in the deep but returns — briefly, perennially, against great odds — to the headwaters where life began.

Her name was Chris, and she developed what she would describe as a "sense of nature," although her existence was primarily urban. She grew up in Santa Rosa, in Sonoma County, and studied science and psychology at Sacramento State. By the time she was finished with school, she was married to the soft-spoken, accommodating Jack Malan and was the mother of two boys. They had moved to Napa in 1978, and Jack had gone from the United States Navy into the county's health program, as a psychological counselor. Chris went into that line of work, too, to supplement the family income.

The Malans bought a piece of property on the flank of Atlas Peak, a rugged, wild promontory in the south of the valley strewn with volcanic rock, and they built a rudimentary house with a carport. It had the feel of an outpost, separated from the road by a long stretch of blacktop and two cattle gates, the first a mechanical device that rose when a button was punched, the second held shut by a piece of chain. Between the two barriers — one to the outside world, the other to the Malans' — cows belonging to a neighbor stared mournfully. No cattle sullied the Malan property, though there were dogs, a mobile home parked on the tarmac, and cars necessary for the relentless commuting that characterized life miles from the nearest store or school.

Chris had always wanted to work with children. She and her husband took foster children into their home, and as a county counselor she dealt with a range of pathologies mostly manifest in adults but rooted in childhood. Addiction and psychosis were often factors, and child neglect and abuse often the result. This was the dark side of the valley, the antithesis of the shimmering reflection thrown by wine and money, unsuspected or ignored by the tourists and often by those catering to them. Large contributions from the Napa Valley Wine Auction went to hospitals and health services every year, to take care of such problems in scruffy urban neighborhoods far from the vineyards and McMansions and symbolized not by the Wine Auction but by the somber presence of the Napa State Hospital.

Counseling helped families at their worst, Chris would say when asked why she was drawn to work both difficult and depressing: "I like helping people at the lowest point of their lives." Some of those years were spent in crisis and psychiatric intervention, working with people who were disturbed and often needed institutionalization. She spent many nights and weekends on the job; often the police were required. She found she was good at dealing with conflict — knowledgeable, committed, physically solid, with full, dark hair and a daunting persistence.

This could be risky. Once she walked up to a house that had been barricaded by the owner — "a biker, huge, covered with tattoos" — and surrounded by police officers, and Chris said, "Hi, I'm here because some people are worried about your kids." The biker told her the kids were fine, and she told him, "I have to see them." Reluctantly he opened the door, and the confrontation was resolved.

A man just out of prison came to the crisis center, jumped from a window, and threatened to slit his own throat. He had to be dissuaded. "That's the kind of work I do," she later explained. "I deal with very crazy people."

A woman and former prisoner became psychotic after drinking too much alcohol, and Chris had her hospitalized. When the woman got out she returned home, put on fatigues and camouflage paint, came back to the hospital with a gun, and started shooting. The police had to wound her in the leg before they could subdue her. Chris learned from the experience that when people focus on you as the source of their problems, it can be dangerous.

The lesson would come back to her in an arena far removed from crisis counseling.

Her "sense of nature" provided a useful alternative. She described herself as humanitarian and deeply concerned about the environment. "This is a fragile world," she would say, "Carl Sagan's small blue dot. If we screw it up, we'll all be miserable."

Her experience in the gritty world of the emotionally damaged carried into the public weal. She sidled up to organizations devoted to environmental causes that tended to coalesce around specific issues, mutate, and reemerge in different form, like mayflies. There was no dearth of these issues in Napa Valley. Her first fight, as she would later tell it, was for a prospective greenbelt around the city of Napa that did not prevail legislatively. Then she joined the board of the fledgling Friends of the Napa River, a polyglot group of outdoors people and conservationists devoted to cleaning up both the water and the riverbanks.

Friends of the Napa River argued that if the primary drainage couldn't be saved, then the county, too, would be lost, that the river was the key to everything else. The U.S. Fish and Wildlife Service had listed the steelhead as a threatened species throughout the San Pablo Bay drainage; someday the federal government might demand changes in farming, construction, and road-building practices, all of which had an impact on the river, so there was an impetus for the locals to act first. Friends of the Napa River also became effectively enmeshed in flood control politics.

Chris soon found herself involved in an effort to prevent some Texans from developing an elevated bit of real estate known as Soscol Ridge. She was learning, taking advice from others, and concerned about the outcome of this fight. She worried that enough wasn't being done. In the house of Moira Johnson Block, a founder of Friends of the Napa River, she met the bearded Volker Eisele, veteran of the vintner wars and reputed master strategist, and Volker tried to reassure her about the outcome of the vote on Soscol Ridge. The development would be defeated, he said, and to drive this home he wagered a lunch on the result. Chris accepted the bet, figuring she would win something either way: if the initiative passed, Soscol Ridge would not be developed, and if it didn't pass, at least she would get a free meal.

The total opposed to the development turned out to be more than eighty percent, and Chris happily paid for lunch. For her, Soscol Ridge had been a watershed. She had clearly seen the face of the enemy — despoilers of natural habitat — and clearly understood that what was needed to defeat them was early involvement and dedicated follow-through, even when the outcome appeared dubious.

Others in the environmental movement viewed Chris as an activist rather than an organizer, more a bulldog than a strategist. An errant pants leg was always attached to development, in her view, and she clamped down on it. Although her sympathies were divided between the hills and the river, the two were inextricably linked. Vineyards were appearing just under every horizon, and no one was acting to stop them. It didn't seem to bother her friends as much as it bothered Chris. Opponents of sprawl could strongly unite for preserving the valley floor, she would say disapprovingly, "but they can't get it together for the hillsides." And gradually a divide began to grow between her and other, less outspoken environmentalists.

Meanwhile, a proposal for a bedroom-community development within the Napa city limits surfaced. It was known as Stanley Ranch, and it required rezoning for high-density housing; this inspired an ad hoc committee opposed to high-end sprawl and "the Santa Rosa trend," and included were Richard Niemann, a schoolteacher and Sierra Club member, Ginny Simms, a former county supervisor and the first woman ever elected to that office, Harold Kelly and Diane Dillon, both long involved in community action, Chris, and others.

For two years they fought Stanley Ranch, lobbying the city council, calling for new studies and public hearings. The Napa city General Plan was subject to an environmental impact review, and they attended these public meetings, spoke out against rezoning, and formed Get a Grip on Growth to launch a referendum if need be. Eventually the city council, faced with lawsuits and the referendum threat, backed down, and Stanley Ranch sank into the increasingly crowded compost heap of potential developments.

But in the midst of the Stanley Ranch fight, something occurred of such cataclysmic severity, a personal crisis in the life of the county crisis counselor so profound, that it overshadowed all other concerns and left her "living every parent's worst nightmare."

Her younger son, Micah, by then eighteen, had gone on a backpacking trip in the Sierras and was sleeping in the car while his friend drove home. His friend dozed at the wheel, crossed the center strip, and collided with an oncoming vehicle. Neither driver was seriously injured, but Micah's spine was broken.

For the eight weeks he was in intensive care he could not move or breathe without the aid of a ventilator. Every night someone slept in the room with him, if not Chris or Jack, then one of their friends. Chris was convinced he would die if left alone; she couldn't spend every night there herself, and she couldn't stop crying when away from him. The doctors told her Micah might someday be able to use a wheelchair, but only by manipulating a straw with his mouth, and Chris hadn't even been told before that her son would be paralyzed. She told the doctors, "No way."

She didn't know how she would prevent this severe limitation, only that she would prevent it. She couldn't talk about her feelings with the social workers or with anybody else. Emotionally exhausted, she had trouble talking at all, but realized that Micah was badly in need not only of love, strength, and technical ability, but also of a strong advocate.

When he was moved from intensive care to rehabilitation, he couldn't speak because of the ventilator, which caused him pain, and he couldn't move his arms because he had injured his rotator cuffs. He communicated by blinking his eyes.

His mother wrote about that time later, on her computer, in a rush of memories, without regard for punctuation: *I would sit and watch from a chair outside in the hall and watch as Micah's friends would just lean over and just talk to him. He couldn't respond because he had a tube in his throat. My life was so wrapped around him and I could think of nothing else but to hang on every breath he took hoping there would be a next. I became completely meshed with him and could hardly think of anything else. It was as if I was in bed with him. Sometimes I left paralyzed and unable to talk or breathe . . . It is hard to explain what a mother feels when a child is injured and you want so much to take the suffering away. The feeling of*

*watching them struggle is unbelievably painful and the weight upon your
heart is hardly bearable. You wonder how God could let a child suffer . . .*

When the injury had improved, Micah found he could write with
a piece of chalk on a board — short, cryptic messages, as in, "I can
breathe." The doctors wanted to do a tracheotomy anyway, and
Chris had said no. She and her sister had a plan for training Micah to
continue breathing without the ventilator, and she wanted it removed. The doctors insisted that Micah wasn't strong enough, that
the tube was necessary for his survival, but Chris said to herself,
"Who are you to say?"

Micah wrote "Family meeting" on his board. When everyone had
gathered at his bedside he wrote "No way operation."

He was eighteen years old and legally of age, and the ventilator
was removed. He began to breathe on his own with great difficulty,
and for two hours they all encouraged him. The nurses clapped, and
then the ventilator was reinserted. Each day Micah went a little
longer without it. This amazed the doctors, who had not believed it
possible.

Each time machines were brought forward to assist him, and each
time Chris fended them off. It took a week and a half to get Micah
sitting up in the wheelchair; the big day came when he was able to
manipulate the motor with his left arm. Then he tried to feed himself. At first he threw the food over his shoulder, and he laughed, saying, "Feeding my monkey," but slowly control came.

The final triumph was going home without a machine, the family
having been trained to take care of him. Jack and Chris had to
refinance their house to pay for everything: a caregiver, a ramp
for the wheelchair, a new addition for Micah. For a long time the
house felt incomplete, the living room sparsely furnished, all activity
centering on the narrow kitchen and the table, where cups of tea
and plates carried from the counter competed with piles of papers,
memos, letters, reports, maps, fliers. Here Chris worked, close to
Micah, who sometimes called from his room on the telephone.

Her son was alive. He could breathe and speak and eat and operate
his wheelchair, a small miracle. Somewhere in the experience Chris
had reached dead-level bottom; nothing worse could ever happen to
her, she thought. She had glimpsed the superficiality of human ambition and understood that few things really matter. These things

will not survive without vigilance and uncompromising will, and she reimmersed herself in the Stanley Ranch fight and the flood management proposal.

As crisis counselor, she worked nights and went to bed midmorning. Some days she stayed up, using the phone, doing paperwork, sending e-mails, and writing on the computer until fatigue settled with the sodden finality of the winter rains: *My choice was narrow. Hard work and trying to make a difference . . . I have learned to be patient. Environmental work is unbelievably frustrating. We fight big money, greed, overconsumption and terrible destruction. We are labeled as extremist, radical and difficult. Our rewards are few and the time we must put in to see a small measure of change is profound. We fear that time is short . . .*

All around her lay evidence of a bigger fight, its causes clear to anyone who bothered to look up: the hillside ordinance wasn't working, obvious but difficult to prove, with little incentive for politicians who might favor stricter regulations but had little political cover. Then, out of the blue, that cover was inadvertently provided by a vintner Chris had never met, Jayson Pahlmeyer.

He felt, he said, "like a Cistercian monk poking around in the wilds of Burgundy not long after the birth of Christ. The Europeans have for thousands of years been deciding where best to plant, and have nailed their *terroir,* whereas the Americans are still figuring theirs out."

For Jayson Pahlmeyer, his reputation now tied to the appearance of his chardonnay in the film *Disclosure,* the hills were clearly the place where the best grapes grew, just as a bank was the place where the money was. So to greatly expand his source of good grapes, and therefore his production of wine, he bought two-hundred-plus steep acres in remote Wooden Valley, an adjunct of Napa Valley by virtue of its drainage into the Napa River. He planned to spend millions to turn eighty acres of it into prime vineyard.

Helen Turley had taken over the making of his wine. She was an acknowledged maven of ripe fruit — "physiologically mature," she called it, and others called it too far gone — low yields, expensive viticulture, manicured vines. She tromped into vineyards like a disheveled Valkyrie, sometimes with Jayson in tow, to sample grapes left so long on the vine they were often black and splitting, attracting wasps, bees, and skunks, and she put the sample bunches into a little colander she carried, with a kind of rolling pin inside, and mashed the grapes up and poured the juice into a glass and tasted it. She would then order that some grapes be "dropped" — cut and left on the ground so as to further concentrate the flavor in those left on the vine — in the final days of harvest, despite the great cost of leaving quality cabernet sauvignon in the dust. This was known as "Helen's way."

Jayson had seen the light because Turley brooked no compromise, would forgo any amount of money offered if her standards weren't met. She was quirky and her husband, a kind of vinous manager, difficult. Jayson had once seen Helen turn down a prospective client because he answered his cell phone while at lunch. She managed to get Robert Parker to taste the wines of all her clients, a huge advantage. Another winemaker would take over from her, common in the musical chairs of quality viticulture, but while she lasted she provided Pahlmeyer with what he needed at the time: big fruit, more exposure.

His vineyard manager, the man responsible for the master plan, the recognized avenue to accredited rocket juice and progenitor of rising cult cabernets, was none other than Dave Abreu. No longer asking about pH, unscathed by the Viader and other contretemps, Abreu wore not Big Ben shirts but those with rearing polo horse and rider stitched above the pectoral, and he charged a lot of money for putting in an acre of vines. Abreu's standard refusal to travel far from Rutherford on jobs had been overcome by Jayson's money and the ambitious scope of his project.

In Jayson's opinion, Abreu was a foul-mouthed genius, a rough, Rutherford-speaking diamond, the Robert Trent Jones of vineyards. Abreu went out and sat in the prospective vineyard and felt the soil, felt the roots of the young vines; he lay down on his side to divine the pattern of the drip valves. He said, "Here . . . hey . . ." and released a torrent that was part appreciation, part abuse, all authoritative. *This is what we're going to do,* he would tell Jason, *this is what's best* — vertical rows, close planting, whatever, and then do it. All of them — Jayson, Helen Turley, Dave Abreu, and his surrogates — were focused on the goal; accepted practices, rules and regulations, seemed to be no impediment when you had a job to do.

The contractor Richard Stadelhofer graded fifty acres of Jayson's property in 1997 without an erosion control permit, removed the vegetation next to a dry creek, and dumped some debris into the streambed without permission from the California Department of Fish and Game. All no-nos, as Jayson later put it, and Stadelhofer got caught. Jayson said he didn't know the permit hadn't been issued, adding that, as a lawyer, he knew that ignorance was no defense. He and Stadelhofer had to pay close to ten thousand dollars in civil penalties, and Jayson lost a year in his vineyard development because he was shut down until the following spring, a big financial hit all by itself.

He agreed to restore some of the slopes above thirty percent to their natural state and to make other improvements. He was criticized by other vintners whose ranks he had eagerly joined for setting a bad example and providing ammunition to vintners' enemies. Jayson stood up in front of them and performed a *mea culpa,* admitting that he and his contractors had made a mistake and, in effect, asking for forgiveness. He hoped that and the mitigation he had agreed to do on the land would counteract the bad publicity.

The criticism of his peers was innocuous compared to that flowing from the environmentally minded community. Jayson was in the green crosshairs now.

Chris Malan received a plea from a woman in Wooden Valley who had assisted her with Micah when he was still in the hospital. The woman now had a crisis of her own: her neighbor, Jayson Pahlmeyer, was putting in big vineyards and subjecting her to dust and the constant drone of chainsaws. He was denuding hillsides remote from the rest of Napa Valley, out of public view. She asked for help.

Chris and one of her neighbors on Atlas Peak Road, Parry Mead, went up in a small aircraft and told the pilot to fly them over all of Napa Valley — Atlas Peak, Pritchard Hill, Howell Mountain, Diamond and Spring mountains, Mount Veeder. They were shocked by what they saw. Parry took a lot of photographs, and the worst, in Chris's view, was Pahlmeyer's new vineyard. She would later call it "the trigger."

Broader involvement was needed to give the hillside ordinance real teeth. Yet another group, Concerned Citizens for Napa Hillsides, was founded, and Parry Mead's photographs were submitted to the local newspaper and to the board of supervisors. Concerned Citizens began to protest hillside conversions and demand that use permits for steeper slopes be required. They insisted that conversions of woodland and chaparral to vineyard on even more gradual slopes be subject to the California Environmental Quality Act, from which the vintners were currently exempted. They wrote letters to the editor. People whose property had been flooded by runoff from development higher up or otherwise affected got in touch with Concerned Citizens and wrote letters of their own, and all this began to have an impact.

The organization was granted a spot on the board of supervisors' agenda, and Chris made a three-hour presentation. Using all the ammunition in the burgeoning file, she and her allies asked for a moratorium on the clearing of all hillsides. A moratorium was feared most by those seeking to profit from the unprecedented business expansion; the wine business was just so good, and all the flat land already in production, and here comes this proposal out of left field seeking to hobble the primary enterprise of Napa Valley. That was the view of most of the vintners. Moratorium was anathema to them, an economic and philosophical abomination sending up a figurative cloud of dust.

The ever-mounting litany of complaints had to be listened to, as always, by supervisor Mel Varrelman of the V-neck sweaters, in the estate planning office with the blue awning. The hillside ordinance had produced some good effects, he thought, the required erosion control plans reducing the turbidity of the river, for instance. But controversial new vineyard "conversions" like Pahlmeyer's, new houses, and the destruction of trees and vegetation wiped those benefits out of the public consciousness.

People were so agitated that Mel's reelection was cast into doubt. Something had to be done. Napa's state senator, Mike Thompson, suggested the formation of an ad hoc committee composed of growers, scientists, environmentalists, soils people, and ordinary citizens to discuss development in the hills and ways to make it more palatable. It was to be chaired by a scientist from the Resource Conservation District.

The idea of it was attacked by developers, Seventh-day Adventists up in Angwin, some vineyard managers and vintners opposed to any government regulation — the usual suspects — but the committee met anyway. It included Volker Eisele, Richard Niemann, a veteran canoeist and river advocate named Jim Hench, a young woman from the Farm Bureau, Joelle Gallagher, representatives of the legal firm of Dickenson, Peatman & Fogarty that often represented developers, a Mondavi vineyard manager, a vintner named Stuart Smith, and a few others. Thompson and Varrelman hoped they would all get along and that this would be the first step in defusing a potentially explosive issue.

At first they seemed to get along, and Varrelman was reelected. He and his fellow supervisors voted to formalize the ad hoc committee, calling it the Watershed Task Force, and they appropriated money to hire a consulting firm to "facilitate" the meetings and eventually to produce a report. The operative word was consensus. Each supervisor was allowed to appoint people to the board. Chris Malan wanted on, of course, but the supervisor for her district thought her too outspoken. Then another, outgoing, lame duck supervisor agreed to appoint her, and Chris was in.

Creating the Watershed Task Force did not, as Varrelman and Thompson had hoped, put the hillside issue to rest. Its head never touched the pillow.

15

THE FIRST MEETING of the Watershed Task Force was held in the St. Helena Public Library. It was already clear that those members opposed to more vineyard construction on steep slopes wanted to address specific provisions in the hillside ordinance, to make them stronger, a common enough environmental goal. Concentrated in the relatively tight confines of Napa Valley were many of the issues of concern to the rest of the country, particularly in the West, and they could be generally summarized as an end to logging and clear-cutting, the establishment of wildlife corridors, and extended "setbacks" — undisturbed areas to be established between streambanks and vineyards and other development — for the benefit of native vegetation and water quality. This meant a river and its tributaries that would support sufficient microorganisms as well as the glamour species like steelhead trout.

Also underlying the whole exercise was a desire by some to prove that the effects of all activity in the valley eventually touched the river, and by others to formally recognize that, though the above might be true, it didn't really matter, because the fish and the people would survive and prosper. This faction, made up of vintners, vineyard developers, contractors, and their representatives, wanted a law that could not be challenged in court, so that work, once undertaken, could proceed. Such a law would at the same time allow vineyards to continue to expand with modest restrictions and relatively little financial pain.

There were those in each camp sharing some views of the other; the hope, as expressed by the organizers, was that commonly agreed-upon procedures would result from this exemplary democratic process.

To Chris Malan, the idea that everyone would agree was ridiculous. Consensus was, in her opinion, a code word for inaction while every other day there was another story in the press about hillside vineyards and their effects. Often Chris was quoted. This clearly bothered some on the task force. One of these people, Stuart Smith, a familiar bearded figure in work boots and an old snap-brim canvas hat with a sweat-stained band, said so. He asked that everybody stop airing in the media the issues to be discussed by the task force, and by everybody he meant Chris.

Of all her fellow task forcers, Stu seemed to her the farthest from her own beliefs and objectives. He owned Smith-Madrone Winery, high on a flank of Spring Mountain, and often spoke in public about the sanctity of farming and property rights. A relatively early arrival in the valley, he had carved his vineyards out of redwood, Douglas fir, and chaparral, and he represented a certain approach to farming and winemaking. That much Chris knew without knowing any details. She considered Stu loud, demanding, occasionally obnoxious, and a curiosity. With his big hairy face, jeans, and rough appearance, he was one of the proverbial mountain men who had conquered the West, but instead of finding the Northwest Passage, he had tamed the landscape for vines.

She was struck at the first meeting with the amount of dirt on Stu Smith's boots. This was symptomatic, she thought. His attitude toward the land seemed to be, Conquer it and make it pay — a view diametrically opposed to her own. She liked to wake up and relish the beauty of the natural landscape, to hear the birds foraging close to the house and the symphony of the wind in the branches during storms, an overall harmony that she wanted to pass on to subsequent generations. She assumed this large, hairy man was missing all that, and wanted to ask, "What kind of battle did you have with your mountain today, Stu?"

He grew up in Santa Monica, where "nature" for most people meant the beach, and "ball" — the oblong sort — was a good measure of male potential. But Stu Smith was a Boy Scout before he was captain of the high school football team, and he knew something of the outdoors not related to the Pacific littoral. Husky, good-looking, smart, he seemed the embodiment of the American dream, going off to the University of California at Berkeley to become an economist and eventually marrying his high school sweetheart, a beautiful, equally smart blonde named Susan.

At Berkeley, Stu, like everybody else, ran into a distraction known as "the war." Vietnam seemed to him a colossal mistake by the American government. It should never have gotten into a conflict in Southeast Asia but, once in, should have sent enough men and equipment to win. That it did not was tragic. This opinion ran counter to most of the students'. At the same time, Stu thought the antiwar movement was justified, and he worried that it would be discredited and its members marginalized after the war ended by association with the failure of the United States to prevail.

He liked discussing politics and taking the contrary position. Stu was good at winning arguments, not so good at losing them, and his vision tended to tunnel, often with no light at the end. "You never win," he would later say of real and philosophical battles. "It's all a matter of personal satisfaction, really, of passion. I understand passion. What I will never understand is passivity, how people can disagree about something and not stand up and say so."

Broadening the view of a budding macroeconomist was a love of the outdoors manifest in hiking and canoeing. Part of Stu's lament about the peace movement was that it contained people concerned about the land, before the term "environmentalist" became so widespread, and that they, too, would be compromised. They were all anti-nuke in those days, and when many of them went into the bureaucracy after college, Stu thought the country could stop worrying about corporations dumping chemicals into the rivers and other sorts of commercial depredation of nature. He considered himself an environmentalist, and he never dreamed that this movement "would come back to bite me in the ass."

He and Susan began to read about wine and vines. Stu enrolled in UC Davis and began to study viticulture; he worked in Napa Valley for a while under the tutelage of André Tchelistcheff, who referred to Stu as "professor." "Back to the land" was a popular phrase, too simple and clichéd to convey the true emotions driving people to physical hardship and financial insecurity as a way of beating the system. Some of the attraction of wine lay in the challenge of making an American success of a fine European commodity and figuring out an exotic substance and the place that produced it. Some of the attraction also lay in creating a life apart.

Stu and Susan knew of a piece of property high on Spring Mountain that belonged to the uncle of an usher in their wedding; they bought it by borrowing from their parents and committing themselves to "sweat equity." Stu was good at that. He knew something of machines, having restored a Model A while in high school, and he was thorough to a fault; he possessed the physical strength required for most anything within an individual's capabilities. His passion for work was fortunate, given the opportunities that abounded on steep slopes that had been cleared and planted in the 1880s and then abandoned during Prohibition. Douglas fir two feet in diameter reared from the same soil. Up there, Stu found an old, fire-hardened redwood grape stake protruding from a tree trunk that had grown to encase it over the years. Madrone trees were everywhere.

He and Susan decided to call their wine Smith-Madrone, and they set out to make it the best. The seventies would seem, in retrospect, a golden era. If you saw somebody in Napa Valley under thirty years of age, you wanted to be his friend. People got together for potluck dinners and guitar playing; there was a wonderful sense of sharing. If you wanted to have a big party, you called up the vintners and they all came, and so did everybody else, right down to the cellar rats. One Friday a month everybody went to lunch at a restaurant, even the old guys — Louis Martini, Peter Mondavi — and it was all great fun and everybody assumed it would last.

Stu planted cabernet sauvignon, pinot noir, chardonnay, and riesling. Cabernet was not yet supreme; people were still experimenting. Stu "felt like a crusader marching off in search of the Holy Grail." Riesling was then a strong campaigner, and he made a good one, and it in turn helped make Smith-Madrone's reputation. Then Freemark Abbey produced a sweet, "late harvest" version from grapes that had been accosted by mold, and although it won a prize in Los Angeles, the sweetness of it turned off the public to riesling. After that, wineries largely abandoned the variety, but not Stu, who hung on because he liked riesling and, as he told people, "I'm a tenacious SOB."

He could also be intimidating by dint of size and a brooding consideration of the assertions of others, before he came back forcefully with his own. But when the Smiths' house accidentally burned in 1975, people were very supportive. A friend brought a case of wine to help them through their difficulties, to resettle and keep going.

Later, the winery rose in the swale in the middle of their vineyard, all wood, with a place to sit up top and enjoy a view much like the one from the century before. It seemed to them that things began to change after Coca-Cola bought Sterling, and more corporations came in, soon followed by the rich. These newcomers hired wine-makers instead of doing the work themselves and seemed to have no commitment to the natural landscape or to long-term environmental concerns. And the price of necessities rose. Gradually people stopped discussing their philosophy of winemaking, and dealing directly with each other, using attorneys instead. The handshake deal disappeared, and camaraderie went the route of dirt on vintners' shoes.

Pinot noir had been a strong contender among the reds — "a wine," Tchelistcheff used to say, "that invites you to drink it." Smith-Madrone's pinot was inviting indeed, but again bad luck prevailed. The seventies were a cool decade, good for pinot, but the eighties were not. Stu held on, though, and didn't finally graft over to chardonnay until 1989. He was late in catching the unprecedented chardonnay wave that lifted so many wineries into the big time and made later, larger successes easier.

By then the Smiths had moved down to St. Helena to live. They were parents, and Stu a recognized vintner committed to his way of life, outspoken, looking as if he belonged on the countercultural side in any argument, a throwback to the sixties, but with a crucial distinction: he regarded property rights as sovereign, and those who tried to tell him what to do as dangerous. Increasingly, this suspicion of authority on the part of public agencies occupied his thoughts.

All around were signs of success, of mergers and infusions of capital that transformed other wineries into landmarks of profitability. At Smith-Madrone, the school of sweat equity was still in session. Stu wasn't interested in pushy outside partners or in the opinions of those who hadn't put in the physical effort, who knew less about the place and the product than the farmer and the winemaker he had become. He continued to do the work, with the help of his brother, and hoped for the best.

The changes Stu and Susan had observed accelerated. Their sentimental vision of the valley became at last irretrievable, as were those
cherished times together, and they were divorced. Stu remarried, and
he threatened to get out of the political involvement that had been a
part of life in the valley for years. But he came back in from a slightly
different direction in the mid-nineties, as a cofounder of something
called Farmers for Napa Valley. This was an inherent rejection of the
Napa Valley Vintners Association and the Napa County Farm Bureau, both of which he believed incapable of effecting the changes
he wanted, given their current leadership. It was also a tacit declaration by Stu and a handful of others that a more radical approach was
required.

Farmers for Napa Valley had no bylaws and no official standing,
but was dedicated to the general cause of property rights. In this way
it echoed some of the ultra-conservative views elsewhere in the
country. Specifically, its purpose was to take control of the Farm Bureau away from what Stu and his allies viewed as environmental ex-
tremists, an effort that would be served by Stu's active participation
in the Watershed Task Force as a counterweight to the formidable
Chris Malan.

Stu continued driving up Spring Mountain every morning in his
beat-up Suburban, taking a right near the summit and meandering
among properties until he reached his own. Slopes hedged with conifers and combed with vineyards led out until the land fell dramatically away toward the green valley floor, the incessant traffic looking
small and insubstantial in the distance. In winter, clouds clung to
the mirroring mountains rising on the other side, and in spring,
the busiest season — things growing, equipment breaking — Stu
worked too hard to notice much else, still hoping for that unique
Napa Valley success, for lightning to strike. In summer, the unforgiv-
ing sunlight winked back at him from proliferating façades of new
houses across the valley.

In the early task force sessions Stu detected what he thought was a
bias against agriculture and private property. This impression was reinforced by the tactics of the environmentalists, mostly urbanites
who wanted to limit activities they didn't share in or understand. He
dismissed it as a combination of ignorance, jealousy, and a desire for
control. There was also the neo-prohibitionist element, never far be-

low the surface in America. Outside the task force gatherings, environmentalists were calling grape growing "alcohol farming," the act of planting a vineyard "graping the land," and wineries "alcohol factories." The words incited and inflamed and demanded similar tactics in response.

Stu liked to tell people that Napa Valley's environmentalists had grown stronger in recent years because of the pathetic response of the wine industry to their demands. He hoped the "greens" would now lose that power by being perceived as unreasonable. Just across the county line in Sonoma, the environmental din was even louder than in Napa Valley. Sonoma was bigger, had more traditional agriculture — cattle, row crops — and more people, a major highway and a bigger city. The loss of pasture and woodland to vineyard conversion there had brought critics out of Santa Rosa and the suburbs, and so entrenched and virulent had this opposition to vineyards become that it was known now as "the Sonoma syndrome."

In other parts of California, the Sonoma syndrome was increasingly evident. When the Kendall-Jackson wine conglomerate cut thousands of oaks in the central coast region in plain sight of the highway — an ego play, in Stu's view — the Sonoma syndrome had been given quite a boost, adversely affecting the entire industry.

Napa was the jewel in the crown of California's viticulture. No other place could command these prices, a fact that annoyed and dismayed vintners in other counties, from Mendocino to the Mexican border. Ernest and Julio Gallo had chosen to make their play for premium wine in Sonoma instead of Napa, and they and many others were envious of Napa's success. This valley was secure under the seemingly ever-ascendant arc of its rocket juice, and naturally a lot of attention focused on Napa, with its allure for wealthy outsiders and the noisy ranks of the urban greens.

The argument wasn't really about the environment, he thought, it was about land use. Those involved in it carried a lot of baggage: growth/no-growth, not-in-my-backyard ("NIMBY"), guilt over having destroyed someplace else to be able to live here. Increasingly, people refused to accept the premise that farming was environmentally friendly, and growers were lumped in with developers by a minority within the environmental movement. The argument Stu used was that the environmentalists were trying to legislate the valley green because they couldn't afford to buy it and that they could well ruin farmers. It was an argument with little proof to sustain it, but still it ran deep in contemporary American conservatism. Some among the vintners thought there were no real environmental problems in the valley, no crisis in "nature," and that any abuses by people were already atoned for by the existence of national parks and other set-aside lands.

The alternative to agriculture in Napa Valley was houses, more valuable even than rocket juice vineyards, more ecologically damaging than vineyards, more insidious than tourists and the fanfare wineries like Beringer, Mondavi, and Niebaum-Coppola. Even the strongest enterprises could fail, as economic history indicated. The port of San Francisco, once the biggest on the West Coast, was now a remnant; Montgomery Street had been the Wall Street of the West, but no more; and the Bank of America and Wells Fargo were owned by outsiders. Once an industry starts spiraling down, it can't be stopped. The same thing, he insisted time and again, could happen here.

Later task force meetings were held in a new office complex next to a strip mall in south Napa, what could have been Anywhere, USA, known as the Gasser Building. Some people on the task force thought the name both appropriate and ironic, since a lot of gas was being expended in discussions of environmental protection in the middle of a development that not so long ago had been open space and wetlands.

Stu would carry his container of coffee from Starbucks into the Gasser Building, put his hat on the table, sit back, and pull at a beard flecked blond and gray. He turned small, unflinching eyes beneath heavy brows on whoever spoke, his big arms crossed, a presence. The one he focused on most often was the county crisis counselor, short, solid, attractive, no more reluctant than he to speak out. Stu had listened to her at numerous board of supervisors meetings and he thought her strident and unreasonable. Chris Malan epitomized for him the urban environmentalist, despite the fact that she owned property on Atlas Peak, making assumptions about water quality and aquatic life that he would not accept.

Stu and others on his side said they wished to spend money on science, to define the problems, whatever they might be, and allow the vineyardists some time to meliorate them. It was in part a delaying tactic, and the environmentalists resisted. Stu liked to say that no one knew enough about the subject; he cited the parable of a bunch of wise men sitting around a table speculating about the number of teeth in a horse's mouth without actually going out and counting them, when in fact the teeth were already being counted by scientists working for different agencies and for environmental organizations.

Consensus was required, but all you had to do to prevent consensus was block the opposition. Chris obviously understood that. She wouldn't accept the possibility that the county government was a neutral factor in this struggle, wouldn't even accept, from the get-go, the county's statistics about the number of planted acres. She claimed to have a study indicating that there were many more planted acres in the county than the county and the wine industry would admit to, which was about thirty-five thousand. Stu and others on the task force couldn't determine who had done this study, but Chris kept citing it as evidence of official skullduggery: *I've got a study here . . .*

It was just one of the tactics that spread doubt and dissension by innuendo, environmental McCarthyism, in Stu's opinion. And it was pissing him off.

16

FOLLOWING THE DEATH of Jack Davies, the boys had asked, Where do we go from here? Their father's legacy had to be dealt with. The family began by establishing a foundation in his name and asking well-wishers to donate money; they announced the fund in the newspaper and discussed how it would be managed, looking to other, similar organizations for guidance. They held a fundraiser. Jamie and Hugh both got up and spoke, emphasizing that the money would be used solely for the preservation of agricultural land and open space. They created a special wine, brut rosé, the proceeds from which would go to the fund, and they took Jim Hickey's suggestion that the wine be called Querencia, a Spanish term meaning a deep, abiding affection for home.

Schramsberg was a larger consideration, a family business with a venerable history and a challenging future. Jamie and her youngest son entered into an unspoken bond to work at it more intensely than before, which was evident to others, and reassuring. But at unexpected moments, for months after Jack's death, Jamie would suddenly find tears running down her cheeks. Sometimes Hugh noticed and sometimes he didn't, but he never spoke of it.

Jamie decided to take the staff to Champagne, an affirmation of Schramsberg's success, a sign of the transition and of the seriousness of the family's intent. Know yourself by the competition, that was the idea. In Schramsberg's case, the competition was the big houses of Reims and Épernay, which in terms of tradition, aloofness, and lavish display outdid even the chateaux of Bordeaux and Burgundy. And these estates in Champagne, just like little Schramsberg, outside

Calistoga, Napa Valley, northern California, depended on customers flush with the times and discerning enough to demand the best.

Hugh organized the trip. The fact that he spoke fluent French, though helpful, was not as important as the enthusiasm he brought to the task. He turned a company jaunt into a quest for general understanding and collective practical knowledge that would serve them all in the future. He had worked as a cellar rat at Moët et Chandon, producer of the legendary Dom Pérignon, named for the monk who supposedly discovered the secret of sparkling wine, and now Hugh was returning as a vintner and proprietor in his own right, staff and mother in tow.

At Roederer, the Schramsberg party was allowed to taste the base wines — those that eventually went into the finished *cuvées,* or blends — and given lunch in the home of the owner. This included tall flutes of Cristal, Roederer's best, its *tête de cuvée,* in an atmosphere of cordiality among equals. The experience was repeated at Pol Roger, where the heir served the Napa crew his *tête de cuvée,* the Winston Churchill.

Then their host brought out a 1980 Schramsberg blanc de blancs that Jack and Jamie had given him on an earlier occasion. Jamie's heart was in her mouth as she watched her wine opened, poured, and critically tasted. After due consideration the renowned Champenois said, "Good body, very lively," and Jamie thought, Praise indeed.

Back in Napa Valley, Hugh stood up before Schramsberg's partners and told them in no uncertain terms that he was committed to the company and to the wines. What he didn't talk about, but what was known among family and friends, was his commitment to the environment. This could conceivably someday conflict with the demands of vineyard and winery, of land acquisition and conversion, of increased production and marketing and estate taxes — of business. The commitments would have to be complementary. Hugh had once declared, "Martin Luther King sucked it up and had a tremendous effect, against tremendous odds," a somewhat grandiose example, but one that moved him.

As a student at Bowdoin College, on the Maine coast, he had lived simply, studying history and Spanish. He spent his junior year in Madrid and in Lima, broadening his experience and his ability to speak Spanish, a measure of privilege but also of intent. Spanish was the second language of California and the first language of the vineyard; it was spoken in the winery as well, and often predominated in the old caves dug by Jacob Schram and expanded by the Davieses, where thousands of bottles of sparkling wine had to be stacked and unstacked in an endless ritual of riddling, storage, disgorging, and packaging, most of it performed by Mexicans. He had worked there also as a cellar rat, long days and nights in the shadow of Spring and Diamond mountains during the time of the Vision 2020 initiative debate. His parents had encouraged him to get involved in the land-use argument; Hugh had re-formed alliances with some old college friends, and he spoke out for the right of the voters to veto big developments in the valley. Like them, he resented the cutting of century-old oaks just up the road from Schramsberg by absentee owners of an ugly commercial winery on Highway 29 known as Beaucanon.

The summer he worked for a congressman in Washington, D.C., his unspoken intention of also serving the environment was not realized. He worked for the Trust for Public Lands, coming closer to that goal, but living in a big city cut him off from the land. Somewhere along the line he realized he could make more of a difference in a place he knew, with land-use problems and also the possibility of a sound ecological future.

He had enrolled in Davis and taken the alternative, enological path that led back to Schramsberg, where he became a familiar sight, the uniquely tall Davies, a grinning ectomorph in hiking boots and shorts in all but the coldest weather, his sleeveless synthetic vests the sort ubiquitous in the high Sierras and his beat-up baseball caps bearing the firm's logo. He moved through the halls and up and down the stairs in the dim old cellar at speed, pausing to consult his clipboard, inseparable from the small spectacles and ready grin.

She grew up in the valley, just down Highway 29 from the turnoff to Schramsberg, not exactly the girl next door, but close. Lily Oliver

loved Napa Valley without reservation, but she resolved to live elsewhere for ten years to see what life was like on the outside.

Earning a liberal arts degree at Pepperdine University, on impulse
she went to a well-known restaurant in Malibu and worked in the
sauté section, just to learn. (She brought her own knives with her.)
Although she wasn't paid she considered this a valuable opportunity
and a privilege. She taught for a time in a private school in Malibu
but couldn't stand the idea of rich kids, five- and six-year-olds acting
like miniature surfers and hitting on the little girls as if they were all
adults. She moved to New York, then back to Los Angeles where she
worked as an interior designer, all the while thinking of her family's
property in Napa Valley.

She and Hugh had gone to the same grammar and junior high
schools in St. Helena but were separated by six years of age. Lily had
been to parties in the vineyard at Schramsberg thrown by the Davies
boys, had listened to the bands and watched revelers full of beer
plunge into the water in the gondolas, all famous stuff, ancient history now. Then one Thanksgiving she was home from L.A., at another neighbor's, playing a board game and listening to the women
talk about eligible bachelors in the valley, and the telephone rang.
Lily answered and heard Hugh Davies inviting them all to a party at
a bar in Calistoga where the musical group the Towne Dandies was
playing.

The two of them met at the bar; they talked for hours. Lily realized that Hugh was different from what she imagined, and accomplished: he spoke Spanish and had a master's degree but at the same
time seemed a free spirit. He had spent time in Spain, Peru, France
— and Australia — but he loved the valley. "It's awesome," he said
with that crooked grin and halting way of talking. A bit off the wall,
maybe, but never flip. Interesting, she thought, and he lived a mile
from her parents' driveway.

A lean, pretty woman with short blond hair and intense blue eyes,
Lily Oliver favored sweaters and pants that could double as equestrian attire, for riding is what she liked most to do. Her family owned
the small winery El Molino, and she had grown up hearing about
and tasting pinot noir and chardonnay and could stand next to Hugh
and trade wine appreciation with him, term for term.

They shared other interests: children, living in the country. He was more drawn to nature than she was, though this was not a problem. She did share his outrage at certain things, like the loss of the heritage live oaks in the pasture across Highway 29 where she had ridden as a child. The removal of the old trees to make way for yet another vineyard was not just unwarranted, it seemed criminal to her, as it did to many who had watched the grand oaks come down at the end of the eighties.

Lily went back to L.A., and she and Hugh met on weekends in San Francisco. Living at opposite ends of California began to look as if it could be a problem. She had vowed to stay away for ten years, and she had made it for seven before she went home.

They moved in together, into the bungalow tucked into the trees off Schramsberg Lane, built in the nineteenth century in the shadow of the Schram place by a man named M'Eckron. House and setting had been described in Robert Louis Stevenson's *Silverado Squatters:* "A rude trail rapidly mounting; a little stream tinkling . . . overhead and on all sides a bower of green and tangled thicket, still fragrant and still flower-bespangled . . . The buckeyes were putting forth their twisted horns of blossom: through all this, we struggled toughly upwards, canted to and fro by the roughness of the trail . . ." The enemy then, as now, was poison oak. "Basking in the sun and silence, concealed from all but the clouds and the mountain birds . . . a bachelor establishment; a little bit of a wooden house, a small cellar hard by in the hillside, and a patch of vines."

Lily parked her horse trailer beside the paddock, where she installed Mack, a gentle thirteen-hundred-pound equestrian presence. She assured the vineyard manager that Mack would not eat Schramsberg's vines.

Her and Hugh's housemates included two honey-colored Labs and two cats. The bungalow, no longer a bachelor pad, was hot in summer and drafty in winter, as it was when Jacob Schram made still wine just up the mountain and Chinese laborers worked in the caves. "You don't have to worry about falling asleep after dinner," Hugh would tell visitors, explaining how he got his reading done — about farming practices, river ecology, winemaking. "It's too cold."

When people asked, as they often did, when he and Lily were get-

ting married, Hugh would just grin. He and Lily got used to not answering this question.

Hugh often wore his winery uniform — boots, vest, sometimes
shorts — to various meetings, but for the Napa Valley Vintners Association he put on more suitable long pants and a polo shirt with
the Schramsberg stitching. As the winery's representative to the
NVVA he was responsible for determining the drift of the industry
and for getting involved in issues that would affect Schramsberg and
the valley. He signed up for one of the committees — community
and industry issues — and at first sat back and listened.

He also attended Farm Bureau meetings. There it didn't matter
what you wore. At the urging of boyhood friends who had risen in
their family businesses, Hugh was emboldened to run for the large,
broadly based Farm Bureau board of directors, but he was defeated.
Disappointed, he felt foolish for overreaching. He was new at the
game, he reminded himself; it was too soon to run when he still had
one foot in the cellar and the other in UC Davis, a lucky spermer yet
to prove himself.

The Watershed Task Force would be better, he thought. Here was
a chance to make a difference for the environment and at the same
time to try to pull together opposing factions of vintners and environmentalists. Theoretically a win-win situation. He agreed with
many growers and vintners that the real enemy was urbanization, although tourism and related development were also major problems.
Agriculture was the only viable alternative to bedroom communities and high-end infestation by McMansions. He was particularly
angered by trophy houses appearing on the ridges, outsized expressions of ego, irremediable scars on a landscape he had been part
of since childhood and which for him possessed an absolute value he
couldn't articulate.

He didn't miss a meeting of the task force in the beginning, despite his heavy work schedule and other obligations. After the first
few months he saw that things weren't going to pan out quite as he
had imagined. Chris Malan and three or four others talked only
about strengthening the ordinance and ignored the fears of the winery owners and contractors about restrictions. They clashed with
Stu Smith, a prominent vintner named Dennis Groth, and other

landowners over the relative value of wildlife, water, and agriculture. Hugh found his sympathies split between the environmentalists and the farmers, and his loyalties, too.

Hugh Davies wished for more common ground. Meanwhile, development went on as before in the hills, with no apparent slackening of the practices that had brought the task force together in the first place.

17

THE POSTMASTER wore a denim shirt with embroidery on the front depicting eagle feathers, and he was barefoot. He smiled at the electric-green parrot on his finger, a half-moon conure from Costa Rica named Ricki Lake, after a minor icon of pop culture. The postmaster said, with affection, "He's very spoiled."

Ricki Lake was allowed the run of the office in St. Helena. That included the smorgasbord of organic seeds, dried fruit, and — Ricki's favorite — blueberries. He flew to the postmaster's shoulder, which was protected from Ricki's droppings by a sleeveless sweater streaked as if with the ammoniac tears of stalactites. Ricki Lake fluttered to the desk and strutted among papers relevant to the affairs of the U.S. Postal Service while the postmaster gazed out the window.

It was Friday afternoon and already the procession had begun on Main Street: Jags, Mercedes, sport-utility vehicles belonging to up-valley residents collecting last-minute items for the weekend, rented convertibles, the odd limo with smoked glass and forked antenna. The postmaster was at that moment considering an unusual step: filing a lawsuit. It would be of such magnitude that it would royally upset the people in those vehicles and many more throughout the valley. In truth, the question for the postmaster was not whether but how to file. He had at his disposal a figurative tire iron of formidable proportions, and as he remarked while feeding Ricki Lake another blueberry, there was an abundance of targets. "So many fenders," he said, "so little time."

Back before the creation of the Watershed Task Force, before Stanley Ranch and shortly after the formation of Friends of the Napa River, Chris Malan heard about Peter Mennen. He was the eccentric St. Helena postmaster, one of a long line of individualists who had been coming to Napa Valley for more than a century to get away from the pressures of life in America, before the valley came to symbolize them. If it hadn't been for the fact that Mennen was wealthy, the interest in him might have stopped right there.

His postal customers considered him a friendly, idiosyncratic, intelligent holdover from the sixties, a "character" who had inherited a fortune and dedicated some of it to environmental causes. Few people knew of the extent of his involvement in these things, and that included Chris.

Friends of the Napa River was sponsoring a river festival, and she decided to call Mennen up and ask him to finance a Klamath River dory, to be offered as a raffle prize, and asking herself, "What do you have to lose?" She looked up his telephone number in the directory and dialed it, and a man with a soft, youthful-sounding voice answered. After she had identified herself, he said, "I've been wondering when you'd call."

During the fight over Stanley Ranch, Chris called Mennen again. She was peripherally involved and wanted him to speak at a gathering in Napa against the project, since Mennen often stood up at public meetings and expressed opposition to development. His letters to the editor were surprisingly hard-hitting for a public servant, but his attention, and his money, was usually focused on organizations operating outside the county. That was the word on Mennen and his wife, Carlene, a figure less outspoken than Mennen himself, as together they engaged by proxy in distant battles in Utah and elsewhere.

The Mennens had political preferences at home, too, but remained apart from the local environmental organizations and indifferent to the reigning social hierarchy. This rendered them sideliners to the greens and irrelevant to the local elite, who tended to assess those in the valley by their access to the celebrated producers of its famous product and who didn't keep up with environmental activities elsewhere in the nation.

Then in 1998 the Mennens held a fundraiser for Mike Thompson, who was running for the U.S. Congress for the first time. They invited most everybody in the valley with any claim to being "environmental," and that included Chris Malan. She took her photographs with her, as was her habit, those taken by Parry Mead from the airplane showing razed land high in the hills, dire evidence of environmental damage, and these included photographs of Jayson Pahlmeyer's new vineyard, put in under the supervision of David Abreu.

The Mennens lived in a modest subdivision in St. Helena, just down the street from Stu Smith and his new wife, Julie Ann, and the Mennens' front yard was quite unlike others on Sylvaner Avenue. No neatly mowed lawn, no lawn at all, in fact, just a postage stamp of natural aridity that annoyed the neighbors, all rock and wild azaleas and a coffeeberry tree that attracted birds in unusual numbers. Inside, the little house had a Southwest feel, nothing fancy, with wooden beams and nice wooden furniture and sliding glass doors overlooking the creek between the Mennens' and the Spottswoode vineyard which also, in season, flowed past Peter Newton's and Buddy Meyer's properties on its way to Sulphur Creek and the Napa River, San Pablo Bay and San Francisco Bay, and finally the Pacific Ocean.

Peter Mennen didn't look like a postmaster to Chris. He was tall and casually dressed, and the clear stems of his glasses disappeared into abundant hair that had turned from blond to off-white without aging him. Carlene, Mennen's physiognomic opposite, was maybe five feet six, with black eyes and a mien more American Indian than Anglo. She had straight black hair much like Chris's and, if truth be told, looked a little bit like Chris: solid, dark complexion, with a transforming smile and a level gaze.

When Chris showed the photographs to her hostess, Carlene said, "You're ruining my dinner."

Undeterred, Chris asked why she and her husband spent money on environmental causes far from Napa when right here there was much to be done. Home was the problem, Chris said, launching into her familiar refrain: people will work, and spend, to protect distant mountains, wild washes, even the Napa Valley floor, but they can't get it together for the hills. The blaze resulting from this exchange would take more than a year to kindle, its provenance indistinct and the chronology of its progress imprecise. But in the end it wouldn't matter who did exactly what, exactly when, for the effect would be profound and there would be more than enough credit and acrimony to go around.

Sometimes he thought about the distance the country had come since his great-grandfather invented a corn remover in a Newark basement, at the end of another century. Then America was, in relative terms, unspoiled. At least large parts of it were. Then, millions of acres in the West retained sufficient beauty and wildness to be included by Theodore Roosevelt in new national parks and national forests; this stretch of California still had remnants of Great Basin Indians in the early twentieth century, including a handful of Wappos of Napa Valley whose forebears had once enlivened the coastal ranges with myriad languages and customs. Redwoods stood tall and thick the entire length of the Mayacamas and other ranges then, and the California dream had been very much alive.

Mennen's Sure Corn Killer had led to other inventions for the temporary melioration of the natural human condition, like perspiration and the growth of facial hair. Deodorants, after-shave lotion, and the like eventually produced a significant fortune, and the great-grandson grew up in its glow, not in Newark but in a mansion in exclusive New Jersey suburbia, vaguely aware from an early age that his world lacked something. Concepts that Peter Mennen later came to understand as privilege, exclusion, loneliness, and guilt attached to an existence over which he had no control and could only oppose obliquely, first through withdrawal, later through rebellion.

Conformity and exclusivity were among the things being rejected in the 1960s, and Peter joined in. "I know what you're against," his father would say, "but what are you for?" And Peter couldn't answer. He didn't yet know that natural beauty was something you could be for, like God and country.

He was accepted by Brown University despite mediocre grades — he was, after all, a Mennen — but failed all but one subject his sophomore year. Young men his age who were not in school or married were being drafted into the army, involved in a military campaign in Southeast Asia becoming a full-fledged war, "Vietnam" a synonym for everything supposedly wrong with America. So Peter bought a motorcycle — a Honda Dream, barely capable of reaching sixty miles an hour on the open road — and took off for Mexico.

He had heard of a cheap university in Mexico City that catered to veterans on the GI Bill and offered a haven for the academically and professionally challenged, as well as those enjoying the honeymoon of a marriage between illicit drugs and industrial democracy. This was inspired by the ready availability of mind-altering substances not so readily available in suburban New Jersey. Peter enrolled. The school was called — ironically, he thought — the University of the Americas, while many of its students had rejected American culture and had no allegiance to the one below the border, either.

Personally, he was on a search but didn't know for what. He still could not answer his father, but felt he was getting closer even as he slipped farther down the slope toward disinheritance, the fate he had been led to believe was his. One night, having inhaled the essence of a green substance he considered essential in those days, he took the Honda Dream over the mountain between Mexico City and the sea, an ancient volcano of great spiritual significance in pre-Columbian times.

Descending at speed, his relaxation and coordination chemically enhanced, he went through a seemingly endless series of curves, courting the precipice, dipping first to one side and then the other, so low that the motorcycle's footrests scraped the pavement and re-leased showers of sparks that blended with stars hanging out in the immense, unmarred Mexican sky. He sensed a coming together of self and surroundings, totally new, even as mind and body separated and the feeling expanded to include the universe. It was sustained ecstasy — no other word for it — and it lasted until he gained the flatland and got off the Dream and stood looking back. He knew he could never again be the person who had made that descent in that way.

"Once you ram through that window," Peter would later say, "you can't go back, even though life's new possibilities might mean ex-treme loneliness. You can't even want to go back."

Later, he wrote a poem about the experience:

> I lie, an open wound, 'neath my devouring lover night
> and bleed to mingle freely with the darkness,
> spread fine as mist 'round the earth's curve;
> and I die in ecstasy, kindling a million stars.

He returned to the United States, unable to shake the memory of that night, and was told he had been disinherited. In search of another window, he took a civil service exam, and to his surprise did well, and went to work in a post office in San Francisco. It was the late sixties, the beatniks gone, the hippies going, love coming in, high boogie time in North Beach and psychedelia in the Haight. Peter collected some experience as a bureaucrat and began to look around for a more peaceful slot.

There was an opening for a postmaster in a town north of San Francisco called St. Helena. It was the next-to-northernmost branch in the region ruled from Oakland, and so unlikely to be hassled by supervisors. He looked it up on a map and found that St. Helena was in the middle of nowhere, just where Peter wanted to be. He applied and got the job on merit.

The lovely little building on Main Street, he discovered, had wood paneling, old metal post boxes, and a vibrant mural from the Depression era showing Anglo-Saxons picking grapes. His office in the southeast corner, directly off the reception area, had two big windows and another door leading into the sorting room. It would be home for a long time.

In 1981, the first year of the Napa Valley Wine Auction, Peter Mennen got into a dispute with the woman organizing that event over the amount of postage required for a mailing. She sent her assistant, a good-looking, dark-haired younger woman named Carlene, to deal with the postmaster. She and Peter hit it off, and although the postage price was not reduced, they began to see each other outside the little building on Main Street.

Carlene seemed to be Peter's polar opposite. She had grown up on a big ranch in Texas, about as far as you could get from the New Jersey gold coast, but both Peter and Carlene had broken off relations with their families. She took this tall, blond, boyish former scion on hikes in the woods, fossil hunting in eastern California and New Mexico, and into canyons and wild lands. He was Ivy League, she seat-of-the-pants, but she taught him something about nature. Together they worked for the eradication of Scotch broom in California, gathering and distributing the seeds of native plants.

At first, Peter had said, "This is so boring." But gradually he came round to an appreciation of the land, something intuitive in Carlene, having been raised on the Red River, where she spent hours watching soft-shell turtles, coyotes, and panthers. She abhorred the land rush there and the practice of wearing out a piece of property before moving on to do the same thing someplace else. She considered that part of Texas "Bible-belted" and hadn't bought into that brand of spirituality. It was just another version, they agreed, of conformity and exclusivity.

Peter was impressed with Carlene's "wildness." Her mother was French, but there were Cherokee and Comanche genes aplenty, and he liked her knowledge and persistence. Over the years Peter would say repeatedly, "Carlene's like water. It always finds its way to where it wants to go."

In 1987 they went up to Mount Shasta, and Carlene read aloud Gary Snyder's "Prayer for the Great Family," after a Mohawk prayer; she asked for guidance to support biological integrity and the wherewithal to do it. This sentimental act had implications more profound than either of them suspected, for after they were married and living in a trailer, having bought the house on Sylvaner that still had to be renovated before they could move in, Peter received a letter at his office from a bank in the Midwest. He opened and read it. The manager of his trust fund, the letter informed him, was requesting a million-dollar raise in her annual fee.

He thought, "What trust fund?"

He read the letter again, then leaned back in his chair and stared at the ceiling. In a rush of elation and rage, he realized that stock in the family company, long reputed to have been left to Peter by his dear grandfather, *had* in fact been left to him, and had sat somewhere all these years without his knowing it. Mennen, Inc., had recently been acquired by Colgate-Palmolive, rendering all such stock public, and so his had surfaced through the inadvertent action of some functionary in a distant countinghouse through whose purview it had passed. Peter was not disinherited, as he had believed. He was not poor. He was, in all likelihood, rich.

He found a lawyer, a hotshot litigator in San Francisco, who looked into the situation and came back and told Peter that he did indeed own stock and that its history was less savory than he had imagined. But if he took the matter to court, some people once close to Peter might go to jail and he might lose the bulk of the money. Peter told the lawyer, "I don't care."

That is just what a litigator wants to hear, but this one didn't work on contingency. The case would require a lot of digging and the pursuit of people who didn't want to be pursued, and the lawyer asked, "How much money do you have?"

Peter had about thirty thousand dollars that was supposed to pay for home renovation — the vegas, the fireplace designed by Carlene, the deck with its redwood ramada where Peter intended to plant wisteria — but it all disappeared into the litigator's account.

While he waited, Peter saw in his mind's eye millions of dollars tumbling toward him, the greenbacks fluttering and turning in the air. They rained down, electrifying, transforming — sixteen million of them. As if in a dream, the case did not make it to court, and all pretension and false rectitude dissolved in a settlement that he felt vindicated decades of moral groping. It was the headiest of moments, a breathless experience, and then a strange thing happened: for the first time he could remember, Peter *wanted* to be rich.

He went outside the post office and saw a Jaguar and wanted it. He saw a trophy house and wanted that, too, not a bungalow on Sylvaner Avenue. He wanted a sailboat, he wanted better clothes, he wanted . . . Going up and down, from the heights of anticipation to the depths of despair, he imagined himself in every enviable position in the valley and then got depressed. He realized that once he had all the possessions and positions, he wouldn't be happy.

It was painful, Carlene thought, watching all this. She would say, "Peter's having a terrible time," and wait for him to come out of it. They talked about what else might be done with the money, about various causes and, specifically, about fish — salmon and steelhead — species emblematic of big trees and clear mountain water, of the best of the West, which meant a lot to both of them, and wilderness. Gradually, Peter began to see that he had enough money either to be rich or to do some good, but not both.

He sat in his office behind the Depression-era mural, staring up, and saw the dollars falling, falling right past him and into a bin at his feet marked "Mennen Environmental Foundation." He wasn't going to be rich after all, and that meant he had to remain a postmaster. This was fine, but the prospect of juggling both his public duties and those of the new environmental enterprise freaked him out. Carlene, who had taught him to eradicate Scotch broom and had prayed on Mount Shasta, said simply, "Why don't you let me do it?"

She went about it in her usual way, first looking into other, larger foundations and discovering that some were fronts providing access to resources for powerful people. Others did good work but wasted time and money by pitting one environmentalist against another. Some projects were good and some just excuses for extracting money. The Mennens' was a piddling foundation compared to most, but it had about six hundred thousand dollars a year to spread around, enough to *do* something.

The way to go, Carlene decided, was to pick a really good cause — there were so many — offer some money, and then bird-dog it. One of the best causes was the inventorying of wilderness in Utah, so it could be preserved, and Carlene got directly involved. She met with ranchers out there, whom she understood, and with native-plants people; she gave public testimony about wilderness before an advisory council, and shook things up. She and Peter started getting invited to things, like the meeting of Conservation International in Washington, D.C., where they showed up in Tevas and jeans only to discover that everybody else had on formal clothes and lots of jewelry. When Harrison Ford asked Peter to sit with him, Peter said, "I have to sit with my wife."

No one in Napa knew these things. Peter and Carlene helped with reforestation in Costa Rica and salmon restoration in Oregon. Carlene got interested in urban sprawl in the Bay Area and in how much money had been raised and spent over the years by the Sierra Club, the Wilderness Society, and the National Conservation League. She thought she could get more bang for the buck with smaller, more tightly focused grants, including those promoting watersheds and recovery of wild-land corridors. These had to be run by people who knew the terrain, she thought. "Don't look for expertise and grant-writing talent," she would say. "Look for passion on the land."

Gradually she and Peter returned, philanthropically speaking, to the place they had never left, where they had begun their lives together, Napa Valley. Then Chris Malan showed up at the fundraiser for Mike Thompson, nearly hysterical about development in the hills and unsure of what to do next. Chris might be overbearing at times, Carlene thought, but she was passionate and she got them to look differently at something they had taken for granted until then.

Carlene delved into the possibility of suing the county, the vintners, or both. Through her contacts in the Sierra Club in San Francisco, she found a lawyer good at such things, and she collected a lot of pertinent information and turned it over to Chris, telling her, in effect, Go for it.

18

TOM LIPPE grew up in faraway Florida but went to law school at Stanford University and spent his free time in the Sierra Nevada. He naturally gravitated toward environmental issues and "social betterment" — his phrase — and by the time he graduated knew he wanted to practice in the public interest. Environmental litigation would be his niche.

In the eighties in northern California that meant the timber wars. Protecting old growth was the emblematic regional struggle, and Lippe represented the Sierra Club and another organization up in Humboldt County against Pacific Lumber, with some success. Along the way he got to know the leadership of the club in San Francisco, where its headquarters was located. He later opened an office just blocks away from the Sierra Club's utilitarian digs in the Mission District.

He now shared a suite with a financial consulting firm in an Embarcadero skyscraper but kept his hair long; he wore open shirts and sport jackets, and rarely talked about strategy. "Litigation is like poker," he would say. "You don't say what cards you had in the last hand" once your opponent folds. And you don't waste a lot of time on sentiment.

In 1998, he got a call from a woman in Napa Valley named Chris Malan. He wasn't surprised to learn that she had heard of him through the Sierra Club; it had often sent him referrals. Malan and other activists in the wine country were concerned about vineyard development in the hills and wanted to know if it could be halted, and Lippe drove up to talk to her.

He found Malan both personable and well informed. Lippe didn't drink wine and knew nothing about it or vineyards, and he couldn't digest all the information on the spot. But it certainly seemed to him that the county had big legal problems, and that there might be work for him. For one thing, the visual evidence was compelling. "Look what's happening up there," he said of the patchwork development.

He thought Napa Valley representative of other places in the United States where success had come down to money versus the environment. Many projects in the hills had been approved piecemeal, allowing developers to assemble big vineyards by doing them as a succession of smaller projects and avoiding more rigorous review. And there was the problem of enforcement — projects uninspected, violations unpunished, wrongdoers unrepentant. No one seemed to be looking at the possible effect of all this on the overall environment, or what would happen if it continued — the effects on wildlife and the river.

Here was a cautionary tale, he thought: do something destructive to the land and try to fix it with technology, and you create other problems as unintended consequences. During storms, underground drainage delivers water too quickly for the river to handle, for instance. Developed hillsides erode. Rocks roll. Species suffer.

Lots of laws applied, at least theoretically. One of these was the Endangered Species Act, savior of old growth — and of the northern spotted owl — and bane of the timber industry. It was a strong law but had its weaknesses, including the need to prove a "taking" — death or injury of an endangered creature as a direct result of activity by human beings. Proving this required a lot of field work by scientists and was very expensive (a million dollars just to get into federal court nowadays). San Pablo Bay was listed by the Environmental Protection Agency as impaired, and so consequently was the Napa River, a major tributary to the bay. The steelhead in the river were officially threatened, so that was a clear opportunity. And there were a few spotted owls in old growth above the west side of the valley.

But there was a better, cheaper, more immediate way, the best card in any potential plaintiff's hand: the California Environmental Quality Act. Known all over the state, either reverentially or contemptuously, as CEQA, the law stated that any project affecting the environment, if it involved "discretionary" decisions by local officials on the specifics, had to be first opened to public comment. The other sort of decision, "ministerial," was for more standard projects and unsuited to those in Napa County because of the variety of the projects themselves and the terrain. Virtually all vineyard development in the hills involved discretionary approval, and to date there had been no public comment on erosion control plans.

Lippe asked Chris for her documentation relating to new vineyards, acquired some erosion control plans from the county planning department, and reviewed it all. He was "dumbfounded," he later said, to discover that the plans were apparently illegal. "There's evidence all over them that the county was exercising discretion."

By that he meant that the planning department had approved projects on their merits without giving the public a chance to weigh in, as required. The irony was that if Napa had not passed a good hillside ordinance requiring certain safeguards and review, all the projects could have been treated as ministerial, rubber-stamped, and exempted. It was the provisions of Napa's hillside ordinance, more stringent than in the rest of California, passed years before and requiring erosion control plans, that had opened Napa up to such potential litigation. From the time the ordinance was passed, Napa County should have been complying with the California Environmental Quality Act, and it wasn't.

If the county thought that its already strong hillside ordinance rendered public review unnecessary, Lippe thought, the county was wrong. Even if there was more environmental protection in Napa because of the hillside ordinance than elsewhere, the requirements of CEQA still applied.

There also existed the possibility of suing individual property owners. If vineyards had been planted in the hills without environmental impact reports, then those same vineyard owners were presumably as liable as the county was. There were plenty of owners to choose from, including vineyards developed in the last few months with nothing more than a declaration from the authorities that they would have no negative impact on the environment. They belonged to all kinds of people, from big boys like Beringer to little start-ups nobody ever heard of to cult producers like Jayson Pahlmeyer. You could almost throw a dart.

A month after meeting with Lippe, Chris and her associates in Concerned Citizens for Napa Hillsides began combing through erosion control plans filed with the county and then comparing those plans with what had taken place on the ground. They needed photographs of work done in the early stages of vineyards to buttress their assertions that the actual work had not conformed to specifics put forward in the erosion control plans. Neighbors came forward with photographs of their own of what was taking place on adjacent properties. Chris saw the relationship between the county and the developers as one big administrative scam. "What was being done by the engineers and the attorneys," she told people, "and what the county was approving, was not what was happening on the landscape."

An almost religious fervor pervaded the search. To back up paper evidence, she had the growing stash of photos showing ecological assault and some scientific evidence from ongoing studies financed by the Mennen Environmental Foundation. Damage to invertebrates, fish, and waterway channels downstream from vineyard development was obvious, all fodder for any future legal action. And there were moles in at least two public agencies in the county providing additional raw data. This all went into the spinning hopper that would eventually spit out a verdict on whether or not to sue.

Chris was adamantly for it, as she had always been. The lawyers were cautious, and the Mennens in between. They now had more than seventy potential targets, should they decide to move. They started narrowing the possibilities, to increase their chances of winning if they did go to court; the criteria that emerged from these sessions were simple: no mom-and-pop operations; vineyard plans that could be challenged within time limits set down by the California Environmental Quality Act; and real, demonstrable environmental damage.

The photographs of early stages of development were crucial. Vivid pictorial evidence could, if need be, prove to a judge that damage had been significant before it was obscured under a sea of trellises and young vines. No decision would be made until all the legal research was in and the lawyers could predict near-certain success. Everyone agreed on all these things. Napa Valley had supposedly the best erosion control and land conservation regulations in the United States. The publicity about any such lawsuit in this, the darling of the wine world, destination of billionaires, would be widespread, and the criticism of the suit relentless. The stakes were just too high, both for the environment and for the environmentalists, to screw up.

Meanwhile, on the Watershed Task Force, Chris found herself in arguments not just with Stu Smith but also with other members. Dennis Groth, owner of the well-known winery of the same name in Oakville, the pink stucco mission-style landmark nicknamed Taco Bell, producer of a notable cabernet, told her in a moment of exasperation, "Some people don't care as much as you do about these species." She took this as an indication that he cared for them not at all, and she thought the county's position not much different. She was convinced now that "the developer/special interest deck was stacked against the conservationists and environmentalists."

In her opinion, both the county planning director and the professional facilitators in charge of task force procedures were tacitly allied with the wineries. They sought the same outcome of all the deliberation, which was hand slaps for the developers and no real follow-up. The first phase of the task force was almost at an end, and concrete change would clearly not emerge. There was a plan for establishing an information center where the citizenry could obtain facts about hillside development and a way of dedicating certain sensitive lands to a public trust; both good ideas, Chris thought, but of little practical use in addressing regulations and penalties for violations.

Worse, there was no firm indication that the county planned to go ahead with the second phase of the task force, as had originally been intended. The second phase was to have looked at the scientific evidence still being collected and to have made hard recommendations for a tougher hillside ordinance. But the board of supervisors delayed authorizing money for the second phase. All this pointed to a legal remedy.

There was a catch, however: the Mennen Environmental Foundation couldn't sue. Its bylaws and tax-exempt status prevented this, although the foundation could, and did, finance the research for the potential suit. It would have to find an organization willing to front as plaintiff if the backers and the lawyers ever decided to file, and finding the right organization was crucial. Public perception of environmental lawsuits was generally good; almost as important as the cause itself was the reputation of the organizations behind it. This could be a factor in the final outcome, and in the outcomes of possible subsequent lawsuits: the more important the organization — the older, larger, more respected, more popular, and more committed — the better.

John Stephens, chair of the Napa group of the Sierra Club, lived on the west side of the city in a blue-collar subdivision with shared driveways and patches of grass. His patch was given over to native species. During the day, Stephens — tall, thin, with owlish glasses and slate-blue eyes — worked as a plumber at the Napa State Hospital, and at night he pursued various environmental goals, including river and forest protection, land conservation, the curtailment of urban sprawl, the preservation of ground water and water in the river and the wells, and numerous others. But what most of these had in common was H_2O — its purity, its increasing scarcity, the declining health of things living in it. The state of the steelhead in the Napa River was in Stephens's estimation "dismal, sickening."

So as a plumber he dealt with the utilitarian aspects of the earth's most precious resource, and as an environmentalist he tried to restrict its use and degradation by human beings. It was a thoroughly contemporary dilemma, and it was mirrored, with variations, in the lives of most people actively involved in aspects of Napa's environmental reforms.

Many of these were discussed around Stephens's dining room table in the west of the city. For years he had been a civil rights and a peace activist as well as what he called "a rocking chair Sierra Clubber," but the Stanley Ranch controversy had galvanized him. Stephens proved adept at dealing with conflicting personalities and was voted onto the local Sierra Club executive committee, known as the ex-com. Its numbers varied from time to time, half the seats on this governing body elected by the valley's entire membership and half by the other ex-com members.

The Sierra Club was famously democratic and grass-roots, but there were certain controls not immediately apparent to the rank and file. Local autonomy — like access to local dues — went only so far, and Stephens soon learned about these limitations. He found the ex-com in Napa to be an "intellectual, quite wordy group," and he had no trouble holding his own. Any member could raise an issue of concern and become the expert in that area and lead the charge, so to speak, as long as the rest of the committee went along. He became the conservation chair, one of many lesser chairs available to those who would sit in them. His soft-spoken persistence and ability to avoid open conflict usually prevailed, and during one meeting he went into the kitchen for a cup of coffee and came back to discover that he had been elected chair of the Napa group.

Membership was extensive in the county, but the vast majority of members weren't actively involved in the group's political activities. Many were only dimly aware of them, their interests tending toward hiking and bird watching and preserving redwoods and treasures like Yosemite. The local environmental nitty-gritty was left to the wordy ex-com members, the core of which in Napa was made up of Stephens, Tyler York, the vice chair, who was a builder and a distributor of organic fertilizer, two other veteran Sierra Clubbers, and a relatively new arrival, Chris Malan. She was voted onto the ex-com by the committee itself. This was due to her keen interest in the issues and a desire by other ex-commers to take advantage of her energy and growing clout. Her insistence on being heard and her reputation for environmental action indicated a dynamo for the resource, not a dilettante. The issues had in recent years become increasingly complicated and divisive, and Chris was made the political chair.

From the beginning she talked, across the embroidered white cloth on John Stephens's dining table, sometimes nibbling a cookie, about the growing need to sue the county for neglecting state environmental laws and to sue specific property owners for wreaking havoc in the hills.

19

JAYSON PAHLMEYER stepped out onto his patio and turned first
to the east and then to the west, his hawklike profile to the wind.
Behind him were the steep slopes of Atlas Peak, littered with
volcanic debris, not the sort of place where a house would logi-
cally stand, but with a view, as visitors often said, to kill for. Miles
straight out from the edge of his swimming pool, the south end of
the valley slipped away through the Napa River estuary and the tule
marshes to San Pablo Bay, gleaming like a doubloon dropped in the
unblinking California sun, while farther out, beyond the fog banks,
stood the intimation of San Francisco, the ghostly white skyline
there one moment, gone the next.

His house had been remodeled in a style he described with pride
as "high-tech Italian industrial," all glass and tile and tubular steel.
The architect had put a lot of effort into rendering the walls the
color of dirt and the angles suggestive of the European ducal antecedents of all-American, ever-striving, results-oriented entrepre-
neurial brass. The house's roofline resembled the blade of a huge
overturned snow shovel, and the blinding south wall reflected the
conjunction of sea, sky, and land.

Inside, the living space was separated from the outside by a kind of
automated clerestory, a glorified garage door fitted with glass panels
that rose on command to allow the dining room table to be rolled
out under the stars. Circular stairs were encased in fiberglass plates at
once reminiscent of fifties industrial breakthrough, foundry discards,
and armor. The gorgeous blue leather chairs in the living room, under a cliff of burnished steel that served as a chimney, complemented
the overall retro feel, as if the creator had found refuge in a universe

of sharp manufactured objects and worker upheaval where he could safely sip his wine, emblematic of Old and New World craft.

In the attached garage lived two monkeys, a spider and a capuchin, both born in captivity. (Jayson Pahlmeyer would never own a monkey from the wild.) They shared the space with his white '64 Cadillac convertible, the last year Caddies had good, clean lines, in his opinion. He owned a powder-pink Cadillac convertible of similar vintage and liked to drive first one and then the other while wearing a high school letter-style jacket and a billed cap bearing his and his wine's name, Pahlmeyer. He would head down the mountain to lunch at Mustard's, his favorite restaurant, or, as he did this morning, in the white Caddy, up Atlas Peak Road.

After a few winding miles he stopped to look at his new vineyard in the distance, overlapping the ridge separating Napa and Wooden valleys. The clearing of chaparral had begun, as Jayson and anyone else taking this dead-end route could plainly see in the spring of 1999, the final step in the ambitious, multimillion-dollar estate that had already caused him grief but was now marching toward completion.

The young vines would be in by the end of summer, as the cowboys had promised. The clearing on the ridge resembled a light green Post-it on the darker flank of mountain running north to south, the natural palisade without a break except for the vineyard. Jayson's Post-it had once been pasture, he argued; he was not destroying old growth. He could have dealt more easily with his critics among the environmentalists if he felt he had the backing of his own peers, but he was shunned by some vintners, despite his *mea culpa* and his lighthearted description of himself as the poster child for the hillside ordinance because his contractor had graded without a permit. A bit of humor doesn't hurt, he kept thinking, and he took it a step further, referring to himself deprecatingly as the Monica Lewinsky of Napa Valley.

But many people were still not amused. He hoped his new vineyard would help put his misdeeds behind him, that people would be forced to recognize the value of what he was doing. Eventually there would be a winery up there. The architect who had made over Jayson's house was developing the concept: three levels, gravity flow, all natural materials blending into the hillside. A stealth structure.

It would be beautiful, with heavy, industrial pipe columns and an elevator made of glass and furnished with chairs and a sofa for wine tasting as one rose with an ever-expanding view of the valley — of creation. A three-dimensional computer model being devised by the architect would allow Jayson to move things around and see what worked, what looked best, once he got his building permit. This was more stunning edge work and the final step in a master plan allowing him — finally, in quantity, on premises — to make a wine to drop you to your knees.

Chris Malan's driveway emerged at a point directly below the ridge where the new Pahlmeyer vineyard was going in. She saw the activity up there every time she left the house to drive down Atlas Peak Road, every day for months, trading her short black raincoat and gold loops for shorts and bobbed hair, noticing first the isolated power pole and then the narrow trail coming down from the ridge and then the clearing. She stopped on one of the countless trips down the mountain to look more closely, and the next time she got out of her Cherokee with a video camera and stood amid volcanic rock and pushed the button. The lens was pointed eastward and upward, and it recorded the weekly progress of chainsaws and Caterpillars.

What Pahlmeyer was doing up on the ridge was apparently legal, but it enraged her and other residents of Atlas Peak Road. The videotaping happened to coincide with the research and strategizing going on among the tight group composed of Malan, the Mennens, and their lawyers. Unbeknownst to Pahlmeyer, he had made each shortlist of possible defendants; whatever evidence was required to sue him was already in the group's possession, including the early aerial photographs. But this continual transformation of a formerly wild place, the final Post-it in the larger Pahlmeyer scheme, in full view of Chris Malan, fueled her and the group's resolve.

The Watershed Task Force's first phase was now completed. There would be a second phase, but neither the supervisors nor the county planning department would tell Chris definitively when. In June 1999 the task force recommendations were formally accepted by the board, and although it did not rule out funding a second phase, the board still had not authorized funds for it.

Chris and her allies took this as evidence that the county thought the issue of the hills had been officially dispensed with and that it would be allowed to pass into political oblivion, if possible. Throughout the summer she telephoned the county offices seeking to learn the fate of the second phase, without success. Then one day she cornered the planning director, Jeff Redding, in the elevator of the county building and demanded to know if the task force would be reconvened.

Redding had come to Napa from Santa Cruz, and he wore his hair in a ponytail. Energetic, generally responsive, he spoke quickly and moved his hands in the air at the same time, as if development and conservation principles were right there, to be grasped by any-one who was interested. But Redding was overworked and stressed by the ever-increasing applications for new vineyards, as well as by the politics surrounding the issue, and he was unable to say which way the task force decision would go.

Chris thought the decision had already been made, and by August she was pushing harder than ever for the lawsuit. The best defen-dants, they all agreed, were the county and three individual busi-nesses that had recently put in vineyards, all of them ignoring the California Environmental Quality Act. The individual defendants would be a little-known partnership then called The Best Cellar/ Vineyard Properties West; an aspiring boutique, Chateau Potelle, managed by a Frenchman living in the Mayacamas; and the owner of the cult wine featured in the movie *Disclosure,* Jayson Pahlmeyer.

The Sierra Club would be the plaintiff, the Mennen Environ-mental Foundation the means. The Napa group ex-com had already agreed to this arrangement, despite the fact that the announcement was bound to be explosive, the outcome transforming. For the first time ever, a well-known, powerful environmental advocacy group was challenging not just development of wild places but the right of Napa's successful, adulated, glamorous industry to prosper and grow. The very basis of the wineries' existence, not just profits, was being cast into doubt, and the result was bound to be acrimony, and worse.

Chris Malan and John Stephens assumed that their decision to sue in the name of the Sierra Club would be sanctioned in the club's upper echelons. The Sierra Club could not be associated with any lawsuit without approval by the litigation department in the national headquarters in San Francisco, but that should be no problem. The lesser lights in Napa assumed the slightly brighter lights in the Redwood chapter in Sonoma, to which the Napa group belonged, and the beacons in the Mission District would all be as enthusiastic about their cause as they were.

The lesser lights were wrong.

Much of the work of the Mennen Environmental Foundation was done in the house on Sylvaner Avenue at the kitchen table, made from a two-hundred-year-old barn gate from Mexico, where light fell from a chandelier of elk antlers and from a lamp made of an old saguaro cactus trunk.

On a shelf stood a tightly woven Pomo basket, given to Carlene Mennen by her friend Yolande Beard, dead now, author of the elegant little book *Wappo,* about Napa Valley's indigenous people. Hanging nearby was a prayer wand of wild turkey and grouse feathers dedicated to the health of Turtle Island, the Cherokee name for planet Earth. The barn gate was spread with letters, press clippings, photocopies of documents relating to half a dozen issues, pads, and reference books. Carlene had no computer on this command deck. She didn't want to be bombarded with e-mails and other time-wasting electronic messages when the really big stuff — wilderness inventories, the health of fish, redwood and live oak preservation — had better ways of making itself known.

This was usually through the resonance of the human voice. The telephone was her chosen instrument, quick, direct, capable of transmitting more than information — resolve, strategic nuance, sometimes anger. Carlene got calls at seven in the morning from Washington, D.C., such as the one from Senator Barbara Boxer, who wanted Carlene to fund a political action committee. Carlene kept up with campaigns all over the country because, in the end, everything was political.

It was after a lobbying trip to Washington and a session in the office of Senator Dianne Feinstein that Carlene had decided to go back to Napa and work on her own. Now while Peter sat in the post office receiving bureaucratic directives about what sort of art to hang on the bathroom walls, Carlene worked away here, "under the canopy," a figurative screen from public view of her string-jerking in twenty different environmental causes, from Utah to Oregon, from the nation's capital to the California coast. She didn't want recognition, she wanted to affect the argument. Her husband called her the Terminator. "Don't try to hide anything from Carlene," Peter Mennen would tell people, laughing. "She's out there, over the curve of the earth. She sees things come up long before the rest of us see them."

One afternoon Peter came home from work and stood at the kitchen sink, eating a leftover sandwich and gazing out into the narrow backyard. The day of legal decision had come. "I have to think things over for weeks," he said, "but Carlene decides immediately. With her, there's no difference between a good idea and an act."

Her philosophy of philanthropy was simple: empower activists with real science, then empower them with real money. She had told Chris Malan to handle oversight on the litigation and report to her. The Mennen Foundation had financed the study of the Napa River, to provide scientific ammunition for the courts and for the political arena; Carlene had helped Chris find the experts to do the ongoing research, part of a wider look at cumulative effects on the watershed, the objective being a long-term recovery plan to restore the river and the wild-land corridors. The fight was no longer about parks and open space, it was about conservation biology and sustainability — more important, harder to win.

Money was credibility, but it could also be destructive. The national assumption nowadays was that if you had a lot of money you had to build an in-your-face mansion and an in-nature's-face vineyard. Those building them didn't want to be told what to do, but they were telling everybody else what to do — accommodate my spectacle, my erosion, my water diversion, my herbicides and pesticides. Well, wine was a luxury, and an economy based on luxury shouldn't be allowed to destroy the landscape.

There was sufficient money in the valley to achieve anything, she knew. The Culinary Institute of America could actively promote local organic food and responsible farming, and the American Center for Wine, Food and the Arts celebrate and support the ecosystem in which it sat, but they had no plans to do so. Vintners, vineyard developers, and promoters of the Center would rather call Chris and people like her radical than look at the radical things they themselves were doing, such as building a tourist attraction in the middle of the floodplain and then diverting the river. They should be thinking about the Dust Bowl, not about Burgundy and Bordeaux. Public agencies shouldn't be assisting agriculture in destroying the hillsides with public money, something that was truly radical, and the supervisors should be protecting the rights of the people and not getting caught up in the idea that grapes are the one true cross.

The vintners couldn't see that maintaining the ecology of the river was important, or that other people were affected by their activities. If they'd take a hard look at this, Carlene thought, something could be worked out. Instead, the vintners were turning the valley into a feudal state.

It was time for democracy to reassert itself. She and Peter had decided on the litigation strategy as a way to refocus the argument. Assisting them was not just Lippe but also Bill Yeates, founder of the Mountain Lion Foundation and a recognized environmental attorney in Sacramento who had led a successful statewide initiative to protect the mountain lion. They had talked to representatives in Congress and with the folks at the Center for Conservation Biology in Oakland. They were ready. The Mennen Environmental Foundation was considering a future suit over water allotments in the county, one part of a years-long strategy. But first things first.

The Redwood chapter of the Sierra Club in Sonoma County had objected to their suing Napa County and the individual landowners. Since the Napa group of the Sierra Club was just one of several within the Redwood chapter, it was at least theoretically obligated to get approval. But the Sonomans didn't want the Napa suit brought because the bad publicity might hurt Sonoma's chances of passing a tough hillside ordinance of its own. A lawsuit in Napa might frighten the Sonoma County Board of Supervisors into enacting weak regulations that would not be subject to the California Environmental Quality Act, so Sonoma wouldn't be sued. This argument was ridiculous, in Carlene's view. The voters over there would demand a strong ordinance, she thought, just as they had in Napa, regardless of what went down in court.

The suit would show how serious the fight had become all over California, the Sonoma syndrome being replaced by the Napa syn-

drome. It was time for everybody to kick it up a notch, but environmentalists in Sonoma were jealous of the resources available to environmentalists east of the Mayacamas. The Napans' influence over
the regional environment rankled the Sonomans, just as the high
prices paid for Napa wine rankled Sonoma's vintners. The Redwood chapter resented the funding available in Napa, and the fact
that the Napa group would get even more attention.

Carlene thought some members of the Sierra Club in Sonoma
were too close to the industry. They had gotten the ear of the Sierra
Club's lawyers in San Francisco and were trying to kill the suit there.
The whole question of so-called radical action was complicated by
warring sentiments within the Sierra Club membership, some veterans demanding an end to logging in the national forests and others,
including the club's leaders, holding a more accommodating view of
the use of public lands. This difference of opinion had resulted in a
schism, the apostate group calling itself the John Muir Sierrans,
which included the legendary David Brower, a mountain climber
and veteran environmentalist. The leadership of the Sierra Club denounced the John Muir Sierrans as unruly and characterized their
movement as an illegal "fire in a trash can" rather than a serious attempt to get back to the club's roots.

At the same time, the leadership was tightening control over individual cadres and strongly discouraging activities at odds with official policy. In the middle of all this the little Napa group arrived
with a lawsuit and the money to pay for it, the target being a highly
celebrated and influential industry that ordinary people did not associate with environmental degradation. The lawsuit could easily
make the club sound radical, if not downright John Muir Sierran,
the opponents of the suit argued. The battle, after all, was over a relatively insignificant, glitzy piece of real estate where, as some Sierra
Clubbers said privately, "the resource is already lost."

The same people feared that actions like the Napa group's could
lessen support for the club, and for environmentalism in general, at a
crucial moment when a presidential campaign was under way and
there was a good chance of placing a true environmentalist, Al Gore,
the current vice president, in the White House. Gore was being
challenged by the Green Party candidate, Ralph Nader, and the Sierra Club grappled with a decision about which man to endorse. All
this demanded caution and restraint.

Carlene had not joined the Sierra Club until 1997. By then the Mennen Foundation had been in existence for a couple of years and she had had the opportunity to appraise several of the big environmental organizations. Some were good and some were death stars, absorbing contributions to pay big salaries and working against sound ecology and biological integrity. The Sierra Club was one of the good ones, she thought, but like all bureaucracies, it had to be watched.

Sizable donations had put her on the club's National Advisory Council, something those in the Redwood chapter didn't know about. Money enabled her, sitting at the barn-gate table on Sylvaner Avenue, under the elkhorn chandelier, to pick up the telephone, immediately reach a lawyer in the Mission District headquarters, and have a meaningful conversation. She then telephoned Bill Yeates in Sacramento and asked him to make the same call.

All summer Chris Malan videotaped activity on the Pahlmeyer Post-it. By the end of August the ground was bare and the last of the vines were going in, the heavy equipment shuttling back and forth, dust plumes rising. It was dry, dry as only the air can be when the wind blows from the desert.

According to existing regulations, all such work was supposed to stop by the first of September, but the work didn't stop. Chris gave the workers a little more time and then, over Labor Day weekend, decided to act. She knew the ropes well enough by now to get a response without having to go through the county planning department, and she called the sheriff. He went up and shut the operation down until the following Tuesday, when it could be reviewed by the appropriate authorities, but by then the story was in the press.

Jayson Pahlmeyer claimed to have obtained oral permission to continue working for a few days, until the grapes were finally planted, but the project stayed on hold. Most of the work was done, but once again his cowboys had run up hard against a deadline, prompting angry comparisons with the Viader vineyard of the decade before and setting the stage for what was to come.

Two weeks later, Tom Lippe drove up to Napa and walked into the courthouse, located between the county administrative building and the district attorney's office. There he filed suit on behalf of the Sierra Club against Napa County for failing to enforce the California Environmental Quality Act, and he filed suit against the three individual defendants for putting in their vineyards.

Two days after that became public knowledge, members of the Watershed Task Force received a letter informing them that the group was being reconvened. The timing was purely coincidental, but it didn't really matter: the spark had already been struck, the fat was in the fire.

III

DIVIDE AND FALL

20

I N THE SIXTIES Lee Stewart had said that Napa Valley could support perhaps half a dozen more wineries. He was known as the Stone, an accredited wise man of nascent winemaking, founder of Souverain Cellars before it became Burgess, long before the creation of Viader and all those other names on Howell Mountain. But within a dozen years there were eighty functioning wineries, and by 1985 close to two hundred. By the turn of the century the number was approaching three hundred, with no end in sight, and Lee Stewart had been demoted in the minds of the very few who still remembered him from the role of seer.

In 1999, Napa Valley contributed more than a billion dollars to the state's overall economy, another indication that something extraordinary had happened both to the perception of wine in America and to the nation's ability to create wealth. Wine made in the Napa Valley, sometimes from grapes and juice trucked in, provided paychecks, directly or indirectly, for thousands of residents, the combined value of which was about two hundred and fifty million dollars. That was a lot of money in historical terms, but relatively little in comparison to what was being made in tourism, wine sales, and real estate. As in the nation as a whole, the wealth of a relatively few grew exponentially compared to that of most Americans.

That same year, fifty-five houses in the valley sold for more than a million dollars each, many of them for several million dollars. In the first six months of 2000, forty more such houses changed hands. But other numbers told another story: the population of the county had increased by more than twelve percent in the last decade, to one hundred and twenty-four thousand citizens, and the vast majority of them resided in the cities of Napa and American Canyon, the hyper-thyroid housing development to the south that had incorporated.

Applications for new wineries and new hillside vineyards prolifer-ated, the challenges to them mounted, and some of the wealthiest and most successful vintners found themselves not just criticized but also fearful.

&

Jack Cakebread's English great-grandfather worked his way around Cape Horn in 1842 as a cabin boy and then labored in the California gold fields. He bought land and fathered thirteen children, nine of whom lived, and signed his curious name with an *X* until the day he died. He left each child a quarter section — one hundred and sixty acres — and his progeny spread thinly over the land in the American way until one of his grandsons was running a garage in Oakland in the middle of the twentieth century.

And that grandson's son washed auto parts in gasoline and swept out the garage from the time he was nine years old. His name was Jack, and by his junior year in high school he was taking the streetcar there after school and riding home with his father, who returned to the garage after supper.

Those were the Cakebreads: workers. They drove on weekends up to the family quarter section, but it was finally sold in 1958, when Jack was attending what he called "the University of General Mo-tors" and preparing to take over the family business. A decade later, Jack had nine mechanics at his command, working, working. Jack's interests were somewhat catholic, however, and included photogra-phy, which he made pay, like everything else.

A photo assignment took him to Napa Valley, and up in an air-plane, and he passed over a twenty-two-acre parcel between High-way 29 and the river that he liked and decided to buy. His mother knew the owner, and Jack purchased the parcel in 1973 for eight hundred dollars an acre, twenty-five hundred dollars down, for land that in two decades would be worth more than ten times that.

André Tchelistcheff, asked his advice by this brash young arrival in the valley and willing to give it for nothing, as Tchelistcheff often did, suggested planting merlot. But Robert Mondavi, also willingly, offered other advice: plant sauvignon blanc. Jack took Mondavi's advice. He also took advice from Louis Martini, Joe Heitz, John Wright, and Jack Davies — most of it good, all of it free. This was before the valley got so competitive and political, and soon Jack was filling bottles with the Cakebread name on them with sauvignon blanc, chardonnay, and cabernet sauvignon.

His name was more suggestive of baked goods than wine. Realizing that he now had to sell the bottles, he went to the library and read the restaurant reviews in Cleveland, which seemed as good a market as any. Then he called up the restaurant with the best review and made a reservation for the next Saturday. He caught the Friday-night redeye to Cleveland after work at the garage, got a special hourly rate at a hotel there so he could change into a tie, and went to look at the menu in the restaurant window. After determining that the dishes were expensive enough, Jack walked in with three bottles of Cakebread wine. The beverage manager tasted and liked the wines. Jack asked him for the name of the best distributor in town, and then he flew home to get the ball rolling by telephone.

Jack repeated the procedure in other cities — Chicago, Detroit, St. Louis, Dallas, New Orleans, Jacksonville. And when beverage managers and wine writers asked why he called his wine Cakebread, he would say, "Ask my great-grandfather."

By then he was running a winery and a garage and doing photography on the side, getting by on very little sleep while his wife, Dolores, got by on little more. If Jack couldn't be back home from a sales trip in time to take care of things at the garage, Dolores did it for him; when they were in Napa, she cooked big meals for a steady stream of family and guests. Then the Cakebreads moved up to the valley full time. Jack drove every morning from Oakville to Oakland, checking on the day's repairs and the parts orders, drove back to Oakville to make wine and have a civilized lunch, hauled back to Oakland to review the garage bills and drive all the cars and make sure the repairs were done right, and then drove home again. Oakville to Oakland and back, twice daily, for nineteen years.

Up at five, to bed at midnight, that was Jack. Ass-busting, flushed, funny, quick with a good story and as quick to anger, working harder and getting luckier. He sold the garage in 1989, when his wine business was belted into the valley's sidecar and riding the steep trajectory of rocket juice, sauvignon blanc, chardonnay, and relentless marketing toward the summit. His sons were involved by then in what was at times a contentious enterprise; before each winery board meeting there was a family meeting, and Jack brought along a basket of clothespins. Anyone could take a clothespin and hand it to another family member, indicating that a "pinch point" existed, a problem that needed talking out. If pinch points weren't talked out, they became "choke points" — that was Jack's theory.

Some people in the valley thought there weren't enough clothespins in the basket, that Italian conversations were as common among descendants of Englishmen as they were among Mondavis and Martinis, but the Cakebread enterprise marched on. Yet another Cakebread winery rose on the east side of Highway 29. More Cakebread wine flowed out; more money flowed in.

It was around the time of the winery definition fight in the late 1980s, Jack thought, that things got so political. He was unhappy with the drift of public opinion and thought the wineries were losing control of their destinies, along with the right to make and market wine as they saw fit. The winery definition, which limited the percentage of grapes allowed in wine bearing the Napa Valley appellation and limited activities at the new wineries, might have some good things in it, Jack told his friends, but mostly it was a wake-up call. The permit process was putting a burden on the county, and the environmentalists were "painting the wineries with a black brush," diminishing their influence in the community.

One of the problems, in Jack's opinion, was the Napa Valley Vintners Association. This, the original marketing and public relations effort, had been started by old man Martini, John Daniel, and a few others before the proliferation of advocacy groups that made the valley sound more like the Balkans than wine country. Since its founding, the NVVA had become large, heterogeneous, and, he thought, politically useless: trying to get two-hundred-plus wineries to unite behind their common interests was "like trying to herd cats." Mostly he disliked the fact that his influence there had waned.

A couple of years passed, the situation getting worse in his view, until at last he decided to do something about it: start his own organization. Its express purposes would be putting out the word about the wineries' needs and problems, influencing local elections, and having some effect in the larger political arena. He told people it would be a positive force, not reactionary but innovative.

There was little a few good men with plenty of resources couldn't do, he told those he wanted to join — not just money, but also secretaries, fax machines, lawyers, public relations people. Those few good men would not be obligated to share either their deliberations or their opinions with outsiders. Invitation only, closed door, a wine country version of Harry Truman's kitchen cabinet.

Consider the state of the valley, advise, bankroll, and wield a big stick, that would be the role of the new Winegrowers of Napa County — or some such name, "winegrowers" being an old-fashioned handle for vintners when vintners knew more about farming and grapes than they did about computers. The Winegrowers could meet at the Cakebread winery, Jack told Dolores, in the morning, before the day's business began, to set a new agenda, and she told Jack, "They won't come for sticky buns."

This was Napa Valley, where culinary distinction was required in all endeavors, and lack of it could doom an otherwise worthy cause. So Dolores made Egg Beaters with abalone and mushrooms, and Jack served the celebrated Cakebread sauvignon blanc — at seven o'clock in the morning.

"Jesus, Jack," said Michael Mondavi, the first time he walked into a meeting of the Winegrowers and was offered a glass.

Jack demanded, "Are you in the wine business or not?"

The Mondavis were, and so were Michael's first cousins from Charles Krug Winery. The "Mon-*day*-vis," as opposed to Robert's "Mon-*dah*-vis," also joined. Members of the Winegrowers could forget their individual differences in the face of common threats, and their ranks came to include, over the next few years, two dozen of the wealthiest, most influential men in the valley, and also those men who came to the meetings of what had come to be called the Breakfast Club to represent their bosses.

Among the members were the Barretts of Chateau Montelena, a winner of the famous Paris tasting of 1976 when their chardonnay was pitted against the most famous white Burgundies; specifically, Jim and his son, Bo, who was married to one of the valley's better known winemakers, Heidi Peterson Barrett. Her efforts had greatly benefited Dalla Valle, Grace, Screaming Eagle, and others, and whose father was Dick Peterson, once the winemaker at Beaulieu, another of the intertwined strands of family and opportunity.

Phelps Vineyards was another member, an important ingredient in any mix of tradition and money. Old Joe Phelps had been one of the first to put real prices on his Napa Valley wine — not California prices, Bordeaux and Burgundy prices. He had already made a fortune in construction — highways, rapid transit, buildings, dams — when he came to the valley and bought seven hundred acres off Taplin Lane, where a rough-hewn structure rose, reflective of forests and rugged individualism.

Justin Meyer, another Winegrower, owned Silver Oak, a notable example of the Napa Valley lightning strike. Ruddy, substantial Justin still ironed his own tuxedo shirts and played the guitar in the local Catholic church. He had studied under the Christian Brothers at old Mount La Salle monastery in the valley. Part of his local fame derived from stiffing Robert Parker when the soon-to-be-famous wine critic first came to Silver Oak and Justin refused to come down and meet him. Parker rated his wines nearly perfect anyway, and that had launched Silver Oak. Now when Justin's new vintages were simultaneously released at his wineries in Oakville and up in the Alexander Valley, they brought in more than a million dollars in a single day.

Bob Trinchero, much more affluent, had turned a mom-and-pop operation — *his* mom and pop — into the symbol of white zinfandel, his Sutter Home winery the Camelot of pink wine from red grapes. People had said the wine would never sell, but it did — in quantities beyond imagining. Trinchero's son was one of several wealthy up-valley residents who shared an enthusiasm for big Harley-Davidson motorcycles, resplendent "hogs" ridden together on clear California days.

John Trefethen was another member, who had inherited the old Eschol winery south of Yountville, designed by Hamden McIntyre, and extensive vineyardland on the north edge of the city of Napa that was immensely valuable. There were other lucky spermers in the Winegrowers: Clarke Swanson, frozen-food heir, and Donald Hess, the Swiss businessman, benefactor, and art collector. And there were the Disney lucky spermers, descendants of the famous Walt, who owned Silverado Vineyards, the winery recently expanded to accommodate crowds and tour buses. Walt's daughter, Diane, raised orchids in her Yountville hothouse while her interests were represented at the Winegrowers by Jack Stuart, the malamute-eyed winery president and also the current president of the Napa Valley Vintners Association.

Another lucky spermer, nursery magnate and racecar collector Gilliland Nickel, had grown up in Muskogee, Oklahoma, and inherited an enormously profitable nursery business that enabled him to move to California, collect Ferraris, maintain a yacht in Sausalito, and otherwise comport himself in a style considered lavish even by Napa Valley standards. Gil's Far Niente winery, once identical to Eschcol/Trefethen's except that it was made mostly of stone, had been renovated to make it appear more fanciful, the long, beautiful roofline shaved and angled eaves added in an architectural arabesque referred to jocularly by staff as a *slonge,* bogus French for "slouch." The trim had been painted turquoise.

One of the most influential of the Winegrowers was Dennis Groth, who went on to become president of the Wine Institute in San Francisco and a member of the Watershed Task Force. As a certified public accountant and former chief financial officer for Atari, he was pulled strongly in the direction of venture capital and the survival of the entrepreneur. Some of his fortune had gone into the big pink mission-style winery on Oakville Cross Road that bore his name.

Bill Harlan, developer and vintner, belonged to the Winegrowers, as did a vineyard manager named Tucker Catlin, who represented a group of investors calling themselves Juliana Vineyards and seeking to develop a large chunk of Pope Valley. Beringer and Franciscan, both of which had big expansions planned to further capitalize on tourism, belonged to the group, as did Cardinale, the latest acquisition of Jess Jackson, the San Francisco attorney turned wine magnate, and a few others.

The Winegrowers, a.k.a. the Breakfast Club, became an institution, at least among its members, and by the fall of 1999 many of them did not attend meetings but instead sent surrogates. Michael Mondavi's was his vice president for public affairs, Herb Schmidt, wearer of the disarming smile and loafers soft as bedroom slippers. Herb was known for keeping two lists, of people he trusted and of people he didn't trust, and was a common sight in Sacramento, Palm Desert, and Washington, D.C.

One person not invited to join was Garen Staglin. In addition to being in a fight with Jack Cakebread, Staglin was a Democrat. He represented, as Jack described it, "Napa burnout. A guy's been trying to hit financial home runs for so long he can't quit, and he comes to Napa to do things differently, and buys land and starts a winery, but not to make a living. He feels entitled to some enjoyment, but then ego takes over. He wants more of whatever he has. What happens when he gets tired of the place and decides to sell out? He prices it too high for a grower to buy. If the wine market goes to hell, and no one else will pay his price, no telling what will happen." What Jack didn't say was that, more likely than not, a member of the Winegrowers would buy Staglin's winery.

Their executive director was a pro-development supervisor who had retired from the board, Fred Negri, and their official adviser a smart young attorney in the law firm of Dickenson, Peatman & Fogarty named Richard Mendelson, an aficionado of wine, an artist who worked in metal, and the brains behind many a decision by Napa Valley vintners. Many Winegrowers and other aspiring vintners yearned for nothing more than for Mendelson to tell them, "I understand."

Exchanges had been frank. "Spit it out," Jack had said, and they still did. The issue of greatest concern now was environmental regulation. The Winegrowers all said repeatedly that they were the true environmentalists, their vineyards proof of this. Their critics were chronic complainers, they added, and worse: radicals out to torpedo the industry, talking about alcohol farming and alcohol factories, running to the courts.

The Winegrowers needed to get the facts out, they felt. They were intimately involved with the land, and their profits not just shared by the community but essential to its well-being. All vintners had to develop better "communications" and flex some legal muscle because the industry was being blamed for things that couldn't be scientifically proven, like a muddy river. "What about runoff from the streets of Calistoga, St. Helena, and Yountville?" someone would ask, and when the question of the ever-falling water table arose, "What about all those holes being dug by weekenders?"

The Winegrowers thought they had neutralized some "troublemakers" in the industry, most notably Volker Eisele. The former UC Berkeley sociologist had been essential in the transformation of the

Farm Bureau from a mere advocate of economic advantage for farmers into what the Winegrowers considered an activist cell of demanding greens. Eisele had been defeated in the Farm Bureau board election, in part because of manipulations behind the scenes by the Winegrowers, while he was visiting relatives in Germany. But there was a bigger threat now. Truly radical enviros from outside the industry had dropped a bomb: the Sierra Club lawsuit.

Filed against the county for failing to enforce its own environmental regulations, the suit had caught many people by surprise. There had been talk of it, but few thought the plaintiffs had the courage to do something so divisive. The emotional effect on the men gathered around the big table in the Pond Room, behind the Cakebread winery, was profound. Unaccustomed to criticism, suddenly they were being condemned by the spiritual heirs of John Muir, and the legitimacy of their way of life was being questioned, and some of them were too angry to discuss this rationally.

They blamed the county for getting them into such a mess, for not shielding the valley from CEQA when the hillside ordinance was first written, for not vowing now to fight the Sierra Club suit to the death — money, countersuits, whatever it took. They discussed having Napa Valley exempted from the California Environmental Quality Act through a state legislative end run, resolving all this with a legal *deus ex machina,* their attorneys and lobbyists descending on a platform of legal brilliance and connections to save them from "Malan/Mennen."

This new phrase for the collective demon was uttered with alliterative disgust, some members wanting to go after them and their lawyers — "carpetbaggers" — who operated out of San Francisco and Sacramento and made their livings suing respectable people — businessmen! — who happened to violate some obscure environmental regulation while engaging in the basic American right to make a profit.

Jack denounced Malan/Mennen as humanoid equivalents of the glassy-winged sharpshooter, the vine-sucking wasp that transmitted a bacteria threatening the vineyards with destruction. Chris Malan was, in Jack's opinion, the worst, either neurotic or craving of attention, a "pot-stirrer" who put men like him on the defensive when they should be on the offensive.

The reaction of members of the Breakfast Club to the mention of

Chris approached the apoplectic. "You never know when she'll bite you on the ankle," someone would say. Her presence on the Watershed Task Force was seen as a travesty that would prevent additional planting in the valley. Many of those vineyards already in existence — like Groth's, Silverado's, and virtually everybody else's in the Winegrowers — would have to be pulled back from streambanks at great cost unless the industry got a grip on the problem, meaning the environmentalists.

There were other culprits. A few of what Jack called "rogues" — Delia Viader, Jayson Pahlmeyer, Dave Abreu, others — had brought the wrath of the uninformed public down onto the head of every vintner. The county should have been tougher on those people in the first place, although many of those sitting in the Pond Room had opposed all restrictions on hillside development when the hillside ordinance was first discussed.

One way to get a grip, they agreed, was through the upcoming supervisorial election. Kathryn Winter, the incumbent, was running, and she could be beaten if her opponent, a political unknown named Bill Dodd, got sufficient support — that is, money. Several Winegrowers had contributed to Kathryn's campaign in the past, despite her closeness with Volker Eisele and other environmentalists. Kathryn had supported a moratorium on new houses in the hills and suggested that she might someday vote for a moratorium on vineyards. She had voted to limit water allotments. She was principled, and these things might in ordinary times be ignored in the interest of continuity. The devil you know is better than the devil you don't. But these were not ordinary times, as everyone agreed.

When Kathryn Winter asked to be allowed to appear before the Breakfast Club, most of the members were impressed that she would dare come. Bob Trinchero had already held a fundraiser for Bill Dodd, and all those men sharing scrambled eggs and sauvignon blanc had spoken with increasing uneasiness of Kathryn's candidacy.

21

S HE HAD A pageboy cut and big brown eyes and she wore business suits, sometimes with pearls. The third woman ever elected to the Napa County Board of Supervisors, she was well aware of the fates of the two who had preceded her. Her most recent predecessor had taken a slow-growth stance at a time when the wine industry felt itself under attack, and had been dumped by a coalition of city businessmen and up-valley vintners demanding less restraint on development, less regulation of winemaking with cheap out-of-county grapes, and fewer obstacles to capitalizing on tourism.

In both cases, the women's male successors had proven embarrassments to those who got them elected, but that was little comfort to the women. Kathryn didn't intend to share their fate. She had a record of responsible votes on land-use and housing issues and had tried to balance the demands of proponents and opponents of growth. The Sierra Club suit had complicated her reelection, the specter of the California Environmental Quality Act threatening the conduct of business and politics in the valley and frightening vintners who were largely ignorant of the law. Some were very angry.

As far as Kathryn could tell, that included every member of the Winegrowers of Napa Valley, Jack Cakebread's conservative, deep-pocketed Breakfast Club. The tendency among its members was to lump all environmentalists together as part of a conspiracy against wine, when in fact there were myriad differences among environmentalists that became more pronounced each day. Kathryn asked to meet with the Winegrowers with the intention of requesting contributions for her campaign, despite the fact that some members were demonizing her. One had gone so far as to call her "the Chris Malan of the board of supervisors."

This was a silly allegation, but it revealed the deep polarization of the valley. The Winegrowers had already scheduled a fundraiser for her opponent, Bill Dodd, and Kathryn hoped the men would give something to her campaign as well, as they had in the past. Balance was more important now than ever.

She called Jack and told him she would like to come to the Pond Room and discuss the race. Jack said fine, but that he wanted to raise "some other issues," without stipulating what those were. She had already consulted with him on the Staglin matter, that long-running battle painful to Jack in part because he and his old friend Robert Mondavi were at odds over the Staglin winery. Jack had taken Kathryn up to his house to show her how close the structure would be to him, but she had remained noncommittal since the winery permit was then still under consideration.

Jack Cakebread was a man of contradictions, she thought. He could seem vulnerable at times, insufferable at others. He made a point of mentioning Volker Eisele, and Jack had gloated. In the tangle of recent political alliances the Winegrowers had become tacit allies of Farmers for Napa Valley, Stu Smith's property rights advocates and the recognized heavy in the worsening fight over regulation and resources. Farmers for Napa Valley was willing to do the dirty work in the ongoing struggle for control of the broadly based, environmentally minded Farm Bureau, while the Winegrowers sat back in anonymity and wrote checks.

One particularly strident voice in the fight was the innocuous-sounding *Jack Neal & Son Vineyard News,* published by the biggest vineyard development company in the valley and edited by a towheaded young man named Mark van Gorder, a friend of Stu Smith's and, in Kathryn's opinion, a propagandist. Van Gorder had portrayed her as an enemy of agriculture. She had kept van Gorder's stories and faxes stored in her garage because, she thought, they revealed a systematic, unprincipled attack on her that had turned especially nasty in June over the issue of a moratorium on hillside development. The idea had come up often as a way of allaying public distaste until a new, better law could be devised. But many in the community of wine hated the idea.

When an item had appeared on the supervisors' agenda — "Discussion and possible direction to staff to prepare an urgency interim ordinance imposing a moratorium on hillside development in Napa County" — a blizzard of faxes had resulted. A marathon hearing on "monster" homes and "houses on steroids," as their opponents called them, was also attended by many people connected in one way or another with developers, and had to be moved to the city council chamber. There, environmentalists and ordinary citizens pleaded with the board for an end to ridgetop residence building, and Kathryn and Mel Varrelman voted for a moratorium on just such structures, but the third vote they needed for a majority, Mike Rippey's, was denied them. This was because, Kathryn thought, Rippey and Varrelman disliked each other, and that had left her holding the bag with Mel.

The vineyards remained the biggest push. She and Mel later went up to look at the reservoir on Howell Mountain that served almost two thousand people, many of them Seventh-day Adventists. Kathryn thought the silt flowing from new vineyards appalling. The supervisors discussed this problem as well, but an emergency measure was not voted on, in part because it would not have passed. Kathryn said publicly that the issue ought to be taken up by the Watershed Task Force, left it at that, and was later surprised to read in *Jack Neal & Son Vineyard News:* "THE NAPA COUNTY BOARD OF SUPERVISORS HAS ENTERTAINED THE IDEA OF A MORATORIUM ON 'HILLSIDE DEVELOPMENT' THREE TIMES! . . . Supervisors Kathryn Winter, Mel Varrelman and Brad Wagenknecht each voted in support of a hillside moratorium . . ."

But she had voted against houses, not vineyards, a fact hidden in the tirade. It continued: "The BOS recently passed a new Groundwater Ordinance that threatens to take away water rights from farmers. They have spent $100,000 on Phase I of the Watershed Task Force and are spending another $100,000 on Phase II . . . to create a Viewshed ordinance that may regulate farming structures on our County hillsides . . . WHAT DO YOU EXPECT WILL HAPPEN IF THE INCUMBENT SUPERVISORS ARE RE-ELECTED FOR ANOTHER FOUR YEARS?"

The implication was that Kathryn was set on destroying agriculture. No reasonable person would credit such drivel, she thought, but the facts were troubling. Van Gorder and Stu Smith were the principal actors in Farmers for Napa Valley, along with Tucker

Catlin, who was also a member of Cakebread's Breakfast Club. In Kathryn's opinion this was a furtive alliance of rednecks and gentry dedicated to undermining not just the Farm Bureau board but also the task force, the board of supervisors, and all regulation of development in the valley.

The old, fruitful connection between environmentalists and farmers was being severed, and Kathryn knew she was the only person who could put it back together.

She had been to the Pond Room before, when the board of supervisors held a retreat there and paid for the privilege. Jack had played the gracious host, managing, as only he could, to be both charming and hostile. The old structure had once served as the center of his operation, before success transformed the Cakebread fortunes, and was now a sentimental reminder of leaner times, a kind of Lincolnesque cabin in the vineyard testifying to the wisdom of working harder to get luckier.

This time Kathryn arrived at the Pond Room at eight-thirty in the morning. The primary election lay several months in the future; there was time to turn things around with these guys. She needed some support from this recognized bastion of male influence, but she wouldn't pander. They were all Republicans, exercised in a momentous year of national and local elections — 2000, the year of Bush/ Gore — and Kathryn was a Democrat as well as a woman. But she intended to tell them what she thought and to trust that their good judgment would prevail over inflamed rhetoric and reaction to change.

She found the Breakfast Club seated around the big table. It had been spread with a white cloth and set off by a vase of yellow daffodils. She recognized John Trefethen, Bill Harlan, Justin Meyer, Dennis Groth, and some other proprietors. Herb Schmidt was there for the Mondavis, Tucker Catlin for Juliana Vineyards, and representatives from Beringer, Phelps, and Far Niente. Silverware lay on the table but the food had already been consumed, and some members were still drinking sauvignon blanc.

Kathryn was offered a cup of coffee and a chair with its back to the window, with jokes made about "the hot seat." She offered a frank appraisal of the environmental problems splitting the county, figuring she owed it to them, that she had nothing to lose. She had already been out campaigning in the Fourth District, asking for votes, and had repeatedly heard people say that development in the hills had gone too far, that something had to be done. She told the men this, and that she was eager to help them address the issues troubling voters and to solve the problems facing the wineries.

Someone said, of those in her district critical of vintners, "Those are just malcontents."

No, she said, opposition came from people not involved in politics and not particularly knowledgeable or opinionated about vineyards, just ordinary citizens who didn't like what they saw and what they read about in the newspapers.

There was a pause. Kathryn looked around at these flushed middle-aged faces, and then there was a rush of denunciations of restrictions, people who advocated restrictions, those who didn't actively oppose restrictions. Groth, recently picked to head the Wine Institute, for which Kathryn's father had once worked, seemed to her openly hostile, as did Justin Meyer, owner of Silver Oak. He was livid as he gripped his wine glass. Bill Harlan said nothing, but glared at her. Shaken, Kathryn wondered what their problem was. Her votes on the board hadn't been much different from those of the other supervisors; the unpopularity of hillside development had been obvious to everyone for a decade, and the Environmental Protection Agency had declared San Pablo Bay and the Napa River impaired. The old hillside ordinance was only partially successful; clearly something more had to be done to fend off the feds and to calm voters' fears. But this observation further angered her hosts.

The question of setbacks was quickly raised — the pulling back of replanted vineyards from edges of the river and streams to allow natural vegetation to grow. Setbacks had become shorthand for limiting profits and were totally unacceptable to this group if setbacks applied to replanted vineyards. Kathryn explained that she couldn't take an official position on setbacks because the matter was still being discussed by the Watershed Task Force, and final recommendations wouldn't be made until the new round of meetings was complete. She expected setbacks to eventually be proven necessary — as did everyone else, including the opponents — but she didn't say that.

Mention of the task force was met with sarcasm. These men viewed it as a theater for environmental bellyaching. It seemed to

Kathryn that they wanted her to oppose setbacks now, regardless of what the ongoing scientific investigation revealed, and that their concerns had little to do with political reality. A real backlash existed against the wineries, as everybody in county government knew, and sooner or later they would have to address it.

John Trefethen raised the possibility of lifting limitations on winery activities, so they could make more money from tourists. "Can we reopen part of the winery definition?" he asked.

Surprised, Kathryn said, "But you're all grandfathered."

They were already allowed to sell things and to conduct commercial activities that more recently built wineries weren't allowed to do, since most of the Winegrowers had been in business longer than their competitors. They were already entitled. But Harlan said pointedly, "*I'm* not."

"If you try to reopen the winery definition in this political climate," Kathryn told them all, "you'll tear the county apart."

Trefethen, she thought, was contemptuous of this idea. He, Clarke Swanson, and the other heirs seemed to Kathryn fatuously unaware of the fact that they had been handed most of what they enjoyed in life and yet wished to avoid all protections for the valley. Self-made strivers like Harlan and Bob Trinchero were no different. "Scratch them," she thought to herself, "and you'll find naked self-interest." Their willingness to scrap the rules, after so many people sacrificed so much to create the agriculture preserve and to maintain some of the natural landscape, made her angry. If everyone had behaved like this over the years, interested only in short-term gain, the valley as they knew it would not exist.

There was something else going on; she struggled to figure out what. These men were accustomed to getting what they wanted, that was clear. They were determined to find a way around environmental regulations, but there was more: they hated all restrictions placed upon them by county, state, and nation, apparently on philosophical grounds and also because these laws gave people without their means some influence. No matter what, they weren't going to be told what to do by a bunch of what they considered to be radicals, or by a female Democrat who had supported the winery definition. They wanted the moon, she decided, and they wanted someone to blame for their difficulties.

She said only, "The planning department couldn't handle a re-opening of the winery definition right now, not with all the applications for new vineyards and the Sierra Club suit."

The collective blood pressure rose again at the mention of the Sierra Club. "We want to make sure the county fights this with all it has," said Jack. There was no doubt in her mind that it meant a lot to him. This was another issue Kathryn couldn't discuss, already knowing as she did that the county was vulnerable to the Sierra Club's charges. She had sat in closed session with the other supervisors and the county counsel and heard the merits of the case, but she couldn't legally say so. But she could say, believing it, "Chris Malan's a kamikaze."

Catlin said, "Well, we're not going down in the plane with her."

The men all laughed bitterly, and Kathryn saw the problem at last: these men all considered themselves victims, deprived of the credit they alone deserved for the valley's success. It was incredible, objectively speaking, but apparently true. Carefully, she suggested that they tell their story more effectively. She was then told that they and other members of the Napa Valley Vintners Association intended to take care of their collective troubles through a massive public relations campaign and more aggressive "marketing," a solution that struck her as ludicrous. They were blinded by their fear of change, she thought, and projecting their anger onto her. She saw that they would attempt to knock her off, just as they and men like them had knocked off women supervisors in the past, with money and an inexperienced, pliant good-old-boy candidate plucked from the ranks of commerce.

She thought they would turn the valley into a circus while publicly touting their achievements, if they could. It was cynical and destructive of the quality of life. So Kathryn took a deep breath and said, "You have a perception problem. People are concerned about destruction of habitat in the hills, and you have to take some responsibility for it. You can't just talk about it, you have to *do* something."

22

PEOPLE ASKED Chris Malan what effect the Sierra Club lawsuit would have on the Watershed Task Force. Wouldn't it
override any recommendations the task force might come up
with, and thereby short-circuit the process of making better law?

She argued that there were two distinct issues involved: the lawsuit, which was about environmental law, and the task force, which
was about land use. Eventually, she said, one would complement the
other. County officials were unofficially telling anyone seeking an
erosion control permit for a new vineyard that approval would be
difficult to obtain before the suit was resolved. So in this way Chris
had managed to shut down hillside vineyard development, accom-
plishing at a stroke what she thought the supervisors should have
done a long time ago.

She told her critics, and they were legion, that if a moratorium
had been put into effect earlier, to last only until scientific studies of
the river could be completed, none of this would have happened.
But the supervisors wouldn't act.

When a clear problem exists, she pointed out, elected officials are
supposed to stop activities, whatever they are, until informed decisions can be made. A dirty river and reservoirs full of silt are clear in-
dications of a problem, but such a rational step as delaying development until the answers could be found was not feasible in this, the
most profitable of wine countries.

The Mennen Environmental Foundation's strategy was more far-
reaching than those outside its tight circle of strategists could imagine. Chris didn't talk about this for the obvious reason that surprise
was a crucial part of success. The strategy included more lawsuits —

possibly requiring a cumulative impact study, requiring setbacks from streams and the river, challenging water allotments — and proposing an initiative on hillside development. So many fenders, so little time. While these possibilities were researched and weighed, the anger directed at Chris from the outside was palpable.

Her enemies on the task force demanded that she resign. When she refused, they took the demand to the county counsel, who said she couldn't legally be removed. Stu Smith, Dennis Groth, and the others were stuck with Chris Malan and her belted raincoat, her carryalls full of documents, her steely but still pretty smile. And the Sierra Club lawsuit continued.

The individual defendants — Jayson Pahlmeyer et al. — were in their turn suing the county, claiming the permits they had been issued were illegal because they hadn't been subjected to the California Environmental Quality Act. Therefore, they argued, the county should pay any and all damages, a highly ironic situation, since the county and the developers had been cohorts. Now they were adversaries.

Pahlmeyer and the others were eager to settle with the Sierra Club. Their lawyers were saying, in effect, "Tell us how much money you want, and let our clients get back to work." Tom Lippe wanted to take the money and move on to the next stage — suing the county for failing to do an environmental impact study, say — but Chris told him, "Hold on." She and the Mennens had another idea.

The defendants were using what was known as the laches defense, implying an unfair seizure of assets. Their claim was that they would suffer undue financial loss from the suit because of work already under way, and that land graded and ready for planting when the suit was filed was theoretically exempt from CEQA. All right, thought Chris. But not those areas where they were just beginning to work, where they were still removing trees and vegetation and making roads. Forty-three of Pahlmeyer's acres were involved in this stage, and smaller plots belonging to Potelle and Stotesbury, all pieces of larger developments. So she said to Lippe and to the Mennens, "Let's go up and see how much work they've actually done."

Lippe argued in court that a laches defense allowed his client, the Sierra Club — but in reality, Chris — to go in and inspect the properties in question, to measure slope and get soil samples and other information to see how much work had really been completed, to see if there was an additional threat to the environment. What Tom Lippe didn't say was that such access to the properties might provide evidence to be used in future lawsuits over the type and degree of development there. The defendants objected to the Sierra Club traipsing all over their land, but the judge overruled them, and soon Chris, a scientist, and other people were up there poking around and measuring and photographing, driving their adversaries wild.

Settlement talks between the county and the Sierra Club were not easy. In essence, the county was waiting to be told what Chris and Lippe — and by extension the Sierra Club — wanted, and had the impression that the plaintiffs didn't really know. They apparently had no exit strategy. The Sierra Club could at that point have demanded almost anything, and gotten it. But then Chris would no longer have the issue, and the public might lose interest, and so the suit would proceed.

The Napa County counsel said that if the lawsuit made it all the way to court, and the Sierra Club won, the county might simply rewrite the hillside ordinance, making it weaker. They would make it so weak that CEQA wouldn't even apply. This would effectively break the state's environmental club, and the county would be free to regulate, or not, in the hills.

Chris and Tom Lippe went out into the hall, and the attorney asked her if the county would actually do that, and she said, "Yes." If the wrong people gained control of the board of supervisors, the board could tell the county counsel to change the ordinance, making it ministerial rather than discretionary. This bureaucratic sleight of hand would permit a rubber stamping of erosion control permits, and then they wouldn't be subject to CEQA. All this discussion of runoff and tough standards would be rendered moot.

Nothing was resolved that day, but Chris walked out of the settlement talks determined to run for the office of supervisor herself. She had seen her opportunity: put the hillsides on the table in a big way, because the other candidates weren't talking about them.

The damage up there was pervasive, and the county's continuing boom assured even more destruction. She would charge the supervisors with taking cover behind the Watershed Task Force, and that included Kathryn Winter. Chris expected her to back some Band-Aid approach when the task force finished its deliberations the following summer; the county would announce that its "experts" had determined what was needed, and dissenters would have to eat their objections. Well, Chris wasn't eating anything. And she wasn't waiting, either.

The primary election was only a few months off, but first there were some people she wanted to consult. One was Peter Mennen. He and Carlene had become a major force in Chris's life; after years of struggling, penniless, for causes she believed in, against people whose motives she considered bad and whose financing was limitless, she had suddenly found money — money! — for monitoring, for scientific studies, for lawsuits, and maybe more. It was a wonderful, heady feeling, and she didn't think it would end. With confidence she telephoned Peter and told him she wanted to run for Kathryn's seat, adding, "If you have a problem with that, please let me know."

He said, "Let *us* know if we can help."

The other person Chris called was Parry Mead. The Mead ranch, just up Atlas Peak Road from the Malan property, provided an example of the alternative to full-scale development. It was there, around the forty-five-acre vineyard set in the middle of thirteen hundred acres of remote, rugged, often precipitous country, that Chris and Parry often walked and talked. They were close friends, two women in their forties, mothers active in causes that often took them far from home. As fellow members of the Watershed Task Force, they had resisted pressure to acquiesce in the demands for more latitude in developing vineyards, for "progress," but their styles were very different.

So were their pasts. Parry considered herself a moderate and thought her history as an activist showed this. She and her father, Giles, sat on the board of their own foundation, which was dedicated to environmental causes. But it did not operate in the manner of the Mennen Foundation, and its goals were different. Giles Mead lived in the original stone ranch house built at the turn of the century, Parry in a modern house nearby, next to one of the old barns. The vineyard provided income to run the ranch. The Meads had placed an easement on the property through the Land Trust of Napa County to prevent it from ever being developed, and they had donated a million dollars to the Land Trust to continue its work. The Mead Foundation funded a variety of projects around the country that either directly effected good land use or broadened knowledge of it. Although the Meads didn't sue, they put their money where their mouths were, as Parry liked to say.

For years, in the mornings, she and Chris had walked and hashed out what they saw as a likely future for the valley. They held differing views, however, and agreed never to let this or their divergent politics affect their friendship.

The possibility of the Sierra Club lawsuit, long before it was filed, had been a topic of discussion. Pressure had to be exerted on the county to bring about change, they had agreed, but legal action should be held in abeyance until it was clear that the task force was unable to bring about change. But by the end of the first phase, Parry had realized more had to be done. She and Giles had met with the Mennens, their lawyer, and Chris at a restaurant in Calistoga, to discuss the pros and cons of going to court, and the Meads, father and daughter, decided not to take part in the suit.

But Parry hoped to moderate reaction to it. As a member of the task force, she could point out that blame should not be assigned just to the wine industry but should be shared by the developers and by the cities — by everybody, in fact. What was happening to the hills and the river was a community responsibility. Parry wanted rules laid down for everybody to observe, but she also wanted a reconciliation among vineyardists, environmentalists, and conservationists.

Chris's actions sometimes got in the way of what she and Parry wanted to accomplish. The Mead Foundation paid to have a scientist come down from Oregon to study the river and its tributaries and report to the county and to the task force. His name was Charley Dewberry, and he had been well received. Then Chris had employed him to conduct a separate study for the Mennens, under the auspices of Friends of the Napa River. Predictably, Stu Smith and Dennis Groth claimed Dewberry was tainted and shouldn't be heeded in his prescriptions for the river's recovery. Parry had publicly defended the scientist, but the men on the task force drove the issue into the ground. After that meeting, Parry went to Chris and said, "This is awful, we lost credibility," but Chris didn't seem to care.

She was so passionate, Parry thought. And Chris's focus was so tight. What resulted from such fervor was often tunnel vision. They talked about this, too, but Chris was fired up, agitated by the exchange with Stu and the others, and Parry realized there was no point in continuing.

They walked, forty-five minutes of brainstorming and scheming. One morning the subject of the board of supervisors arose, and Chris said, "Things are getting hot. I don't want to make you mad, but I'm considering running for the board."

"Great," said Parry, then realized which seat Chris was talking about — Kathryn's. "Why run against her? We already have our position well represented in this district." And Kathryn was a friend.

"It's very nice of you to defend her," said Chris.

Parry pointed out that she was also defending the work they had all done over the years that could be jeopardized by splitting the environmental vote. But Chris said only that she appreciated Parry's general endorsement of the idea of her running. She didn't seem to hear the other part.

"You're losing sight of the objective," Parry told her gently. "You've brought the county to its knees. This would put everything at risk."

Later, Parry called her repeatedly, from the ranch, from New Mexico, trying to persuade Chris not to run. But her friend was a runaway freight train, caught up in the idea of single-handedly taking control of the county's future. They walked and talked some more but, Parry felt, to no avail.

Not long after the meeting in Jack Cakebread's Pond Room, Kathryn Winter received a telephone call from a friend in Napa. This friend informed her that a woman was going around Kathryn's district saying she was running for supervisor and talking about "saving the hillsides."

Kathryn made some calls and learned that the woman was Chris Malan. She couldn't believe it. Why would Chris undertake anything so reckless? She telephoned Chris and asked if she was running, and Chris said yes, just to keep the hillside issue before the public. Kathryn asked her to come to her condo off the Silverado Trail so they could discuss the matter, thinking there was still time to get a handle on this.

A fourth-generation San Franciscan, Kathryn had grown up in the Central Valley and witnessed the destruction of farmland there and near Chico, where she had taught school for a time. She deplored what had transpired around Stanford University, with the proliferation of the computer companies, and didn't want something similar to happen to Napa Valley.

Her voting as a supervisor indicated this, but she was an environmentalist with a small *e*. She had carefully distanced herself from the more radical elements of the movement, and her refusal to appoint Chris to the Watershed Task Force had proven this. The decision irked Chris, but it was done in good faith because Kathryn wanted the task force, an experiment in civic cooperation, to work. Chris's presence was always polarizing.

Although Kathryn had supported the moratorium on new steroid houses in the hills, she had refused to oppose all vineyard development up there. She had joined with others in condemning the Sierra Club lawsuit as divisive and potentially damaging. There was so much at stake, not the least of which was Kathryn's job, and Chris had to be made to understand this.

She didn't show up for the meeting. Kathryn was scheduled to go door-to-door canvassing with a local supporter at lunchtime, and had to cancel. That was a squandering of valuable support, but she figured the meeting with Chris was more important.

The longer Kathryn waited, the angrier she got. Finally Chris arrived, three hours late, having been up in an airplane, leaning out the window taking more photographs of hillside destruction. All over the valley now, whenever people heard or saw a helicopter, they said, "There's Chris Malan," and often it was. Cold, tired, in a foul mood, Chris told Kathryn, without preliminaries, "I'm running against Bill Dodd, not against you."

Kathryn pointed out that Chris would in fact be running against both of them. Doing so, she would split the environmental vote and perhaps siphon off enough of it to force the election into a runoff. Possibly — unthinkably — she could throw the whole thing to the Chamber of Commerce candidate at the outset. Kathryn assured her that, after the election, she would sit down with her and work out a plan for the watershed, if only Chris would reconsider.

But Chris didn't seem to be listening. She said she wouldn't run if Kathryn signed a piece of literature calling for tough new regula-

tions for the hillsides, and if she put together a meeting with the big
vintners and brought Chris along to talk to them about the problems. Kathryn said she would think about it, knowing that such a
meeting would be a fiasco, that it would lose votes, not gain them.

Chris seemed to her intransigent, dogmatic, either misunder-
standing the consequences of what she was doing or indifferent to
them. Kathryn had been carrying water for the environmentalists for
years. Now, when she needed them, Chris was threatening to turn
the election into a personal vendetta against her and everyone who
had, at one time or another in the past, dismissed her or simply not
gone along with some aspect of Chris's agenda. Kathryn thought
this was the result of several things: Chris's exposure in the media,
the strong reaction to the Sierra Club lawsuit by everybody from the
county counsel to the Napa Valley Vintners Association, the heady
rush of power, and Chris's access to Mennen money.

Chris's ultimate goal, Kathryn now believed, was not a moratorium on new hillside development but an end to all agriculture in
the hills, period. That, or nothing. Win, or take the ship down in a
blaze of self-destructive glory.

Everyone was calling, telling Chris not to run. This included even
her friends in the Sierra Club. She told them, "Dodd won't win."

She had talked to him, she added. Dodd didn't know diddly about
the hillsides. "Who will be in the runoff?" Chris then asked, and answered her own question. "Kathryn and Dodd, that's who." And
then Chris would work for Kathryn during the runoff campaign;
she would keep the hillside issue before the public, going door-to-
door, as she was doing now, saying, "Let's talk, people."

In the end, Kathryn would be reelected because voters hated development in the hills. No one would be able to deny why Kathryn
had been reelected — the hills! — least of all Kathryn Winter.

Volker Eisele called and argued with Chris. She could well get
Kathryn defeated, he told her, which would be a major environmental disaster. When she disagreed, Volker shouted at her. She didn't
know what she was doing, he said; her motives were murky. Chris
hung up thinking Volker was too close to agriculture.

She got a call from Ginny Simms, a fellow member of Friends of the Napa River with whom Chris had worked on other projects. They were both totally committed, and they met and talked for two hours. Ginny was a walking database who worked on elections all the time, but she admitted that she didn't know a lot about the watershed. She vowed to work for it anyway if Chris would just reconsider. "Don't run against Kathryn," she pleaded.

"Kathryn won't do what's needed," Chris told her. Kathryn would have to agree to walk door-to-door with Chris, handing out the signed literature denouncing hillside vineyards, before Chris would consider withdrawing her name. Ginny said she would talk to Kathryn about this possibility. "I'll get back to you on that," she added, but she never did.

23

JEFF REDDING saw, as if in a dream, an end to life as he knew it. The impetus for that dream was the Sierra Club lawsuit. His waking life, already complicated, had become stressful by any standard applied to county planners, land-use planning being the profession he had been trained for at the University of Southern California and had pursued in freewheeling Santa Cruz before coming to Napa. Almost overnight, following the announcement of the lawsuit, applications for vineyards had doubled, people fearing that if their projects weren't approved immediately and soon begun, they never would be.

Redding had to deal with all their conflicting demands that applications be approved, or rejected, that standards of erosion control be raised, or lowered, that the Sierra Club lawsuit be treated as a regulatory fait accompli, or ignored, that new planners be hired and those remaining reorganized and made more efficient, that the board of supervisors be prepared for the unpredictable future, that he, Jeff Redding, alone, push the Watershed Task Force in a direction the wine industry could live with, or that moderate environmentalists wanted, or that the radical greens would not sue over — again. And that he provide a framework for a moratorium on new houses in the hills and an environmental impact report for the county, when he had no time to spend with his wife and children, when . . .

When it got too bad, he drove down to Vallejo. There, in a big room where Korean devotees of the martial arts gathered — people without vineyards or steroid houses — gripping sword and dagger, ponytail flying, Jeff performed intensely physical moves that left him drenched in sweat and obliterated, if only for the moment, all the tensions tearing at the referee in a land-use war in this, the prime crucible of high-end American real estate.

He had moved to Napa in 1987, after Jim Hickey hired him. Jeff felt that this new county had a lot in common with Santa Cruz. It was a tourist destination with much community involvement and an interest in affordable housing and resource protection. He could advance his career in Napa and at the same time advance the causes of open space and agriculture.

Environmental planning and resource management had figured prominently in his studies, but the big picture for Redding was the relationship between man and the world around him, an interest shared by Hickey, the big, white-haired county planner then spending a lot of time in front of the board of supervisors and the planning commission. The supervisors had agreed that Hickey needed help. Later, the supervisors took Jeff to lunch, without his boss, and both Jeff and Hickey realized they were looking for a replacement for Hickey. Hickey had always believed that part of his job was telling elected officials what he thought, regardless of the political implications, but the board elected in 1988 had tipped away from resource protection, toward development, and some of its members resented the fact that Hickey had publicly asked the big question, "What is a winery?" That had started the whole winery definition battle, allowing in more regulation.

Jeff got Jim Hickey's job. The lesson there was that politicians have no respect for expertise or good works if these go against their interests. Now Redding was in a similar situation, the butt of conflicting demands, lightning rod for a department overwhelmed by work, burgeoning scientific data, and demands for increased enforcement of regulations. And now there was this lawsuit.

A marked shift in community values had occurred in the last two years, he thought. The valley was awash in dollars, the stock market was booming, interest rates were low. An unprecedented amount of cash was going into development. The hillside ordinance had reduced erosion somewhat, but not enough for most Napans. Wildlife habitat, including that for fish, and tree preservation had also surfaced as real considerations for the public, ignored at the peril of politicians and those working for the county. The Sierra Club suit indicated how far some members of that public were willing to go. At the same time, the constituents with the most money — the vintners — resented and opposed the shift in community values, blaming it on newcomers and city dwellers.

First you're part of the solution, Hickey used to say, then you're part of the problem. Lately people viewed Jeff as part of the problem. A new supervisorial election loomed, and if the board tipped again, as it had a decade earlier, Jeff might find himself in Hickey's predicament. Not only might the supervisors stop asking his advice, they might stop paying him.

Yet he was doing his job to the best of his — and, he firmly believed, to the best of anybody's — ability. It was Jeff who had gotten the Watershed Task Force on track after the board authorized it, the county having already tried the bottom-up approach to solving the problem. On hillside development, they had brought the stakeholders together and used the planning department's expertise to come up with a hillside ordinance, only to discover, as Jeff often said, that the public didn't like the result. What he didn't say was that the county neglected to vigorously enforce its own regulations, another problem entirely.

The county had decided to involve the public from the beginning, form a task force, hire a mediator, and resolve this hillside thing out in the open. They were on their way, Jeff had thought, and then along came the Sierra Club suit. Not only did it upset the apple cart, it also gave people wildly different expectations of how it might be resolved. While lawyers for the club, the county, and the individual defendants jockeyed for position, consensus and flexibility on the basic issues went out the window. Jeff wondered if the Sierra Club intended to bring about this confusion.

He had asked of the club's representatives, "I know what your position is, but what's your interest?" The answer was equivocal, and that lack of clarity was producing anxiety on all levels. Everyone knew implicitly that new vineyard development in the hills was unofficially on hold, but the planning department's proposed guidelines for new hillside residences had also been delayed. This was potentially harmful because single-family homes were a greater threat to the valley than anything else, including hillside vineyards. Most people didn't realize that there were still six thousand legal parcels in the hills waiting to have houses built on them, and that there were few rules about what could be built.

Jeff often asked people on both sides of the argument, "Do we see ourselves as Sausalito?" Invariably, people said no, but the same thing could happen in Napa Valley, houses everywhere, if the citizens weren't careful.

The wine industry had some culpability in the present mess, he thought, by not getting their message out. They spent more on marketing wine in New York than on explaining themselves in Napa Valley. For instance, Jeff's own children couldn't understand why there was agricultural land right here, just an hour from San Francisco, when everywhere else the land was paved over.

The population would double by the year 2020, the cities growing fastest, surrounded by fragile ag lands. The quality of the valley's product was very good, but that wasn't enough to automatically assure the survival of agriculture. The building of homes also meant building in opposition to agriculture; it was axiomatic.

"If we're ag," Jeff often said, "let's make sure we set agricultural standards and then let people farm. Don't choose the future by default. Stop thinking as individualists within the community rather than as *part* of the community. Don't let Chris Malan and Peter Mennen define the argument" — and in the process make Jeff Redding's life miserable.

His father, an economist working for the Foreign Service, had always kept a résumé out there, in case a better opportunity came along or a job proved intolerable. Keeping a résumé out there had suddenly become a Redding family tradition.

Jayson Pahlmeyer's answering machine informed callers: "This is Jayson. Please leave a message while I uncork a powerful Pahlmeyer merlot."

His travel schedule brimmed with wine promoting events, his bank account with the proceeds, his large presence — slicked-back hair, new Dickensian eyeglasses — with confidence, but increasingly he found himself talking penance. He was no longer just a fine wine producer and owner of a capital-inhaling new vineyard, he was the object of a lawsuit by one of the most powerful environmental organizations on the planet, one started by a saint of nature lovers, John Muir, who had attempted to prevent the construction of the Hetch Hetchy Dam in the Sierras and the despoiling of Yosemite and other pristine places. The club had hundreds of thousands of dues-paying members, and he imagined that they were all mad at Jayson Pahlmeyer.

The lawsuit had effectively shut down all new agricultural projects in the hills and brought new condemnation of Jayson, but also some grudging sympathy: some vintners had decided that their enemies' enemy was their friend. "I planted what was already a cow pasture," Jayson repeatedly told them on the telephone, at Vintners Association meetings, at Mustard's, "and what's lost in all this is that *I didn't cause any damage!*"

If his story was made into a movie, he thought, it would go like this: Cult vintner brings secret grape clones to the United States and makes a notable success. He raises money and tells a cowboy to put in a primo rocket-juice vineyard, pronto, at any cost, and is then attacked by eco-zealots. The ending of the film was as yet unclear. Perfectly clear was monoculture-as-villain, along with "alcohol factories," miracle-grow aristocrats with recently buried pasts in microchips, condo developments and other, less salubrious means of fortune accumulation, and other businessmen, no longer envisioned as daring entrepreneurs but as exploiters and elitists.

Jayson had been at home the day he heard about the suit. The papers were served at the Pahlmeyer Vineyards office down in Napa, in the revamped industrial section overlooking the Napa River, and his partner, Michael Haas, had telephoned him with the news. Jayson had felt his stomach drop. This was the crowning blow, after all the previous bad publicity, and he saw the future unfolding, as he had been trained to do as a lawyer, with many possible outcomes of the lawsuit, few of them entirely beneficial and none pleasant.

What really scared the vintners were the words "moratorium" and "radical setbacks." The suit would add fuel to those fears. A legal end to planting in the hills, to clearing and planting within a few hundred feet of streams, would mean suffering serious opportunity and capital losses and the personal effrontery of the have-nots.

Another hated word was "restoration." Returning vineyardland to wildlife habitat sounded less than draconian to the average American, but not to vintners who were outraged by the lawsuit. Their shared pain gave Jayson some comfort. Wines like his were still the driving consideration among present and aspiring vintners, cult labels contributing to the symbiotic relationship among wine, second and third homes, upscale tourism, art collecting, heavy-duty land-scaping, and all the elements of the boom that danced bellybutton to bellybutton in the valley, grinding out lucre. In such an environment even slow-growth advocates and old-time responsible farmers were tempted to forget the rules. That was human nature, but the rules were before the public now.

Jayson had to finish his million-dollar project on the ridge, so close to completion he could taste it. One day it would include a three-level, gravity-flow winery, and maybe a chateau that Chris Malan would have to look at every morning on her way down to Napa. But settling the lawsuit would mean reapplying for an erosion control permit, paying legal costs of the Sierra Club and the county — unless his suit against the county for damages proved success-ful — and contributing thousands of dollars to some environmental organization stipulated by the plaintiffs.

That was the most galling suggestion of all those made by the Si-erra Club lawyer. Jayson told anyone calling to ask about the lawsuit, "It's known as extortion," as he sipped a Pahlmeyer red in one of his blue leather chairs. "There were eighty other vintners like me with hillside projects. Malan and the Sierra Club could have gone after all of them, but they didn't. Maybe that would have caused too much dissension. Frankly, I don't know why they picked me. It's a mystery. I'm the one that got caught in the crosshairs. I feel like a wildebeest singled out from the herd."

If he reapplied for a permit to finish his vineyard, "Chris will stand up in front of the board of supervisors and say I shouldn't get it without an environmental review . . . She's been able to marshal in-credible power as a private citizen. And once they get CEQA, she'll have her private pulpit. She can take any vineyard granted a permit right back to court."

This fear was making its way beyond the mountainous confines of Napa Valley to the halls of the capitol in Sacramento. It raised red flags from Mendocino to Santa Barbara and threatened to do on a large scale what the Sierra Club had failed to do locally: rally envi-ronmentalists. Chris Malan was quoted as saying, "California's in for the fight of our time," and Jayson felt that the words were directed at him. The boy from Oakland who made a wine to drop you . . . Eve-rybody had heard that phrase by now. But his marketing image was being overshadowed by that of the cult wine producer who let the eco-zealots into Eden.

At the other end of the valley, Stu Smith wore rubber boots and a rough canvas jacket in the cold of a winter morning. He gazed down at his little winery in the swale, next to the olive trees, before the day's work began. When he and his first wife, Susan, had come to the valley, they had lived in a trailer, without water, and bathed in the Napa River when someone invited them to dinner. The marriage had failed, and now Stu's new wife, Julie Ann, was pregnant. In middle age, the Old Testament–visaged Stu found himself faced with the prospect of being father to an infant again, in uncertain times.

The spectacular beauty of a new day on Spring Mountain, full of light and smells of the earth, was complicated by the knowledge that Stu couldn't do with that earth exactly what he pleased. He still didn't have a use permit from the county to add more vineyard on the far side of his property, a couple of acres that was visible from where he stood on the grassy knoll, leveled for hosting barbecues and greened over by the rains. And he wasn't going to get a use permit any time soon. The so-called Napa County Department of Conservation, Development and Planning, Jeff Redding's bailiwick, had been cowed, he thought, first by the fear of objections from citizens, and second by the Sierra Club lawsuit.

Stu had hoped to have the land graded the following summer and vines in the ground, not possible now. The fact that the slope would just sit there supporting grass and a few conifers really chapped him. What did the ability of Chris Malan and the Sierra Club to stick their noses into other people's projects have to do with agriculture? He refused to accept the possibility that these involved the public interest. No one would address, straight on, his concerns in this factional democracy, not the county, not the Vintners Association, not the Farm Bureau, and he said aloud, into the morning, "It's just *farming.*"

But it was farming in a very delicate place, just one reason that environmentalism had become what Stu called "the Zeitgeist of the twenty-first century. Reasonable people won't stand up and say that what the environmentalists are doing is wrong." He ignored the fact that many reasonable people agreed with the environmentalists' objectives, and he argued that if this kept up for another ten years, the environmental movement brooking no compromise, taking no prisoners, it would be dead, a victim of its own methods.

His opposition to government control had been shaped by experiences in the valley from the beginning. To clear his land in the seventies, he'd had to hire a forester and develop a timber harvest plan, as required by law. He remembered the first Douglas fir that fell, the feelings of sadness at the visual destruction, the elation inherent in the heady smell of fresh-cut wood. He had been reminded of this by a line in Francis Ford Coppola's *Apocalypse Now*, "I love the smell of napalm in the morning," not an association most people would have made.

A month into the project, the county had tried to shut him down with a moratorium on timber cutting. Stu had thrown the inspector off his land, pointing out that timber was regulated by the state, not the county, the last time he would have absolute legal right on his side. Someone from the Upper Napa Valley Associates, the old environmental group, now defunct, had called and accused Stu of tourist development. Stu had called Jack Davies for advice, and Jack had sagely asked who was representing Stu, only twenty-two years old and not aware that he might need a lawyer. Jack hadn't been helpful, but he'd been gracious.

People who had known Stu for a long time thought he had stopped distinguishing between Malan/Mennen and the broader coalition of environmentalists. Even those on its fringe, people concerned enough to speak out in favor of some minor form of regulation, were condemned by Stu: "Tits on a boar." It was time for commitment, he said repeatedly. You were either on the right side of the argument or hopelessly out of it. He often cited Neville Chamberlain, the man who failed to recognize the threat represented by Adolf Hitler, as the avatar of the appeaser now being emulated in Napa Valley, waffling on important issues, particularly property rights.

A woman who had known Stu for years had said, "He's turned into a crank." He was aware that such things were being said, but he had never been good at taking direction. He was defensive above all about his land, his only real, appreciating asset, and determined that those he opposed would take him seriously. He was also aware that some of them were afraid of him.

A registered Republican, Stu despised the party's current makeup, which he considered racist and intolerant. He was disgusted by the impeachment proceedings in the Republican Congress against President Bill Clinton, a naked exercise of the abuse of power by the bigoted, Anglo-Saxon old guard, he thought. They salivated so heavily over the prospect of destroying the president for sexual misdeeds that the American people caught on and condemned the politicians more than the sex.

Real Republicans were, in Stu's view, more Lincolnian. They believed in responsible ownership of land, in Adam Smith's laissez faire, free and open debate. What Abraham Lincoln might have thought of Farmers for Napa Valley and its tacit alliance with the Breakfast Club was not discussed.

He felt that the Sierra Club lawsuit had been a slap in the face of the people, the county, the politicians, and the Watershed Task Force. It had thrown everything into chaos, proving how divisive environmentalists had become. The county might be able to control the wine industry, but it couldn't control Malan/Mennen, and now everything required an erosion control plan. Even replacing existing vineyards was affected by the de facto moratorium brought on by a couple of people with no connection to agriculture, in a county that already had the most progressive hillside ordinance in California. If the wine business failed as a result of all this, nothing would prevent the valley from becoming a bedroom community.

Anyone would prefer trees to vineyards, he recognized, but vineyards were a hell of a lot better than concrete. The environmentalists should be coming to growers, saying, "Thank you, but maybe you could do some things a little differently," and offering their help and support. Instead, they portrayed growers as the Evil Empire and equated vineyards with development. Many of Stu's associates in the loose coalition of Farmers for Napa Valley *were* developers, or represented developers, but Stu insisted that this didn't affect the basic justness of the cause.

The inviolability of private property, the right of a landowner to do with his land what he wished, was threatened by what he called radical environmentalists and their fellow travelers in the bureaucracy. His friend Mark van Gorder, in the employ of the biggest vineyard management company in the valley and the editor of the *Vineyard News,* spoke of "the People's Republic of Napa where you're supposed to maintain the land for others' benefit." That about summed things up as far as Farmers for Napa Valley was concerned.

The umbrella of property rights also covered members of the Winegrowers, Jack Cakebread's Breakfast Club. The big boys had all moved into the hills — Beringer, Cakebread, Trefethen, Hess, Duckhorn — but they weren't talking about it. They and others like them needed Stu and Mark to take decisive political positions the Winegrowers were afraid to espouse publicly. And the umbrella covered new arrivals in the valley who understood nothing about the land or farming, turning those tasks over to experts who often agreed with Stu.

It was a bitter irony that he didn't respect his wealthy allies and couldn't stand some of them; he felt like the American Civil Liberties Union defending skinhead neo-Nazis. But in troubled times you overlook minor distinctions; your enemy's enemy is your friend.

24

THE RAINS CAME in January and sometimes fell for whole days. Wet vines blanketed the valley, the few knobby, old-fashioned head-pruned stumps left resembling dwarfs strung hand-to-hand across the earth, vastly outnumbered by spindly young canes in replanted vineyards and the strong contenders in productive middle age that draped the trellises, waiting for spring.

Viewed from a moving car, the interlinking vines formed an organic matrix, spinning out alleyways and cordons in dizzying geometric combinations. To some viewers this was an orderly inspiration, to others an endless array of bars and wire binding the landscape.

On clear days the air was crisp and clean. New mustard in the fields and vineyards glowed a vibrant yellow, and the hillsides looked lush in the sun, the steeper slopes a subtle green suggesting that all was well below the earth's turning, slowly evolving surface.

The county resting upon it, despite its legal difficulties, was prosperous as never before, a bright reflection of the nation to which it belonged, flush with the years of ascending value in real estate, stocks, and almost every talent and commodity of an enduring and seemingly invulnerable democracy. Relatively few people suspected that this would dramatically change within this new year; no one foresaw the disaster that was to follow.

Guy Kay drove down to Napa from St. Helena as he had done regularly for more than a year now, to attend another session of the Watershed Task Force. He had been making similar trips for almost thirty years, participating in group discussions, committee meetings, legislative sessions, all manner of information-swapping endeavors aimed at preserving both Napa Valley and its agriculture. He would never have said so, but many people considered Guy one of the few members of the task force, if not the only member, with no political objective other than this, and no ulterior motives.

A retiree, he wore the white sneakers, chinos, and sleeveless sweater of the officially leisured, but his duties seemed as relentless as ever. He had studied forestry in college, then botany. He had spent a great deal of his life looking at birds while his profession had changed plumage a number of times: microbiologist in a chocolate factory owned by Nestlé, the Swiss conglomerate, manager of another Nestlé factory producing freeze-dried coffee, supervisor of bottling in a large winery — Beringer — after it was acquired by Nestlé and before it was sold to Texas investors.

Now, in addition to consulting for Beringer and leading a life of reasonable contentment, Guy performed in the interest of what he thought of generally as "habitat." A member of the task force, he told people he hoped the group "could come up with something helpful for the hillsides." It was more complicated than that, of course; rewriting the conservation ordinance was an incredible opportunity. All the issues were concentrated in it, and public agencies fascinated by the potential. Stewardship programs in Napa County had already scored some successes — Huichica, Sulphur, Garnet, and Dry creeks. If the valley could pull off the cleansing of its own river and keep the federal agencies from issuing mandates somewhere down the line, it would be viewed all over the United States as a signal success and at home as an extension of the sentiment that had produced the ag preserve back in the sixties.

Guy had a dream of the perfect hillside ordinance. It would be site specific, since the two sides of the valley were so different, the hills to the east volcanic and those to the west sedimentary: two different worlds with different subsets of potential problems. There would be a tiered system to address them, at once protecting the watershed, renewing the river, and recognizing the rights of owners of existing vineyards. It would allow for some development, meet the various legalities, reassure property owners, and satisfy the environmentalists.

He described himself politically as "a little left of center on the environment." Eventually he would have to say publicly what he thought of the whole scheme to improve wildlife habitat, but not quite yet. For more than a year he had been waiting for information on the establishment of wildlife corridors, those broad, natural avenues that enabled wildlife to move freely in the hills. This was a sensitive issue, as were setbacks, removing vineyards from fragile stream- and riverbanks so they wouldn't erode. The vintners had to realize that some compromises had to come, and it would be better if they did the right thing through persuasion rather than regulation.

That was the idea, and the opportunity was within grasp, Guy thought. It would be a shame to squander this chance. The task force represented the whole spectrum of opinion in Napa Valley, ranging from give-it-back-to-the-Indians on the one side to let-us-do-anything-and-you'll-love-it on the other. The county was under the watchful eye of the U.S. government, because of the state of the Napa River, and everybody wanted to do something about this, some for pure environmental reasons, some to forestall federal regulation. But Stu Smith and Chris Malan had clashed, waging the battle of the letters in the newspapers, and then the Sierra Club lawsuit hit and everything was up in the air.

Guy was convinced that the suit was a terrible mistake, even from the perspective of the more extreme environmentalists. The county already had a conservation ordinance. It needed improving, and this could be accomplished through science and paid for by the county. The Sierra Club, by asserting that the current ordinance wasn't being properly enforced, would get better enforcement of the same old, flawed rules. At the same time, it put in jeopardy two good supervisors, Kathryn Winter and Mike Rippey, and brought out of the woodwork opponents of all restraints on development.

He was already suspicious of the Sierra Club. The national office had endorsed the idea of allowing mountain bikes into wilderness areas because the bikes were popular with young people interested in the outdoors. Guy thought the Sierra Club did it just to expand membership, when the leadership knew that bikes were wilderness shrinkers and did a lot of damage. He had written to the club three times protesting this, and three times received a form letter and a package of promotional material. Guy's allegiance then went to the Wilderness Society.

He considered Chris Malan naive, unaware that politics is the art of the possible, not the ideal. The case of Charley Dewberry, the Oregonian student of rivers, was a case in point. Dewberry — bald,

thick spectacles, an engaging manner, unpretentious — had made
his presentation to the task force, talking about the health of streams
beginning at the ridgelines and explaining how macroinvertebrates
— the critters under rocks — produce food for fish. Much of the
science the task force had to absorb was numbingly detailed, and
those presenting it — soils experts, biologists, hydrologists, botanists
— accustomed to the rigors of academic and governmental posi-
tion-taking.

Dewberry was different: lucid, compelling in every argument,
from the importance of leaving woody debris in the river as nurseries for fish and microorganisms to the inescapability that everything
in a watershed comes down to the river eventually. Then Friends of
the Napa River hired Dewberry to do a study establishing baseline
information about tributaries and the river's main stem from which
recommendations could be made about what should be done to
improve things. But the grant for the study was paid for by Peter
Mennen, and this was used to compromise Dewberry. Wearing
scuba gear, he discovered a great many more organisms in the river
than anyone had thought possible, and although some would argue
that this revealed the river's basic health, most would see it as evidence of a vital, fragile, important source of life. Nevertheless, the
scientist was cast by Stu, Dennis, and others as an advocate rather
than a scientist because of the source of his funding. Dewberry
wasn't for sale to anyone, but critics of change used the incident to
discredit his work and further delay the process.

The aftereffects of a flawed political decision like Chris's to run
for Kathryn's seat could last for decades. Back in the time of the winery definition, the Napa Valley Vintners Association had helped
knock off a good county supervisor who happened to be a woman
and as a result suffered a public relations disaster. The new city at the
bottom of the valley, American Canyon, had been incorporated, and
now there was no stopping its expansion. The board of supervisors
had swung leftward in the next election, after the Vintners lost both
credibility and influence, but by then the damage was already done.
The Vintners withdrew from the public arena, creating a vacuum
filled by Jack Cakebread's Winegrowers. Now a small group of
wealthy middle-aged men who thought they should have what they
wanted because they controlled most of the acreage in the valley
gathered over breakfast to manipulate the political discussion.

To them, the idea of restraint was an insult. They were attempting to unseat an honest, dedicated supervisor — Kathryn Winter — and rejoicing in Chris's decision to enter the race because it greatly improved their candidate's chance of success.

The big room in the Gasser Building contained a long center table and a blackboard (white, actually) set up by the facilitators. Strips of paper had been taped to the windows to afford some privacy. There was an ice chest just inside the door, full of bottled water, and extra chairs set out for spectators.

Stu Smith sat with his Starbucks cup, still wearing his anorak. He leaned back in his chair, beard on chest, and made a droll comment about the theatricality of Guy Kay's broad-brimmed canvas hat. Taking it off, Guy said, "I have to keep my thinking machine warm."

The planning director, Jeff Redding, sat at the head of the table, ponytail down his back, smiling and on edge. Important environmental decisions rode on the outcome of these proceedings, and maybe Redding's job.

Nearby sat Hugh Davies in a wrinkled green pullover, squinting through his ovoid wire-rimmed glasses at the day's agenda. Increasingly Hugh reminded Guy of Jack Davies — the same attention to detail, the same passion, a touch of his father's restraint.

Other task force members straggled in: Dennis Groth, a member of Cakebread's Breakfast Club, outwardly easygoing and inwardly attuned as only a certified public accountant can be; Parry Mead, of Atlas Peak Road, a student of art and a principal in her own family's environmental foundation. This twosome, Groth and Mead, had very different interests and perspectives, yet they got along.

The same could be said for most of the fourteen or fifteen people who spread their winter coats on the backs of chairs and arrayed their papers, steeling themselves for tedium and possibly some unpleasantness. As yet there was no sign of Chris Malan.

In the spectators' section Guy recognized the woman from the Audubon Society, dedicated advocate of wildlife, and the wiry, white-haired figure in a lumberjack shirt, a piece of string tied to the stems of his glasses. This self-described "river rat" and Sierra Club member, Jim Hench, was a retired electrical engineer who had helped set up the first oceangoing computerized sonar system in the sixties, one of many interesting people who had shown up in the valley over the years.

Guy Kay knew everybody in the room, and much of their history. Where else in the United States could one find such a diverse group of knowledgeable people committed to effecting ecological change? Many places, he suspected, but here the issue had taken on special significance because of the federal government's interest in the river and the fame of Napa Valley. Many people felt that the entire nation was watching.

The meeting was brought to order by the chief facilitator, an outsider with a toothbrush mustache and a tie bearing the images of fish. He drove into the valley once a month to conduct these meetings and had proven himself a paragon of patience. Now he announced that yet another task force would be formed in the spring, after phase two of the current one, to weigh technical questions related to sedimentation in the river; it would be called the TMDL Study Group, the acronym referring to "total maximum daily load," a technical term from the federal Clean Water Act and a mantra repeated in every discussion of land use nowadays, reflecting how far the discussion had progressed. Of particular concern were the pathogens, nutrients, and sediments in the river that had caused the EPA to list the bay it fed as impaired.

Environmental concern had waxed and waned in the county over the years, and now was in sharp ascendancy. Guy had become involved in the 1970s in the discussion of riparian versus appropriated rights. He had been on the side of maintaining corridors along waterways when not many people thought about such things, but after the winery definition fight, environmental considerations got more serious. The big vintners wanted to maximize the dollars, as he often put it, but democracy worked only when the people at the top restrained themselves and agreed to forgo some commercial opportunity for the common good. And there was no evidence of such restraint in either the county or the country.

Guy had earlier sat on the planning commission, where his actions reflected this view, to the displeasure of his bosses at Beringer. He told them at the time that it was in their interest to have him on the board, whether or not they and the parent company, Nestlé, agreed with him, that someone from the company should be publicly involved. "What I do on the commission has nothing to do with my duties here," he had said.

The task force had accomplished much, the facilitator was reminding the members. A watershed information center would be established, and the dissemination of information done by disinterested third parties, not those with a financial interest in the outcome. Stake-holders would be replaced by "data-holders" in the information center.

A discussion followed about who these data-holders might be. "I'd be more comfortable with a nonprofit doing it," said Parry Mead, as opposed to a quasi-official agency that might not be immune from political pressure. But just then Chris Malan entered, wearing a trench coat and carrying a big floppy bag full of campaign literature. She smiled and grimaced at the fact that she was forty-five minutes late, and took the empty chair next to Stu Smith. He glanced at her, expressionless, and the subject shifted to the river.

A scientist had been brought in to discuss hydrology and river morphology. His plaid shirt, Levi's, and stubble were casual even by California standards, his easel blooming with charts, and he filled the air with geomorphic terms — "weathered rocks," "soft sedimentaries," "shallow volcanics" — and with riverine ones — "channeling," "entrenchment." The overarching question was the likelihood of erosion and whether or not it could be prevented. The answer tended to be lost in the details, but the overall impression was that it could.

After a while Chris said, "It's clear this whole setup is for ameliorating differing views of what the problem is and what in fact constitutes relevant science."

The unfazed scientist went on to discuss runoff on the west side of the valley, more prone to eroding than the east side. He uncovered a bar graph indicating that ripping the soil improved absorption of rainwater, and showed slides of erosion control featuring black plastic pipes and catchment basins for holding runoff. "Leaving natural vegetation downstream is very effective," he said, and was listing other possibilities when Chris announced, "This is a whitewash . . . They're trying to show that some areas are more prone to erosion than others, so they can eliminate whole areas as being in danger."

Guy was losing patience with her, as was most everyone else

in the room — including, on occasion, her allies — but no one showed it. Exasperation was an indication of weakness. They had heard all this before, been through the arguments in slightly different form, and they knew that real agreement was not possible. Guy asked the task force facilitator when they were going to get to the discussion of wildlife corridors.

Not until the next session, Guy was told. "We're heading toward some answers," added the facilitator. "Please bear with us."

"How many more meetings are going to be taken up with these presentations?" asked Chris.

She wanted to get on with making recommendations for a new ordinance, but nothing could be rushed here. And then politics came forcefully into the discussion as Stu raised his hand and said that someone he knew in the valley had called the national headquarters of the Sierra Club, to ask questions relating to the club's activities in Napa, "and he was referred to Chris Malan. I thought no one here was supposed to be an official spokesperson for the litigant."

"You can't be a litigant and a negotiator at the same time," said Dennis Groth, and stared at Chris.

"I'm not the Sierra Club's official spokesperson," she answered pleasantly.

The facilitator suggested that the person spoken to in San Francisco might have made a mistake, and Richard Niemann, a member of the Napa group, said, "Yes, it must have been a communications breakdown."

Guy Kay reminded himself of the bright side of all this. The county had come under pressure because of an impaired river and had responded, instead of sticking its head in the sand. But the extreme environmentalists weren't easy to work with. They could well win their legal battle against the county, he thought, and lose the war.

Dennis Groth decided to be a hard-ass. When it came time to vote on the final recommendations of the task force, he was not going to pretend that everyone agreed and that consensus prevailed, or that the objectives of the opposition were acceptable. Meanwhile, he would bring like-minded people on the task force together at his winery, to decide what had to be done to counter Malan and her allies. Stu Smith was key to any action that would effectively block the greens, more passionate about the issues even than Dennis and willing to stand behind his arguments and take the heat.

People who knew Dennis already considered him the iron fist in the velvet glove, a sharp contrast to both Stu's bare-knuckled defense of property rights and Jack Cakebread's quick verbal provocations. When Dennis raised his hand in task force meetings, his palm was invariably turned inward, a deceptively fey gesture; other members knew that his remarks would be astute and unequivocally in favor of the economic elements in any argument. Dennis had disputed with Chris, Parry Mead, Richard Niemann, and others over the number of planted acres in the county, water quality, wild species, and what was acceptable science. Underlying it all was an ideological resistance to all regulation and a belief in the hallowed right of free enterprise and capital accumulation that befitted a successful CPA.

The year before, when the environmentalists on the task force issued their joint memo calling for protection of native vegetation and new rules for existing vineyards, Dennis had sent a note to Bob Steinhauer, Beringer's representative on the Winegrowers and a Watershed Task Force alternate. "Bob," Dennis wrote, "the vintners need to get upset over the direction this group wants to take. These recommendations would stop *all* vineyard development." There was no balance, he added, "between the economy and nature. It is time for us to get active and maybe even get a little unreasonable ourselves."

After the Sierra Club lawsuit was announced, Dennis wrote a letter to the supervisors, the planning director, and other officials describing Chris as "a shrill voice" and the real one behind the lawsuit. "If she will not resign, the Board of Supervisors should demand her resignation."

When this did not occur, Dennis threatened to resign in protest, "in a highly public way," but changed his mind because, if he resigned, he would be gone and Chris would still be there. So he would stay on as a hard-ass, demanding cost-benefit analyses and, like Stu Smith, solid data proving assertions about water quality and agricultural effects on soil and species. All this would take time, and if it turned into a biologist's full-employment act, at public expense, so be it.

After the task force meeting, Dennis went back to his big pink stucco winery on the Oakville Cross Road. People might call it Taco Bell, but in fact it was mission architecture. He went up the broad front steps and past heavy doors into the cool, arching interior. He nodded to the clerk at the retail counter and mounted the stairs to the left that led to the business department. His second-floor office overlooked the back courtyard and the littoral of Conn Creek beyond, with vineyards spread all around on the flats, proof that superior cabernet came readily from the valley floor. But much of his vineyards bordered the creek, which was a tributary of the Napa River. All vineyards had to be replanted periodically, and the hillside controversy, in raising questions about erosion, had brought the question of so-called replants to the fore. Now there was a hue and cry for moving all vineyards as much as three hundred feet from streambanks, which would mean a major hit on revenue.

His computer was on, the geometric screen saver mutating every few seconds to provide a different aspect of what resembled a luminous, futuristic city. A few entries on his calculator told exactly how big that revenue hit would be for Groth Vineyards and Winery. Setbacks of a couple hundred feet on six or seven acres that produced between three and four tons of grapes per acre translated into a loss of about twenty tons of fruit. Since there were sixty-four cases of wine in a ton, that meant nearly thirteen hundred cases of wine that would not be made and sold, or a loss of a million dollars a year.

Dennis had once explained this to Chris Malan and a scientist from the Regional Water Quality Control Board. They had looked at Dennis as if to say, So what? "If it needs to be done," Chris had said, "it needs to be done," and Dennis had felt the hair stand up on the back of his neck.

That had been the moment of truth, the realization that they would never understand his position and he would never accept theirs. Yes, hard-ass was the only attitude now. He and the others were through making concessions and taking chances. When Kathryn Winter asked him for a campaign donation, he laughed in her face.

That she had showed up at a Winegrowers breakfast at all surprised some members, and got her some credit, but then she had read them a letter from a constituent on Soda Canyon Road complaining of the loss of open space and asking how this had happened. After Kathryn had left, the men agreed that if the guy who had written the letter wanted to control his environment, he should have bought it, and that the board of supervisors should have written back to him explaining how a free society works.

Now Kathryn and Chris were opponents in the supervisors' race, an unexpected turn of events and a stroke of luck almost too good to believe, assuring at the very least a runoff between Kathryn and Bill Dodd later in the fall and possibly handing the office to a proponent of development and economic expansion. Malan's announcement had overjoyed the Winegrowers and others in their camp, although no one said so publicly.

The biggest remaining problem, Dennis thought, was not Kathryn Winter or even Chris Malan; it was Peter Mennen. Seemingly harmless at the time of the winery definition fight, when he stood up at public meetings and said he didn't hear frogs anymore in Napa Valley, that vineyard development had eradicated them, Mennen had since inherited a lot of money. He wrote letters to the editor calling wine "flavored alcohol" and a fine cabernet "a bottle of arrogance," sentiments that Dennis thought would discredit him, but they hadn't.

Peter Mennen no longer seemed harmless to Dennis Groth. He seemed dangerous.

25

PERCHED ON MY SHOULDER as I write this letter, like a small but powerful conscience, is a little parrot known to the world as 'Ricki Lake.' He lives at the St. Helena post office, and under his watchful eye we humans here go about our curious business. Several times each day Ricki becomes restless and announces with increasing urgency his longing to fly. He waits impatiently while I walk around shutting down the overhead fans, then he's off, circling above the workroom floor and darting among the lights and other hanging paraphernalia with amazing speed and agility. And as he makes his rounds, he calls out over and over to his flock.

"But, of course, there is no flock . . . I hope you will reflect not only on Ricki's plight, but on a problem just as serious that is taking place, not in distant jungles, but very close to home. I ask you to think about our own small piece of the Ark here in Napa County . . . And it is not starving indigents struggling for survival that are destroying our forested hills and driving our tapestry of natural beauty to extinction.

"It is the minions of extraordinarily wealthy individuals and corporations who are . . . extirpating the diversity and ruining the livability of this treasure called Napa Valley most of us love. The next time you read or hear some polished pitchman for the wine industry tell you to feel good about the violence being done to our hillsides because they are preserving 'open space,' go stare at a blank wall . . .

"I absolutely refuse to accept the destruction of everything I find beautiful here . . . just so we can offer the world a little more flavored alcohol. Are we obliged to sit still while our landed gentry, this new breed of feudal lords in their absurd castles on the ridgetops, rapes the public trust and destroys the natural beauty that made this valley a slice of heaven on earth, for no better reason than to sell some stranger a bottle of arrogance?"

The letter appeared in the *St. Helena Star* a month before the election. It was signed by the postmaster and read by a large proportion of the citizenry. Most of Mennen's customers already knew of the residency of Ricki Lake in the post office, and that his owner went about his duties there without shoes. Mennen was a familiar sight, too, on Main Street, wearing Teva sandals and blue jeans, strolling toward Gillwood's, smiling at people and wondering now who would smile back. He ate the lunch special almost every day — smoked turkey and avocado was his favorite — and traded quips with the servers, all members of the proletariat who did smile back.

At times he felt overcome by the combined demands of job and avocation. In the Mennen Environmental Foundation's grant-making report and guidelines, the cover printed with Anasazi stick figures from the canyonlands of the Southwest and with the words "air to breathe, water to drink, room to think, space to grow," lay evidence of the foundation's priorities: protection of wild lands in the West, tropical and temperate rain forests, and salmon habitat. Juggling these concerns with those of the post office was more demanding than people seemed to realize.

Peter's unapologetic lodging of Ricki Lake on government property, like Ricki's flights over the heads of mail sorters and the array of seeds on the postmaster's desk, exceeded the customary accommodation of a pet by its owner. Peter told visitors, "I've learned so much from this little bird. My own spiritual life has grown immensely just by being around him."

But there were limits, some people said, to the passions of a nature-loving refugee from the sixties who had described himself at that time as "a long-haired freak" and was still stricken with prelapsarian permissiveness.

Peter had been in St. Helena for a quarter of a century, longer than many of his critics, as consistently unconventional as he was pleasant. Word of Ricki's perambulations, like the disorder of his owner's official existence and the unconventionality of the staff, reached beyond the post office. These things, like Peter's involvement in community affairs, had garnered support from residents who valued a pocket of remnant individuality in a valley once notorious for it, but phrases like "feudal lords" and "bottle of arrogance" resonated.

Postmasters were supposedly invulnerable to outside pressure, but after the filing of the Sierra Club lawsuit, loud complaints about the postmaster began to be heard beyond the valley. Assertions that the St. Helena post office was being run by a bunch of Aquarian throwbacks found their way to the Postal Service's district manager in Oakland. Peter had been subjected to audits in the past, but pressure from his superiors increased, and then came a notice that an inspector was being sent up to St. Helena to look around.

The staff dreaded this visit, but Peter went about his business as ever, in his ammonia-streaked sleeveless sweater, occasionally holding Ricki over the wastebasket, absorbed in the latest endeavor of the Mennen Foundation. Evidence of this sat in cardboard boxes on the floor of his office, circulars with the potential to end all hillside development. For after backing the lawsuit and Chris Malan's candidacy for supervisor, the Mennen Foundation had printed seventy thousand "ballots" emblazoned with disturbing color photographs of hacked-off redwood stumps on Mount Veeder, ugly erosion west of Yountville, a D-9 ripping the earth, and dust devils dancing on denuded land above Milliken Reservoir.

"SAVE OUR HILLS" demanded the headline above the photographs. On the flip side, Peter addressed all "concerned Napa County residents," and warned that "this beautiful valley we love, with splendid oaks . . . and magnificent redwoods . . . is being destroyed before our eyes . . . We are so concerned about the great damage being done . . . that we decided to write this letter and include the attached petition, and then personally pay to have it sent to residents like you all across the county. No big corporation, no marketing company, no special interests are paying for or promoting this letter. This is personal. This is from the heart. This is from us. This is to you.

"We are not losing our county to runaway urban development, like Silicon Valley . . . But sadly, even though we are fighting a winning battle against strip malls and sprawl, we are watching everything we and most of you love being destroyed by an industry we once thought would be our salvation — the wine business. The charm, beauty and varied wildlife we once took for granted and made Napa County such a wonderful place to live are being smashed by armies of bulldozers ripping through the hills . . .

"This strip mining of our woodland watershed and its conversion to barren, pesticide-laden dirt is having a massive secondary impact on many other lives . . . Without trees and shrubs to hold in the soil, most of the rainfall that used to soak into the ground and recharge our underground water supply is now 'engineered' to race down the slopes as runoff . . .

"That same polluted water races down to local reservoirs, upon which many Napa Valley residents depend, filling them with silt and ruining water quality. Other tainted streams run directly into the Napa River . . . It has to stop!"

Recipients of the material were being asked to review it and return the petition, signed, as an indication of support. The accumulated names could then be shown to the board of supervisors and eventually used as a base for an initiative that would force a legal end to hillside development.

The printing and mailing cost the Mennen Environmental Foundation upward of fifty thousand dollars. It had been Carlene's original intention to go door-to-door with a petition, collecting signatures. Peter had said, "Let's do it by mail instead." Let stamps do the walking.

Now he secretly feared that the mailing would be a bust, that he was going out on a very feeble limb indeed.

But within a week there were enough returning envelopes to require Carlene to load them into her car and drive them to a friend's house for sorting. If Carlene's idea had been simply to build a database, the effort was already a success, but the effect of the mailing went far beyond that. Everybody in the valley, from Calistoga to south Napa, was seeing, in glaring color, photographic evidence of the destruction of nature; they were reading that this was directly related to bottles of so-called arrogance. Many were responding.

Ricki Lake flew round and round the main room while the inspection team dispatched from Oakland stood below, gaping. The two women carried clipboards; they were clearly angered by the spectacle of feathered flight in this outpost of the United States Postal Service.

The inspectors disapproved of the poster in the women's restroom showing a hard-bodied man in something skimpy, and the light switch portrayed as, well, a man's penis. They didn't like the seeds on Peter's desk much, either. One of the women took photographs of the seeds, and, annoyed, Peter told her, "This isn't representative of what goes on here," and swept them away. The inspector just scuttled around the desk and took photos of the seeds now on the floor.

Then the women sat down and told Peter what they thought was wrong with his post office: Ricki Lake was unhealthy, the place was dirty, the employees indifferent and improperly dressed. There were earrings . . . Listening to these women, after watching them photograph and scribble on their clipboards, Peter realized that things had changed forever in America and that he, Peter Mennen, was endangered. He represented the last of the old ways in the postal system, where a sense of freedom had made him so love the institution in the first place, before its symbol, the eagle, had been stylized into a clutch of geometric shapes replacing the likeness of a real bird and before post offices had turned into philatelic versions of Denny's, the workers forced to look and dress and act alike.

The system had become a totalitarian business, postmasters called "station managers" and required to squeeze out the last drop of profit. The old post office had believed in providing a service without going into the customer's pocket from behind; now it was the same as every other commercial enterprise on the horizon, demanding maximum money for the least amount of effort, cold and indifferent.

Peter said in his own defense, "You don't understand that individuality among employees doesn't necessarily detract from efficiency. And the presence of animals can have a soothing effect upon people."

Eventually the acting manager of post office operations in Oakland drove to St. Helena to tear down the poster in the women's restroom. He went back to Oakland and wrote Peter a letter headed "Indecent Pictures — Women's Restroom" and stipulating that "during the Retail Performance Improvement Team visit . . . questionable/indecent pictures and light fixture was observed by one of the team . . . Your response to the team was, 'It was not your business what went on in the women's restroom.'"

". . . As a Postmaster/Manager you can delegate some of your responsibilities, but you can not delegate your accountability. This letter serves notice that you are required to perform all the duties of a Postmaster . . . You should also be aware that failure to carry out these duties might result in corrective action."

The Retail Performance Improvement Team's report was included. It contained ten recommendations for change, including the one that window clerks be required to wear ties, and another that Peter remove the display of historical objects, which "were beautiful, but this space should be used to display 'Postal' retail and packaging products that generate revenue . . .

"There were indecent (objectionable) pictures lining the walls of the ladies restroom. The light plate was a picture of a man with the switch as the man's privates . . . The Postmaster, who greeted the team in a sweater, jeans and sandals, keeps a parrot 'Ricky [sic] Lake' in his office . . . The bird was flying around in the distribution/carrier section. The Postmaster's office contains two large cages, and the carpeting and desk were covered with bird droppings and bird food . . . He had a laissez-faire attitude and did not give any indication that things would change . . . The atmosphere in the office is relaxed and kicked back, very unprofessional."

Peter drew a smiley face on the report and tacked it to the bulletin board, first scribbling, "All Employees — Please read!!"

Instead of immediately getting rid of Ricki, Peter found another conure parrot, a female, to live with Ricki at the post office. Her wings were clipped, yet her ardor for her new companion was so great that she fell from the perch each time Ricki left it. Peter wanted Ricki to pay more attention to her, and perhaps eventually produce a brood, but Ricki maintained his affection for Peter. Consequently, the female regarded her human rival with great misgiving; it occurred to Peter that Sartre had written a play about a similar situation, called *No Exit*.

He found a couple in North Carolina who took care of wild birds as a calling, and they agreed to take Ricki and his new companion. The Mennen Foundation provided a grant for the construction of a geodesic wire dome in which the birds might soar and otherwise live a more natural life than in the post office. Peter knew that the female's feathers would return after the next molt, and by then she and

Ricki would be relatively free under the North Carolina sky, and perhaps — who could say? — they would produce little Rickis.

Ricki's days were numbered at the post office. And so, Peter suspected, were his.

Stu Smith, living just up Sylvaner Avenue from the Mennens, had dinner in the early February darkness at the Rutherford Grill with his wife, Julie Ann. First they warmed their hands at the outdoor brazier, and after settling into a booth talked about the election. Stu thought the mass mailing of the petition, with its color photographs and charges about the wine industry, had marginalized the opposition. Malan/Mennen had used all their power to work outside the system, doing great damage, and now the system would come back to crush them.

He drank a little red wine and felt better about things. There would be a reaction against extreme environmentalism. If Kathryn Winter managed to be reelected, she wouldn't do Chris any favors, and neither would Mel Varrelman. Kathryn had gotten the message that a large part of her constituency was upset with her, and she had realized what Stu and his allies were up against in having to deal with Chris and Peter. In ten years, he figured, the environmental movement in the valley would be dead.

Stu compared the Mennens to other moneyed families in the past — the Medicis, the Rockefellers. He once thought the Mennens might put together an effective coalition in the valley, but that notion had evaporated when he read Peter's references to flavored alcohol and bottles of arrogance. That and the Sierra Club suit had driven various competing groups to a kind of consensus, and members of the Winegrowers, the Grape Growers (the other agricultural group), and even the Farm Bureau met at the offices of the legal firm Dickenson, Peatman & Fogarty to hash out a strategy with Richard Mendelson, the vintners' lawyer of choice. The objective was to create an ordinance that would enable vineyard development to continue and thwart Mennen should he ask, "What are the cumulative impacts of all projects?" Then Peter couldn't shut down the valley completely until that question could be answered, a process that would take years.

The Malan/Mennen challenge to approval by the county for new vineyards may have been just an insistence that the existing law be obeyed, but it had ignited a lot of passion, including Stu's. When the board of the Farm Bureau considered an interim hillside ordinance, he decided it was a giveaway of more farmers' rights and appeared defiantly before the board. "Nothing's more dangerous than a drowning man," he had told the directors. Faced with the loss of his livelihood, he would fight to the death, though in fact he was not faced with the loss of his livelihood. And the people most visibly associated with Farmers for Napa Valley worked for someone else. But, again, Stu felt that didn't affect the basic soundness of the principle.

After what Stu laughingly called his "meltdown," the Farm Bureau president telephoned and asked him to apologize for threatening the board. Stu had refused. "I mentioned the name Neville Chamberlain," he recalled over dinner, "and he didn't know who I was talking about. He didn't know what I meant by appeasement."

He shook his head. "Mennen and Malan are the Hitlers of today," he said. Warming to the subject, he went on, "They're the religious jihad of the ayatollah, with no flexibility. Consequently, they're going to break . . . It all goes back to Pahlmeyer. He did a good project without a permit, which is better than a lousy project with a permit."

The unintended consequences of that act were still unfolding like the petals of a big, exotic flower.

26

JAYSON PAHLMEYER met his architect and one of his attorneys at the Valley Store, south of the Silverado Country Club, on Saturday morning. The architect had designed the makeover of Jayson's house and produced a plan for the winery that, if all went well, would rise in the middle of Jayson's contentious vineyard. The attorney, Richard Mendelson, strategizer, guru of appellations, was not the lawyer representing Jayson in the Sierra Club suit but was the man to retain when you were applying for a permit to build a winery. Also along for the jaunt was Jayson's partner, the agreeable Michael Haas. The men would all tour Jayson's new vineyard, so Mendelson could get the lay of the land and the idea of the winery fixed in his mind, and then they would go down to lunch at Mustard's.

They piled into a big white Suburban, in vests and canvas hats and thick-soled shoes, and headed east, the architect in the back with Michael and an armload of blueprints in cardboard tubes. Jayson's jacket, bought at Mustard's, bore the droll message "Too Many Wines." Mendelson wore a pale orange cashmere sweater with the sleeves pulled down over his hands, to ward off the cold. His eyes behind oval glasses were pale green, and sloping brows gave him a look of perpetual concern, a professional advantage.

Mendelson was "the one with the juice," but he remained a bit of a mystery. Too smart to believe all the copy put out by the industry about free enterprise and entrepreneur-farmers, he nevertheless represented its denizens well and kept a cool head when they were losing theirs. Mendelson could tell them that the property rights argument against government regulation, for instance, was "a nonstarter" and sound so reasonable that most people would accept it, with the possible exception of Stu Smith.

The polished Mendelson spoke French; he often cited French antecedents for land-use decisions. He was equally conversant with the arguments for developmental restraint in hills, and with the ways around them. "We have a resource here that is as scarce as any biological resource," he said when the subject of environmentalism arose, as it inevitably did whenever people gathered nowadays, "and that's prime vineyardland."

One of the many ironies of the current fight over the future of the landscape was the fact that Mendelson had once been a good friend of Tom Lippe. Mendelson and the lawyer who had filed the Sierra Club lawsuit had attended Stanford Law School at the same time and spent many hours together, talking about the future. Tom had already committed himself to public interest law and to the environment, Richard to wine and, clearly now, to making money. If Mendelson had run into his old friend again, he would have asked him if he preferred to see houses where the vines grew. And Lippe would have told Mendelson that he was surprised at the route Mendelson had taken, and that Mendelson was not the person Lippe thought him to be.

In addition to practicing law, Mendelson was a sculptor, his antic, two-dimensional figures cut out of steel displayed in restaurant interiors, on the edges of clients' driveways, and in gardens, whimsical silhouettes showing that the guru of appellations was on the artistic as well as the legal verge. His life-size cutout of stylized dancers, welded at head and toe, stood in the conference room of his law firm in Napa, in sharp contrast to the dour furnishings of bread-and-butter legal services and the no-nonsense attitude of old Joe Peatman. Some visitors found the contrast amusing, though none said so.

After passing through Wooden Valley, the Suburban turned onto a sharply mounting dirt road. The architect got out to open the gate, and Jayson started to drive away without him. "Sorry," he said, "I'll get it right next time."

But he did the same thing at the second gate, so eager was he to show off his long-suffering project, slamming on the brakes, then driving on past new vineyards on steep slopes. They all got out to inspect the catchment basin designed to trap eroded soil, and Mendelson said, "You've got quite an investment here. This is a genuine estate vineyard."

Jayson was touched. He said "Thank you" with real gratitude, and explained that he sometimes bought five times the amount of grapes he needed at harvest, to make sure quality was assured, and bulked out all that didn't pass the quality test. This was a great extra expense, since he had to pay the winemaker on a volume basis. As Michael Haas put it, "We have to pay her to tell us what's not any good."

There were twenty-five hundred vines to the acre here; theoretically, the owners could get ten to twelve tons of grapes from a single acre. They intended to ask for a permit for a winery capable of processing that much juice, just in case they ever had to — a relatively big operation.

Beyond the last, highest bit of vineyard, Napa Valley opened up, the foreground sprinkled with live oaks and volcanic rock, Mount Diablo lowering far to the south, and to the right Atlas Peak. Chris Malan's house was down there somewhere. She had come out of nowhere to marshal incredible power, Jayson thought. He and other vintners, like Dennis Groth and Jack Cakebread, could sit around all day saying she was a screwball, but Chris knew all the buzzwords, and she wasn't going away.

The lawyer representing Jayson in the Sierra Club lawsuit had reported back from the settlement talks with more bad news. Chris Malan wanted Jayson to go back to the county for a new erosion control plan, which he didn't intend to do because she could then stand up before the planning commission or the board of supervisors and say he shouldn't be allowed to proceed because of cumulative impacts. That was the big phrase now — cumulative impacts — very important, yet nobody knew precisely what they were. This was a tremendous advantage for the environmentalists, and until cumulative impacts could be measured, everything was on hold.

Jayson was convinced that Chris really wanted him to return this land to forest. She and her cohorts had used the legal system to get access to his property — to trespass, in his view — drilling holes and taking soil samples and photographing. She, Peter Mennen, and Tom Lippe had something else in mind farther down the line, Jayson suspected.

In turn, he had sued the county for issuing the illegal permit, which he claimed had gotten him into trouble in the first . . . well, the second — no, the third — place, insisting that he was an innocent party, incurring big legal fees because of the county's flawed review process. Whether or not he would prevail against the county he didn't know, but he was afraid neither he nor the county would prevail against the Sierra Club because the county had clearly exercised discretion in granting vineyard permits.

Lippe had offered to settle the suit against Jayson and the other two vineyards if they would go back before the county for their projects, pay Lippe sixty thousand dollars in legal fees, and donate thirty thousand dollars to some environmental fund Chris Malan cooked up. "And I haven't done anything wrong!" Jayson said repeatedly. "It's known as extortion. I'm delayed in putting in my last forty acres, more than eighty tons of high-quality fruit worth nine hundred dollars a case." That was about a four-million-dollar penalty.

He had spent many sleepless nights wondering why Lippe and Malan had picked on relatively little guys like him instead of Mondavi or Beringer, which would have attracted more attention. There were eighty other vineyard operators that could have been sued, all of them nervously waiting for the statute of limitations to run out on their projects. Jayson had been only four days away from finishing his, and now he was ready to pay whatever it took to get free of Chris Malan. Like a prizefighter, he was down for the count.

The architect was saying that the winery would overlook Napa Valley but pay tribute to Wooden Valley, which drained into the same river. "This is a chance to make a gesture, psychologically important in identifying this prominent appellation . . . On the edge of the vineyard the winery will nestle in, very much a part of it, farming merging with wine, moving grapes in a graceful way . . . The building won't be that much different from Dominus — stunning, primitive . . . Driving up, you might say, 'What's so great about that?' but on inspection you'll see a powerful entity, a wonderful enclosure for wonderful wine . . ."

Mendelson asked, "Are you a minimalist?" Then he asked, "Is this cut-and-cover or excavation?"

"We're imagining several small cuts, with a stone retaining wall."

"Explain to me what you're cutting into."

The architect did: volcanic soil, rock.

Jayson added, "If you looked up here from the valley floor after the winery was built, you would still see an unbroken ridgeline."

He told Mendelson that he wanted, in addition to a winery permit, a permit for a chateau that could be built near the edge of the property presently occupied by a solitary marsh hawk, "in case some rich guy comes along and wants to buy the whole thing." Such a house, were it ever to be built, would sit under the horizon but still be visible from Atlas Peak Road. Jayson wanted the permit now because a new hillside ordinance might someday prevent it, and Richard Mendelson intoned, "Understood."

Chris Malan's life had become busy even by her standards, but that was okay. In addition to home duties and work, she had the county and "real parties" — Pahlmeyer et al. — to deal with, and she was about to be deposed by their lawyers. This would be very contentious and required some preparation. And then there were the demands of membership on the Watershed Task Force, Friends of the Napa River, and the Sierra Club, and of course there was the election.

She went door-to-door in the Fourth District, handing out beeswax candles in biodegradable containers that said "Save Our Hills" and talking up the hillside issue. The pressure on her to withdraw had lapsed into sullen silence on the part of many former allies. The Napa group of the Sierra Club had refused to endorse her, supporting Kathryn Winter instead; now Chris had to sit in ex-com meetings with some people who resented her candidacy and discuss "stuff" with them — legal strategy and ways of dealing with Jeff Redding and the board of supervisors — as if there were no controversial campaign in progress. If this peculiar state of affairs made the other Sierra Clubbers uncomfortable, it didn't bother Chris a bit. She had the backing of the Mennens and a few stalwart greens; she was funded, and impervious, and eventually everybody would thank her for keeping the issue before the public, she thought.

Chris knew she wouldn't be elected. She believed there would be a runoff election in the fall between Kathryn and Bill Dodd, the Chamber of Commerce candidate, the rich boy from the city who had inherited his family's Culligan water business and would be recognized as a political neophyte unequal to the challenges of governing Napa Valley in the twenty-first century. Chris would help bring that recognition home. She would endorse Kathryn after the primary, after Chris had extracted a promise from her to get tough on hillside development, and help her win.

The situation in Napa — her situation — reflected the national contest in which the Democrat, Al Gore, was being challenged by the Green Party candidate, Ralph Nader. Well, she thought, they would all ride to glory in November, the environmental mainstreamers winning and the more committed, so-called radicals having kept the environment right up there with other big issues, like housing and the economy.

On the overcast Saturday afternoon before the Super Tuesday primaries, a collection of cars and vans pulled into the parking lot outside the Albertson's grocery store in north Napa. An unusual troupe assembled on the tarmac: a yellow and black bulldozer made of cardboard and slats, placed over the electronic wheelchair driven by Micah Malan, in blue sunglasses; a symbolic redwood tree made of cloth, with artificial boughs, worn by a young woman in black stretch tights, the girlfriend of Chris Malan's older son, Josh, who shook her limbs in preparation for some political theater the likes of which had rarely been seen in the valley; and the *pièce de résistance,* an outsized spotted owl constructed of bits of turkey feathers, fashioned into a hood and sewn onto a cloak draping the shoulders of another leotarded reenactor. She was widely recognized in the county as the comely "deer lady" who regularly got up at various public forums to speak on behalf of wild animals.

Shoppers stocking up for the weekend saw the troupe strung out along Trancas Avenue, dramatizing "the rape of the land," the bulldozer making mock assaults on the redwood, the redwood languishing, the spotted owl flapping disconsolately. A handful of supporters brandished placards — "Save Our Hills," "Be Healthy," "Vote for Chris Malan" — and called out to the passing motorists, some of whom honked in sympathy. Most were puzzled by this demonstration, dampened by the drizzle that began to fall.

The troupe scooted for cover under Albertson's portico and there competed for space with shoppers seeking carts and with boys on bikes delighted with the spectacle. "You can't block the entrance," said a butcher who had come out in his stained apron. Chris assured him they wouldn't. In her thin raincoat, she too looked bedraggled, trying to keep her umbrella over the redwood, the owl, and her son the bulldozer.

"Let's try Target," suggested her husband, Jack.

The whole road show moved back toward the vans, the light already going, the women in their costumes soaked and cold, the bulldozer's paint glistening with rain, threatening to dissolve. The cardboard blade drooped, but the driver's blue-goggled face was smiling.

27

D AWN ON Election Day bled a silvery luminescence over
the eastern mountains. Shrouds of fog drifted north against
the emerging face of gray rock, and dark volcanic blades
pierced the tattered mat of forest.

Up in Chiles Valley, that remote adjunct of the larger appellation,
digger pines woke mournfully. The clumps of distant oaks looked
impenetrable in the scant light. Volker Eisele made his pot of tea and
prepared to deal by telephone with last-minute stratagems. When he
first came to Napa County back in 1967, what had most appealed to
him was the vibrant green of the hillsides offset by the bright yellow
of blooming wild mustard. He and Liesel had repeatedly driven up
from Berkeley after that; it took them a long time to understand this
new place, its flora and fauna far more complicated than most visitors and many residents suspected.

Living in Napa Valley and environs for more than thirty years, he
had come to realize that things that appear to be static are not. Rocks
would ultimately win the removal battle, no matter how much
heavy equipment is thrown at them, because replacements are constantly being pushed up by an earth on the move. No amount of expense would prevail over geology in the long run.

You learned such things through experience, as farmers had been
doing for eons. Only gradually do you come to understand what
erosion and slippage, riparian corridors, and biodiversity really mean.
One of the first things you learn is that natural processes take time.
People who don't live in a natural setting — absentee owners, day-
trippers — don't feel this. And most of those involved in agriculture
in the year 2000 had the work done by others. The new managerial

class also lived away, in a city or in one of Napa's gigantic subdivisions. Only the Mexicans really understood the place, because they stayed, in worker housing and sometimes in their cars, driving the tractors, pruning, doing the things owners had once done for themselves. By dealing with the demands of agriculture and of nature, the Mexicans had become not just essential but also the unacknowledged masters of Napa Valley.

The disconnect between the land and the investments of the owners made it difficult for them to understand the land they owned, or even to talk about it. Yet their radical altering of the landscape would have long-term consequences. Many of these were unforeseen by the people causing them, a problem that was not just Napa's but also the nation's. Because quality grapes were now so valuable, trees were being pulled out on an unprecedented scale all along California's coastal ranges. The massive loss of oaks, and numerous plant and animal species, was, like the consequent erosion, a real and unmitigated disaster, and it was going on all over America.

Relatively few people realized that fourteen tons of topsoil *per acre per year* was being washed into the Napa River. Thousands of years were required for a mere inch of topsoil to form. Stu Smith would no doubt say that the old hillside ordinance had reduced erosion by seventy percent, but that still left five to six tons of topsoil lost per acre per year, whereas in an oak forest the loss was less than a ton, and sometimes it was zero.

Volker had encountered what he thought was the first mention of erosion in Western literature, in one of Plato's dialogues, the *Critias*: ". . . all the richer and softer parts of the soil having fallen away," says Critias, about three hundred and fifty years before the birth of Christ, "and the mere skeleton of the land being left . . . Moreover, the land reaped the benefit of the annual rainfall, not as now losing the water which flows off the bare earth into the sea."

A ban on hydraulic mining had been the first law seeking to control erosion in California. Today mudslides in various parts of the state were the result of deforestation, as everyone knew. Everyone also knew that trees should not be cut on five-acre plots in the Sierra Nevada, but it was impossible to control the local jurisdictions. Patchwork destruction continued, as did the loss of agricultural land, because there were no state laws to protect these resources.

The original immigrants to Napa Valley had farmed right to the water's edge. This had allowed in pernicious species of plants and insects and exponentially increased erosion. The situation had worsened for a century and a half, the local elite too greedy to effect change, and then came the roaring 1990s, with everybody getting rich and few people willing to consider the consequences. Larger setbacks of all vineyards from the river and creeks should be required, a tough, expensive moral choice that would mean good water, enduring flora and fauna, and less erosion caused by raindrops colliding with bare earth.

Napa's native vegetation — oaks, shrubs, and chaparral — helped bind the soil, but grapevines did not. The rainwater was soaked up by the layers of clay in the vineyards, which then tended to slide, and artificial drains had to be put in to move the water rapidly off the hillsides, much more rapidly than it would naturally move. Consequently, the creekbeds were overloaded. Then the banks began to erode, too, so a problem that started high up with clearing and derocking worked its way steadily downhill to the lowest point, the river.

The big floods in China that everyone was reading about were directly attributable to human activity, a fact no one denied. But citing what happened on the Yangtze River, however relevant, to change minds on the board of supervisors was next to impossible. The Clean Water Act had been an attempt to address this difficult question on a national scale, using science. Only Guy Kay on the Watershed Task Force had the guts to talk about ground water, while Stu Smith and Dennis Groth called for more science. The prototypical hard-charging Napa Valley vintner, faced with regulations affecting his pocketbook, claimed suddenly to be incapable of making tough decisions and in need of experts. Well, Volker thought, when the science finally arrived, the Winegrowers and the so-called Farmers for Napa Valley weren't going to like it.

The desertification of North Africa, like the destruction of Sicily's farming, had been scientifically attributed to the cutting of trees. But science wasn't required to understand erosion, not if you had some experience with the land. You didn't need science to know that the Napa River was in trouble; all you needed to do was look at it. The river was full of silt, dangerously low in season, too warm. The salmon were gone and steelhead threatened. People hadn't been taught to notice these things; they didn't understand the connection between trees and available water. The most influential among them — corporate executives, shrewd entrepreneurs, career politicians — were ignorant of basic natural processes.

Local officials most anywhere in the country would allow a thousand applicants to clear and grade twenty-acre plots, but if a Japanese investor, say, came in and cleared and graded twenty thousand acres, there would be an outcry. That was the paradox. There had been great advances in environmental awareness since the seventies, but the result was uneven. Environmentalists had yet to make it plain to the general public that clean water was a universal need, as important to an Oakland ghetto as to Napa Valley.

Peter Mennen and Chris Malan knew this, and their rage was understandable when one looked at what was going on in the hills. But though their motivation was good, Volker believed, their actions hurt the cause. When you undertake an extreme action like a lawsuit, you must know where it will lead. Volker was convinced that Malan/Mennen didn't know. Environmental impact reports were not the answer to Napa's problems, because an EIR addressed the process, not the substance. In the end, it was a political document that could be fudged and then voted on.

Napa Valley was California in microcosm: bracketing mountains, plenty of sun, the capacity to grow more than two hundred different crops. The question was how to sustain it. If the resources couldn't be preserved here, they couldn't be preserved anywhere, and the chances looked slimmer today than they had six months ago.

The problem wasn't just in the valley, it wasn't just Californian, but national. While Volker mused, the Sierra Club was compiling figures about the effects of urban sprawl on America, and would conclude that the loss of farmland, open space, and wildlife habitat amounted to 2.2 million acres every year. Four million miles of roads adversely affected fully one fifth of the continental United States, if one considered air, water, and noise pollution. According to Defenders of Wildlife, habitat loss was the main threat to eighty percent of endangered species. The Environmental Protection Agency estimated that between 70,000 and 90,000 acres of wetlands were lost every year. Thirty-eight percent of estuary miles were impaired, by EPA standards, and almost half that could be attributed to urban runoff.

Chris Malan didn't understand the issues, Volker thought, including the primary one of farming versus residential development. Either that or she didn't care. This had been proven to his satisfaction by her support of an initiative launched by developers, Measure G, for a commercial and residential community at the moribund, historic Aetna Springs resort. The developers had put a great deal of money into that struggle and were overwhelmingly defeated in the vote just six weeks earlier. The defeat was a relief to most people living up-valley, but that victory was overshadowed by today's supervisorial election and all it portended.

If Chris managed to siphon off enough votes to force Kathryn Winter into a runoff, the pro-growth lobby would be encouraged. And if the "bad boys" won outright, unlikely but not impossible, they would think all their problems solved.

Volker's telephone was ringing.

The rain — gentle, persistent — did not bode well for incumbents, whose supporters tended to stay home on Election Day.

By evening, the pavements of Napa glistened under the streetlights. Inside the handsome Victorian not far from the courthouse, in a dining room devoid of wallpaper, snacks and soft drinks had been set out for the supporters of Chris Malan. A dozen people milled about, in a preponderance of comfortable shoes and ponytails, among them some members of Napa's Green Party. There was no television in evidence, no one rushing over from the courthouse with the latest poll results, the atmosphere more akin to that of a church social than the culminating ceremony of a political war.

Chris wore a black pantsuit and smiled with assurance, not of the outcome of the election but of the rightness of her part in it. She had brought her mother with her, a short, sturdy woman with a bright gold pin on her lapel who accepted a glass of sparkling water. She said proudly of her daughter, "Once she makes up her mind, that's it."

Moira Johnson Block arrived, in a welter of rain and good wishes, for what was a brief, obligatory visit to a fellow founder of Friends of the Napa River. Moira swept the hat from her head, revealing bobbed white hair, and announced, "We're in a crucible here. We could lose the whole thing. Ten years ago, we thought we had the development problem solved, but we were wrong."

A few blocks away, in a storefront on Third Street, Bill Dodd's campaign headquarters filled with the sound of the rock group Queen, singing "We Are the Champions." The tables were spread with red cloths and enhanced with open bottles of wine donated by Cakebread, Sutter Home, and other members of the Breakfast Club.

The candidate wore an open-necked orange shirt beneath a jacket, but there were ties in evidence, too, and scarves about the necks of carefully tended women looking askance at visitors not known to them. Business associates, friends, and family watched the latest election results, brought by runners from the courthouse and posted on a board, and the candidate — thinning hair, the practiced smile of a fifty-year-old novice at the end of a long, unexpectedly fortuitous campaign — watched as closely as anyone. Satisfaction was evident about the eyes, but more so a growing sense of amazement reflected in every face in this noisy Republican enclosure.

Two blocks in the direction of the river and one block over, the grand old Napa County Landmarks Building shone in the rain. Inside, under high ceilings and elaborate moldings installed in a more heroic age, a medley of political enthusiasts had gathered on the faded gray carpet: a few jackets but no ties, heavy sweaters, some facial hair among the men, the women more casual than their counterparts over on Third, but no less determined. There was no canned rock in the Landmarks Building, which would have interfered with the television set and with the earnest conversations conducted while sipping Stag's Leap and Eisele cabernet sauvignon and sampling chips and melon slices.

The subjects were as various as the district attorney's reluctance to prosecute developers and the northernmost reaches of the tide in the Napa River. Underlying it all, including familiarities exchanged among people who had known each other and worked together for years, was concern for the fate of candidates Kathryn Winter and Mike Rippey. These incumbent supervisors were Democrats, the ascendant party in the state, but not in the county or the nation. The complications of the past six months had affected the mood of what should already have been a victory celebration. Not since the winery definition fight more than a decade before, when a woman supervisor went down to defeat, had such doubts inhabited the brows and the words of the party faithful.

The challenge was not just from the community of developers and dedicated commercial interests, the usual suspects, like Rippey's opponent from the feathery edge of American Canyon's right wing. "This is a portentous time," Rippey said, not having bothered to remove his coat because of the chill both outside and in. "This is similar to the time when the ag preserve was created."

The relatively small but determined band of radical greens and uncompromising idealists, those willing to spend hours reading obscure county documents and to stop their secondhand cars on the Silverado Trail to rescue injured raccoons, had in the past overcome reservations about "the establishment" to cast their votes for Democrats. But by the spring of 2000, grape growing was perceived as elitist and this vote as elusive and potentially dangerous, and everybody in the big room knew it. And less committed or sophisticated voters were put off by the squabbles among environmentalists.

The latest returns were loudly announced by Kathryn's husband, Mick. Mike Rippey was ahead, but Kathryn had received only thirty-six percent of votes cast so far in the Fourth District.

Sitting on a folding chair, Kathryn smiled and shook her head. A suggestion that she analyze the results precinct by precinct was rejected. "I already know which ones are for me," she said. "I'm not going to do that to myself."

Moira Johnson Block made an entrance similar to the one she had made earlier at the big Victorian. She asked Parry Mead, "What are we going to do tomorrow morning if Dodd wins? *What are we going to do?*"

Chris's total had climbed to almost ten percent and then stuck. But it was more than anyone had expected Chris to get, and it might just be enough to deprive the county of a runoff. Parry said, "Chris brought the county to its knees, and then she had to run. If Dodd wins, I'm afraid she'll lose all credibility," and Moira said, "She's finished."

Shortly before eleven P.M., Kathryn's cell phone rang. She went off to one side to take the call. "This could be a squeaker," said Mick, but it already was. Looking fondly at his wife, he added, "She's a trouper."

The crowd had thinned. Red rings of dried cabernet marked the abandoned glasses, and a bunch of white-and-purple campaign signs with the wooden sticks attached, leftovers from the battle of the roadsides, stood upside down in a corner.

Kathryn came back and sat beside Parry. "Your friend is doing it," she said, without accusation, and Parry said, "Chris caused some voters to go to Dodd because they didn't understand the controversy over the hills and wanted to get away from it."

"She drove away some voters, and she took some."

"The industry guys on the task force will be so smug," said Parry. "I see all the work we've done going by the boards. We'll keep going, but it will be so much harder."

After a bit, Kathryn said reflectively, "Chris has had some hard knocks. She has a level of frustration, and I became the target. It's approaching an obsession."

Mixed with the incoming local results were those from the presidential primaries. Republican Senator John McCain had not fared well against George W. Bush, the governor of Texas. "McCain's being attacked by the Christian right as an agent of evil brought out the reactionaries," someone observed. And although Vice President Al Gore had prevailed as expected, across that distant victory lay the lengthening shadow of Ralph Nader — the Chris Malan, someone said, of the national campaign.

Volker walked over and kissed Kathryn on the cheek. "We're all here," he told her. She smiled up at him, but in that gesture was all the exhaustion of months of frustration and disappointment.

The final results came in well after midnight. Dodd had received slightly more than half the votes, precluding a runoff election in the fall. He had won.

Volker busied himself picking up empty wine glasses and putting them back into cardboard boxes, helped by young Tom Gamble, lucky spermer and grape grower, who wore a dramatic white cowboy hat with a big feather in the brim, even indoors.

"It's incredibly bad," said Volker. "The bad boys will be ecstatic."

28

J ACK CAKEBREAD told everyone who asked that he had expected
Bill Dodd to win, if not in the primary, then in the runoff. The
fact that there would be no runoff was desirable, he added, since
a runoff could be devastating, with all that time for adversaries to
attack Dodd's lack of experience and to whip up emotion. He also
told people that Dodd would have beaten Kathryn Winter even if
Chris Malan hadn't been the wild card, but few other observers
agreed.

Comparisons with the national primaries were inevitable. Jack
heard them repeatedly: Super Tuesday in America and in Napa
County had pitted sharply divergent personalities and issues; just as
George W. Bush had to brand himself a reformer to counter John
McCain's campaign reform message, Bill Dodd had to declare himself aware of the environment, particularly the river, as important to
valley life. And just as the Texas friends of Bush had spent millions
attacking McCain, who was Jack's choice, Peter Mennen had sent
out an inflammatory mailing showing gullies and severed redwoods
— in color!

A shadowy group of businessmen had taken advantage of all the
confusion and mudslinging to run anonymous ads in the newspaper
attacking the board of supervisors for stymieing development in the
valley's south end. There was an equivalent of that on a national
scale, too, but the only comparisons that mattered were that a pro-
business candidate was in and that environmentalists had been revealed as making up less than half of the voting public.

At last the Winegrowers had someone on the board of supervisors, Jack said, "who'll listen." Now the Breakfast Club could get on with blunting the effects of the California Environmental Quality Act, diluting the recommendations of the Watershed Task Force, and taking over the Farm Bureau's board of directors. And Jack could resume working harder, although at the moment he couldn't imagine getting any luckier.

The Winegrowers threw a small, discreet celebration party for members of the Farmers for Napa Valley and invited Stu Smith and others who had helped behind the scenes. Everyone was pleased not just with the outcome of the primary but also about Malan's disruptive candidacy, a great favor.

Stu admitted that he was surprised that Bill Dodd won the primary. Maybe the message was out that the wine industry wanted a little more respect. And now that Chris Malan had been marginalized, he told people, the environmental community would turn on her "and eat her for lunch."

It was typical of the environmentalists, he thought: they would destroy a movement based on ideals rather than compromise. The environmentalists wanted to use up all the oxygen in the valley, but they weren't going to be allowed to. It was going to become a very different place in the future.

Kathryn Winter had been the best thing the Sierra Club ever had going for it, but wasn't radical enough, and so the enviros had treated her like Socrates. Stu reminded people, "And they stoned Socrates."

As vice president for public affairs for Robert Mondavi, Inc., Herb Schmidt had to be circumspect about political associations. He represented Mondavi on the Winegrowers but was also the company rep in Sacramento and Washington, D.C., and in other venues affecting the sale of Mondavi wine and the image of Mondavi, Inc. Public relations, while not his official duty, was always his unofficial concern. Herb knew that environmentalism was here to stay, that it triggered strong emotions, and that the corporation could be damaged down the line if certain perceptions became widespread.

He operated out of the tasteful innocuousness of Mondavi's new office complex atop the winery, walking soundlessly in his soft loafers on beige carpeting past the offices of Robert and his wife, Margrit Biever, and sometimes past Michael's. Herb knew his place. He never referred to the aging Robert Mondavi as "Bob," as many people did, always as "Mr. Mondavi." He referred to Robert Mondavi's elder son, the chief executive officer, as "Michael," never "Mike," although his younger brother, Timothy, was most definitely "Tim."

Michael had experimented for a time with an approximation of his father's illustrious name, publicly referring to himself as "Robert Michael Mondavi." But there could be only one Mr. Mondavi at a time. Although Michael was still in line for that title, he already had the power. Much of his father's time was spent trying to get Michael's attention, after Robert had neglected Michael when he was a boy because of the demands of the new business.

Herb didn't say this, but others working for the company did: the great tragedy of Robert Mondavi's life was allowing his winery to go public and thus losing control. Robert had to watch the amenities of a family estate bent to the tyranny of quarterly profits, and the best wines overshadowed by its second, cheaper Woodbridge line, made from grapes grown far from Napa Valley.

In the past, the Robert Mondavi Winery had been special. Now it was just another corporation, part of a trend that started with Heublein's taking over Inglenook back in the sixties. Robert had then made the best wine he could; now the overriding concern was volume, price points, and partnerships with other large international producers. Italian conversations continued among Robert's heirs over where the company was headed, and other stories reflected on the family, like the one about Michael inviting the fire department to train its men by burning down his old house, so he could build a new one and take a tax deduction.

Michael didn't command the respect his father commanded, nor the loyalty. Employees and former employees speculated that a larger corporation would sooner or later come in with an offer for this one, and the children would take the money. Or the board would hire a go-getting new CEO, because without an overachiever you can't run a five-million-case winery. Then the family would be history at the Robert Mondavi Winery.

Herb Schmidt was a realist. He moved as easily among the corporation's principals as he did among the big issues — international trade, labeling, flavored wine, Pierce's disease, the California Environmental Quality Act. A master of the indirect advisory, Herb could effectively suggest to the chief operating officer of Mondavi, Inc., that attending some luncheon was not worth his time, and add that he, Herb, was off to "the desert" to play golf with someone worth playing golf with, and not give offense. He could smile in that way of his, not exactly ingratiating, indicating that he knew something worth knowing, something that would redound to the company's benefit, adding a little humor and sometimes handing out a business card with his name rendered in an Italianate version of the family's: *Huberto Schmidtavi*.

Herb knew how to deal with wealthy or well-connected and sometimes prickly individuals. Laurance Rockefeller had once given him a ticket to New York, when Herb was a young man from the suburbs of Detroit, and told him, "I want to talk to you." Herb had gone to New York, talked, and found himself running resorts for Rockefeller in the sunny Caribbean, before moving on to the Tetons. He had gone on to manage Meadowood for Bill Harlan and his partners; Robin Lail had worked there, and introduced him to the Mondavis.

Now Herb had the job of positioning what was still the most famous Napa Valley name in an increasingly demanding political framework; increasingly demanding was this question of the environment. He thought the public recognized the positive contributions of the wine industry to the valley: few social problems, green vistas, jobs. But the Winegrowers' own survey had revealed a drop in public approval of the wineries, and this was related to vineyard development. Herb didn't believe there was an environmental crisis in the valley, only a *perceived* crisis — but a problem nonetheless.

At his suggestion, Mondavi, Inc., had given a thousand dollars to Bill Dodd's campaign. It had also given a thousand dollars to Kathryn Winter's, just in case. But Kathryn was too much of a single-issue person, the issue being land use. And she was insufficiently ambiguous to be a good politician. The Winegrowers disliked the fact that she wanted to amend the county's General Plan to include habitat protection and favored the original erosion control ordinance. Herb admitted that the ordinance had been a good thing — a law hated by both the political right and the political left. But the Sierra Club suit had thrown the whole question back into the county's lap, and harmed Kathryn indirectly.

Herb was one of the men who had come up with the idea of having Napa County exempted from CEQA. Since the county already had an ordinance, he could make a case that the intent of the law was not to punish people. The idea had gotten some traction in Sacramento where, as Herb told people, "much bigger forces heard about our proposal and said, 'Hey, that's a good idea.'" Other counties in California were watching Napa carefully, aware that they, too, could get hit with a suit. Napa Valley was a special place with special problems, and if the exemption argument proved effective with the legislature, maybe it could be pushed on a national scale. Who knew? Maybe they could get Napa Valley exempted from the Endangered Species and Clean Water acts.

But no one wanted to be perceived as anti-environment. What Mondavi, Inc. — what the industry, in fact — needed was a public relations person to deal specifically with the environmentalists, to listen to their demands and deflect their criticism and their lawsuits, someone with special qualifications.

Kathryn Winter tried to cope with defeat in an honorable way, by continuing her work as a lame-duck supervisor, listening to supporters' laments, and ignoring the self-satisfied comments of those who had contributed to her defeat. Added to this burden was the knowledge that her beloved brother had a malignant melanoma in his right leg that would probably kill him, knowledge she had carried with her during the campaign and that at times rendered her nearly immobile.

Everybody was telling her that she had done a good job, that Chris had cast doubt on her as an environmentalist and driven people to Bill Dodd. Kathryn believed that this was so, but the knowledge didn't assuage the hurt. She had put her soul into her job, and told the truth as she saw it, and the outcome was disastrous. Supposedly, if you do a good job, you win; that was the American way, but not in politics.

She felt cheated. If there had been a runoff election, she would have had a chance to fight it out with Dodd over the issues. Many of his workers had been paid, something Kathryn couldn't afford. But what had really defeated her was Chris, an almost comical misstep by Malan/Mennen and a stroke of pure, decisive dumb luck for Dodd.

Two days after the election, Kathryn received a telephone call from Herb Schmidt. Sounding as if nothing had happened, he told her, "I've got a great idea. Want to hear it?"

She didn't, but said, "Yeah, Herb."

"Why don't you come to work for the Mondavis?"

Kathryn's mouth literally fell open.

"You'd be a great liaison to the environmentalists," he went on. "You could tell them about all the good things the Mondavis are doing. I'm going to put you in next year's budget. Will you think about it?"

Stunned, she hung up. If they liked her so much, she asked herself, thought her so capable, why had they worked so hard to defeat her? It all came down on her at that moment: the loss, the melanoma, the stupidity, the cynicism. She got into the shower, turned on the hot water, and stood under it for half an hour, crying.

Peter Mennen had gone to bed before the election tallies started coming in, and no one had called him with the results. He heard of them the next morning on the radio.

He hadn't actually wanted Chris to win, of course, just to make a point, but apparently Kathryn had been too cold to the voters in Soda Canyon and other areas threatened with development even to make it into a runoff. Now all the cards were up in the air, and who knew how they would come down? Meanwhile, he, Carlene, and Chris could go to Bill Dodd with their five thousand signatures collected from the mailing, showing him that they had a solid base and could affect Dodd's reelection. "Hey," Peter said of the outcome of the election, "if you've got lemons, make lemonade."

He was not going to get depressed about all the acrimony in the valley. There was too much work to be done. He believed not only in the correctness of the cause but also in the agent he and Carlene had chosen. As he had believed earlier, he believed still: "Thank God for Chris Malan."

★

She told all who asked: "Dodd picked up all my points and then attacked Kathryn . . . There's some disappointment, but, going door-to-door, I was shocked by the number of people who didn't know there was a problem in the hills. Now they do. I have no regrets."

Chris and the Mennens had enough signatures to mount a voter initiative to stop all hillside development. They had the Sierra Club suits and the long-term legal strategy; various clocks were ticking.

Within days of the election, she had fired off an e-mail to all her supporters and interested parties. "Hi to you all," she began, and went on to explain why she had run, what she thought had happened, and to ask for help in launching an initiative. "This time I would clearly like to know where my environmental friends and the friends of the environment stand . . . The money machine is too powerful and wine grapes are revered in a very elite portion of our population that controls the media and the mystique of our time. I am not stopping . . .

"I wake up each day in these glorious oak woodlands. The woods are alive with insects and sometimes the noise of it astounds me. When a tree falls you can feel the weight of it for miles. The birds are foraging in the rain. The bluebirds are coming back to nest already. They flock on the ground around the perennial grasses. Occasionally I see the falcons and golden eagles flying. The coyotes howl at the crisp, cold, moonlit night . . ."

Not long afterward, the Mennen Foundation received an anonymous letter, also addressed to Chris, the Sierra Club, and the Communist Party of California. Chris wangled a copy from Peter and, after reading it, informed the sheriff that she had received a death threat.

"NAPA COUNTY AGRICULTURISTS WERE ALLIES OF YOURS FOR THE LAST 30 YEARS. IN THE NAME OF PRESERVATION OF AGRICULTURE IN NAPA COUNTY, WE GAVE UP PARTS OF OUR PROPERTY RIGHTS. AS A RESULT, NAPA AGRICULTURE WAS PRESERVED, OUR LOCAL ECONOMY THRIVED AND OUR WAY OF LIFE . . . THE PROBLEM IS, ENVIRONMENTALISTS LIKE YOURSELVES ARE NEVER SATISFIED. THERE'S ALWAYS ANOTHER CAUSE TO FIGHT FOR THAT'S JUST A BIT MORE RADICAL THAN THE ONE BEFORE IT. I AM CONVINCED YOU WILL NEVER BE SATISFIED UNTIL

YOU HAVE STOPPED GROWTH, STIFLED THE ECONOMY AND HAVE
EVERYONE EATING YOUR BRAND OF NOURISHMENT . . . YOU
KNOW WE AGRICULTURISTS ARE NOT DESTROYING THE ENVI-
RONMENT. YOUR PROPAGANDA IS INFLAMMATORY AND FALSE.
WE WINE INDUSTRY FOLKS ARE GOING TO RESIST YOU . . . THE
RESISTANCE WILL BE MILITANT IF NECESSARY. WATCH YOUR
BACK. YOU'VE STARTED A WAR."

Soon after that, Chris's husband, Jack, told her he had a permit to
carry a pistol. She didn't know much about pistols, but his looked
like a .45 semiautomatic, the kind used by the infantry in World War
Two. She laughingly told people that Jack carried it wherever he
went now, even to the woodpile.

IV

TURTLE ISLAND

29

ROUGHLY one hundred and forty million years before the creation of the Watershed Task Force and the Sierra Club lawsuit, the land in question lay at the bottom of a warm, shallow sea. It wasn't yet part of the continental mass; it wasn't even a valley, just a formless geologic embryo in briny anonymity miles west of a chain of volcanic islands produced by grinding tectonic plates. These shaped and reshaped the earth's surface, and as they nosed into the magma, or mounted one another, they produced rifts and upthrusts in a spectacular terrestrial coupling accompanied by deep-time pyrotechnics.

To the west of the land in question, the sea's ancient floor, part of the Pacific plate, plowed under the basin supporting it. This plate was overridden by the California crust, part of the continent, and it pushed up a rubble of older rock and sediments that would overlay the rising coastline and extend for miles inland, oceanic debris evident today in the soft, rounded hills and unstable soils of Carneros and elsewhere. Meanwhile, the Pacific plate — six thousand miles in breadth, forty miles deep — continued eastward, increasing the friction, suffusing the grinding rock with entrained seawater and producing violent eruptions along the line of fire that became the Sierra Nevada.

Eonic floods would wash much of this debris westward to mingle in the confusion of rock littering the continent's new coast. Five million years ago, the grating of one plate against another along a line now known as the San Andreas Fault reached these latitudes. The Pacific plate was drifting northward at an average annual rate

of only inches and setting off new eruptions along the length of
the plate's migrating edge. Faulting and uplift produced sheer gray,
pocked cliffs on the eastern perimeter of this land still without
a name, under the brow of low mountains, long before stags
leaped and mythic gods like Atlas flowered in the human imagination.

The vast, tempestuous ocean steadily rose, inundating the new
land. Four million years ago the San Andreas Fault was compressed
and temporarily contained, causing dramatic upheavals and with
them a folded, precipitous, gorgeous, confusing landscape much like
that seen today. By the same process, the earth's crust was pulled at
and stretched thin, and at one such point formed a depression that
became the unique, structurally varied, mineral-rich province of
Napa Valley.

The life that overspread this region was as diverse as its geology. Half
the myriad plants growing in the coastal areas of what became California, and in adjacent valleys and defiles, were found nowhere else.
The same could be said of some nine thousand species of insects.
Aquatic and upland birds at times darkened the sky, filled at others
with massive islands of moisture drifting on the wind from the
ocean. The western slopes of successive ranges, recipients of that
rain, supported towering walls of redwoods, Douglas fir, and associated biota that held and slowly released moisture that continually fed
the streams and the river. These raged in season with salmon and
steelhead; enormous grizzly bears and stately tule elk, before those
names were invented, ranged freely in country that must have, by
virtue of climate, abundance, and beauty, been paradisiacal.

Homo sapiens arrived from the north about eighteen thousand
years before the present, and their numbers grew and spread over the
ensuing millennia to include hundreds of separate groups. They
occupied the coastal mountains, with languages almost as diverse,
and intricate systems of trade and communication developed. Less
than three hundred years ago, when Europeans first made contact
with the indigenous population, there must have been one hundred
thousand natives already in residence between what is now the
Klamath River in Oregon and San Francisco Bay.

This relatively dense population subsisted on resources so abundant that human demands were absorbed within the natural rhythms of the land. The people burned and ditched to facilitate agriculture and the gathering of food, and built weirs for snaring fish, but the forests and lowlands, the long expanses of river, the marshes and expanding bays pulsed with life just as they had "forever."

Roughly a thousand Yukian-speaking natives occupied what became Napa, eastern Sonoma, and southern Lake counties, going back as far as four thousand years. The Napa Valley settlement was larger than the others and traded with both the Indians to the west (Pomos) and those to the east (Wintuns), the currency shells and beads.

The Napa group's tools and weapons were often fashioned from the residue of old volcanoes that had spewed lava and tuffaceous ash but also left troves of obsidian still found on the east side of the valley. Peaceful, intimately connected to the ways and interests of neighbors beyond the steep, densely wooded mountains, the Indians fished with ease and retreated from the river only temporarily in spawning season to make way for marauding grizzlies.

The name associated with this discreet group, Napa, or Nappa, has been variously interpreted to mean "grizzly," "harpoon point," "fish," "house," and "bounteous place." The conquering Spanish called them *guapo,* which over time became the corruption Wappo.

Spain's soldiers and priests established missions from San Diego to Sonoma, bringing with them the criolla, or mission, grape. Throughout California they burned villages, food supplies, and tools, driving the Indians to the missions, where they were indentured in the dual interests of converting heathens to Christianity and acquiring labor.

In this bounteous place, the Wappos' numbers began to dwindle, as they did elsewhere in California. The Spaniards' successors, the Anglo Europeans, adopted the scorched earth practice in dealing with intransigent natives, systemically attacking and killing any group perceived as an impediment to the prospects of gaining land and, more importantly, gold.

The natives' way of life wrecked, their dependency on their conquerors increased, paradoxically, as they sought food, shelter, and work from them. The total native population of northern California had been reduced by nine tenths in the century and a half since the arrival of the Europeans.

George Yount, who made his way from Missouri to San Francisco in 1833, obtained a Spanish land grant of almost twelve thousand acres in Napa after converting to Catholicism. He planted the first vines on his Caymus ranch, and dealt humanely with the remnant people there, but many who followed him did not. The discovery of gold in 1848 changed the face of the Sierra foothills and of coastal valleys like Napa, and the social disposition of much of California succumbed to the enduring spirit of bonanza.

In 1850, settlers still had difficulty enticing their horses into some rivers that, during the migration of Chinook salmon, boiled with life, but the effects of prospecting and settlement rapidly increased. Thousands of new arrivals dislodged earth near the headwaters of countless streams and rivers and filled the lower concourses with silt and gravel. It is estimated that hydraulic mining carried more than a billion cubic yards of such debris from the Sierras into the Sacramento River delta, and subsequently into San Francisco Bay, a human reenactment of earlier geological cataclysm.

The "reclamation" of lands obliterated more than seven hundred and fifty square miles of tidal marsh in that period, and farming and ranching had a similar, if less catastrophic, effect on rivers and waterways throughout the valleys of northern California.

Yet Napa remained a place of beauty and incredible fertility. Paintings of the late nineteenth century reveal a verdant land flanked on two sides by green mountains, under drifting clouds, and on the valley floor a seemingly inexhaustible fecundity. Everything is suffused with a light almost numinous, and everywhere — on the flats, in the tributary valleys, up narrow canyons — and in all seasons, even when dust covers the roads, there is water.

Standing and rushing, in vernal pools and crystalline tributaries, in deep, reflecting bays dense with the distant prospect of birds, water promised regeneration. The labor, and even the habitations, of people were only subtly imprinted on a larger canvas of life.

". . . spreading away in matchless loveliness, these valleys, where our merchant-princes even now delight to plant gardens like Eden and to build palaces to embosom a new social life."

This was written in 1868 by a certain "doctor of divinity" named Charles Wadsworth, in San Francisco. Napa was surely one of the Edens he had in mind, and old Gustave Niebaum, builder of Inglenook, was about to qualify as a merchant-prince. This could not be said for the struggling Germans — Charles Krug, the Beringer brothers, Jacob Schram — but the impulses were the same: a love and some knowledge of wine, access to the valley, determination to develop a dream.

Old Schram's success on the flanks of Diamond Mountain would have a legacy in part literary. A budding English writer and consumptive named Robert Louis Stevenson brought his new wife, Fanny, and an enduring romanticism to Napa Valley in 1880. "It is difficult for a European to imagine Calistoga," Stevenson later wrote in *Silverado Squatters,* his brief, alternately affectionate and acerbic memoir on what was still relatively wild country, "the whole place is so new, and of such an occidental pattern; the very name, I hear, was invented at a supper-party by the man who found the springs."

Stevenson described the California vineyard in general as "one of man's outposts in the wilderness . . . There is nothing here to remind you of the Rhine or the Rhone, of the low *côte d'or,* or the infamous and scabby deserts of Champagne; but all is green, solitary, covert."

The wine, he acknowledged, had potential. He sagely predicted that the eventual success of California wine was connected to something larger: "All things in this new land are moving further on . . . This stir of change and these perpetual echoes of the moving footfall, haunt the land."

He and Fanny moved into a rude cabin on the steppe of Mount St. Helena. The greatest threats were poison oak and rattlesnakes, neither of much concern to Stevenson. He exercised daily within earshot of the rattlers. The easily gotten gold in these environs had mostly been extracted, but the newlyweds were not interested in lucre. They wanted, and apparently found, a brief idyll "in our mountain hermitage."

The memoir was serialized in *Century Illustrated* in 1883 but received no notice in Napa, despite the fact that it was the first book written about the valley by an outsider. Stevenson was probably considered too critical of some of the ruder examples of early California enterprise, for even after the international success of his *Treasure Island* and *The Strange Case of Dr. Jekyll and Mr. Hyde,* neither he nor *Silverado Squatters* was mentioned in the *Calistogan* or the *Register* when Stevenson died in Samoa in 1894.

Jacob Schram, the immigrant winemaker and erstwhile itinerant barber, had been well treated by the author, as Stevenson had been by the German enophile. While Fanny was entertained by "stout, smiling Mrs. Schram" on the veranda, the men descended to the cellar to sample his New World wines. In the penumbral gloom of tunnels dug by Chinese laborers, Schram "followed every sip and read my face with proud anxiety. I tasted all. I tasted every variety and shade of Schramsberger." He added that "these are but experiments."

On the walls of Schramsberg's Tower Room, in the year 2000, hung framed photographs of Jack Davies with Presidents Nixon, Ford, and Reagan, Brezhnev and Gorbachev. Tall windows provided a panoramic, if narrow, view of native flora: oaks, Douglas fir, a flowering plum, and the gigantic eucalyptus. It was raining, and the Spanish moss close to the windows held suspended raindrops. Inside, the white cloth on the big round table was spread with clipboards, loose sheets of notepaper, a basket of water crackers, four cloaked bottles, and an array of slender glasses half filled with pale, golden wine through which rose columns of very fine bubbles.

Seated around the table were Hugh, the associate winemaker; Mike, the winemaker and general manager; Amy, the enologist; and Craig, in charge of the vineyards. These titles were so fungible as to be almost superfluous, since duties overlapped and, with the exception of Amy's chemical analyses, were often shared or offloaded onto someone else when new demands arose, as they invariably did. This was the nucleus of Schramsberg's winemaking operation, a business whose international reach was indicated by the photographs on the wall. The members were in their thirties, or about to be. All had attended the University of California at Davis and wore shoes with thick soles to ward off the cold of the concrete floor of the downstairs winery.

The morning's tasting was of "late-disgorged" wines, those that had been allowed to age on the lees for nine years, and of younger wines treated with "dosage," blends of wine and brandy that improve flavor and add depth. The wines had recently been opened and poured, and included blanc de blancs (white wine made from white grapes, mostly chardonnay) and blanc de noirs (rose-tinted wine made from pinot noir).

Each person carefully picked up first one and then another of the glasses, looked at the wine, smelled and then tasted it. For several minutes the room was filled with the sounds of sniffs and sighs and grunts, of liquid sloshed around in mouths and dispelled into cylindrical plastic containers, of pencils scratching on paper. When the tasting was done, the talk began — of tastes (cider, melon, dust, malt, yeast, soy, caramel), smells (cheese, cookies, "honey graham cracker," citrus, squash, nectar, spice), and feel (beeswax, steely, chewy). Then the cloaks were removed from the bottles and the identities revealed.

The consensus was that the barrel-fermented dosage was best. The lees of those wines were periodically stirred, which improved the wine's complexity and that of the sparkling wine to which it was later added, the object of all this.

After the tasting, the glasses were rinsed and upended in the drying rack, and each member of the team went his own way. Hugh had business in the cellar and a lot on his plate in addition: the Watershed Task Force, the community and industry issues committee of the Napa Valley Vintners Association that he chaired, the board of directors of the Farm Bureau to which he hoped to be elected in the summer, and marriage.

Outside, he discovered that the rain had stopped. A patch of blue showed high up in the watershed, where Napa and Sonoma counties met, and he stood for a moment on the rough-hewn steps, under the towering eucalyptus, wondering how big the tree was when his father first arrived. The seed pods on the tarmac had been run over by passing trucks, and a sharp, minty smell hung in the fresh morning air.

Hugh finally left the winery at 6:30 that evening, the light still strong, and drove a short distance down the long approach road to the bungalow tucked into the trees. A big silver horse trailer was parked below, next to a small paddock made of steel bars, set up by Lily to contain her thousand-pound-plus horse, Mack. Lily met Hugh on the porch in sweater and riding pants, her short blond hair framing blue eyes. She smiled, reining in her black Great Dane. "Behave, Hamlet," she said to the dog.

They decided to go into Calistoga for dinner but, once there, found their favorite spot, Wappo, full. So they went to Cin Cin, a new restaurant. Talk during the meal was of the hillsides and the California Environmental Quality Act. Hugh said, "We've got to save the planet," and asked, with a slightly lopsided grin, "Why not start here?"

But his activities bothered some of his late father's friends. As head of the industry and community issues committee, he had urged the membership to back a resolution opposing the exemption of California's vineyards from CEQA review. He and others on the committee didn't think the vineyards should receive special privileges that went against environmental integrity; he didn't want the vintners to be perceived as selfish. The resolution passed unanimously in his committee, but before he could present it to the Vintners' full board, he had received a call in his office from Joe Phelps. "Now Hugh," Joe had said paternally, "this isn't a good idea."

The older men in the organization didn't want the Vintners on record as opposing some action that might eventually benefit them. Hugh had respectfully listened to his father's friend, surprised that he was so insistent, and explained his position. Hugh hadn't backed down, but he had slept poorly the night before the meeting of the Vintners' board. He had gone before it to present the committee's vote, and not a single board member agreed with him.

"What did I do wrong?" he later asked, and the older members of the board had smiled and said, "Things are more complicated than you think," and, "We move a little more slowly than that," and, "We don't want to take a position on something that probably will never come to a vote anyway."

But the vineyards shouldn't be exempt from environmental laws affecting everyone else, a position any socially responsible group had to embrace. "This is where the Vintners should be," Hugh said now, over dinner and a bottle of California wine made from Rhone Valley grapes, one more bit of vinous symbiosis.

30

THE NINETIES had officially ended with the coming of the new year, but the decade still flourished in early 2000. Some unpleasant premonitions were felt, and voiced, on Wall Street, and a barely perceptible softness in the valley's real estate market, but the price of land — like that of good wine — remained high.

The expectations of those wanting to preserve what was left of the valley were centered, now that the election was over, on the outcome of the Sierra Club lawsuit and all it implied. The effects of the suit itself filtered down to people not ordinarily concerned about runoff and distant clear-cuts, and made them think about the valley in a new way.

Since going to work for Niebaum-Coppola, Norm had found himself increasingly aware of contradictions. People praised the valley as a place of beauty, then sought first and foremost to exploit it. Such things had not been of much interest to him before, but the newspaper and television stories and the evidence that lay all about — merchandise flooding the tasting rooms, the sight of mansions in the hills — engendered something in Norm that surprised him.

He decided to write down some of what he was thinking: "I have never speculated about the connection between the little acts of unethical behavior and the developmental issues," he wrote. "Since the '80s, when Ronald Reagan set the example for getting away with all that you can, I've watched the ethical debate shrivel . . . With the devaluation of the dollar under Reagan/Bush, Napa properties were a bargain for the French and Japanese corporations with the vision to invest in the valley. Do you suppose they or the Coppolas were any more, or less, likely to make ethical decisions affecting their investments than a corporation based in Connecticut?"

By that he meant Heublein, former owner of Inglenook, now Niebaum-Coppola. A corporate mentality seemed to have taken over even the boutique wineries. "For the destruction of riparian habitat on Atlas Peak, Pahlmeyer received a slap on the wrist for doing it without permits. The message that was sent to others planning vineyard expansion was that after taking into consideration the amount of time saved, it cost about the same amount of money to ignore the law. Heck, you might not even get caught!"

Some things never change, he thought. Gustave Niebaum had exploited his property in Rutherford and the Chinese laborers who helped build the chateau and reroute Navalle Creek, paying them a pittance. Looking around, Norm saw weird connections between past and present reality not featured in the chateau's promotional literature or on the signs on the walls. Like busloads of prosperous Asians showing up every day to race through the chateau with their cameras, buying clothing and trinkets; old movie paraphernalia overtaking wine as the historical product of note.

Management wanted to expand Mammarella's Café, which had been built in the winery, and applied to the county for permits. When they heard that a county official would do a walk-through, everybody on duty, including Norm, ran around removing merchandise not related to wine — kitchen ware, fancy trivets, plates, even loaves of bread — and replacing it with wine.

Once the head of the county planning department had shown up unannounced with a video camera. He was Jeff Redding, a pleasant fellow with a ponytail, and he made a pictorial record of all the gewgaws on the shelves. He had told management that they didn't pass "the smell test," that they had to limit their sales to items more closely related to wine and remove the electric sign in the courtyard that continuously fed fluorescent messages to the tourists. This had caused quite a stir. Francis had been furious and at first threatened not to comply, but eventually the sign was dismantled with a crane and the concrete pad broken up with jackhammers.

Taking all the extraneous items off the shelves had been less successful. Anyone visiting the chateau and the different tasting bars and salesrooms would see things for sale that had nothing to do with the winery's history or its ultimate product. Norm had seen all of them. In Mammarella's there were for sale Francis's specially designed espresso cups for eighty-five dollars, as well as yo-yos, mechanical birds, bocce balls, juggling balls, binoculars, chocolates, flashlights, chessboards, cigars, cards, board games, olive oil, spaghetti sauce (arrabbiata, pomodoro basilico, puttanesca), straw hats, sandals, two sailboats (one for sixty-five dollars, another for one hundred and forty dollars — "One's a toy, the other a work of art"), and, of course, inexpensive rosso, bianco, and rosé Coppola wine.

In the bigger main shop, the press of merchandise, and the prices, increased dramatically. In wooden cases cunningly built to increase the illusion of depth there was all manner of clothing, lavender sachets, candlesticks, candles, handbags, and glasses of all kinds, including the now-absolutely-necessary-in-the-view-of-the-knowledge-able-taster Riedel wine glasses (ninety dollars apiece), and there was the equivalent of a small bookstore. The wine had to be strategically placed to emphasize other upscale stuff for which the designers and the folks in the office intended for the tourists to avidly reach.

Upstairs, near the gleaming red Tucker, was the glass case containing costumes from *Bram Stoker's Dracula,* a bamboo cage designed to hold a human being, and a surfboard, all related to movies. Another case contained the movie awards. Everywhere you looked there was a reference to Francis.

The number of buses increased, evidence of the effectiveness of Niebaum-Coppola marketing. The winery was the only one Norm knew of with a representative specifically for meeting concierges, hoteliers, country club managers, and anyone else dealing with high-end tourists, to get them to send guests en masse to N-C. The Japanese alone accounted for two, three, even four buses a day. They all paid twenty dollars for the tour and then were left to shop in what Norm called "the Gump's of Napa Valley," a reference to San Francisco's famed specialty store, which actually did less business now than N-C. It struck him as absurd to charge clueless people for being exposed to N-C wine made from Central Valley and central coast grapes.

Increasingly, the courtyard and foyer of Gustave Niebaum's fabulous structure reminded Norm of Disneyland, the crowds largely indifferent to the architecture and the tradition of fine wine, and most of them oblivious. A few paused at the door of the Captain's Room, where old Gustave had once sampled wines made at great expense, as had his great-grandnephew John Daniel. Now the Captain's Room was passed by gawkers after celluloid products. They might as well have been glancing into an Egyptian tomb and wondering what rituals had required all the stained glass and carved oak chairs.

After each hectic weekend, Norm and his colleagues would look around and ask, "Who's left? . . . Who got fired?"

It was disconcerting working at a place where you didn't know what would happen next. At times, arriving in the morning, dreading the prospect of dealing with hundreds more tourists, Norm felt as if he were entering through a fake doorway, that he would discover broom handles propping up a facsimile of the towering stone façade designed by old Hamden McIntyre.

At other times he felt overwhelmed by a feeling of loss, and sympathetic to his employer. N-C was simply doing what Beringer, Mondavi, and others did. If commercialization was overwhelming what was true and good in the nation, if this was what America was becoming, Norm asked himself, why shouldn't Napa Valley and Inglenook/N-C reflect it?

In April, the grand three-hundred-year-old oak in front of the Niebaum house toppled onto that architectural gem, the tree's roots having rotted after prolonged watering of the surrounding lawn. The oak missed the turret but broke through the roof and filigree trim — Eastlake influence — and part of the wraparound porch. A limb went through the window that John Daniel's wife, Betty, had had boarded up during her reclusive period. No one was hurt, although Eleanor Coppola was at home at the time.

The family held a ceremony for the tree on the following Sunday. The tasting staff was allowed brief, staggered visits. Norm went and listened to Robin Lail, John Daniel's daughter, speak of sitting in a swing under the oak's spreading branches as a child. She now had her own travel business and seemed to have gotten over the loss of the family estate and all it represented. Also speaking was Rafael Rodriguez, the Mexican immigrant who had worked on the estate for almost half a century. Rafael was in semiretirement, a symbol of the past, and well treated by the Coppolas. He delivered a moving eulogy to the tree. Francis spoke of the cost of finding a suitable replacement, appearing to squeeze out a tear.

Norm went back to the winery. In the foyer of the chateau stood a cylindrical device known as a zoetrope, built in the 1830s. It was made of metal, with slots cut into the sides at regular intervals, and the photographs inside seemed to come to life when the cylinder was spun. This was due to a phenomenon known as the persistence of vision. The zoetrope — the name of Francis's company — had offered the first glimpse of animation, the first thrilling illusion of movement, but instead of augmenting the historical significance of movies, this innocent device was used to authenticate its blatant commercial successors. So was the romance of Inglenook used to sell sandals and sailboats.

The compromises Norm felt he was making were no worse than those made by other winery employees, and some benefits were better. Many people he knew in the industry had their own tales to tell of ego and exploitation. These employees also had to speak purple wine prose to visitors while being secretly aware of the tricks of the winemaking trade, like filtering out the yeast from fermented wine and then adding some juice to bring up the sweetness, and blending in a younger vintage to perk up the package, and letting the grapes hang on the vines until almost rotten, to soften the tannins, and then adding water to tone down the sweetness. Some of these same knowledgeable employees had to pick up leaves by hand that fell onto pebbly paths and listen to pompous invocations of celebrities from Robert Parker to the Dalai Lama.

Somebody should write about life in the trenches, he thought, but no journalists showing up in the tasting rooms seemed inclined to. Who wanted to read that stuff? they would ask. And what wine writer wanted to lose his portion of foie gras and long-macerated cabernet sauvignon?

Norm decided to leave Niebaum-Coppola. Maybe he would leave the valley. It felt increasingly insular, almost claustrophobic. Deprived of its early promise, wine had not delivered him into a world of enlightenment or culture; it had indentured him as surely as it had indentured the Italians and the Chinese in the nineteenth century.

31

TOM LIPPE, sitting in his office in San Francisco's Embarcadero, wrote a letter in late March to attorneys representing the county and the three private parties in the suit — Pahlmeyer Vineyards, Chateau Potelle, and Vineyard Properties West. He shared office space with an investment firm ("responsible lender") on the sixteenth floor, the lobby offering views of Treasure Island, and on the walls reproductions of Van Gogh, Renoir, and Monet. But Tom Lippe still wore no tie.

In the letter, he laid out the already agreed-upon terms, including the big admission by the county that it had exercised "discretion" in approving erosion control plans and that these were therefore subject to the California Environmental Quality Act. Environmental impact studies would be necessary for future projects, and some public comment. Earth-moving activity was prohibited on parts of the vineyards in question, and the size of sediment-holding basins would be increased. All three defendants would split the Sierra Club's legal fees, which amounted to one hundred and thirty-five thousand dollars.

In addition, each defendant had to pay ten thousand dollars into "a mutually agreeable non-profit foundation . . . to be used for the purpose of studying the environmental impacts of vineyard conversions in Napa County." And the Sierra Club — which in reality meant Chris Malan — could decide which fund.

Tom had talked informally to Richard Mendelson during the course of the suit. Richard wasn't involved, but he provided some background about Napa and the people there, without giving anything away, and seemed to think that the suit had restricted the vint-

ners' efforts to perfect their planting and their product. Actions like
the Sierra Club suit could eventually lead to houses in Napa Valley,
Mendelson had said, instead of vineyards. Tom knew that Richard
spent a lot of time in France, that he spoke publicly about appellations and agriculture abroad, and about threats like tourism and development. But he seemed very conservative now, insisting above all
on the freedom to farm and saying that if there was a moratorium, it
should be on houses.

When they had been at Stanford together, talking about everything from art to politics, Richard — with his pale green eyes and
soft, intelligent voice — had at least seemed to share Tom's activist
values — environmental protection, social justice — but Tom wondered now if he had. During the course of their friendly, if measured,
conversation these decades later, Tom had avoided discussing limitations on any future suits.

His trips up to the valley took him far from the hectic activity sixteen stories below, on the street. Tom could always find a parking
place in Napa. He always picked his time to take the Bay Bridge, to
avoid the worst traffic, and once in the valley of the grape felt more
relaxed. Sometimes he went for a run there and reflected on the fact
that the struggle over land use in Napa County was important for
the rest of California and maybe for America. The presidential campaign pitted two candidates against each other who seemed different, but weren't: oil man and environmentalist were in Lippe's mind
products of the same undesirable establishment. He would probably
vote for Ralph Nader because the country needed a viable third
party and candidates who wouldn't compromise.

Meanwhile, he was looking into the behavior of the county and
those in it who wanted another vineyard in a place already saturated
with them. He'd heard that the county was preparing an environmental impact study for the whole valley, but each prospective vineyard would still need its own EIR. Cumulative impacts would have
to be reckoned with, too.

Everyone agreed on the basics as outlined in Tom's letter, with the
exception of Jayson Pahlmeyer. He wanted an alternative to donat-
ing ten thousand in cash and offered to give up development rights
on twenty acres at the edge of his project and let the Napa County
Land Trust manage it. Pahlmeyer couldn't stomach the idea of turn-

ing money over to a cause dear to Chris. The development rights on the land were worth a lot more than ten grand, so nobody could legitimately object. The final details of the settlement were yet to be worked out, but it was essentially a done deal.

In the house on Sylvaner, Carlene Mennen sat over the usual array of material on the table made from the Mexican barn gate, her long, glossy black hair framing her face as she studied papers relating to water diversion in northern California, the Utah wilderness, campaign fundraising, forestry, mountain lions, salmon, the Sierra Club lawsuit, and Napa River macroinvertebrates. The Mennen Environmental Foundation had put upward of a hundred thousand dollars into studying the river, from its smallest inhabitants to its historical use by human beings.

The victory with the lawsuit was about to be announced, and Carlene thought it would counter some of the criticism over the loss of Kathryn Winter's seat on the board of supervisors. Carlene was relieved that Chris had lost the election, but Chris had gotten more than ten percent of the vote. Not bad at all, and better than many had expected. Chris had kept the issue of hillside development before the public, which was the reason the Mennens had financed her in first place.

More important was the long-term legal strategy of which the lawsuit was just the opening gun. Chris had wanted to go to trial and get those vintners up there testifying, but that had frightened the lawyers. They, and Carlene and Peter, wanted a settlement with the county, and one with the individual growers that acknowledged the county had made a mistake in not complying with CEQA. Environmental impact reports would now be required before any slope over five degrees could be developed, and the county would have to consider the total impact of development on the river.

The plaintiffs also wanted money from the individual defendants that could be used in future lawsuits, but if Chris pushed too much, their own lawyers argued, they could lose the whole ballgame. Carlene and Peter had agreed, and this had made Chris mad. But there was nothing she could do about it because she didn't control the funding of the suit, Carlene did.

Sometimes success was harder to handle than failure, Carlene thought. The county and the vineyard operators were on the run; it was just a matter now of sorting out the details and getting Jayson Pahlmeyer to either pony up the money in damages, as the others agreed to do, or forgo some development rights. Because scientists had been allowed on the Pahlmeyer property during discovery, to take soil samples and collect other information, they now had material that might be used in a future lawsuit against him, one alleging bad business practices or some other violation. One way or another, they had Pahlmeyer where they wanted him.

The telephone rang. It was Peter, about to leave the office. She told him about recent developments in another resource fight, and he said, "You're the most articulate 'dumb blonde' I ever met."

Carlene had to laugh. Her hair was downright raven, not blond. From where she sat, she could see the prayer wand hanging on the screen in the living room, the wild turkey and grouse feathers beautiful in the natural light. Carlene, too, was dedicated to the salvation of Turtle Island. She never stopped thinking about her projects and even dreamed about them; there was no difference between the way she lived and what she did, and her doctor had once asked her, "When did you last have any fun?"

Carlene couldn't answer in a way that satisfied him, though she should have said that what she did, while not technically fun, was much better.

Most of the foundation work and supervision of projects was funneled through Carlene. So were the checks to finance them. Decisions were made jointly by husband and wife, but the standards were hers, and they were absolute. Many people thought that Peter was the final arbiter, and lately Chris had been acting as if she thought that, too.

Carlene didn't care what people thought. She listened to what they said about their hopes, intentions, and needs, but if someone crossed her, she could reveal a nasty temper.

Peter was perturbed by the sudden downturn in the stock market. Two weeks before, the Mennen Environmental Foundation had been a lot richer. Everybody was hoping that this was an aberration, that the market would rebound, but if it didn't, well, there was money left. This was fortunate, he reminded himself, because there were plenty of projects and plenty of people who needed setting right. So many fenders, so little time.

He and Carlene thought of themselves as fixers, but so much was happening so fast that they still felt they were putting Band-Aids on broken limbs. At the same time, his squabble with the Postal Service had intensified, distracting him from the other business. The bureaucracy was after Ricki Lake; it was, in Peter's opinion, after him, too, but he was fighting back.

In response to the official objections to Ricki's flying around the post office, Peter had obtained a letter from a psychotherapist saying that he needed the bird in his office to help relieve his anxiety. There was even a name for it: "service pet." The psychotherapist insisted that Ricki was Peter's enabler and a therapeutic necessity.

Peter laughed aloud when he thought about the discomfort this must cause his superiors. He was taking a stand for the individual, something he thought as important as the environment, against the standardizers, the homogenizers, the breakers-down-of-the-little-guy who had to be checked here and there or they would take over the country. Nobody at the St. Helena post office was likely to "go postal" because Peter didn't treat his employees like objects. He allowed a woman to wear a cotton miniskirt instead of the uniform because the polyester irritated her skin, and a man to keep his hair long. He exempted another from wearing a tie. All this displeased the inspectors. Because he gave the employees some say in their own lives, in an otherwise highly regimented system, they were happier, better workers.

Sitting in his office with Ricki on his shoulder, Peter gazed at the trees in the park across Main Street, so green in April, the sky so blue. Few little guys got a chance to object to injustice, he thought. None had the chance to object as he did, to have some influence, and that angered people who were accustomed to the little guy keeping out of the way and his mouth shut, people like the members of the Winegrowers. One of them, Herb Schmidt, the Mondavi political operative in Italian loafers, had written a letter to the *Napa Register* accusing Peter and Carlene of trying to buy the election by financing the petition opposing hillside development. "While the Mennens' attempt to corrupt the political process here in Napa failed," he wrote, ". . . we do need to remain vigilant to these type of campaigns."

What did that mean? Did it include the campaign waged by the Winegrowers — presumably with the participation of Mondavi, Inc. — to heavily finance Kathryn Winter's opponent and have Napa exempted from the California Environmental Quality Act and suspend environmental protections? That backfired in Sacramento and made the sponsors look like fools, but there was no letter from Schmidt explaining that fiasco.

Peter thought he saw the hands of vintners on his continuing problems with the postal establishment. That added zest and common cause to the fight. He had planned to retire, peaceably, in two months, and had even turned down a request by a television producer to do a take-out on Peter and Ricki Lake, one featuring them strolling along the streets of St. Helena, because the bureaucrats opposed it. But now, after all the demands that Ricki be exiled and that he retire, Peter intended to go out with a bang, and maybe with some financial largess for a worthy cause.

In twenty-four years he had developed a lot of contacts in the post office, he knew a lot about regulations and strategy. A friend and counselor for the Postal Service wrote a letter to Peter's superiors on Peter's behalf, saying that he was "INCREDULOUS when informed that the Postmaster's manager . . . had again made inappropriate comments. Apparently he told the Postmaster that IF HE WOULD RETIRE IN JUNE, THAT HE WOULD NOT ORDER THE REMOVAL OF THE BIRD. You should be aware that there is a word for this type of conduct, and it is known as 'Constructive Discharge.' Mr. Mennen stated that . . . the bird is necessary for his emotional well being. I understand that the bird is certified as a therapy pet . . . I was also informed that Mr. Mennen was disciplined for an item in the ladies room. There is also a word for this type of conduct, and it is known as 'Retaliation.' The problem now becomes rather evident . . .

"I only made one visit to the St. Helena Post Office . . . and found the office and the people to be extremely pleasant. As a former Customer Service Supervisor . . . I am familiar with customer service excellence . . . The Postmaster's therapist and various members of his LEGAL TEAM have contacted me regarding [management's] latest actions. Included are those involving the St. Helena Bird (an endangered conure species). The agency may also want to consider that there has also been mention of Mr. Mennen having access to legal representation including Johnnie Cochrane and F. Lee Bailey. It has been mentioned that any and all monies from the agency through the legal process would be donated to an environmental charity . . ."

So it went.

Ever since the experience on the motorcycle in Mexico, Peter had felt himself nudged by some powerful force into the right path. It was as if a hand descended each time and pushed him back toward the necessary, difficult way. He could almost hear the voice: "No, Peter . . . Back over here now. This is what needs to be done." The last time was when he was tempted to be merely wealthy — "piss-ant rich" — instead of environmentally significant. The hand had descended, and Peter had seen that he must live ethically if he was to pursue ethical goals. Otherwise, it wouldn't work.

Fortunately Peter had Carlene to take care of the big picture, because he was a detail person. He was reminded of the group of Bedouin in the desert that he had read about. When shown a Rorschach print, instead of looking at the whole thing, the Bedouin concentrated on the edges, where they saw little projections that reminded them of gun barrels above a sand dune. That was him, he thought: Peter Mennen. Gun barrels on the big, rolling sand dunes.

That night, he left his old pickup with the license plate reading ODD DUCK parked at the curb. Carlene was off taking care of some business, and Peter got out his BMW 540, which lived quietly and anonymously in the garage. A limited edition made for use in Germany, one of the few such cars in the United States, it had been augmented with a supercharger at a specialty auto shop down south, and modifications done on the gearbox and differential made the car "blindingly fast," as he put it whenever asked. The Department of Motor Vehicles would have liked to get inside the "black box" containing the computer settings and make the car a little less juicy, but Peter was resisting that bureaucratic interference, too.

He took the sleek white car, his one concession to the dark side — the evil reign of the internal combustion engine — through the back streets of St. Helena and up the Silverado Trail. It was his favorite road in the valley and always reminded him of an inspiring paragraph written by Edward Abbey, in his environmental classic *Desert*

Solitaire, which began: "May your trails be crooked, winding, lonesome, dangerous, leading to the most amazing view."

As he gathered speed, the night in Mexico so long ago came again to mind. Peter was no longer a very young man in search of himself, but an established philanthropist and political activist on his way to Pacifico, in Calistoga, for enchilada suiza. But the effect was similar: speed, exhilaration, insight. The car took the curves with ease at eighty miles an hour, a banked loop no problem whatsoever. Inside, all was quiet, immaculate. On extended road trips up north, and to Utah, Peter didn't allow snacks in the car. The BMW was his one technological obsession, one for which he made no apologies.

A Mercedes loomed on the Trail, also headed north. As the BMW approached from the rear, the Mercedes speeded up. The license plate was local, but Peter didn't recognize it or the driver watching him intently in the rearview mirror. Peter deftly pressed the accelerator. The supercharger gasped, feeding exhaust back into the maelstrom of combustion, and the car leapt forward, pinning his back to the seat. The Mercedes struggled to match this velocity, trailing smoke. Peter could plainly see the driver now, the picture of success in the valley, a florid face above a blue blazer. The man scowled, stressing his machine, but the 540 ate its lunch.

32

THE PAPERWEIGHT had been turned upside down, and inside it was furiously snowing.

That was the image Jeff Redding carried with him everywhere — to the planning department, to the martial arts studio, home. The Sierra Club suit had changed things forever and done nothing to alleviate his problems. It had made them worse. It wasn't an official defeat for the county until the county, too, threw in the towel, which it would eventually do, but so far nothing had been clarified. New applications for vineyards had trebled; landowners persisted in seeking forgiveness, rather than permission, for their projects; illegal grading was going on at an accelerated — rampant — pace; and the county was incapable of keeping up with it all.

As planning director, Jeff continued to be blamed by both sides. No amount of exercise could alleviate the tension he now felt. He made a public statement about the private parties in the suit agreeing to modify their erosion control plans, bravely adding that the county was not affected "in any way." Environmental review of all proposed new projects would continue, he said. No problem. But he had to do an environmental review of each project, with Malan/Mennen/Sierra Club waiting in the wings to challenge him on grounds of "cumulative impacts" on the river. An environmental impact report would eventually have to be done for the whole county, and the river's total maximum daily load of sediment — the dreaded TMDL — was being quantified by a federally funded research team. The study might take years to complete and would no doubt open doors to more legal maneuvers.

The county planning department wasn't equipped to deal with all this. It wasn't sufficiently staffed to handle the flood of applications for new vineyards. Jeff was frantically trying to hire people in a job market sucked dry by the dot-com boom, which had also inflated salaries and other expectations.

The collective will of the defendants — Pahlmeyer, Chateau Potelle, and Stotesbury (or Vineyard Properties West, as it was also called) — had proven to be zero. They should have stood up to the Sierra Club and gone through with a trial, airing the issues, motives, and maybe solutions, too. If that had happened, Jeff believed, the defendants would have prevailed, the Sierra Club would have been hung out to dry, and the county would have received recognition for what was a good erosion control ordinance, relatively speaking.

That ordinance had simply been contravened by a few renegades. The vintner community should have publicly turned its back on them, like the judges in the movie *Bloodsport* who turned their backs on an opponent of Van Damme's when he got too rough and killed a guy. Censorship, real and lasting. But instead the vintners had stayed in the background, afraid that by speaking out against the violations they might damage their own interests down the line.

As for the Sierra Club, Jeff had asked, "I know what your position is, but what's your interest?" The lack of clarity had produced anxiety on all levels. The Sierra Club had put the county and the vintners on notice, and everybody was sitting around waiting for someone else to blink, while Jeff's workload had become all-consuming.

Was the Sierra Club's interest a healthier watershed, he wondered, or something more draconian? It was implicitly clear to everyone that the effects of CEQA could eventually shut down agriculture, while single-family residential development went forward without review by the county. He also wondered what would happen in the next five years, the true test of Napa Valley's future. After the recommendations of the Watershed Task Force were made, whatever they turned out to be, there could still be surreptitious efforts on both sides to prevent them from being enacted. There could be business as usual in the hills, or none.

Even a pessimist had something to be optimistic about: at least the questions of development and its effect on the water were before the public. The agencies were attempting to address it. But the Sierra Club remained an unknown. Many people feared that Peter Mennen would back an initiative to shut things down in the hills once and for all — the ultimate test of both the environmentalists' and the public's will.

Jeff was saying to the Sierra Club, through intermediaries: Help us. Don't file more lawsuits. It doesn't help the environment, hurts it, driving up illegal activities by those seeking to avoid the system. Let's work together. But whether or not the Sierra Club was listening was anybody's guess.

What *was* its interest? What was its goal? Was the Sierra Club an organization or a person? These questions would not go away. The county was finally enforcing the requirements of CEQA, with deafening objections, and people were calling the planning department to ask if the Sierra Club was interested in their single-acre family vineyard, if they were to be sued next, everybody gun-shy. The easy part had been done, a gotcha on the county over CEQA, but what was the Sierra Club's endgame?

The question haunted him, and he hoped he would be around in a few years to find out the answer. He continued going down to Vallejo to do his martial arts, working off the tension, moving through the big room, slashing, twirling, sweating, getting out of his skin. Others were there doing the same thing. They knew little about land use in Napa County, but they, too — like the members of the Watershed Task Force — noticed that Jeff Redding had cut off his ponytail.

Jayson Pahlmeyer read the *Register* with dismay and rising anger. Specifically he read, and reread, under the headline "Everybody's a Winner in the Sierra Club Settlement," the letter by John Stephens, chair of the Napa group of the Sierra Club. Jayson had never seen Stephens, wouldn't have recognized his rail-thin, bespectacled figure or his postage-stamp front yard devoted to native plants, where Jayson's fate had been freely discussed, but he found himself resenting Stephens and his associates with newfound passion.

"We are happy Pahlmeyer, Chateau Potelle, and Stotesbury Vineyards joined with the Napa Sierra Club in a mutual agreement," Stephens began, in the most reasonable of voices, ". . . that all three projects would come under the more careful scrutiny" of CEQA, "signaling a new age of better farming practices." He pointed out that each defendant had agreed to "help pay for environmental studies on the impacts of hillside vineyard conversions" and "in a spirit of putting the past behind us . . . agreed also to pay for our own court costs."

In a spirit of putting the past behind us!

"Very often," Stephens went on, "those who are in the midst of historic events fail to see the significance of the individual roles they play . . . Gone are the days of gross exploitation . . . savvy vineyard developers will be factoring in the projected additional costs of an environmental review and allowing more time for their projects. We see this as a turning point for our valley . . . protecting wildlife and the people downstream will become as universally accepted as the seat belts in our cars and the nutritional labels on our food. We have all won in this joint settlement."

Jayson thought, "We've *all* won?" No sooner had he finished rereading this published letter than he set about addressing it, first as a letter to the editor and then, on second thought, as a direct response to Stephens. Jayson wasn't a lawyer for nothing, and a good attorney knew a few things about spin. If he wasn't savvy, his wine wouldn't be nearly as popular.

His position was that the Sierra Club had not ushered in a new age of better farming, but had extorted money and development concessions affecting fewer than three acres "out of a total of more than 1600 acres," as he wrote, adding that these acres of new development were scattered among more than ninety property owners. In terms of individual land use, this was a pittance, "a low blow. If we had seen a copy of your letter before signing the settlement agreement, we would rather have gone through the trial. Your letter unnecessarily rubbed salt in the wounds . . . If Sierra Club had truly believed that there was an environmental crisis posed by hillside development in general, it would have sued each and every one of the 90-plus who held approved erosion control plans . . . Given our potential losses and the fact that we had no standing to defend the County's approval process, we had little option but to try to settle this suit . . . not in the 'spirit of putting the past behind us,' but rather as one would react with a revolver aimed at one's head . . . .

"Only after some years have passed will someone be able to truly assess the carnage this lawsuit wrought . . . Our settlement, rather than being a cause to celebrate, closes an ugly chapter of an ongoing book about Napa Valley."

"He's my favorite lunchtime customer," announced the manager of Mustard's, where Jayson had gone for lunch, "a great bon vivant. Bring Jayson something good from the back," he told the waitress.

"He's putting together some French sauvignon blancs for our blind tasting," Jayson said to his guest, of the manager who was helping the cult-label owner with ongoing research into different types and styles of wine. For in addition to his Napa Valley holdings, Jayson owned vineyards in Sonoma County and was about to launch his expensive pinot noir.

The bar was packed. White tablecloths around the room supported the bottles and the elbows of eager diners, several of them from Silicon Valley, the financial boom having been in effect so long that no one could imagine it ending, like the owner of the pearl-gray Jaguar parked prominently out front with a beautiful companion in a navy-blue knit. Jayson had already shared a glass of his recently released chardonnay — the same label that appeared in *Disclosure* — with a hair stylist and her boyfriend, an off-duty chef, who were relaxing valley-style with an array of glasses before them and on their faces the satisfaction of locals who know what to order. Jayson told them, before taking his place on the banquette under the window, how long the wine spent in oak and how much mouthwatering acid had been preserved and when the grapes were picked and why.

"A vine is like a male *Homo sapiens*. For the first third of his life he's vigorous, and then as he ages he loses productivity, and in old age he's slower and wiser . . . After forty years the vine is putting all its energy into a few clusters — even, consistent. The French have never stepped back and considered this . . . My goal is to make the best wine in the world — better than the French."

He had also brought along a bottle of Pahlmeyer merlot and a pinot noir from another winery. Both were opened by the waitress. People dropping by to say hello were offered a splash of the powerful Pahlmeyer red and a short rap by the vintner. This was his favorite restaurant. He ordered seared ahi to follow the appetizer, in a good mood despite his loss to the Sierra Club. "They cost the taxpayers a lot of money, they got no real concessions from us" — modifications on fewer than three acres of new vineyard, and the giving up of some development rights presently negotiated by Jayson. "The Land Trust doesn't want to be in a position of serving as a regulatory agency, they don't want to look like a bagman. I'm doing it because I believe in it — like a peasant giving up a one-acre plot to the Catholic Church."

He sampled the pinot, pulling air in over the wine, and swallowed. The lips were pursed, the eyes reflective behind gold-rimmed lenses. But instead of evaluating it, he said, "Some people called me up in the beginning and gave me hell for not getting a permit. They made me feel like a scumbag. Well, the Sierra Club should have chosen Mondavi, Beringer, Phelps. If they had, those guys would have stood up at a press conference and said, 'We're being persecuted,' and never have paid Lippe's fees. The Napa Valley Vintners Association would have rallied round them."

By now the assertion that he and a couple of other relative newcomers were singled out and sued was thoroughly familiar. What was missing was any recognition of the fact that excesses had taken place all over the valley, and were still taking place, though on a much reduced scale; and that these excesses were relevant to what was happening to the valley and to the country.

The pinot was okay, he said, but nothing great, one of hundreds tasted and pondered by him in a long quest. "It's only in good economies," he said reflectively, "when things are humming along, that people look around and say, 'Hey, this hurts the environment.' In a depression, where the hell are the environmentalists? All you have to do is travel the world and look at people scratching out a living — firewood in Uganda, rain forests in Brazil — to see why. You can't say, 'Don't cut that tree' when somebody's starving. You're not worried about sludge in a creek when you're trying to support your family. Environmentalism's a kind of luxury."

He sampled his merlot, and his eyes closed for a moment. But instead of commenting on it, he returned to the subject of Chris Malan. "She was there in 1990, when the land was first cleared, and she didn't say anything. Those people before me had gone broke, and I came in, and . . ." He trailed off. Then, "Chris knows all the buzzwords. She'll be ready the next time I have a project. It'll take me eight years to get a use permit for my winery. All my work is now in political preparation for this. It's a sad comment. 'How stupid can you get, trying to plant a vineyard in Napa Valley?' Well, now it's going to be, 'How stupid can you get, trying to build a winery?' In Napa Valley!"

The first step toward approval, he added, was taking Mendelson up there. Next would come a supervisor — Bill Dodd — and then Jeff Redding and his people, then the planning commission — "the major, major, major stumbling block. In the good old days it was the land you had to get, and financing, and a good contractor. Now it doesn't matter what the land and the winery cost, it's getting the government to approve it."

The couple from Silicon Valley moved toward the door, all eyes on the navy-blue knit, worn by the sort of companion once seen with movie stars, not software and IPO beneficiaries. Bread crumbs littered Jayson's table, swept away by the busboy. "It was all a scheme to raise money for mercenary lawyers," he said, back to the Sierra Club, "and radical environmentalists. Environmental extortion, that's what it was!"

At last the seared ahi arrived. Jayson tasted it. "I can see a time coming in America when you have no idea what you will be allowed to do with your own land," he mused, a realization, however oblique, that land is finite and population infinite, and eventually society will act to end uses antithetical to human well-being. "But the lawsuit could backfire"; in the short term, it could encourage politicians to pass fewer, less rigorous regulations.

Much remained up in the air. The Watershed Task Force had to finish its deliberations. Lawyers working for the Mennens were looking at new possibilities, as everyone knew, for suing. But Jayson's long, expensive bad dream was over, or so he thought. "I settled the suit because I wanted to get on with my life. My vineyard's more or less in now. I'm set. And I'm telling you, I'm gonna make a wine that drops you to your knees."

33

VOLKER EISELE returned from a marketing trip that had taken him to Charleston and other southern cities and found in his mailbox a flier from Farmers for Napa Valley. Stu Smith, Mark van Gorder, and the other "bad boys" were urging grape growers to jettison the current board of directors of the Farm Bureau and replace it with people like them, an unwelcome homecoming message.

For years the Farm Bureau had been a bastion of sensible land use in the county. In other parts of America, the prime concern of such bureaus was not farming but the protection of future options of farmers, including that of selling out to developers. In Napa County, the Farm Bureau acted to preserve land and involve itself in other questions affecting agriculture. The board had taken positions considered anathema by Jack Cakebread's Breakfast Club and Stu Smith's Farmers for Napa Valley. The latest of these was the Farm Bureau's opposition to the bill in Sacramento that would have exempted vineyards from environmental review — something the Napa Valley Vintners Association had failed to do, despite Hugh Davies's efforts. Such a law would have been bad for both the land and the reputations of real farmers, a proposition devised as a blunt instrument to strike down Malan/Mennen. It had failed to garner enough support.

But the Farm Bureau board was under attack from within. Volker talked by telephone to his ally on the board, the young Tom Gamble. He, like Beth Novak Milliken, Jon-Mark Chappellet, Rich Salvestrin, Hugh Davies, and other younger people who had grown up in the valley, was determined to fight. Volker and Tom discussed what steps to take to counter the Farmers for Napa Valley letter, and Volker called it "a declaration of war."

He walked — in bulky sweater, scuffed leather shoes (no running gear here), and old khakis — and tried to order recent events in his own mind. Kathryn Winter's loss in the election was just now sinking in. If she had been stronger, and clearer on the environmental issues, she might have won, bringing Chris Malan along with her instead of in opposition. That would have prevented the voters from thinking something was wrong with Kathryn in the eyes of the environmentalists, and Kathryn should have made no attempt whatsoever to placate the Winegrowers, telling them straight out that what the Breakfast Club was doing was wrong.

Mel Varrelman, the most enduring supervisor, would have to be the leader of the county on environmental issues, and Mel was looking decidedly weary. If he lost his seat in the next election or decided not to run, the developers could end up with a three-to-two majority on the board.

The failure of the bill put forward by the Winegrowers to exempt vineyards from environmental review had been proof of bad intentions by the big vintners. It had brought everybody together in opposition, but Malan/Mennen remained an unreckonable. If they had been patient, in five years they could have sued the county in federal court, after insufficient progress had been made to clean up the river, and won a huge victory. The Sierra Club lawsuit was still a big win, but Malan/Mennen and their lawyers weren't exploiting it as they should have. The settlement with the county could have included a moratorium on all development in the hills, until its effects could be accurately calibrated, since the county was desperate, but the Sierra Club didn't insist. Malan/Mennen could have demanded more than CEQA review and environmental impact reports; they could have gotten tough, specific regulations, but they hadn't.

The next step might well be a voter initiative to put the question of hillside development and resource protection squarely and unequivocally before the public for an up or down vote; if it passed, it would be a far-reaching victory on a par with the creation of the ag preserve. If it failed, it would be a disaster, indicating that anti-development forces were not representative of the majority of the population.

The question would be whether or not to help Malan/Mennen.

So far the Farm Bureau and the allied Grape Growers Association had taken on both sides, attacking the right — the Winegrowers and Farmers for Napa Valley — for seeking to have Napa Valley exempted from CEQA, and the left — Malan/Mennen — for sabotaging Kathryn Winter's candidacy. An initiative would require cooperation, and whether the disparate elements among the environmentalists could achieve this was uncertain.

Among growers, stream setbacks were the big issue now, and the chief subject of discussion on the Watershed Task Force. Water in the stream running through the Eisele property would eventually find its way down to Lake Hennessey, and in the rainy season it might make it past the dam, to Conn Creek, flow past Dennis Groth's and other valley-floor vineyards, and into the Napa River.

A regulation that new vineyards stop well short of the banks of such streams was almost certain, and also that replanted vineyards be required to pull back to some degree. This posed a big political problem, since setbacks cost money. Fewer vines per acre in riparian areas meant fewer grapes, fewer grapes meant less wine, and less wine meant lower profits. Of this, people like Jack Stuart, who oversaw Silverado Vineyards for the Disneys and who was the current president of the Napa Valley Vintners Association, complained bitterly.

Easter Sunday broke clear and bright in Chiles Valley. Volker's son, Alexander, had been up at 4:30 to turn on the sprinklers in the vineyard for frost protection. The young, developing fruit was coated with water, which would turn to ice and, paradoxically it seemed, protect the fruit itself from freezing. This was the most vulnerable time in the grape's life cycle, frost protection required a lot of water, and water was limited, including that stored in the pond at the top of the vineyard, crucial for irrigation and for the survival of the bass, frogs, turtles, and a myriad of unseen aquatic life in the long dry season soon to follow. Water was also sustenance for everything else, from wild Canada goslings to the mountain lions whose tracks were often visible in the fine dust bordering the pond.

Volker was to cook the celebratory Easter meal. First he went to church in St. Helena and listened to Father Brenkle ask for money and blankets for homeless farm workers. There were many of them, and they were an embarrassment despite the fact that the valley paid higher wages than other places and so attracted more migrant labor. The demand for additional housing was complicated because houses, even low-income ones, replaced agriculture. But to point out these difficulties was to be criticized for lacking compassion. You can't fight Jesus, Volker thought; He was the original homeless person.

The menu was tournedos Rossini served with a 1983 Château Margaux given to Volker by a friend, followed by a dessert of crème Portuguese complemented by a German Auslese, a late-harvest wine made of riesling, that fabulous grape that got little respect in the Chardonnay Republic, known also as the United States of America.

First Volker opened a bottle Pol Roger, and he and Liesel sat down in the living room, the late-afternoon sun angling sharply through the windows to illuminate their flutes of golden, effervescent wine and the spines of books — Goethe, Schiller, Mann, many titles in his native German.

Alexander arrived with his girlfriend, as dark-haired as Alexander was fair, with dark, radiant eyes. She carried a basket of candied fruit and flowers, and she set it down on the coffee table. They toasted the holiday and lamented the absence of Christiane, the Eiseles' daughter, who was studying medicine at Tulane University.

An easy merriment took over despite the fact that language was never simple at the Eiseles'. German prevailed except when there were guests, and even then the conversation rocked back and forth between English and German, taught to the children when they were growing up in Chiles Valley. The occasional French phrase was also tossed in, when nothing else would serve, and Spanish, too.

Father and son discussed the night's weather forecast in English. Volker asked not only the projected low temperature but also the dew point, and then he went into the kitchen to finish cooking. After some clattering of pans he returned in an apron to say that the tournedos — filet mignon resting on artichoke hearts, topped with foie gras and a slice of truffle — were almost ready. When they were, the others were to go directly into the dining room and eat while the food was hot.

Through the big windows, the lower vineyard was kindled by the setting sun; already there was a chill in the air.

Tom Gamble was known for his white straw cowboy hat with the outsized feather in the band and for a prominent Adam's apple that performed vertical arabesques when he talked ardently about something, which was often. He liked to say, "I've come about half a mile in my life," meaning from Oakville Cross Road to the property where he now lived, north of Yountville, but by a circuitous route that had included a college degree in English literature at UC Davis and a stint as a film producer in southern California. Now he was a husband, father, cattle rancher, and grape grower, but it was the job of member of the board of directors of the Farm Bureau that defined him in the minds of many.

A lucky spermer, a product of the Procter and Gamble alliance in the nineteenth century, he had a colorful family history that included a famine ship from Ireland and a fortune made from selling soap and candles to the Union army. The Gambles came on to California in the early years of the twentieth century; Tom's grandfather and his great-uncle had registered their cattle brand in the Berryessa Valley in 1918, and part of that ranch still existed. From it the two men directly marketed their own meat, taking a page from the wine industry: a specialty product reflecting microclimate, meticulous husbandry, and organic farming will sell. "Boutique beef" wasn't the sales line, but it was the idea.

Tom owned hundreds of acres on the valley floor. There was nothing pretentious about the house, the furnishings, or the view. From where he sat, in an airy living room, he could see mostly vines and oaks. No pleached fruit trees, no long visual throw to the Mayacamas, but beautiful.

Each generation of Gambles had attempted to do something "meaningful," a concept not limited to financial advantage; his contribution, he hoped, was in helping preserve the valley for agriculture. In a complicated world, that came down to thwarting not just developers but also property rights advocates and environmental purists who played into developers' hands. Grapes were the product that had pushed almost all cattle and row crops out of the county, so valuable that it supported the agricultural preserve in an age of otherwise irresistible residential development. New fortunes, and new romance, flowed from an ancient drink. Without it, Napa Valley would become pavement.

The Farm Bureau was currently reviewing all conservation measures in the county. The success of wine, and the prolonged economic boom, had imperiled the place where it was produced by increasing the population and diminishing support for agriculture among the public. There were only eight thousand valley residents involved with wine and grapes, out of roughly sixty thousand voters who were largely turned off by big houses and flamboyant lifestyles. A balance had to be struck, Tom thought, between a total shutdown of the industry and replacing every tree with a vine. To achieve balance, the growers and vintners had to agree to some limits and tell their stories convincingly to the people in the cities. They were able to market wine successfully in Taipei and Baton Rouge, but couldn't make the case for grape growing to people in Napa city or American Canyon.

Tom often said, "We exist only by the political will of the people." Without public support, farming was dead. The Watershed Task Force had been an attempt to address the objections to agricultural development in the hills, but unfortunately it had turned into a slugfest.

Sometimes Tom thought all the political contentiousness, not just on the Watershed Task Force but also abroad in the valley — and he included the Sierra Club lawsuit and the friction within the Farm Bureau membership in this — flowed from the clash of two powerful wills, Chris Malan's and Stu Smith's. Their dislike of each other, and all that the other represented, had crystallized in an opposition that was calculated, implacable, and irrational.

The often-stated opinion making the rounds in the valley among those most sympathetic to vineyard development was "If somebody had told the bitch to shut up, none of this would have happened." While Tom didn't believe that, and certainly didn't repeat it, there was an element of truth there: the perception that no one was standing up to Malan/Mennen had been reinforced by the settlement of the lawsuit.

The antipathy directed toward Chris from every corner had played into the hands of those trying to take over the Farm Bureau. There was no logical connection, since the current board had nothing in common with Malan/Mennen, despite the fact that the board favored restrictions on the planting of steep slopes and zoning that discouraged the breakup of large parcels of agricultural land. Those were the traditional values of the Farm Bureau and the Grape Growers Association with which it was aligned, but sometimes people forgot that.

Tom had been a member since the eighties. His two years on the board had been a rite of passage because the whole world was changing with the boom, and the Farm Bureau with it. At first he had gone to the meetings and just listened, trying to understand the issues that were piling up — ground water, hillsides, population growth, regulation. The struggle for control of the board was already under way, but Tom hadn't yet realized it. Then he started seeing letters from the group headed by Stu Smith and Mark Neal, the vineyard developer, complaining about the leadership's refusal to "stand up for farmers' rights."

The small operator, so often lauded by politicians who then acted to help the corporate farmer, suffered most from too much regulation, so the balance could be struck there. But the property rights advocates wanted no restraints, including zoning and environmental ones. The landowner was inviolate, in their view, which was precisely what the big operators wanted. In Tom's opinion, the powerful winery interests were goading Stu on, when Stu's concerns were more traditional land use, like planting and harvesting timber, not creating roadside attractions and parking lots.

In the previous election, Volker Eisele had been voted off the board by the membership after that calculated campaign casting him as radical and heavy-handed. But Tom had seen him in debates and thought him effective. In that election, the Farm Bureau board had behaved in a gentlemanly fashion, putting forward its own nominated slate of directors without too much fanfare, and four of them had lost to Farmers for Napa Valley candidates, including Hugh Davies, Tom's friend.

The meetings of the Farm Bureau that followed were contentious and unpleasant, the bare-knuckle tactics of Farmers for Napa Valley much in evidence. This detracted from the leadership's reputation in a conservative organization like the Farm Bureau whose members didn't want to see it torn apart by the sort of politics witnessed in Sacramento and Washington, D.C. The president, Rich Salvestrin, let everyone have his say, but the fabric of the organization was constantly torn over conservation issues.

The Farm Bureau's effectiveness in county politics was diminished as a result, the aim of Farmers for Napa Valley, the rump group. Now Farmers had put forward a full slate of its own: twenty-four candidates for the board, proof that the group wasn't interested in balance between conservation and property rights, but in control.

Stu was often described as a libertarian. Mel Varrelman, the supervisor, considered him to be an anarchist. During the debate over setbacks, which most of the board favored, Stu had stood up at a meeting of the board of directors, packed by Farmers for Napa Valley, and said that if setbacks were approved, he would do everything in his power to bring down the board and the Farm Bureau itself. A deathly silence had followed. People had stared at Stu. The board didn't know much parliamentary procedure, and so no one made a motion; the process had broken down.

A big, argumentative, biblically bearded figure could be intimidating, and Stu had it honed to a fine edge. Sometimes Tom had the impression that Stu cared more about himself than he did about others. Stu had become a lightning rod, taking the hits for others, and he seemed to revel in it. His whole life was wrapped up in this.

When Volker had been on the Farm Bureau board, debate was orderly, productive. The irony was that Volker and Stu had a lot in common. Both were small, independent farmers involved in the issues, both believed passionately in their positions, and neither had any use for Chris Malan. And yet they were miles apart in the scheme of the new century.

The board was reeling, its neck in the noose with these environmental debates. Maybe it would wither as an effective force. The Bureau had taken its lead from the agricultural preserve, the idea that farmers would sacrifice some economic advantages for the right to farm. The same sorts who had opposed creating the ag preserve back in the sixties, people like John Daniel of Inglenook, would no doubt be on the side of Farmers for Napa Valley today. Some things never changed.

A new Farm Bureau election was scheduled for July, when Hugh Davies was to try again. He had shown courage over the past year in the Napa Valley Vintners Association, and would be a good addition to the Farm Bureau board, if elected. Tom had grown up with Hugh's brother Bill, the two of them riding ten-speeds through the vineyards, hunting jackrabbits and getting five dollars an ear as part of pest control. (They had to switch from shotguns to .22 rifles after puncturing an irrigation line.) Hugh's father had been a mentor to Tom when the young Gamble was trying to figure out the ethics of a particular situation. Jack Davies had taught him the steps in any decision, and the value of leading by example, always juggling private and public commitments, ready to hear the opposing argument.

At some point agriculture would not be able to do the best thing for the environment and for agriculture, too. There would have to be compromise. It wasn't realistic to expect the return of the grizzly and the tule elk, but the growers could make the valley better, for wildlife and people both.

34

THE WATERSHED TASK FORCE gathered on a warm afternoon in early June in the Gasser Building. The usual suspects
took their seats around the big table as if nothing of any consequence had happened in recent months, as if Kathryn Winter had
not lost her seat on the county board of supervisors, and the Sierra
Club hadn't won its lawsuit, and the Farm Bureau wasn't being
fought over with passionate, take-no-prisoners intensity, and the
Vintners Association wasn't lurching one way and another over environmental issues.

Task force members sipped soda and Calistoga water and, as always, consulted the printout containing the day's business, while
outside on Trancas Street, the traffic ceaselessly passed.

As if he hadn't cut his ponytail and weren't working himself to
distraction, as if his planning department weren't in disarray, Jeff
Redding stood up and made a little speech. He welcomed everyone
to the thirteenth meeting, and suggested, "Let's switch seats." It was a
serious attempt to break up familiar patterns of behavior — if people sat in different places, maybe they would have different reactions
to issues — but only Hugh Davies stood. He immediately saw his
mistake in taking the suggestion at face value, grinned in embarrassment, and sat down again.

"You're all to make recommendations to the board of supervisors," Jeff continued, performing the little two-step, back, forward. "I
urge you all to find some common ground, get away from discussing
principles — i.e., should government be regulating these things. We
are already, so let's deal with the issues . . . If we can't get consensus

here, we're not going to get it in the next arena," by which he meant
the board of supervisors.

Unresolved issues included oak tree removal, slope criteria, biology, and replants. The distance that replanted vineyards had to be
from waterways was the crux of the profit problem in the eyes
of Dennis Groth and people like him in the Breakfast Club. One of
them, Bo Barrett, had written a letter protesting the creation of
more extensive riparian areas. A law requiring Chateau Montelena
to pull back from streams would cost the winery millions of dollars,
Barrett claimed. The point this had made to most everyone, however, was that cult wineries were taking in a great deal more money
than people realized and that their owners might be expected to sacrifice a fraction of it for the general good.

The facilitator took over. "We're back to replants," he said, "because we're still not sure what we're supposed to tell the board when
the time comes."

There was a proposal for a one-hundred-foot setback from
streams, half of it "no touch" and half for use in turning around farm
machinery, but not for planting. About half the members wanted a
twenty-five-foot no-touch zone next to water and a twenty-five-
foot turnaround, and the other half wanted fifty feet in each category. A vote was to be taken, but first Dennis raised his hand — palm
turned inward, as usual.

"I have a question that may impact people's decisions. I've given a
lot of thought to this issue in relation to all these lawsuits. If we
change the rules on setbacks, we may get hung up in a similar litigation limbo . . . If we can't maintain present production levels, every
vineyard and winery owner in Napa Valley should oppose this with
his life."

Jeff pointed out that any replant rule could still be challenged under a new ordinance, and all plans would have to be accompanied by
an environmental impact report. "The question is, what should we
do here?" he asked. "We've talked about this for weeks."

Hugh said, "This is a loaded question, one for the scientists. Is it
fair to ask them to weigh in here? I'm more inclined to live and die
by their recommendations."

Phil Blake, from the Resource Conservation District headquarters — balding, with a dramatic, bristly black mustache — did weigh

in, but cautiously. His job was to advise prospective vineyardists and recommend where and how erosion control devices could be deployed, and he spoke in a soft, reasonable voice of buffer zones for water quality and filtering and "zone structures."

While Blake spoke, Stu Smith sat with his eyes closed, but he wasn't asleep.

"Every scenario is out there in Napa Valley," Blake said. "These numbers we're throwing out, they're just numbers. We need numbers as a place to start, and in a few years they'll need revisiting." But he didn't say what the right numbers happened to be.

Finally, a biologist for the California Department of Fish and Game, the agency often caught between the developers and the environmentalists, said what was on many minds. A big, affable man who in addition to being a scientist was also a game warden, and who had to deal with infractions on the ground, far from the theorizing and the balance sheets at the top of the food chain, betrayed not exasperation but something close to it. "The bigger the setback, the better the resource," he said, meaning the river. "It may be bad for business, but if it wasn't, we wouldn't be here."

That summed it up, but such an unequivocal statement about the reality of nature versus profit wasn't welcomed by half the task force members. However, it was neither challenged by them nor discussed by the environmentalists; everybody was down to specifics now.

There was some talk of enforcement of new rules — how it would be done and monitored. Eventually they had to vote on the proposal for a hundred-foot setback; they had to go on record. Parry Mead said, "In the hope that there's some life left in this dead horse, I want to say that it behooves us to support this modest proposal. It's not written in stone, and we're at a critical juncture right now."

Richard Niemann pointed out that "any proposals for less than one hundred feet are political and economic, not biological."

The facilitator said, "This is not 'I love it,' but just something to drop in the supervisors' laps."

The hundred feet lost by a narrow margin, and the facilitator added, "A little more consensus for change, but not much."

They took a break.

◈

Stu Smith was a month behind with his vineyard work, but the demands of politics took precedence. It made him angry, getting out of his big, battered all-terrain vehicle on the flat spot overlooking Smith-Madrone, the wedding grove below him and the air full of the smell of red dirt in the sun, to think that he was doing all this extra work for a bunch of idiots out of New York, Los Angeles, and Silicon Valley who didn't understand what was at stake.

The last year and a half had been brutal for Smith-Madrone. There wasn't enough chardonnay, and he and his brother, Charley, worked all the time, Charley making the wine and Stu the vineyard/banker/wine tech/sales guy. The winery partnership was a corkscrew of family and friends that needed straightening out, but Stu didn't have the time or the money right now. He was a new father living in his mother's old house, also partly responsible for two growing sons by his previous marriage, keeping up with two older daughters, and trying to live a life.

He was passionately involved in this watershed stuff. The argument was now focused on about one percent of the land — that in vineyard near streams — when everybody should be talking about population, traffic, big houses, and the survival of small business in a rural county under siege by gentrified dot-commers and other rich outsiders.

He could hear the bulldozer clearing a section of his land next to the vineyard where some timber was being cut. It would net him about eighty thousand dollars. That was peanuts compared to his redwoods near the border of Bothe State Park, six feet thick and worth upward of two million dollars. That was a real temptation. A lawyer from Save the Redwoods had come around to look at them and talk about possibly paying Stu not to cut them. Stu wanted to do that, but he didn't want the word to get out because then people would call him a tree-hugger.

He tarried over his view of the valley, reminding himself that the road to hell was paved with good intentions. He didn't believe that Chris Malan and Peter Mennen were evil; they were just wrong. At least he knew where they stood. County officials were shiftier. Jeff Redding, trying to deflect the popular uprising against vineyard development, suggested that a cumulative impact study was in progress without actually saying so. Either he was way ahead of Stu in understanding how vineyards would flourish in the county or he had mastered a language Stu had yet to learn.

Jeff was getting it from both sides, of course. The enviros would sue the county again if projects were approved without environmental impact reports, and the vintners would sue the county if they didn't get what they wanted. Meanwhile, Jeff was acting like a king, nodding this way and that, using what sounded to Stu like doublespeak while his department struggled under the ever-increasing load of mostly unfinished work. Stu was sure that Chris Malan, had he asked her, would agree about Jeff's opaqueness, as would others on both sides of the argument. Stu saw the permitting process, indeed the whole drama engulfing the valley, as a kind of California *Rashomon* — a tale told very differently from different points of view.

The Farm Bureau election was the big thing now. Stu and his allies wanted to change its direction and get their story out about farming — its benefits to the community, its requirements. They also wanted their opponents to get what Stu thought they had coming — a sound drubbing — and to have no choice but to effect some radical changes. That would mean putting representatives in the Chambers of Commerce in the valley, for instance, and in Rotary, and to stop acting high and mighty all the time.

The Vintners Association was even snottier, Stu thought. Most of the officers of the Vintners, like the president, Jack Stuart, got where they were by ducking the issues. It was one reason Jack Cakebread had gone off to form the Winegrowers, because the Vintners wouldn't *deal,* but the Breakfast Club had similar problems. At the party the Winegrowers threw for Farmers for Napa Valley, Jack Cakebread told Stu that they had hired a publicist to get the word out, and Stu had responded that the county didn't want to hear from a publicist. It wanted to hear from *them.*

Jack had gone on to say that they would win the election with Bill Dodd, and Stu had said, "Go tell the people yourself," but Jack had glossed over this forceful suggestion.

Farmers for Napa Valley was about to disappear as an organization, though in fact it had never formally existed. Stu, van Gorder, Neal, Tucker Catlin, and others had held a "come to Jesus meeting" in the beginning and rejected the idea of dues and elections; it would be a shadow organization dedicated to getting a dozen directors on the Farm Bureau board, half the total. Even ten directors would be a victory. After that, Farmers for Napa Valley would fade away like an old soldier.

The real shadowy society, Stu thought, was the Farm Bureau, which was continually eluding efforts to control and change its course. It would not release a membership list, and it wasn't legally required to do so. Farmers for Napa Valley had demanded one anyway, so they could contact members individually, and were complaining for being denied. Stu was running as a write-in candidate against people like Hugh Davies, put up by the Farm Bureau nominating committee, when nominations should, in Stu's view, be member-driven, not board-driven.

Volker Eisele was the key to controlling the Farm Bureau, though he held no official position. Stu had to admire him despite their differences. Volker worked at the committee level, where things got done; he ran things from behind the scenes, through his influence on the staff — the *éminence grise,* listened to by everyone, including the executive director. Jon-Mark Chappellet, like Hugh Davies another establishment candidate, had said when approached by Stu that he wasn't voting for any Farmers for Napa Valley candidates. Now that was straightforward, and commendable. At least Stu knew where Jon-Mark stood. Others had been wishy-washy. There had been silence and cold shoulders among Stu's country club–type friends, but in the end, he thought, he and others rattling the Farm Bureau's cage would prevail.

35

THE CAMEO GOLF COURSE and croquet court under a line of conifers on steep, rugged hills seemed to have been created by God out of lava, soil, water, and wind-driven spores just to support the Wine Auction. A huge white tent rose every summer on the green and filled with bidders luxuriating in the product and ambience of the American Provence, seduced by sun, wine, and lofting air redolent of pine and precious dust.

The Napa Valley Wine Auction had grown in two decades from one huge white tent to two, the first a kind of cloth passageway lined with oils of California landscapes and flowers. It opened onto Meadowood's lush fairway and the larger spectacle of mountain, Douglas firs, and an encampment of smaller white tents dispensing sparkling wine and caviar. The crowd quickly swelled to fill the space, a preponderance of the men in black tie, the women in evening gowns. There was the odd expression of individuality — Michael Martini in a big silver bolo, Garen Staglin in a tailored, brocaded shirt, and a sport jacket and tie on Mel Varrelman, a guest and ever the egalitarian. But mostly the crowd had gone along with the formality desired by the Vintners, people moving in a kind of paseo around the lawn before going into the big tent to take their assigned positions, in every other hand a glass of effervescence.

Two hundred vintners were making themselves momentarily available to two thousand visitors who had paid two thousand dollars a couple to attend. The vintners would dine at individual tables and add their wines to those already selected for a dinner that was a logistical tour de force: a thousand volunteers, the same number of lobsters and pounds of lamb and wild mushrooms, forty cases of baby turnips, ten cases of basil, two thousand fresh grape leaves, twenty-two hundred sugar decorations, and twenty-seven hundred wine glasses.

Hugh and Lily had been assigned to table B10, he youthful and eager-looking in his tuxedo, his fiancée content with a modest sleeveless dress that showed off the trim shoulders of an equestrienne, touched by the tips of her straight blond hair. They attempted to entertain their assigned guests, mostly strangers who had paid for the privilege of associating with the valley's elite and bidding on their wines at tomorrow's auction.

Earlier, at Schramsberg, other strangers from points as distant as Los Gatos and Mobile had formed teams in the vineyard grove and competed in the firing of corks from Schramsberg bottles and the tossing of rings onto the necks of champagne bottles, hand-riddling to a stopwatch and running in a relay race with more corks carried in spoons. Hugh had managed it all with the enthusiasm and good spirits of a camp counselor, saying, "I just want the best team to win." It was all part of the auction weekend.

Under the big tent at Meadowood, a couple from Reno kept getting up to search out other vintners, to present them with Make-A-Wish Foundation awards they had brought with them in red cardboard boxes, but mostly the guests showed the requisite decorum. The wines were varied, all from the valley, natural complements to the lobster and lamb. Hugh had an imperial of cold Schramsberg delivered to the table and, grinning, opened it with panache, firing the cork into the air. It fell unseen among the sea of diners, and he went around the table with the big bottle cradled in his arms, pouring.

On the stage, under revolving colored lights, caressed by fog from a machine, Patti LaBelle performed briefly; after the show, members and guests fanned out into the night. Hugh and Lily tarried to chat with Mel Varrelman, who in his previous incarnation had been Hugh's teacher. Also present was the woman who had taught Hugh library science, and she playfully reminded him, "You never got an A." They all laughed. Hugh said, "Come on, nobody gets an A in library science," and for a moment the auction seemed local again, an echo of the early years in a valley that had changed beyond either generation's dreams or expectations.

★

By afternoon of the following day, the residue of dinner had been cleared away and the vast white tent sheltered the same people, in shorts and open shirts or blouses cut for the heat. Flamboyant straw hats punctuated the bright, colorful sea of bidders in which paddles with numbers printed on them bobbed like buoys. The auctioneer's patter alternated with the booming Motown bumper sound. Two thousand people had before them the catalogue of offered lots to be bid on, each described by the vintners producing the wine. Each vintner had been asked to speculate, here in print, about the valley a century hence, and what they would put into a time capsule.

An early lot — Beringer's — was stuck at a mere one hundred thousand dollars for twelve bottles of cabernet, one nine-liter bottle "etched with our name . . . showcased in a wine cradle handcrafted from exotic hardwoods," and "a custom-made commemorative 'beverage of champions' varsity jacket," until the auctioneer threw in a meal with a professional football player who had been in retirement for a decade but whose remnant fame was enough to double the price.

Sprinkled throughout the audience were the recognizable faces of most every notable in the valley, from cult-wine producer to part-time resident from southern California or Silicon Valley. Vintners often sat with friends and clients who were also prospective bidders, for that was the way it was done at the auction.

Ann Colgin, seated at a center table, wore a straw hat and her red-orange lipstick. She had written in the auction catalogue that she would "include in my time capsule a magnum of my 1997 Cabernet Sauvignon and a corkscrew — which may be an antique." Her lot brought two hundred thousand dollars, and she said, "Not too bad, huh?" But soon ten bottles of Araujo Estate cabernet brought two hundred and seventy thousand dollars. So did eight bottles of Dalla Valle Maya, and Colgin was history.

A line of servers performed a triumphal march; members of the Hoopla Club bestowed hugs, and Motown gave way to rock-and-roll.

At the Staglins' table, directly below the auctioneer, anticipation mounted. Six large bottles of Staglin Family Vineyard wine and twelve Tuscan crystal glasses lay under the gavel, as well as dinner for

twelve with Garen and Shari. She had written that she would include in her time capsule, "underneath our fountain, just at the back
of our sculpture garden . . . a laminated photograph of our family . . .
a Barbie doll . . . and a bottle of 1992 Staglin Family Vineyard
Cabernet Sauvignon."

Bidding stopped at one hundred and fifty thousand dollars, and
Garen leapt to his feet. He waved two fingers in the air. The auctioneer, already prompted, announced that the lot was being split in two,
a neat bit of legerdemain that instantly pushed the price to three
hundred thousand.

"Roll over Beethoven, bring Tchaikovsky the news . . ."

Half a million dollars was then spent for three days and four nights
of tastings, dinners, concerts, and a film screening in the homes of
Dick and Ann Grace ("What will Napa Valley be like in the year
3000? Unless we are vigilant, Disneyland!") and Francis and Eleanor Coppola, whose winemaker would include in the Niebaum-
Coppola time capsule "a pair of bellbottoms and all 200 of my wife's
wooden bowls . . . Napa Valley will be designated an agricultural national park, America's first."

The smell of cooking salmon rolled through the tent, from a
thirty-foot trench full of blazing split oak over which were suspended the slabs of pink meat on poles: Northwest Coast Indian
cuisine, to feed what was left of this throng once the bidding was
done.

An imperial of Screaming Eagle ("In my time capsule I would
place the weight tags with current winery price per ton," wrote the
owner. "This should be good for a big laugh") brought half a million
dollars, the highest price ever paid for a single bottle of wine. A ten-
magnum vertical of Harlan Estate cabernet went for seven hundred
and fifty thousand dollars, both prices paid by a white-haired former
dot-commer, a cofounder of Cisco Systems living in Incline Village
in the Sierras who bore a striking resemblance to a dead movie star.
Thus the winner of the auction, in terms of money paid for one's
wine, was Bill Harlan, who had written that he would leave in his
time capsule "a message defining our original dream, philosophy
and values," but neglecting to say what those things were.

The total raised for the valley charities, primarily health care, was
almost ten million dollars. This was roughly twice what had been

raised the year before, and a record, of course, for records were what the auction was all about now.

❧

The next morning, Sunday, Hugh got up and put on his shorts, hiking boots, and the Tuolumne T-shirt he had brought back from an excursion to Yosemite, and drove up to the big house.

He, Jamie, and Volker Eisele were to walk in the hills above Schramsberg. Volker was already waiting on the porch, the antithesis of backpacking chic: no synthetic vest, no fanny pack, no baseball cap, just an old Windbreaker and those scuffed leather shoes. His white hair and ruddy countenance glowed in the morning light above the railing of the old Schram house. Jamie appeared next to him in sweats, cap, and the worn pack of the habitual hiker, and they all set off up the old wagon road behind the cellar.

They passed the prospect of additional vineyards that had been purchased in the 1980s, some planted to cabernet now, and entered Bothe State Park. It had been named for the man who donated the land to the state after providing horseback rides and other family diversions there in the early years of the twentieth century. The park was easily accessible, a wild retreat used and appreciated by relatively few in the valley. One difficulty in the advocacy of good land use, Volker was pointing out, was that the average American had little real experience with nature. To many Americans, the natural world was an abstract notion. Western lands in America were burdened with a history of economic possibility, a tabula rasa upon which one wrote one's fondest wishes, whether for wealth, status, or solitude, often with little understanding of the place itself.

The champions of Manifest Destiny had used the language to fit their needs and ambitions, rendering the notions of wildness and the natural state undesirable. Thus "vacant" became a pejorative, suggesting idleness and lost opportunity, rather than the truth. "Improved" land was in fact the opposite: cut-over, graded, ready for even more extreme diminishment. These ideas were so deeply ingrained in the national compulsion for expansion as to be inviolable. The only way to change them was a revolution in thinking, and time was growing short.

The trail led to Ritchey Creek and the grove of redwoods where impromptu memorials for Jack had been held. The threesome passed that spot and mounted along the wooded canyon between Diamond and Spring mountains, Hugh leading with characteristic springiness — the Davies gait (chin tucked, eyes upward-gazing) — pointing out the Douglas firs, redwoods, and tanbark oaks once used for treating hides by white settlers, and before that by the Indians. Also live and black oak. Volker knew the Latin names — Liesel had drilled them into him — and he took an obvious delight in intoning them: "*Quercus agrifolia, Quercus kelloggii, Quercus . . .*"

Higher up, they passed through a stand of manzanita, the trunks red, smooth to the touch. Following lightning fires, these were some of the first plants to regenerate. After that came the madrones, then the redwoods. The valley had been heavily logged from about 1850 to 1870, when St. Helena was a lumbering town; the cut reached all but the least accessible trees on the Mayacamas. The pick-and-cut method of the past, which left some cover and small trees under which the replacements might sprout and grow, had been preferable to present-day clear-cutting.

Leavings of the earlier timber boom were still evident in moldering stumps from which new redwoods had sprouted, reaching for the sky.

The younger hiker had romped up and down these mountains as a child. Hugh knew it was a three-hour bushwhack to the top of Diamond Mountain. He had bushwhacked down the other side and up Spring Mountain. The woods had been and still were his backyard. In his thirties now, he remarked on the spread of the outsized leaves of the black oak, the gnarly endurance of the madrones.

They passed blooming chamise higher up and, in the open, monkeyflower, blue brodiaea, and an orchid no one could identify. Gaining a view of the eastern mountains, the whole sweep of chaparral and conifer from the Palisades to Howell Mountain, they could see only one house and the Oat Hill Mine Road, where Hugh and Jamie had hiked two months before, on Earth Day. Between here and there lay the valley floor, like an island in the sun.

"All that land should be bought and put into a park," said Volker, of the land under the Palisades. Hugh, ever practical, said, "That's a lot of money."

As an academic exercise, they estimated that four thousand acres needed such protection. At five thousand dollars an acre for remote, "unimproved" land, that was twenty million dollars. "It's worth more than that," said Hugh. "It's because we've all driven up the price with development. If you made it impossible to build on, by law, the price would reflect the reality."

"Twenty million dollars," Jamie said. "We raised half that yesterday at the auction." And none of that money would go toward land conservation.

"The thing to do," said Volker, "would be to raise a million and then leverage it. You could get the state to come in and pay for some of the land. Start by expanding Robert Louis Stevenson State Park."

"I could get behind that," said Hugh.

Jamie was thinking about mountain lions. They were occasionally spotted in these hills; she gave two thoughts to walking alone here, without the dog, but today the threat was utterly remote. The sun was hot, and they stopped for lunch in a grove on Coyote Mountain. Talk returned to the Wine Auction and the precedent it had set, earning twice as much money as the year before. This was gratifying, but tempering that satisfaction was the spectacle of it, which could be interpreted by the outside world as overindulgent, rampant consumerism.

What kind of example did it set, Volker wondered aloud, for young people in the valley and beyond? How did a parent say no to a wish for a sport-utility van or a vacation in Baja when adults were spending money with such abandon? So many ambitions came together at the auction, not just for cult wines but also for status, celebrity, for greater access to the prosperous "wine country" tourists.

On the descent, Volker and Hugh discussed the Napa Valley Vintners' position on setbacks. Absence of a position was more accurate. As chairman of the community and industry issues committee, Hugh had to be sure the wishes of the members were presented to the Vintner board when it met the following week. Volker said, "You're lucky that as chairman you don't have to make your own views known. You can let others speak, and guide the outcome."

A complicating factor was the fight over the Farm Bureau, an organization far removed from the Vintners in both types of members and issues, but related through the medium of wine. Tom Gamble feared that an endorsement of setbacks at this volatile time by any candidate for the board of directors might endanger the future of the Farm Bureau. Stu Smith and the Farmers for Napa Valley would use such endorsements as evidence that the Bureau had sold out to "radical" environmentalists and try to ride that misconception to victory in July.

Then Volker and Hugh talked about the Watershed Task Force, that seemingly innocuous endeavor that in little more than a year had taken on a larger significance. In its deliberations and personalities resided an aspect of the future, not just of the hillsides and the Napa River, but the community as such. The comity of the valley, its environmental health and rural character, rode on the outcome of the task force and on control of the Farm Bureau.

Walking together, kicking up dust, the men reminded Jamie, trailing behind, of the brackets of environmental concern in the valley before the war over the hillsides. Volker had been considered an extremist in the days of the winery definition fight a dozen years before, when Jack, too, had been wary of him, coming as he did from a different world. Business versus Berkeley. Volker no longer seemed radical even to his enemies, thanks to Chris Malan and Peter Mennen. Jamie wondered if this was because Volker was better known now, and a member of the Vintners himself, active there as well as in other organizations. Or was it that the center had shifted and the issues were better understood by everyone?

Hugh was a good blend of businessman and conservationist, mindful of the economic needs of his peers but serious about preserving the valley. It was an uncomfortable position for him to be in, subject to opportunism by his late father's friends and to the demands of his own heart.

Back at the winery, the tasting room was full of tourists. A couple exiting looked at the hikers curiously, wondering how these scruffy people had gained access to the comely grounds of Schramsberg. Hugh just smiled and nodded.

He spotted a cat in the shade of the overhanging roof, and picked it up. "Hey, Pete," he said, stroking the nervous cellar pet. "He lives in fear of the dogs. Whenever he sees them he runs, and of course they chase him. If only he would lie still."

36

I T WAS A COOL July, the mornings clammy under a blanket of cloud that burned off before lunch, the afternoons sunny and dry, and the roads crowded with trucks pulling heavy equipment on flatbeds, bound for the hills, and with pickups, SUVs, tourists' convertibles, and the more basic vehicles of the Mexican laborers. They could be seen working in the vineyards in tight, isolated groups, sometimes obscured by the vines, the only evidence of their presence a port-a-john set at the edge of a road and a collection of water coolers. The vastness of the leaves was punctuated by straw hats and colorful bandanas, and passersby who stopped for a moment and rolled down their windows could hear, in the pauses between rumbling transport, a staccato language that was not English.

In the evenings the sun cut diagonally across the Mayacamas and, just before darkness settled, turned Mount St. Helena into an incandescent lavender atoll in a blue-green sea. In that moment all evidence of human industry was subsumed in the transient beauty and tranquility of a distant, fabled land.

As a child, Lily had ridden bareback along the Napa River, in the shade of trees in the meadow near Bale Lane, past the big old oaks before they were cut by newcomers to make way for more vineyard. She didn't share Hugh's passion for the wilderness, but she valued it. Usually he went off alone on treks in the Yosemite and the ranges of northern California; she knew how important it was to him, and was glad he could get away.

He worked so hard; sometimes his boots and bedroll went un-
packed for days after he got back from a hiking trip and was overwhelmed with work. He tried to get production costs down — less
wrap for the bottles, fewer people hired from outside to operate
equipment — and he wanted to extend his efforts to the vineyard,
but he couldn't do it all. And he put a little extra into everything he
did because he cared so much about this "experiment" that was
Schramsberg, and Napa Valley.

Hugh dreamed of going organic, and someday would, and meanwhile made less money than his contemporaries in almost any other
business, from catering to computers. It wasn't just winery business
that ate up the hours, but also the reading of documents that flowed
into their lives in an unending stream: Watershed Task Force reports,
Farm Bureau missives, material relating to the committee he chaired
for the Napa Valley Vintners Association. He was conscientious, one
of the few, Lily felt sure, who read every page of that stuff, often repeatedly, up night after night on the couch in the old M'Eckron
house, stacks of papers around him, after she went to bed, often reading past midnight in his down vest and Aussie boots, and was up
again before dawn.

Some on the Vintner board weren't very nice to Hugh, Lily
thought. That made her mad. The fact that she could do nothing
about it was frustrating. Hugh cared about the environment, and was
willing to stick his neck out when others his age wouldn't dream of
doing so. After the last meeting of the board, he presented his committee's case for setbacks, and took the heat, and no one patted him
on the back for a job well done. Hugh thought the Vintners should
be on record as favoring a modest increase in riparian habitat, but
some of the older men had scorned him. And no ally called later to
commiserate.

"I don't want to be everybody's least-favorite vintner," Hugh had
said, dispirited, but he wasn't about to change his position. "There's
no doubt about the environmental benefits of setbacks. Now is the
time to suck it up and do it, when times are good and we can better
afford it. Some of the big boys have made an incredible amount of
money."

Hugh sometimes asked, "Do I want to champion the environment at all costs and risk losing everything — my mind, and finances?" He wondered aloud how his father would have felt about

setbacks and protecting the hillsides, certain that Jack would have been in favor of them. But how forcefully would he have spoken out?

Sometimes Jack Davies's conservation efforts had run afoul of his Republicanism. As far as Hugh knew, his father had voted for Republican candidates until the final years of his life, when he switched over and voted for Democrats, including President Bill Clinton. If some members of the Vintners identified Hugh with Volker Eisele, Hugh thought, so be it. You can't worry too much about those things. There had been people who disapproved of Jack Davies, too, like John Daniel, heir to the Niebaum fortune, and old Louis Stralla, mayor of St. Helena. Both of them had hated the idea of an agricultural preserve and fought savagely to defeat it, and now they — and Inglenook — were gone, and the ag preserve had endured.

Linda Reiff had watched Hugh's performance in the Napa Valley Vintners Association with interest and approval. As executive director of the Vintners, she couldn't be too public about this, but she probably agreed with most everything he said and wished that there were more members like Hugh.

Slim, intense, with short blond hair, Linda was a native of the Sacramento Valley and had worked for a congressman before being hired by the Vintners. Her intelligence and stylishness were not lost on the directors, who hoped she could restore credibility and purpose to an organization seen as rudderless after the debacle of the winery definition fight a decade earlier.

This she tried to do, but her job had been made tougher by the rump group that formed within vintner ranks, Jack Cakebread's Winegrowers/Breakfast Club. A haven for men who did not want to compromise and who believed that their financial gain was synonymous with the general good, the Winegrowers wished to undo the winery definition, to acquire more latitude in catering to tourists, and to assure that vintners generally had a free hand in the valley. Linda and the then president of the Vintners, another young woman, Beth Novak Milliken, heir to the Spottswoode Winery, were in favor of the Vintners opening up on environmental and worker housing issues.

The fact that the Vinters Association was being run by these two women offended some men. The women were nevertheless invited early on to meet with the Winegrowers, and told that the organization was to be called the Napa Valley Winegrowers Association. No, said Linda, that's too close to the Vintners' name; it would put the new group on a par with the Vintners in the mind of the public. Essentially the women were told not to worry their pretty little heads about it, but the men ultimately saw the rightness of this and took the women's advice, calling themselves the Winegrowers of Napa County instead.

Linda Reiff and Beth Milliken knew that the Vintners had to protect the integrity of Napa Valley's name as well as promote its wines. They worked for acceptance of geographic designations on labels, to keep the Napa name off bottles of wine made elsewhere and from grapes not grown in the valley. Again they were told not to worry their pretty little heads about geographic brands, that the Winegrowers would handle it; again the women kept at the issue, and supported the legislation that was finally passed.

Linda felt that if the Vintners didn't take strong positions on other important matters, like the recommendations then being considered by the Watershed Task Force, people like Jack Cakebread and Stu Smith would always step forward and claim to speak for the industry.

Then came setbacks — Winegrower shorthand for the expropriation by environmentalists of vineyardlands. This was the most discussed topic since the Sierra Club lawsuit, and its proponents were a ready replacement for Malan and Mennen as objects of vituperation. The task force recommendations for stricter slope standards, an end to the cutting of trees, establishment of an information center, and other proposals were merely annoying to the Winegrowers, if acceptable, but not setbacks. Setbacks were different: whatever the measurements proved finally to be, they would cost money.

One way to obstruct them was the ploy of having Napa Valley excluded from the requirements of the California Environmental Quality Act by the state legislature. The Breakfast Club and its lobbyist attempted to do this, and Herb Schmidt, in charge of the Mondavis' political affairs, and Tom Shelton, no longer president of the Vintners but still a member of the Breakfast Club, had argued that the Vintners mustn't oppose the proposed legislation, SB 1810. However, the Vintner committee chaired by Hugh Davies had voted unanimously to oppose it, and that diverse group included some representatives in the Breakfast Club. So the two men telephoned every Vintner board member and told him not to agree to oppose 1810.

The Winegrowers' spin was that the bill was pro-environment because it would prove to other counties that they, too, could pass erosion control ordinances and not be challenged under the rules of CEQA. Some people thought the argument a hoot, and said so, although the fact that the Winegrowers would use and push it so hard both surprised and saddened many of their colleagues.

The Winegrowers' efforts in Sacramento had proved a public relations disaster, showing how out of touch they were to think they could make themselves immune to laws everybody else had to respect. And they proved that Chris Malan, whatever people thought of her, had forced the industry to deal with real issues.

Tom Shelton's successor as president of the Vintners had been the smooth, affable Jack Stuart, the malamute-eyed chief executive at Silverado Vineyards who seemed incapable of deciding between environmental and economic requirements. Many vintners considered Jack Stuart ineffectual, and intolerant — as were most representatives of the big wineries — of anything that cost his employers money. He could speak fondly of nature and then complain of setbacks that would affect Silverado's vineyards along the river. Silverado could have set an example, acting to preserve an ailing natural resource, the Disney family emulating the land ethic inherent in the European aristocracies after which so many vintners hankered, from the de Latours to the Staglins, instead of expanding its winery to accommodate tour buses.

At a Vintner committee meeting, David Graves of Saintsbury had addressed the question of the county's right to enforce its own land-use laws, including "police powers." Jack Stuart interrupted him to say, "That phrase, 'police powers,' makes me nervous." Graves began to explain this basic governmental concept, and Jack told him, "Don't talk so glibly to me."

This outburst revealed to other members present the tension within the Vintners surrounding all environmental questions, and how different the organization was from that founded by Louis Martini, John Daniel, and a handful of others seeking only to market the products of a few obscure Napa Valley wineries in a then indifferent world.

Jack Stuart was overheard at a dinner party in St. Helena saying that the money raised at the auction was beginning to be an embarrassment; the word "obscene" was being used by some critics of the industry for the showy spending of millions of dollars on cult wines by instant millionaires who then bragged about it. This came at a time when powerful vintners wanted the valley placed above environmental law. It had been suggested to Stuart that a portion of the Napa Valley Wine Auction proceeds be dedicated to the acquisition of land that could then be protected, perhaps along the river, rather than to the valley's already flush medical establishment, but that subject was too loaded politically for Stuart, a president eager for his term to end.

Hugh Davies — young, committed, energetic — put in the time; everybody said so. He had convincingly presented his committee's recommendation for setbacks to the Vintner board, only to be criticized by the older cohort. Clarke Swanson had loudly asked who represented the Vintners on the Watershed Task Force. "It sure isn't Hugh Davies," Swanson had said.

Watching that exchange, others in the meeting were struck by the transformation of a red-faced middle-aged man fulminating about vintner autonomy into a seeming adolescent, and of a thirty-something in funny glasses speaking of community and the environment into a concerned, reasoning adult. Some of them wanted to see Hugh on the board of the Vintners, and he would eventually be elected to it, as would Swanson, an indication of how diverse the organization was.

And Hugh was already running for the board of directors of the Farm Bureau, light-years from the Vintners in social cachet. Traditionally, there was little cooperation between the two organizations, and sometimes outright hostility. Proverbial Italian loafers and hobnail boots attempted to step all over each other. Hugh Davies could conceivably be a link at the top between those who staged the Napa Valley Wine Auction and those who grew the grapes.

37

TOM GAMBLE was being called a tree-hugger, and worse. He was told by a farmer from another county, while on a trip to Washington, D.C., that the farmer had heard Tom was "pink" on land use. He had heard it from a member of the Winegrowers. An heir to the Gamble fortune and a cattle rancher and grower of high-quality wine grapes, Tom thought he would make an unlikely Communist. It was a stupid, dishonest charge, but indicative of the increasingly nasty debate over the valley's future and control of the Farm Bureau.

At the Napa Valley Wine Auction, he overheard a vineyard manager ask the head of a big winery to help get the tree-huggers off the Farm Bureau board. Sitting at home, under a poster of *Abilene,* with Ernest Borgnine, Tom supposed that he and the others *were* tree-huggers, because they enjoyed looking out their windows at live oaks and eucalyptus and, if they lived higher up, Douglas firs and redwoods.

Tom was the vice president of the Farm Bureau. Every morning he tuned in to local talk radio and had to listen as callers supporting Farmers for Napa Valley denigrated the agricultural preserve as a historic compromise and a "mistake." He had listened in disbelief to assertions that trees weren't particularly attractive and that Napa Valley wasn't visually exceptional and that preserving its reputed beauty was no reason to violate the sanctity of property rights. Tom thought all this outrageous. The moderator was sympathetic to the Farmers, and predicted open clashes at the Farm Bureau meetings.

Farmers for Napa Valley trashed the Bureau it wanted to control, yet as board members Stu, Tucker Catlin of Juliana Vineyards, and a couple of others did nothing productive. Stu played the tough guy, while Tucker played the wily diplomat. The two of them used the democratic process to try to gain power but, Tom thought, if they got it, they would boot out the democrats.

Stu and Tucker attacked the procedure for the upcoming election. The Farm Bureau president, Rich Salvestrin, had written a letter to the members defending the Bureau against charges that it was run by an elite, and the insurgents objected to the use of official stationery to do this. Their real objective was getting their hands on the Farm Bureau mailing list, off-limits to all but the administrators. Rich had refused, but only after checking with lawyers working for the California Farm Bureau Federation — a small, satisfying victory for the "insiders."

There were often fireworks in the board meetings. The Bureau supported geographic labeling to keep unscrupulous producers from ripping off the Napa Valley name. It was committed to fight the glassy-winged sharpshooter, the pest that had wiped out the Temecula vineyards. The Bureau was in favor of the status quo ante for setbacks, but only until the total maximum daily load study could be done and the requirements for riparian habitat made clear. These three things were all uncontroversial, but not SB 1810, which would exempt the county from CEQA. The Bureau refused to endorse the bill, and this and any other expression of environmental concern brought harsh statements from the opposition.

Tom felt burned out. He found himself on the other side of the setback issue from Volker and Hugh, who favored stricter requirements for all new vineyards, including replanted ones. But as vice president of the Bureau, Tom knew that there was only so much he could do with his constituency at any one time. Hugh argued that if the Farm Bureau took no meaningful position on setbacks, it would be barbecued by an irate public for doing nothing to help the river. But Tom's position remained no position, just like the Vintners'. Hold with the status quo and avoid losing control of the Farm Bureau board, then address replants.

Hugh was part of all this now. He was a good friend of Tom's, and often identified with Volker Eisele, who had been knocked off the board the year before. Volker had made a lot of enemies among the anti-environmental factions in the last twenty years and become such a lightning rod, but his influence behind the scenes was incalculable. Hugh had lost last year, too, and the stakes and the rhetoric were now even higher. If Hugh lost again, it would be bad for the Bureau and bad for Hugh, who had stuck his neck out in the Vintners and on the Watershed Task Force. Hugh could use some affirmation.

The election was to be held on the old Krug winery grounds. Twenty-four board seats to fill, and Farmers for Napa Valley putting up a full slate, as well as candidates for president and vice president. The voting would take place during the picnic, a Farm Bureau annual tradition and as much a social as a political event. This year, people were predicting unpleasantness.

A week and a half before the big day, Tom went to his office on Railroad Avenue in St. Helena, with its view through green tree branches of the Safeway parking lot, and met with other Farm Bureau volunteers. They were preparing a mailing of endorsements of the board's slate and a letter to be sent to members, signed collectively by some of the valley's best-known and most successful vintners and growers, among them Jamie Davies, Bob Phillips, and Andy Beckstoffer. That letter laid out the charges against the Farmers for Napa Valley candidates and called on the membership to reject policies ultimately harmful to agriculture.

"We don't have your endorsement yet," Tom told Jon-Mark Chappellet, who spoke for his father and his brother, Donn and Cyril. "It can be verbal — I'll worry about the paperwork later."

"You have it. My dad's all in favor of this."

Tall, lean, with broad shoulders, starter beard, squinty eyes, shaved head, and a single gold earring, Jon-Mark was a piratical-looking tennis enthusiast who had been teaching high school kids in Oakland when he received a call one day from his brother. "How would you like to get paid to eat in some really nice restaurants?" Cyril had asked him, as an inducement to join the family business. Since then Jon-Mark had become not just a Chappellet vice president but an active member of the Farm Bureau and another heir to an established winery estate whose sympathies — and efforts — extended to conservation. Jon-Mark Chappellet was the only lucky spermer in the valley with a bumper sticker on his pickup from KPFA, Berkeley's left-wing radio station.

Now he said, "If these guys get six members on the board again, that'll be good because it'll give them an outlet."

But if they got seven seats, it could be a real problem. All that was needed for a quorum was thirteen board members, and about half the members didn't show up for every meeting. "That means seven votes could be a majority. And if they get ten, it's over."

The old Krug winery had been purchased by Cesare Mondavi, the father of Robert and Peter, back in 1943. Since then the family had split, with Robert going his own way. After changing the pronunciation of his name, Robert had achieved a critical and economic success not enjoyed by the Mon-*day*-vis he left behind. But what a beautiful property it still was, untouched since the sixties, harking back to an earlier era, with a long expanse of lawn dominated by enormous oaks and a handful of redwoods blocking the sun that set behind Greystone, just across Highway 29. Tables had been set up on the grass, each supporting a single potted plant and chairs waiting to be unfolded. The arriving guests appeared to have much more in common with traditional valley life than those seen at the Wine Auction dinner the previous month: no limos in the parking lot and more pickups than SUVs or sedans. No designer outfits or tuxedos, just jeans, chinos, shorts, and an equal mix of baseball caps and straw cowboy hats.

The biggest of these, Tom Gamble's ten-gallon hat with the feather in the band, was stationed by the table where people picked up their name tags, as much a host as anyone. Early arrivals included Jon-Mark and Cyril Chappellet, Alexander Eisele, Stu Smith, and Bo Barrett of Chateau Montelena. Dennis Groth wore a planter's hat, and he and his wife moved a bit regally through the assembling crowd, smiling and shaking hands. Jayson Pahlmeyer arrived gripping a roll of raffle tickets. But this year few other vintners were in evidence, the Farm Bureau picnic now being seen as the venue of the up-valley proletariat.

The voting table was everyone's first stop, then the drinks table, where an array of Napa Valley wines were poured by volunteers. Conversation in discrete groups forming under the big oaks was about the prospects for the harvest, soon to get under way, the need for sulfuring grapes to prevent mildew, and the difficulty of obtaining an erosion control permit. The Sierra Club lawsuit, as if by prior agreement, seemed off-limits, as did the election on this, the day the makeup of the board was finally to be decided.

Hugh and Lily sat down at the table with Tom. Hugh wore a Schramsberg polo shirt with a hole in it and hiking boots he had bought after climbing Mount Shasta with some Schramsberg sales reps and getting blisters from his old ones; Lily still had on her riding pants and stubby spurs.

Dinner was shish kebabs, hot sausages, potato salad, ripe tomatoes, and caesar salad. Rich Salvestrin, the president, stood and spoke of growers' concerns: the shortage of farm worker housing, conservation regulations, eradicating the glassy-winged sharpshooter, the one subject on which everybody was in agreement. "All the other issues won't be issues if we don't find a solution to the sharpshooter." He mentioned the need to find "common ground . . . It's been a rough year," and thanked his wife for her support. "I'm breaking up here . . . I love you. That's all I've got."

The votes were still being counted while the raffle tickets were drawn. Tom Gamble won a wheelbarrow, and a suitcase, and six bottles of Beringer sauvignon blanc. "Fix!" someone shouted, laughter rising from the tables. He offered up the wheelbarrow to be auctioned off a second time, and won again. "Fix! . . . Fix! . . ." It was loaded with his other winnings, and Tom wheeled it back to the table, trying not to laugh.

Then came the election results. Methodically the names of the twenty-two winning board members were read over the loudspeakers. Tom's name was included among the victors, close to the end. Hugh rushed back to the table and sat, leaning forward, elbows on knees, listening. When his name was finally read, he said, "Who else got on? Who . . . ," and Tom said, "Sounds like we got them all."

It was an anticlimax, if not a rout. People had expected arguments, maybe even fistfights, but now well-wishers came by the table to shake hands. Tom said, "It's easy to be magnanimous in victory. I hope somebody's magnanimous in defeat."

The losers, Stu Smith among them, stood off to one side. Mark van Gorder, official mouthpiece of Farmers for Napa Valley, his hair in disarray, was clearly angry. He glanced uneasily in the direction of his employer, Mark Neal, owner of the big vineyard management company and subsidizer of the Farmers' rhetoric. "He's going to make so much money because of all the regulation this board's going to let in," van Gorder said, but Neal ignored him. "It's what happened in Silicon Valley," van Gorder went on, "so much regulation that the farmers finally decided to sell out. Wait till the Sierra Club comes in with more lawsuits," and then, "The band plays on," meaning that the fight wasn't over yet, but van Gorder's boss turned and walked away.

Stu stood with his arms crossed. "A straight party-line vote" was as close as he would come to criticism. "I'm tired of going to meetings anyway. I'm going to start watching *West Wing* on Wednesday nights." And he went out to his Suburban alone.

Tom Gamble, still in the white cowboy hat, stayed behind to help stack the tables and folding chairs.

38

I T WAS A CLASSIC valley scene: a Mexican standing in a field or a
garden or a driveway, a cigarette dangling from his lips, hands on
hips, staring at a pile of material that had to be dealt with — dirt,
rock, vine cuttings, pumice, bottles, lumber, plastic pipe. He sucked
smoke, concentrating, and a minute later the cigarette was gone and
the work began, the air about him hazed with dust.

The pickers who arrived for harvest were in the vineyards before
light, carrying plastic bins, slinging dirt against the vines to dislodge
rattlesnakes, and wading into arduous labor no one else would —
could — do, under a relentlessly rising sun, work that scarred the
hands and left clothes sweat-soaked and tinted with Napa Valley
terroir. Picking was performed at precise moments, when sugar in the
grapes attained the desired degree of concentration; every other eth-
nic group available in northern California had tried this task at one
time or another, and every other group had failed the tests of endurance and reliability.

The pickers were paid twice the rate they would have received in
the Central Valley, and so they came in their low-slung cars and in
vans, and slept in them when there were no beds to be had, which
was often, or in the vineyards, or down by the river, out of sight of
the tourists and the landowners. Their work usually done by noon,
they rested in the heat of the day, or tinkered with an engine, or
called home; all over the valley, men hung on to pay phones as if they
were lovers.

Harvest under way, pickups and gondolas stood with tourists' cars
in the long lines between Dean & DeLuca and the bridge over Sulphur Creek in St. Helena. The sidewalks were crowded with stroll-

ers, who wore a familiar expression as if thinking to themselves: Is this the place we've heard of, and what's all the fuss about? They asked the clerks in Steve's Hardware, the Model Bakery, and Main Street Books if they had a restroom, and if there was a winery within walking distance. They clearly expected such things to exist in easy proximity, and the lack puzzled and disappointed them. After all, this was Napa Valley, yet the choices were limited, the visitors thrown back upon themselves, with nothing to do but walk and eat and drink, glimpsing between the sheltering branches of trees and the façades of reconditioned storefronts the deep green mountains that seemed distant and untouchable.

"They won."

Stu Smith stood in his living room on Sylvaner, declaiming on the Farm Bureau election and surveying the clutter of camping equipment — sleeping bags, tents, a cooler, water bottles, stacked packages of ramen, all to be loaded into the battered Suburban. His son the contemplative Sam, already on his voyage through teendom, had asked about the election. Stu said it had been a party-line vote, although it hadn't really been, and then had to explain what a party-line vote was. The canoe trip the next day would take father and sons to Oregon, and Stu, stroking his salt-and-pepper beard, Spring Mountain dust on his boots, was thinking more of equipment than politics.

"Hugh Davies is naive," he added, a description he thought applied to most board members. "They won't condemn the tactics and objectives of the environmentalists, they won't bite the bullet. And compromise is tantamount to long-term defeat." But Sam had lost interest.

It was early evening. Stu got a bottle of Stony Hill gewurztraminer from the refrigerator and took it out to the patio, where he sat holding his new daughter, Charlotte Ruth. This was what he called "the time of the long shadows," when all grew quiet in the valley and you could look past the yard and the makeshift skateboard jump and spreading branches to a darkening, radiant blue sky. It was what drew him to the valley in the first place, he said, a sad bit of irony — the shadows and the trees that cast them.

The Farm Bureau election was just another step in the process of defining the future. He had over the last year and a half become convinced that there are basically two types of human beings who would inhabit that future, in the valley and in America: those who assume the other person will do the right thing and those who insist on laws to force the same result. A presumed positive versus a presumed negative.

The environmentalists thought they could solve everything with laws, but in Stu's opinion laws weren't going to stop people like Delia Viader. She had been dynamiting up on Howell Mountain again, in plain view of Highway 29, during this discussion of erosion and ordinances and candidates, putting in more vineyard. And the county had cited her for operating without an approved permit, a dozen years after the Bell Canyon Reservoir disaster. The Viader vineyard had, indirectly, been the origin of the fight over hillside erosion and the ongoing role of agriculture in the valley, and now Viader was in trouble once more. It was as if nothing had been accomplished, this action yet another arrow in the environmentalists' quiver.

Jack Cakebread, who was putting in a vineyard above Viader's, had told his attorney about Delia's activities, and the attorney had called Mel Varrelman, who in turn called the county. Dave Abreu wasn't involved this time, since Delia didn't need him anymore, having learned enough in the ensuing years to supervise the work herself, including the hiring of a dynamiter.

The solution to such problems proposed by those Stu called "the numbnuts" — the environmentalists, specifically Chris Malan and her allies — was a more strict law. That was no solution at all, he believed. They wanted a one-year limit on the issuing of erosion control permits by the county, but they didn't realize how long it took to draw up a good plan in the first place, and that people will then rush to get the work done or act prematurely. The unhappy results affected both the land and politics.

Stu planned to abandon the latter. He was allowing Farmers for Napa Valley to quietly expire, but the struggle wasn't quite over. The band had one more number: he intended to challenge the Farm Bureau election on grounds that the staff and the officers prevented the opposition from soliciting votes from the general membership, and get the election set aside. And he would write to the general counsel of the state Farm Bureau Federation in Sacramento and ask for the membership list that had been denied him, even if a futile gesture. If the Napa County Farm Bureau still didn't make it available, Stu was out of there.

The unintended consequences of all that had transpired — the hillside ordinance, the Watershed Task Force, the Sierra Club lawsuit, the elections — were divisive and wouldn't be tallied for a long time. One unintended consequence was Peter Mennen's being forced out of the St. Helena post office, which Stu suspected was painful for him. Peter would no longer be the postal system's most colorful character, and the town was losing something valuable because of this. There would be other casualties, maybe including Stu himself. He wanted to put in a few more acres of vineyard and do some replants without being bothered by officialdom. "Give me the right to farm the hills," he liked to say, "and I'll go away."

Farmers had to be optimistic, starting over each year — a renewal of the spirit. It was a fantastic life, but the new people were missing that fundamental concept because the real work was done by someone else. Stu loved the wine business, but it too had changed beyond recognition. He had become, as he often said now, "a dinosaur, a little guy with small funds who doesn't belong in this market, doesn't drive an eighty-thousand-dollar car, have interior and exterior decorators and butlers, and dinner twice a week at Tra Vigne." His letter to Sacramento would be a parting shot — a reminiscent, sunset move — and he himself just a footnote to the valley's history. He wanted that citation to read "I told you so."

Volker Eisele had been in San Ramon on business the night of the Farm Bureau election, but he heard of the results immediately by cell phone. For once, he thought, all our efforts paid off. Then he went down to the hotel bar for a celebratory brandy.

It seemed to Volker that for the last thirty-five years environmentalism had reigned in California, with liberals in power. But that was starting to change. He saw no broad political will for environmental protection now. Private property rights ideology ruled supreme, despite the results of this local election; the bad boys were still winning.

Citizens might not like what was happening to the land, but very few were willing to take a stand. Volker was the *éminence grise,* but he needed the support of the new generation. It was up to Tom Gamble, Hugh Davies, Jon-Mark Chappellet, Beth Milliken, and other, younger growers and vintners who would have to continue the fight. That meant more, improved regulation — something for the environment, something for agriculture. But farmers had to align themselves formally with environmentalism, rather than with developers, or perish as a consequence.

People as committed as Chris Malan would always be with us, he thought. They were necessary, and had to be convinced that agriculture was a positive force. And they required better leadership. The Sierra Club, credited with a big victory with its lawsuit, had in fact failed, settling for the terms of the California Environmental Quality Act when it could have forced the county to immediately improve the hillside ordinance. The Sierra Club could have pledged to bring no new lawsuits until the completion of the total maximum daily load study of the river, forcing the federal government to get this finished and preventing the sniping by the Winegrowers. Chris and Peter had brought the county to its knees, and then let it up.

Shortly after returning home, Volker went for a walk on his property across the road. He and Liesel had given the development rights to the Land Trust but retained the land. A big Douglas fir stood in the middle of it; all around, Doug fir sprouts battled the dense undergrowth, reaching for the light. The steep Chiles Valley hills seemed to press against his far vineyard, close enough to touch. The infinitely variable complexity of soil, slope, and sun had produced and continued to produce a unique commodity, Napa Valley wine.

Everybody wanted a piece of the terrain, including the dot-commers and other nouveaux riches who were tourists first, householders second. This was nothing new. Long ago, a branch of the Rothschild banking family moved to France, and the French laughed at them, too. They created a coat of arms and bought an estate in Bordeaux, for the association of land and gentility, the same thing that was happening in Napa Valley today. Wine labels were the twenty-first-century equivalent of a coat of arms, except that the Napa Valley nouveaux riches wanted to continue making money.

The message of all that had transpired was pretty simple, he thought, bushwhacking downhill toward the house. In the end everything depends on place and its natural composition; geology is destiny.

Some Mexican pickers would stay beyond harvest, to tend the vineyards, do the landscaping, and generally keep afloat the delicate balance of nature and human demands on it. If they had opinions about land use and water quality, they were not sought out or listened to. But without these people there would have been no argument over hillside vineyards or setbacks, no patios and no exotic gardens, no cult cabernets, no Dean & DeLuca, no muscle houses, no aura of beautiful, natural invincibility.

39

TALK OF spraying to kill the glassy-winged sharpshooter, the little wasp from the south with the potential to destroy Napa Valley's vineyards, greatly alarmed Chris Malan. If they tried to spray poison on her land from the air, she told people, she would find something in herself — she didn't say what this was — and "go to the wall."

Sitting at the kitchen table in a sweatshirt that said "Wild & Free," her dark hair tied up in a blue ribbon, a mug of warmed-over tea before her, she asked one caller, "What about air quality? What about the health of microorganisms and frogs? And people? All this is being weighed against a bottle of wine." This, she thought, was clearly wrong. "There will be a fierce battle if it happens. One segment of the population can't do something like that to another segment and get away with it."

The siding had been pulled off the house, to get at the termites, but otherwise construction was finally finished and Micah happy in his new wing. Parked in the driveway was a customized pickup specially equipped with a lift for his wheelchair and levers all over the steering column, so Micah could drive it himself. Her son had wheels now, thanks to the insurance settlement, and space of his own. Things had settled down domestically, although some mornings Jack rose as early as three-thirty to drive to his youth counseling job in San Francisco and avoid the killer traffic feeding the San Francisco Bay Bridge.

Chris sipped her tea and perused the papers spread out on the table. There was so much going on, not just the Watershed Task Force but also the spraying threat, and making sure Jayson Pahlmeyer actually granted development rights on that piece of property to the Land Trust in the aftermath of the Sierra Club suit. If he didn't, he would look like a jerk, the Land Trust would be outraged, and he would still have to pay ten thousand dollars to an as yet unspecified environmental fund.

There was the new litigation she and Tom Lippe were working on: possible suits against individuals for unfair business practices and against the county for approving new vineyard plans when those plans hadn't been properly evaluated. The planning department was issuing "neg decs" — negative declarations — on new vineyards, which meant no bad effects from erosion, but Chris and her friends were keeping a close eye on those. The argument that only the big wineries could afford to do EIRs, and therefore most small operators were theoretically being kept off the land and unfairly out of competition, left Chris cold. This was about environmental protection, not equal opportunity.

There was more resistance now within the ex-com of the Napa group of the Sierra Club to suing the county. One of the ex-com members, Tyler York, seemed to Chris more interested in agriculture than nature. Tyler was in the organic fertilizer business, and she considered him a mole in contact with Jeff Redding and other officials, working against new lawsuits and making Chris's life difficult. Others thought he was simply trying to reach some accord among the valley's various green and grower factions.

Acting on Tom Lippe's advice, she had brought up in the ex-com the possibility of suing the state over water allotments that went to vineyards, wineries, and other commercial endeavors, and were the lifeblood of development. The Sierra Club would again act as plaintiff, and Peter Mennen as financer. John Stephens, chair of the Napa group, liked the idea and decided that he had thought it up himself, which was fine with Chris. Tyler didn't object to suing the state, either, but again they had hit a snag higher up the chain of command in the Redwood chapter.

A Mendocino woman who had for years been trying to sue on water allotments went through the roof, reaming the Napa group in a conference call, saying the Napans didn't know what they were doing and that their suit, if filed, would ruin the suit in Mendocino. She was saying, in essence, butt out. Chris couldn't understand why this woman was so angry, and then she mentioned the Mennens, and

Chris understood. Some of the money from the Mennen Environmental Foundation could be channeled out of Napa County, the woman suggested, to projects like hers, and Chris realized she was jealous of her and of her funding. The Mennens' contributions were the mother's milk of legal action, and the woman wanted some of it and the power that came with it.

As soon as Chris recognized this "personality thing," she pulled back from that particular suit. That was the way she had learned to deal with such internal opposition: take a different route, avoid unproductive arguments. Many environmentalists got caught up in personality conflicts, but not Chris. She and Tom Lippe weren't butting out, they were just putting water allotments on hold while moving on to other projects.

It was clear to Chris now that she needed another good organization in whose name to sue. The Sierra Club would always be a possibility, but the problems with Tyler York and the ex-com made it increasingly difficult. So Chris familiarized herself with various out-of-county groups that might be willing to lend their names to lawsuits financed by someone else — Baykeepers, the Oak Foundation, others. There were suits being researched against the state and county over timber harvest plans and the destruction of oak trees. Lippe had sent the merits of one such suit to Chris to study, and she had passed it along to Peter. He liked it and said he would be responsible for between fifteen thousand and fifty thousand dollars on the oaks, and fifty thousand on water, but first they had to find an organization to serve as coplaintiff.

Lining up these organizations was a drag. It would be far better to have one already in place, willing to sue, and that had given Chris the idea of turning herself into a charitable organization: Chris Malan, 501(c)(3). It would have to have a name, of course. Having such an entity in place would shortcut the process and get the legal balls rolling immediately. Then they wouldn't need the Sierra Club or anybody else; they would be free to wage war against the exploiters and all those abusing nature.

When she mentioned this to Peter, he seemed to like the idea. He would fund it, he said, and Chris would do all the legwork. But then Carlene weighed in.

She had other ideas. Chris's tax-exempt group had to be set up a certain way, Carlene said, with lots of rules. Carlene could be a problem, Chris knew; sometimes Chris had to go around her. She could do this because she had such a good relationship with Peter, but not in the case of Chris's prospective nonprofit, she discovered. Carlene wanted a friend of hers, a woman in Utah who had received Mennen Foundation grants, to sit on the board of any organization the Mennens financed. They all took part in a conference call, and the woman questioned Chris's ability to manage a nonprofit group. She said Chris didn't have the time to do all that was required, that she was already working for the county and involved in too many causes. She asked how Chris would raise additional funds, and what the bylaws would be, and on and on.

It was a power play, Chris thought. The woman clearly believed that Chris exercised too much influence on the Mennens, and wanted to counter that — the conflict Chris had with the Mendocino woman all over again. This Utah woman was competing for funds, too, and her criticism gave Peter cold feet. Then everybody who had been lined up as potential board members started to bail out of Chris's new, as yet nonexistent nonprofit, and Chris thought, "Talk about corporate takeover — a takeover of a 501(c)(3)!"

Peter felt awful about it. He told Chris that she should go forward on her own, and Chris tried, but was then blocked by one of the Mennens' attorneys. "My God," she thought, "what next?" The lawyer didn't want the Mennen Foundation overexposed and didn't like all the negative publicity resulting from the original Sierra Club suit. He seemed to think the foundation might suffer at the hands of resentful individuals, and possibly at the hands of the feds, and that Chris was taking too many chances. Things got very complicated. Mennen Foundation funding was to be consolidated, he said, and Chris realized that her access to the money had just become much more limited.

Well, she wasn't going to get hung up on all that. If something doesn't work, move on. She had wanted to call her organization the Watershed Recovery Alliance, and went so far as to register the name in Sacramento, before the bottom fell out of the deal. This raised suspicions on the Sierra Club's Napa group ex-com, where her intentions were questioned, as if Chris were trying to make an end run and sue the county on her own. Tyler York, with the organic fertilizer business, gravelly voice, and eyes of an old-time gunfighter, demanded to know who was on her board — no one! — and where the money would come from — the Mennens (hello!) — and wouldn't accept her explanations. Tyler sent her six e-mails asking if this new group was real.

Meanwhile, the county was feeling pressured by a potential barrage of suits from her unformed nonprofit, and that made county officials more difficult to deal with. Who cares? Chris said. Let the county sweat out whether or not it's getting sued again. But this wasn't a common sentiment on the ex-com.

She had been warned about politics in the Sierra Club before she joined, and now was convinced that Tyler and others were out to get her. They were interested in cooperating with the county and the Vintners, in cutting deals and getting invited to lunch, and she was interested in change. Tyler was right about the need for better communications with the county, but officials were going to lunch with him and trying to get him to go back and nail Chris to the cross, she thought. And these internal struggles played havoc with the overall legal strategy that she, Lippe, and the Mennens had worked out in the simpler glory days.

In the midst of all this, Chris had unexpectedly been invited to lunch herself, by none other than Jack Stuart, president of the Napa Valley Vintners Association and head of Silverado Vineyards, the Disneys' winery. The Vintners was conducting an outreach program, and Stuart had drawn her name, although he didn't tell her this. At his suggestion they met at the ABC on Third Street in Napa, a funky place she wouldn't have thought Stuart would know of, and the meeting proved to be a revelation to her. Stuart struck her as nice, well spoken, empathetic, admitting that he was a conservationist who wanted the hillsides preserved. He and his colleagues, he added, didn't like to look up and see bald spots or even breaks in the forest, didn't like the idea of hills eroding into the river. He said all the right things until they got to setbacks, and then Stuart admitted that he opposed the moving of vineyards away from the river because of the economic damage to the owners, including, of course, the Disneys.

That's always the problem, Chris thought. As soon as something affects these guys financially, there's a sticking point, then an about-face. That was why you had to sue people; if you didn't sue, people would never do what was right.

Carlene realized that she and Peter had gotten too close to Chris Malan.

Her relationship with Chris was characterized by Carlene as akin to that between gas fumes and lit matches. Back when Carlene agreed to fund the macroinvertebrate study of the Napa River, she told Chris to apply for the grants like everybody else. She couldn't just blow by people, but Chris wasn't listening. Carlene had never met anyone so determined, and she had worked with many activists, from the top echelons of the Sierra Club and the Wilderness Society to rock-ribbed defenders of the Utah canyon country. Chris didn't like to be challenged, she didn't want to be told what had to be done to get, and keep, funding. She didn't seem to understand that there were rules.

When Chris decided to form her own organization, she had asked for a litigation budget of eighty thousand dollars over three years. Carlene had asked her, "Where is the money coming from?"

"Peter will give it to me."

Then Chris added, almost casually, that she wanted to share an office with Peter. Carlene listened, as always. Then she told Chris that most of what she had in mind wasn't possible.

Chris said, "I'll just ask Peter."

It seemed to Carlene that Chris had forgotten who ran the Mennen Environmental Foundation. That same person read all the proposals, made the decisions, bird-dogged the projects, and wrote the checks. That person was Carlene, who also happened to be Peter Mennen's wife.

Peter kept getting calls from Chris. He was stressed out by all these developments, trying to dance and run at the same time, as Carlene put it. She was afraid Peter would have some kind of emotional breakdown. Chris's demands, the problems at the post office, Ricki Lake's departure, and a lactose buildup in his muscles pointed toward disaster, and increasingly she was worried about him.

People always misread Peter. If you asked him for something, he would probably grant it. But if you went too far, Peter either got nasty or he checked out. Napa Valley and all its issues were more his thing than Carlene's, and they had gotten too intense, and Peter had to leave town for a while, to get away from it all.

Chris kept calling. Every time the telephone rang at seven A.M.,

Carlene knew who it was. That, of course, was also part of Chris's appeal: persistence. Don't take no for an answer. People like her were necessary in the movement, to assume extreme positions and attract the heat and condemnation so those behind the scenes could move the goalpost a quarter inch in the right direction.

Carlene had used organizations in the same way, to achieve her and the Mennen Foundation's goals. The Sierra Club was a case in point. It had been too slow a target to get out of the crosshairs when Chris and Tom Lippe zeroed in on that organization as a good one to use against the county. The Sierra Club had national clout; a suit in its name would attract a lot of attention and support. But now that suit was won, and all these new possibilities had fallen into Carlene's lap, and she had to deal with them, too. If she didn't deal, the Mennen Environmental Foundation, still healthy financially, would be swamped.

Chris was unofficially involving it in all kinds of potential litigation and studies. If she had an idea, she pursued it, without a proposal or a budget. The foundation was getting legal and other bills, and Carlene didn't know what they were for. The fund was hemorrhaging. It was time, she decided, to yank Chris back to reality.

She had decided that everything would be funneled through Bill Yeates in Sacramento, the lawyer who had started the Mountain Lion Foundation and created a legal entity to serve as a clearinghouse for environmental action. Yeates was an experienced environmentalist, patient, but no pushover. He was convinced that Napa Valley could be a demonstration model for the state and the nation on river cleanup and enlightened development. He would be paid to do the homework on all potential litigation being discussed by Chris and Tom Lippe, and pass on it.

Chris didn't like that. She "bucked and pitched." In Bill Yeates's opinion, Chris thought the Mennens' money was her money, too. When Bill told Chris she had to work through him, Chris said she didn't have to, that Peter had said she didn't. She won't listen, Bill told Carlene. "She goes right through you."

Carlene had to explain to Chris that to form a nonprofit Chris would have to develop a membership base, learn to write grant proposals and abide by them, come up with sound litigation protocols, and work with experienced lawyers in developing an initiative opposed to hillside development. Carlene gave her the five thousand names the Mennen Foundation had collected from the petition mailed during the supervisors' race and suggested that she write a letter to all those people, tell them about the new organization and ask for a ten-dollar membership fee. The list was a powerful tool, Carlene reminded her. An organization like the one Chris envisioned needed a broad funding base, and although it was no fun to have to raise money, without that broad base you lose your nonprofit status. But Chris didn't seem interested in that kind of funding.

Carlene also gave her the names of some powerful people in the movement who might agree to be on her board, and Chris sent each of them a copy of her proposal letter for the 501(c)(3) and then called them up and told them what they would be doing. She didn't understand how things worked, that you have to listen, as well as instruct, to work with others. After that, Carlene couldn't persuade any of those people to serve on Chris's board, much less as her treasurer.

Carlene decided to reinforce the firewall between Chris and the foundation, between themselves and the rest of the valley. Everybody was running around trying to find out who was driving the bus, wanting so much from the Mennens — letters, speeches, organizational assistance, and, of course, money. The stress load was too great. Carlene was putting in sixty hours a week with all that and her other projects beyond the Mayacamas and the Howell ranges, and Chris blowing past her time and again.

Chris Malan was the George Patton of Napa Valley, Carlene decided. Her thing was the *only* thing. If Carlene hadn't liked and valued her, she would have tried to stop her. Instead, the Mennens were going to salvage and protect themselves and as much of what was out in the big, aching natural world as they could.

Ricki Lake was gone. Peter flew to North Carolina to see that he was all right, and to turn a symbolic spadeful of dirt for the raising of the aviary dome that would house his former, feathered, cherished office mate. The spade's handle was festooned with the colors of Ricki Lake — green, blue, and gold — for the Mennen Environmental Foundation was paying for Ricki's dome, which would also be home to Lucy, the female conure, and all the other abandoned tropical birds needing refuge.

Back in St. Helena, Peter received from the grateful couple running the aviary a video of Ricki flying with Lucy, who had regained some of her plumage, the two of them obviously in love, nuzzling each other on the perch and flying in tandem. Ricki had a new life and no doubt had forgotten the St. Helena post office and his solitary flights above the heads of the fine, if unconventional, postal staff that was now burdened with an increased workload, without distraction by a beloved service pet. But at least Ricki Lake was happy.

This condition did not extend to Ricki's former owner. Peter would forget to answer telephone calls and to take his wallet to the supermarket; everything seemed unreal to him, some part of himself lost. He wouldn't go back to the post office and was relieved by this decision, but at the same time angry at the bureaucracy he had served so long and which had worked, in his opinion, to make his life miserable. He was still trying to get an emotional handle on this.

He rented a little office in a private home on the edge of Sulphur Creek, overlooking the new park that the foundation was creating there, in the heart of St. Helena. Gradually he assembled the papers and books that would constitute his new existence, hoping the distraction he felt would end. Periodically he sent off letters to Postal Service bureaucrats in Oakland and elsewhere, pointing out the errors of their past ways in no uncertain terms and eliciting intemperate responses that gave him some satisfaction. A lawsuit was a possibility for him, but then there were so many legal actions possible, and pending. The various issues massed at the portals of his consciousness like cars at the entrance to the Caldecott Tunnel under the Berkeley hills, a traffic jam of daunting proportions.

One of the issues was still Jayson Pahlmeyer. There were the three options for going after him again — through the foundation, through the county's district attorney, and through the state's attorney general, all of whom had been made aware of the potential for a suit, for alleged bad business practices having to do with the installation of his new vineyard. Another target being discussed was a developer of oak woodlands in the Mayacamas and a member of the Watershed Task Force whom Chris wanted to nail.

So many fenders, so little time. There was the suit brought against a concrete manufacturer for dumping some of its product into the Sulphur Creek bed, the alternately real and nonexistent waterway within view of the patio of Peter's new office, depending on the season. That one was being settled out of court, which was a relief. This, the foundation's second legal victory in a year, would bring eighty thousand dollars to the restoration of the creekbanks and to reimburse the lawyers. Chris Malan had been the only one willing to testify in that case, once again her iron-bound determination a factor in success.

Peter hoped for more cooperation on the Sulphur Creek front. Sometimes he felt the weight of disapproval in a community that should value his contributions; he had spent his time and money on causes he believed in, but some people — vintners and developers — vilified him, and this had come to matter lately, in conjunction with the post office tumult, the departure of Ricki Lake, and the issues and possible new lawsuits. He felt some of the purpose of the foundation slipping. Carlene was worn out with the struggles of the last two years, and there was no clear way for Chris to act directly on her own and the foundation's interests. Her tax-exempt organization had not come together, and Peter felt guilty about that.

He spent his days in the little office, his desk no longer littered with seeds and blueberries. Deer harbored in the oak grove next door, and a pair of acorn woodpeckers, both beautiful and comical. The creek was dry as dust in summer, but come winter the banks would turn green and the creek fill with water coming down from the mountains.

He and Carlene took a trip to Utah and returned tanned and refreshed. Peter had gotten a speeding ticket in the BMW 540 but otherwise avoided the long arm of the law. He and Carlene had seen two pronghorn antelope, among his favored residents of the arid regions, and prairie chickens, another favored species.

The first day back, he drove to the office in his old Jeep pickup with the ODD DUCK license plate and found many messages waiting on his answering machine. First he called Bill Yeates. "We're deciding where to put all the money for next year," Peter told him. "We're getting seriously into the wilderness stuff in Utah." He called Mel Varrelman and talked about making a pro-environmental presentation to the county board of supervisors. Then he called Chris.

She sounded fine. They had a brief, friendly conversation and talked about attending a public hearing on the glassy-winged sharp-shooter and the need to spray. Finally Peter told her, "I've got to go. I have to mail Ricki Lake his blueberries."

After that errand, he sat in the office and looked at the dry creekbed. He recalled an earlier trip, to Yellowstone, where he and Carlene had gone to witness the release of wolves into the wild. The Sierra Club had kissed the Mennens' feet to get money for that project, Peter immediately willing to give it but Carlene, skeptical out of the womb, wanting something in return. She got it — help with her plans for halting timber cutting in the national forests — and had given the Sierra Club fifty thousand dollars.

She and Peter had heard the wolves howling up and down the Yellowstone. One night they parked, and received the sort of gift that comes with true commitment: the sight of a herd of elk emerging from the deep, primordial forest and pausing on a knoll next to their car to gaze at the moon. All had been silence. Time went on forever. The moon lost its yellow richness, and paled, and the elk turned and melted back into the trees.

Thinking about it in the hot light of harvest time, Peter knew that would always be a magic moment in his life. He wouldn't have experienced it but for Carlene. She was refocused now, using those who tried to use her as pawns in her chess games, reminding him of the time long ago, in Mexico City, in the park where he and his classmates read and tossed Frisbees, of the wagon used for taking children around the park. Each seat had a little steering wheel, and each child turned his, thinking he was in charge, while the old man pushing the wagon went right where he intended to go.

Peter could grasp the essential point of any argument, but then he didn't know what to do with it. Carlene knew. The foundation would not become obsolete, because she kept everything in her head, a constantly spinning Rubik's cube, figuring out relationships, motives, moves, objectives. She saw the hole in the hedge, as Loren Eiseley, the naturalist, had once written. Everyone else marched past it, but Carlene dashed through.

40

THE FINAL MEETING of the Watershed Task Force took place not in the Gasser Building but in the county administrative offices in the center of Napa, home of the planning department and the supervisors' chambers, where countless land-use issues had been debated and voted on over the years. The room had a view of the western hills, the sun flaming out over Sonoma County and throwing the sawtooth edge of the Mayacamas into sharp relief on this crystalline fall day. The touch of coolness in the air promised change.

All members had brought with them a thick spiral binder with a pale green cover printed with the words "Napa River Watershed Task Force Phase II Final Report." The official recommendations, in part still fungible, were general guidelines for the county, without hard science and a minimum of the soft sort. Science was to be undertaken in great seriousness by yet another task force, to follow this one, its members conversant in such things as water quality and biological diversity, and who would be carefully chosen by the organizers to move the recommendations along toward enactment, without political dissension.

Here everything remained open to discussion, but the window was closing fast. The environmentalists on this task force still wanted the county to attach to any new vineyard project a requirement for an environmental impact study, and the ag people and developers wanted to preserve the status quo ante, which meant merely conforming to the hillside ordinance that had been in place for a decade.

Chris Malan and Stu Smith sat in opposition across the table.

Others filled in around them, in approximation of their old consultative slots. There were fewer spectators now, the meetings having dragged on for months longer than anyone anticipated. A collective weariness was evident in the lack of both bonhomie and acrimony; they drank from bottles of Calistoga water and cans of soda and listened to the familiar, soothing tone of the facilitator. "We're going to pick up items not reviewed a second time," he said. "We left off last time with the timber harvest and conversion plan exemption."

The members discussed the proposed "overlay plan" and various restrictions on cutting trees, Jeff Redding reminding them that they had spent two years talking about this, among other subjects. "The longer we wait, the less likely the ordinance will be effected," he warned.

The task force moved on to a discussion of limiting the timber cut and paying property owners for timber rights. Stu said, "I don't like the word 'prohibit.' As long as Napa Valley uses timber, we have an obligation to harvest our own and not get it from British Columbia."

Chris said, "If it was only timber harvesting, maybe it wouldn't be such a problem. But this is a conversion," meaning changing woodlands to vineyards and lots, "a permanent loss."

Richard Niemann suggested using the word "regulate" in place of "prohibit." Jeff nodded, as if these things were actually being decided, Stu pulling at his beard, Chris watching faces. Dennis Groth said the task force's fundamental job was to decide whether something warranted concern, and Chris said, "This is a major issue with me and with a lot of the public. We need a clear recommendation on ending cutting," and called for a vote.

"Ending the cutting of trees is anti-ag," said Stu, "and I'll never change my mind. I'm with Chris, let's vote and move on."

The facilitator reduced the issue to be voted on to an innocuous recommendation that the board of supervisors look into tree removal in sensitive areas. "Anybody disagree?"

Dennis Groth raised his hand, palm inward. "This is a worthless recommendation. It doesn't deserve to be written down."

"I've been saying this from day one," said Chris.

And so it went.

At one point Stu held up the thick, impressively bound report. He said, "This document reminds me of the health-care debate, which was so complicated, and aggressive, and got nowhere . . . I want to make sure you know I'm not in agreement with many of these things."

The facilitator nodded. "We have to decide how we will report this out. If there are any real deal-breakers, we need to get to them."

In the men's room, during the break, Dennis and Stu stood at the urinals and remarked on the futility of it all. Stu said, of the opposition, "The more they talk, the worse they look," but there was resignation in his voice.

Dennis thought the real issue wasn't trees or even setbacks — which would cost him millions in revenue from his cabernet sauvignon, described by him when it was young as possessing undertones of "coffee and chocolate" that mature into aromas of "cedar and cigar box" — but estate taxes. The burden a family like his bore in passing along intact such a prestigious label, and the land it entailed, was tremendous, and unappreciated by the likes of Chris Malan. When he died, his children would have to come up with fifty-five percent of the value of Groth vineyards, a dilemma his corporate competitors did not face because the laws vastly favored that leviathan of the economic system, the corporation, arguably the most potent force in modern America, with unfair advantages and insistence on profit above all else. The corporation could not die, unlike its human counterparts.

Dennis decried this, but it was the system he had earlier served and the one that made him rich. The irony was obvious. He was a product of the thing that had exerted an almost universally bad effect on the valley, from the disaster of Heublein's arrival in the 1960s to the present, and arguably the biggest long-term threat, since land for houses produced a great deal more profit than land under vines, regardless of the grapes' quality, and could well prove irresistible to those for whom profit was all.

After the break, the facilitator dealt with some "cleanup points." Then Jeff Redding told how the recommendations would be presented to the board of supervisors, what all this had boiled down to: the task force would request that a new hillside ordinance be passed, one that required environmental impact reports, and that an information center be established, and a land conservancy. Advance plans would be necessary for timber cutting, and there would be setbacks, but these needn't be determined until the "science" was formally in. "We can do a minority report," he added, to accommodate dissenters, if they wished, but no one did; there were other, better ways to oppose new regulation, as everyone knew.

"I want you all there," said Jeff, of the supervisors' meeting to come, "to give weight to the process." It would include more public comment, more discussion, and perhaps the creation of the other task force.

The facilitator said, "You all deserve to give each other a round of applause."

There was some weary clapping. Guy Kay stood up, put on his straw hat, and said, as he was leaving, "There is a merciful God."

Mel Varrelman, Napa County supervisor, the man who, as much as anyone, had initiated the Watershed Task Force, looked back on it as a necessary lesson in the futility of confrontational politics. Napa Valley had been in the forefront of land-use debates for years, and the old hillside ordinance was proof of this. Now there was to be a new ordinance.

In his view the real nut-buster in the task force recommendations was setbacks for replanted vineyards. The problem, of course, was loss of income. The equity argument. Mel understood it, being an estate planner, and he had mulled over the idea of imposing a cap on the amount of money a vineyard might lose by being further separated from the river — one percent, say, of revenue, although he had heard people talking as much as five percent. Collectively, that meant millions, and no one knew for sure how many. It couldn't be proven, until the studies were done, that setbacks would fix the river, but the tacit understanding on both sides of the argument was that setbacks would be hugely influential on its health.

Meanwhile, there were almost one hundred applications for new vineyards out there, and no one knew how many more appeals Tom Lippe would file, and how many lawsuits. If Malan/Mennen was successful with attack and counterattack, and if Chris Malan's public comments were indicative — that she would like to see vineyards rolled back and more diverse farming — then in Mel's opinion the

wine industry could well fail. This twin assault by extreme environmentalism and the glassy-winged sharpshooter could bring down
the curtain, and everything they had fought over for all those years
would be in vain. All the ordinances would get reenacted, and Napa
would become an urban county.

If agriculture failed, even tourism would eventually go. People
from all over the country wouldn't come to Napa if it looked just
like home; the dot-commers would take their billions elsewhere.
The limousines would become endangered, and limo wines become
mere SUV, Volvo, and pickup wines — which, come to think of it,
was the way it used to be.

The irony remained: if the county hadn't already had a good ordinance, the Sierra Club lawsuit would never have happened. Mel had
told John Stephens, head of the Napa group, that everybody now
had to get behind the cart and push, but Stephens had just listened.
That owlish, expressionless face — no affect, no mercy. Malan, too,
seemed uninterested in agriculture. She had supported the development of Aetna Springs during the supervisorial race, saying the residences were better than vineyards, a clear signal of priorities.

Mel thought that the assumption by the Sierra Club — that the
attitude of the body politic toward environmentalism wouldn't
change if the vineyards became history — was wrong. The super-
structure was a three-legged stool: ag, the political leadership, and the
body politic. All three legs were needed to maintain open space, and
the fights were getting harder. They demanded draconian tactics
now. He thought Kathryn Winter should have been tougher in her
campaign, that she should have run a television spot showing a
stretch limo pulling up and dispensing cash, an accurate, if uncompromising, reflection of what took place. As in football, you have to
knock your opponent on his ass to win. But Kathryn wouldn't do it.
She tried to run a popular campaign — just like that of Kathleen
McCullough, who had lost ten years before — and she didn't have a
chance against a candidate like Bill Dodd in the current political
arena.

Mel was removing himself from all this, although as yet he hadn't
told anyone but his wife. He'd been a significant part of one of the
stool's legs for too many years and would not seek reelection in 2002,
although he had no idea who would replace him. He could imagine
one of the Farmers for Napa Valley running, and a number of other

people. But not Mel. He would concentrate on estate planning in the office with the blue awning ("Go Bears"), talking on the phone, for a change to more clients than constituents, and try to make a new, sunset life in the place he had chosen years before.

Guy Kay — former Beringer executive, environmentalist, member of many boards over the years and a force in more political arguments — lived in a bungalow on a back street in St. Helena, just down the block from the middle school and within walking distance of the post office and the movie theater. He moved about his house in a polo shirt, shorts, and sneakers, well hatted when he stepped out into the sun, eyes bright blue behind steel-rimmed spectacles. Here many strands of civic and political life of the valley crossed, though most people living in it didn't suspect this; since retiring from Beringer, Guy had undergone open-heart surgery but felt fine, and he and his wife, Connie, were secure, which mattered to him. But he had done a great deal of work for no payment, and he wanted to continue doing so.

The Watershed Task Force, he thought, had been worth the struggle. It had been a steep learning curve for everybody, but particularly for the private property rights guys. Some had been forced for the first time in their lives to consider alternatives to their views, and one or two had softened, even if barely perceptibly. Those who didn't, and called for science to bail them out, were soon going to be drowning in it.

When the arguments got convoluted and egocentric, Guy tuned out. He could have done so literally, with his hearing aid, but he refrained, trying to keep in view the enduring big picture: agricultural preserve first, then the winery definition, and now a growing ecological awareness that came down to the health of the watershed.

It would take five to ten years to shake all this out. The ag preserve had fostered the idea back in the sixties, and one unintended consequence of this had been the second "gold rush" in the late twentieth century — the flooding in of tourists and wealthy second-home owners entranced with the physical beauty of the place. But its preservation was ongoing, and he saw the momentum now on the environmental side.

They were all living in an ecological incongruity: immense houses and a county General Plan that said people should live in the cities. The privileged would have to give greater access to the countryside to those urban dwellers or the political pressure would increase to the point of detonation. It was possible that things would come full circle up-valley, that an organization like the Vintners would go back to its roots, which was agriculture, its members rubbing shoulders with farmers instead of the dot-commers and entrepreneurs stepping out of limos.

The county needed a board of supervisors sympathetic to the findings of the Watershed Task Force. Guy didn't know if the newly elected Bill Dodd had the guts to stand up to some of his backers, like Jack Cakebread, when it came to setbacks. It seemed obvious to Guy that the hydrology of the Napa River was knowable, that it wouldn't take much to adjust the General Plan to the particulars of recovery once the scientists made their reckoning. He wanted to be part of the conservancy responsible for the riparian lands and had asked Mel Varrelman to toss Guy's hat into the ring when the supervisors started choosing directors. He was encouraged by the seeds of volunteer activity on creeks around the valley.

Guy wanted to nourish a culture of creeks, so all landowners, big and small, would do the right thing without being compelled, would do it by second nature.

41

Hugh left the little house early in the morning and set out through the fog in shorts, a down vest, and a battered Schramsberg cap emblazoned with a rampant frog. The pickup smelled of dust, the air clammy and cold. He noted his mileage from the day before on the clipboard and reset the trip odometer. He hadn't found time the night before, tired as he was. A hydraulic line had broken on the forklift, and then the auger, used to move pumice from the press to the dump truck, got jammed by a horseshoe. A horseshoe! It had found its way into the press but had not, thank God, shut the beast down.

He drove south. From Highway 29 he could see under the gray mat of clouds a single luminous patch near Howell Mountain and in its center the suggestion of blue sky; it was like looking up through a crevice in the bottom of a deep, sunlit sea. The streets of St. Helena were deserted on this Saturday, the marquee above the movie theater dark, the lights on in the Model Bakery, where bread and coffee were being readied for tourists who would soon be arriving. Across the street, newspapers were stacked on the pavement outside Keller's Market, and the Closed sign in the Green Valley Café was crooked, like an exhausted smile.

Half an hour later, he turned south off Cuttings Wharf Road into the sparsely populated, still rural enclave of Carneros. He often thought how nice it would be to live here, at the south end of the valley, amid spacious, gently undulating hills largely devoid of people, closer to the Golden Gate and accessible to San Francisco without the nightmare of Interstate 80 and the Bay Bridge. A horse stood eating hay outside a barn above a vineyard, a country idyll from an earlier time. Under walnut trees were strewn a dozen cars belonging to the pickers: clothing and bedding on the seats, from the mirrors dangling talismans of another civilization. In the open trunks were tools and water bottles and coolers full of food with an inherent heat to match the sun's, when it finally broke through.

Carneros was known for fog and lingering coolness in summer. From it came very good chardonnay and pinot noir, the classic two-some of Champagne. There was no sign of straw hats and colorful bandanas among the vines, no tractor pulling the big bins into which the grapes were dumped, essential elements in any harvest landscape. Hugh parked and approached the vineyard manager, a heavyset man in a soiled baseball cap brooming dirt and star thistle from the concrete pad. "Where are they?" Hugh asked.

"On the west side."

"I said the *east* side."

Hugh was running, his tall, skinny frame bobbing up and down between the vines. He spent a lot of time running in the vineyards nowadays, mostly collecting samples in plastic shopping bags, to be taken back to the winery and analyzed for sugar and acid content so precise times could be set for picking. Running on the job was a way to exercise when there was no time otherwise, usually no one about but Hugh, the jackrabbits, and an occasional coyote, all of them racing around for one reason or another. These vines were so overgrown with weeds and suckers that long views were nonexistent — not a typical source of Schramsberg fruit, but a good one nonetheless.

Hugh would have to talk to the owner about improving his vineyard practices or the three-year contract wouldn't be renewed, but first he had to find the crew in this vinous jungle and get them over to where the grapes were riper before it was too late.

He found the crew easily, and shouted — respectfully — in Spanish for everyone to move back to the east side of the vineyard. Immediately the air was full of staccato appraisals of this new development by the pickers. They emerged with their plastic tubs, the colorful medley of caps, straws, knotted handkerchiefs, soiled pants, shirts buttoned at the wrists for protection against the vines and leaves, and dirty boots, all donned seven mornings a week for a job that started before dawn and continued furiously until the required number of bins were filled or the sun climbed too high. A knife with a short, curved, sharp blade was attached to each man's wrist by a piece of cord, rawhide, or a bit of ribbon. Wielding it, they could drop clusters into the bins with amazing speed.

The pickers passed the concrete pad and waded into fresh vines, the parley replaced by the drumming of grape clusters against the bottoms of the plastic tubs.

Some pinot had already been dumped into big half-ton containers, waiting to be loaded onto a flatbed, the grapes tightly packed, a deep, glossy blue-black. Smooth to the touch, sweet to taste, they lingered on the palate, a quick evaluation repeated hundreds of times between July and October. Bite into a seed and release the tannin, bitter on the tongue; Hugh allowed the glycerinlike fruit to slide down, and spat skin and pips into the dust.

He began to paw through the clusters by hand, tossing the green ones to the ground. "We don't want green grapes," he said, controlling his disapproval. There had been a minor screwup, corrected now. "You know that. *No uvas verdes,*" he called to the crew boss, who passed the words on, giving rise to another burst of Spanish.

The chastened vineyard manager helped cull the unwanted fruit. Together he and Hugh also tossed the clusters affected by botrytis, a clotted gray mold that attacked and fed on the moisture in the grapes, leaving shriveled, nasty-looking, very sweet fruit with a flavor all its own. It was botrytis that produced the great dessert wines of the world — the Sauternes and Trockenbeerenauslese — but it had no place in the *cuvées* of Schramsberg.

While they worked, the owner of the property appeared in sweat-shirt and jeans, looking like any other Anglo laborer and not the San Francisco physician that he was, up for the weekend to participate in the crush. He mounted the forklift and began to load a half-ton bin onto the flatbed, prompting the appearance of the Mexican forklift operator who had been hired for that purpose. He complained loudly to the vineyard manager that his job was being usurped, if by the *patrono,* and had to be waved away. The vineyard manager muttered, "I wish the owner would just stay home."

It was eight-thirty when Hugh got back into the pickup. As he was driving west, his cell phone rang. It was Lily, calling to say good morning. He said, "Hi," and, "A little screwup at the first vineyard, but things are fine." They chatted briefly, and he put the phone back into his pocket.

He crossed the Sonoma County line. The next vineyard was run by two brothers, old-time growers, as neat as the previous one had been riotous. Hugh had stipulated that the picking was to include specific rows, and there at the far end of them the crew could be seen, bending to the task. As he approached on foot he could hear the Spanish, as constant in the vineyards during harvest as birdsong in spring, and see the big bins behind the tractor brimming with glossy, green-gold clusters of chardonnay. *Vitis vinifera,* the species to which all these grapes belonged, had the power — and the price — to galvanize growers and mesmerize absentee owners like the doctor from San Francisco. For many of them, it wasn't just the money, or a bottle with their name on it, but the association with something at once basic and mysterious.

Five tons would come out of this vineyard in three hours from when picking began, and it would be worth just under ten thousand dollars. That was about nine hundred dollars for the contents of one of those scuffed plastic bins bouncing along behind the tractor. No other legal crop came close to fine wine grapes for profitability, not artichokes, avocados, kiwis, macadamias. The quality of this chardonnay was excellent. Like the pinot noir, it would be hauled to the winery on a flatbed and crushed as one lot, so the juice could be isolated, analyzed, and evaluated, the initial step in a complicated process. By the time the juice from row 90 was drunk as J. Schram — if it made the cut — many more harvests would come and go.

He asked the crew boss to cull the green fruit. *"Deja las uvas verdes!"*

Just pointing out the problem could improve the ultimate quality of the juice. These men wanted to do the right thing, and it occurred to Hugh that he might never see many of them again, so diverse and fluid was the workforce.

Some green fruit would get in. Well, it would add to the acidity necessary for good sparkling wine. They could deal with any excess back at the winery. If this was France, they would simply have added sugar, but chaptalization was illegal in the United States, and unnecessary, given all the sunlight in California that built sweetness naturally.

Hugh drove to another part of the vineyard, fished a plastic bag and a knife out of his toolbox. He raced up and down the rows, tak-

ing samples, feeling the weight of the fruit, spooking jackrabbits
with long ears and powerful legs that accelerated away from him.

Schramsberg's production would be up again this year. Hugh's father
would have been happy with things, he thought. Mounting production was a sign not just of good economic times but also of steadily
improving quality. Fruit from fifty-five different vineyards showed
the care and layers of sensibility going into the *cuvées*. It would have
been nice to own more of those vineyards, but a decision had been
made before his time, when much of the available money went
into marketing. At that time people needed to be introduced —
and reintroduced — to the notion of sparkling wine as something
other than a lubricant for wedding receptions, and as a product
of northern California that was on par with its French competitors.
At Schramsberg, they had pushed their wines into the most demanding markets on the East Coast, but still had trouble cracking
Europe. This was a continuing challenge, as his father had said it
would be.

Jack Davies had always told his sons: reevaluate, readjust. Now
Napa's success seemed to have outstripped the valley's ability to ab-
sorb schemes to exploit it. Development, symbolized by the "castles"
Hugh deplored, seemed unstoppable, as were real estate prices. Vineyard sourcing had begun in his father's time, when Jack Davies talked
a lot about blending different sources — the Champagne model.
But gradually he had realized that it wasn't practical to keep the
Napa Valley appellation, which meant using only Napa Valley fruit,
and thereby limiting Schramsberg's potential to develop in quality.
Now fruit came not just from Napa and Sonoma counties but also
from Anderson Valley, a beautiful stretch of country to the north,
and from the central coast.

He called Craig, the vineyard manager and general troubleshooter, on his cell phone. Hugh said the two loads were on their
way, and told Craig about what time they would arrive. Then he
pulled off Las Amigas Road into a vineyard, got out of the pickup,
and began to take more samples. He could hear the gas guns going
off, scattering the birds, and he could see fingers of San Pablo Bay
probing far inland, the still water a crucial element in a dreamy landscape. He bit into a cluster of grapes still on the vine, stooping, and

judged by the taste that this crop would need to be picked the following week.

Hugh didn't use a refractometer for measuring the sugar content
of grapes in the field, but waited for the fruit to be crushed and analyzed at the winery. But he estimated that the combined sugars of
this lot would be about nineteen percent, lean but okay. The cool
weather was slowing everybody down this year; he knew that if
there was a heat spike, the valley was going to be an even busier
place. Everybody would be hustling to get fruit in before sugars
went through the roof.

He labeled the bags, put them in the truck, and headed east again.
Everywhere they were cutting the old eucalyptus trees, which was a
shame. The "eucks" were messy but handsome, the rows of stumps
left along the secondary roads reminding him of pathetic teeth in a
discarded denture. The cutting eliminated shade that might retard
grape growth, but trees — and shade — were essential elements in a
sense of well-being here. Sunlight, like that breaking through now
up-valley, was powerful and unrelenting.

He turned south on Highway 29. From the overpass, he could see
the broad loops of the Napa River as it blended with San Pablo
Bay, a nineteenth-century view despite the factory sitting in the
floodplain. Stands of eucks nestled in the oxbows threw deep shadows, drawing the mind away from tasks at hand. Hugh was brought
back to reality by the sight of sprawl on Napa city's lower flank, a vast
flatland punctuated with warehouses and lined with proliferating
services, from lumberyards to eateries. This back side of Napa Valley
was home to the less-than-scenic and potentially the undoing of the
whole: by courting development here, the city and the county had
lost control of the present, and perhaps the future.

The new, burgeoning city of American Canyon was eating the
surrounding countryside, reaching for the big hills off to the east,
now carpeted in grapes, where a few years ago none were grown.
Some people stood to make a killing if all the proposed commercial
and residential projects went through. Hugh opened two separate
padlocked gates, to get to what was, paradoxically, very good fruit
grown in an industrial wasteland.

He was hungry by the time the pickup was again pointed north.
He took the Silverado Trail to avoid the traffic, trying not to look up

at the castles but, as always, failing. How could people be so insensitive as to build up there, spoiling what was an indescribably beautiful, inspirational view? What sort of person would insist on having that perspective for himself while spoiling everyone else's?

One of the most productive times he had spent on the Watershed Task Force was the day the members had all visited sites for prospective homes and vineyards on Mount Veeder, and talked about the problems. For once — once — they had all seemed to have a common purpose. Hugh knew that if he had not been raised looking at vineyards, he might see them differently now, might see them as Chris Malan and Peter Mennen did, and he wished he could convey to them his vision.

Going up the long, steep road to Schramsberg, he noticed some motion in the driveway outside his little house. It was Lily, in her riding breeches. He slammed on the brakes.

"Come to lunch," she called.

"In a minute. I've got to stop by the winery first."

Driving on, he felt guilty: he was making Lily a crush widow before he had made her a bride.

On the roof of the winery, north side, stood an artifact of grape processing: a chute once used to suck grapes out of bins and deliver them to the press far below. Installed in 1982 by Jack Davies, it was then considered a marvel of enlightened fruit manipulation, one that bruised the grapes less than the customary dumping and added to the efficiency of the crush. Now it was a mechanical dinosaur.

Across from it, rearing against a backdrop of mountain, exposed to the elements, was the latest in juice extraction: the redoubtable Bucher press, a big, hollow steel cylinder nested in steel catwalks and stairs, capable of squeezing juice out of twelve tons of full-cluster grapes at a time. The internal bladder was strong enough to resist such alien objects as rocks — even the horseshoe that had passed through the day before without puncturing the bladder but clogged the auger that delivers the seeds and skins to a waiting truck. The horseshoe had been secured to the railing with a plastic zip strip, a symbol of good fortune and a hopeful gesture to the gods of harvest.

Hugh couldn't look at the Bucher without feeling pride. It was a beast, but a highly sophisticated and expensive one. The one hundred thousand dollars it had cost was considerably less than was required to excavate the hillside and pour an elevated concrete pad for the trucks, so they could unload and the forklift hoist the grapes into the Bucher. Made in Germany, it extracted the juice without bruising the fruit and releasing unwanted elements that could affect the taste. Three different phases of crushing lasted about four hours. It was mechanically complicated, thoroughly computerized, and sometimes developed problems that had to be scoped out by the company's local reps, who would appear at the winery on short notice and climb into the beast's belly.

Mario, one of the winery workers, sat on the forklift, his face shaded by the brim of a baseball cap, next to a stack of white plastic bins containing a half ton of chardonnay each that awaited the next press run. Below him, the beast wheezed and growled, rotated, throbbed, and discharged. The most valuable lot of juice was the initial "free run" — one hundred and fifty gallons per ton of the very best quality, bound eventually for the J. Schram and for the Reserve. The free run had already been pumped through plastic hoses to a refrigerated steel tank down in the winery, where it would be chilled to forty degrees and left for two days while the solids settled out.

The second, "press run" would produce fewer gallons. These would find their way into the less prestigious blends. The third, "heavy pressing," or "second *taille*," would produce about thirty-five gallons, to be sold off in bulk to producers of lower-end chardonnay. All told, the juice cost Schramsberg twelve dollars a gallon to produce, and the second *taille* would return about five dollars a gallon when sold off, a source of income not available to the winery pre-Bucher.

An undergraduate from Davis, Alisa, stood by the computer screen, an angular young woman with a ready smile. She had the natural adaptability of a good winemaker, Hugh thought. Alisa was shaded from the California sun by a Schramsberg billed cap, and the control panel she studied shaded by a piece of cardboard while she deciphered the hieroglyphics on the control panel. When the time came, she opened the trapdoors electronically for the new batch, and Mario began to dump the bins. After each was emptied, Hugh, wielding the hose, washed the remaining leaves and grapes onto the concrete. There Pio, Jamie's black Lab, pounced to eat the grapes, their sweet stickiness as irresistible to her as the jet of water she then frolicked in. Pio was sometimes sick at sundown from eating too much chardonnay, but for the moment she couldn't have been happier.

It was a fine day, sunny at last, not too hot. The sugars were a little low, but later in the week these would rise, with riper fruit arriving. From the concrete pad Hugh could see across the valley to the new Viader vineyard, starkly visible above, a dusty patch on the alternately green and parched slopes of Howell Mountain. The last of the bins was dumped, and then he walked down to the winery.

42

AT'S PROPERTY overlooking the valley was among the most beautiful and coveted, and that was saying a lot in that neighborhood. Increasingly, Pat stayed home, enjoying the view and working — always working — wondering how much longer to pursue the old ideal of wine and all it could embody. Pat had not gone to the Napa Valley Wine Auction or to the Farm Bureau picnic; took no part in the Napa Valley Vintners' soul-searching on setbacks and the advisability of having the valley exempted from environmental regulation; did not participate in the outreach program where vintners talked to people in the community about their problems; had not participated in the Winegrowers of Napa County's breakfast meetings at Jack Cakebread's, the Farmers for Napa Valley's murky plotting, or the Watershed Task Force's endless deliberating.

By rights Pat could have done any of these things, being a ranking winemaker with historical bona fides and a knowledgeable, successful viticulturist. But Pat continued to view with skepticism the material pretensions of some of the valley's prominent citizens and the political machinations of their adversaries. The fact that this year's Wine Auction raised so much money seemed obscene. Pat was not a snob but a bit of a misanthrope, pushed farther in that direction by the realization in middle age that success does not necessarily bring contentment. After years of achievement, the feeling of loss was difficult to attribute, but it was related to money and excess. That ten million dollars indicated that wine was no longer linked to culture and civilized living, but to celebrity, to showing off.

In recent months Pat's notion of pigs in glass houses had thus been reinforced, but equally dismaying was the behavior of some of the pigs' critics. The environmentalists were, in Pat's opinion, after power as well as the preservation of nature. What would the Sierra Clubbers do with Napa Valley if they controlled it? What would be their chosen next step in the valley's evolution?

The question of the valley's future continued to be asked — in public meetings, in the newspapers, at celebratory dinners, in every restaurant from Celadon to Catahoula. Sometimes, Pat thought, it might be a relief if the whole thing failed, if the valley's prized industry and everything dependent upon it came crashing down. That would mean starting from scratch, without the money and the glamour and the fights. Then Pat — whose cynicism had been shaped by a combination of success and the realization that in America, even in a business as ancient and august as wine, success is often insubstantial and fleeting — could make wine for fun again, without having to seek the commercial praise necessary for big success.

At other moments, looking out over the valley, Pat admitted that this would never return to a sleepy retreat for dedicated people wanting only to make good wine. Success was ingrained now. Too much of the valley was owned by the wealthy and by corporations. In the future, probably half the labels on wine bottles would disappear, bought up by others with irresistible fortunes, and things would get even fancier and more expensive. Barring some catastrophe, Napa Valley would increasingly resemble Bordeaux and Burgundy, the land under tighter and tighter control.

The environmentalists should be pleased with such a development, Pat thought, the valley maxed-out as far as new vineyards were concerned, new houses on the ridgelines having become so obnoxious as to be banned. Lately the stock market had shown signs of real, perhaps lasting weakness, and there was trouble in Silicon Valley. Although it had not yet affected real estate prices in this one, it well might.

A multimillionaire from that world had not long ago offered an astronomical sum for Pat's little redoubt. Pat had thought of what it would be like to be really rich, removed from the demands of nature and wine critics, but then where to live? There was no suitable answer as Pat watched the westering sun break into bright shards on the forested lip of the Mayacamas.

A small, unorthodox element in the Schramsberg *cuvée* was flora, a grape chosen by Jack Davies almost half a century before to add complexity to the wine. Every year this crop was pressed at Napa Valley Wine Company, the custom crusher on Highway 29, and while there to oversee the handling of the flora, Hugh walked between two of the old buildings that had once belonged to Inglenook. Suddenly he found himself looking up at a new "castle" being built on the hill above the Oakville Grade, rumored to be Madonna's, a house truly steroidal, with different elevations cut into the hillside and vast interior spaces to be linked by some kind of corridor.

He felt a rush of bitter resentment and wondered if it was worth the pain of living in a beautiful place like Napa if you had to repeatedly look at things that made you unhappy. You tried to live responsibly and were constantly slammed by your new neighbors' aesthetic and ecological transgressions. And if this was disconcerting now, what would it be like in twenty-five years? By then, the population of California would be double what it now was, and the future of the valley no longer up for grabs.

Sometimes Hugh and Lily talked about picking up and moving to Australia. It was the size of the United States, with half California's population. They could start a vineyard and live out their lives in tranquility, a powerful attraction. Underlying it was the age-old American allure of lighting out for the territory, counteracted somewhat by the memory of his father's admonition to be *in* the world, not to become a winemaking equivalent of a basket weaver.

This impulse to light out had other problems. The basic desire to start over was responsible for the subduing of the western United States in the nineteenth century, leading to the making of great fortunes as well as unprecedented damage to the land. It had created the modern version of California. It was the same impulse that brought his parents north from Los Angeles to a place between two coastal ranges notable for prunes, grapes, and dust, not yet renowned.

Yes, Australia beckoned. The last place, a great untrammeled grove. Its draw was space, sixty or seventy percent of it uninhabitable, people spread like leaves in a wreath about a forbidding arid center that required much of a day to fly across. A friend there had suggested settling near Margaret River, in the west of Australia, a sylvan paradise with oceans and open lands and big trees. Except for the kangaroos, it was a land much like California had been in the early twentieth century, full of promise. In Australia, you could still top a hill and see . . . nothing! You could still do that in the high Sierras, too, as Hugh had many times, but there you came across other trekkers and their leavings. Always you were mindful of more to come, while overhead the ceaseless jet trails served as wispy reminders of the ceaseless cargo of human freight bound for the Golden State.

But to leave Napa Valley would be a cop-out of sorts. You couldn't just run away from problems, as insistent as they were. This was a jewel still in existence, and somebody had to stay and see that it wasn't shattered.

The last load from Carneros was delivered late the following day and dumped into the Bucher press after dark. Four bins short of crushing the twelve tons, the power went out. Hugh, Craig, Alisa, and Matt, the temporary cellar rat from Australia, would within the hour learn that some unkempt bamboo on Larkmead Lane had brought down a power line, but at the moment lights sputtered and ten tons of grapes were already in the press. The weight of the fruit on that below caused a steady stream of chardonnay juice to flow through the plastic hose, and a big refrigeration unit sighed to a halt as if stunned by the absolute blackness of the night.

Much of the harvest sat in the tall metal tanks down in the winery. This was a fortune in juice without the protection of coolly circulating ethylene glycol, which could mean the difference between elegant wine and that cooked by the relentlessly rising heat of fermentation.

They all ran into the winery, Craig's headlamp bobbing, leapt down the long, twisting stairway, and picked their way by flashlight to the circuit breaker boxes on the far wall. There they experimentally flipped switches, to no avail. Hugh raced back up the stairs and called Pacific Gas and Electric and got a recording in Sacramento telling him that the company was aware of the outage.

The plastic hose from the press had to be disconnected from the line leading into the winery, and the bin emptied by hand with plastic buckets, and the juice carried below. While they were doing this, Lily arrived with Hamlet, the Great Dane, two yellow Labs, Pio, and a flashlight. "What's up?" she asked.

Hugh explained as the four dogs raced about in the darkness, enjoying the excitement. Then he called PG&E again, with the same result. Everyone stood around trying to decide what to do next.

"They've hosed us," said Craig, meaning the power company had abandoned them, with twenty thousand dollars' worth of chardonnay in the press and billions of microorganisms waiting to attack it.

Someone suggested, "Let's go eat."

They piled into pickups, dropped off the dogs, and headed north into Calistoga. The Puerto Vallarta restaurant occupied an alleyway next to a supermarket parking lot where tables and chairs had been set out under grass umbrellas, a bit of transplanted coastal Mexico redolent of refried beans and corn tortillas. Everybody had beer and attacked the chips and salsa. As a kid Hugh had gotten his hair cut in the little barbershop at the end of the alley, and he loved this place. He yipped along with the cornets blaring from the jukebox, happy in crisis, but Lily frowned him into silence. This was serious stuff, this blackout.

Craig relieved the tension by describing two years spent running a winery in China, where he had to get drunk with his grape suppliers and was finally flown out with symptoms of a mysterious disease that later went away. Suddenly things didn't seem so bad here in the valley. Matt talked of Australia, where he and Hugh had met and worked together.

"Is anybody at our winery?" someone asked, and Craig said, "Yes, Jacob."

The ghost of Jacob Schram would keep an eye on things while his spiritual descendants dug into steamy enchiladas, carnitas, soft tacos, salsa verde, but not the camarones al diablo, because this specialty was too infused with peppers and gastronomically demanding for what would surely be a very long night.

Driving back up the long, winding approach to Schramsberg, Hugh stopped to let Lily off at the little house. "Wait," she said, and kissed him on the lips.

The problem, they discovered, was the main switch. It refused to be pushed into place, and lurking there, it seemed, was the possibility of electrocution and general pandemonium. So they all climbed to the office and sat in individual puddles of flashlight while Hugh telephoned PG&E again. "This is Pacific Gas and Electric," said the recording, audible over the speaker phone. "We deliver energy."

"No, you don't!"

Eventually a human being came on the line to tell them that another human being working for PG&E was on the way and had been for well over an hour. Hugh played the beam of his flashlight on bottles and framed photos, as if seeing them for the first time. There was still twenty thousand dollars' worth of chardonnay in the crusher, and hundreds of thousands of dollars' worth of juice in the big fermenters that needed circulating glycol, and nothing they could do. He sent Alisa home, across the mountains to Sonoma, because she had to be back again in the morning; he sent Matt off to his girlfriend, who worked at Mumm, and Hugh and Craig traipsed into the winery to check the thermometers.

The tanks were still coolish, but the temperature had reached sixty-five degrees. "We're going to be in trouble if we have to wait until tomorrow," said Craig, and it was after eleven. Both young men, curious about the state of the juice in these conditions, some of it weeks old and well into fermentation, climbed to the catwalk above the tanks and moved along, flipping heavy metal lids that echoed in the darkness. They peered down into deep pools of chardonnay and pinot noir, their flashlight beams reflecting off the vast ceiling.

Only then did the electrician show up. He leaned heavily on the circuit breaker, flooding the winery with electric light and filling the air with the hum of machinery.

When ninety percent of the grapes were in, the annual harvest party was held, bringing together everyone who had taken part in crush and those from the vineyard, the salesroom, the winery, the front office, and their families, all gathered in the wooded grove that had contained so many Schramsberg events in the past. The old pinot vines around it had been cleared away, and the land ripped and made ready for cabernet vines that would fuel the new cabernet program.

Hugh stood up in an ersatz Hawaiian shirt and said, "Nothing went wrong this year," prompting laughter. He said it again, in Spanish. "There was the door taken off with a forklift," he continued, and chardonnay juice that went into a pinot tank, and the power outage. He thanked everyone, and then the hired DJ began to play a medley of Mexican and Anglo songs.

The sun felt very warm. A piñata suspended from one of the olive trees was under attack. The kids all took turns swiping at it with sticks until at last the paper parted and dumped into the dust hard candy wrapped in cellophane. The colors shone brightly in the sunlight, and eager children dove for the treasure, crying out with delight.

It proved to be a strange fall. An earthquake wrought damage from Yountville south to the city of Napa but barely interrupted dreams in more blessed St. Helena; there was rain and uncharacteristic coolness followed by muggy weather as clouds obscured the sun. Then real heat settled in that sent anyone yet with grapes to harvest scrambling, before the sugars got out of hand.

A moratorium on ridgeline houses was discussed by the elected officials, again, but no action taken despite continuing vocal opposition to the McMansions. A shift in public opinion concerning affordable housing for workers was discernible at civic meetings and in letters to the editor. And pressure for more control of vineyard development was eased somewhat by the recommendations of the Watershed Task Force, presented to the board of supervisors with requisite ceremony.

There were close to two dozen recommendations, and they ranged from the creation of the information center to enhanced setbacks for new vineyards. The ticklish question of setbacks for replanted vineyards was left for that time when the total maximum daily load study was completed and the "science" accounted for.

The value of the recommendations was more symbolic than specifically binding, in the minds of many people who had followed the issues, one of these being Mel Varrelman, the supervisor most directly affected by the acrimony surrounding them. Mel thought the task force had established beyond doubt the importance of "canopy" — trees — in the county's watershed, undisturbed riparian corridors for the benefit of the river and wildlife, and the setbacks. Now those three things really were no-brainers.

He and the other supervisors created an oversight committee — another task force in all but name — to hone and condense and move the recommendations forward, to be confronted at some time in an uncertain future and made law.

Guy Kay, still believing, apparently, in a merciful God, accepted a seat on the new committee. Guy thought the single greatest contribution to the process had been the study done by the scientist Charley Dewberry, the one who had donned scuba gear and actually gotten into the river to look at it. Some conservative members of the task force had tried to discredit Dewberry, but his study, even if sponsored by Friends of the Napa River and paid for first with Mead money and then with that of the Mennens, indicated a great diversity of life there, more than anyone suspected, and made undeniable the river's value as a resource in its own right, one worthy of perpetuating. "The light bulb has been turned on," Guy said afterward, of public awareness of the river arising from the task force, "and now it can't be turned off."

Jim Hickey continued to work on his history of the agricultural preserve; he still climbed into his pickup and drove around the valley, looking at all the development. He had said a decade earlier, and still said, "If Napa Valley can't be saved, no place can," but sometimes the problems seemed insurmountable, the valley inching toward a status like that of Plymouth Rock.

One day Hickey read in the newspaper about the miniature winery built by Mondavi, Inc., in Disney's new theme park, California Adventure, down the coast. It was to be called the Golden Valley Winery and set on a terraced acre of vines. Substituting for actual winemaking would be a video, and for winemakers there would be "wine ambassadors."

Hickey immediately wrote another letter that would never be published in the *Napa Register:* "In one glorious defining moment the Napa Valley bonded with Disneyland — the mother of all tourist attractions. You can now see the Napa Valley in Disneyland and every day you can see more of Disneyland in the Napa Valley. Two world class facilities joined together by the green of tourist dollars . . . It's a goofy world we live in."

THE STOCK MARKET decline grew more precipitous, and leading it was some accumulated wreckage down in Silicon Valley. Initial public offerings dried up, as did the more flamboyant evidence of wealth in Napa Valley. Fewer day-trippers got out of limousines, and realtors noted the absence of young millionaires offering three-point-two for a modest house: "the children" had vanished.

Property values were holding, but there were more million-dollar-plus houses available. The following year, 2001, a vineyard sold for three hundred thousand dollars an acre, a new record. The real question on many minds was whether the price of fine wine would fall. The current vintage coming onto the market was mediocre, which didn't help, and all over the valley people were cutting back on services, one eye on stocks, the other on the ratings. Arbor mulch replaced decomposed granite in many gardens; the importation of balled trees from the Pacific Northwest slowed.

Jeff Redding, the county planning director, was fired that spring by the board of supervisors, despite the fact that he had cut his ponytail. In an unrelated incident, Jayson Pahlmeyer, who thought himself finally free of the courts, received a letter from the district attorney's office informing him that he might be prosecuted for alleged bad business practices, a charge related to the way his vineyard had been put in. Jayson viewed this as more collateral damage from the Sierra Club lawsuit and realized that he might never be entirely free of it.

Mel Varrelman decided not to run for reelection as supervisor, easing his conscience with the knowledge that Guy Kay, of the sen-

sible hats, would run in his place. Guy might bring about some reconciliation between wealthy vintners and environmentalists.

Hugh Davies and Lily Oliver were married in Baja. On their return, they moved back into the little house on the Schramsberg
property with several dogs and a cat.

The terrorist attacks of September 11 in New York and Washington,
D.C., initially affected the tourist trade, but not for long. People did
not have to fly to get to Napa Valley, and many Californians began to
choose it instead of Hawaii or other, more distant destinations. And
what they found when they came to the valley seemed far removed
from the problems of a nation involved in a global conflict.

Concern over wine sales was warranted, but only in part. Merely
expensive cabernet sauvignon suffered, but the cults continued to
move. Apparently, the price of the most expensive wine was impervious to recession, war, and pestilence.

Chris Malan, with the assistance of the attorney Tom Lippe, considered suing the county again, with the continued backing of the
Mennens. They sought to force the county to perform a program-
matic environmental impact study that would require scientific data
still being gathered by federal agencies, and so add years to the de
facto moratorium already in effect on hillside development.

Late in 2001, at the San Francisco headquarters of the Sierra Club,
Lippe, Chris, and her friend Parry Mead met with a representative of
the club and some from Napa's vintner and agricultural communities. These included Linda Reiff, of the Napa Valley Vintners Association, and Tom Gamble and Volker Eisele of the Farm Bureau, and
they were struck by Chris's assurance and single-mindedness, as if
the election had never occurred. They hoped the Sierra Club would
not pursue this confrontational course in the new century, and said
so, but the Mennens had established a donor-advised legal fund
within the Sierra Club, and suing Napa County was a prime objective. The legal wrangling seemed about to begin anew.

One dim, wet day in St. Helena, on the bank of Sulphur Creek, Peter
Mennen looked down and saw an apparition: a gray shadow cours-

ing upstream toward the Mayacamas Mountains. It was a steelhead trout, miraculously suspended in clear flowing water that would disappear when the rains were gone. Two feet long, utterly wild, beautiful, this fish would push toward the headwaters until she could go no farther, there to deposit her eggs before turning tail and racing back to the sea.

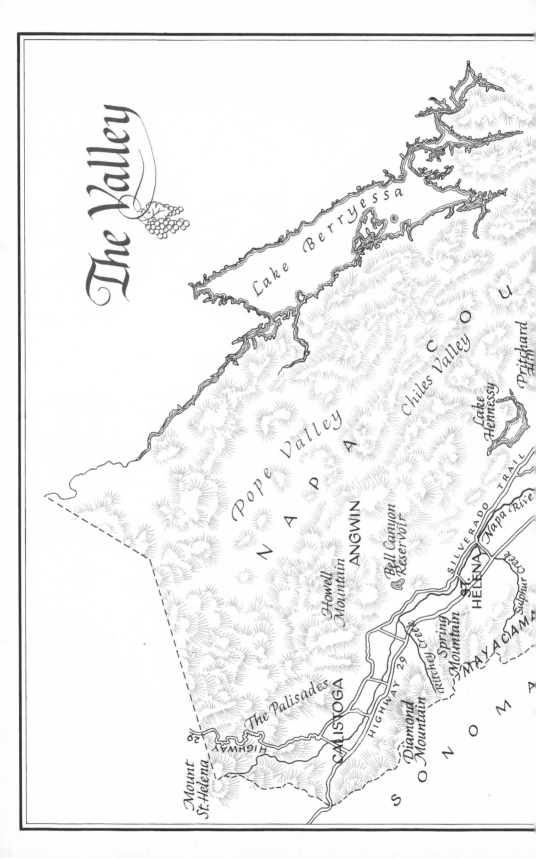